Israel Zinberg

A HISTORY OF
JEWISH
LITERATURE

TRANSLATED AND EDITED BY BERNARD MARTIN

The German-Polish
Cultural Center

HEBREW UNION COLLEGE PRESS
CINCINNATI, OHIO
KTAV PUBLISHING HOUSE, INC.
NEW YORK, NEW YORK
1975

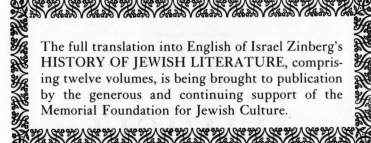

The full translation into English of Israel Zinberg's
HISTORY OF JEWISH LITERATURE, compris-
ing twelve volumes, is being brought to publication
by the generous and continuing support of the
Memorial Foundation for Jewish Culture.

Library of Congress Cataloging in Publication Data

Zinberg, Israel, 1873–1938.
    The German-Polish cultural center.
    (His A history of Jewish literature ; v. 6)
    Translation of Der Daytsh-Poylisher kultur tsenter,
which was published as v. 5 of the author's Di geshikhte
fun der literatur bay Yidn.
    Includes bibliographical references and index.
    1. Hebrew literature, Medieval—History and
criticism. 2. Rabbinical literature—History and
criticism. 3. Jewish learning and scholarship.
I. Title.
PF5008.Z5313   vol. 6   [PJ5016]   89294'09'002   75-11546
ISBN 0-87068-464-7

Contents

PART SEVEN: THE GERMAN-POLISH CULTURAL CENTER
BOOK ONE

Chapter One: **THE CENTER OF CULTURE IN ANCIENT KIEV; ABRAHAM KIRIMI AND MOSES OF KIEV** /

3

The economic role of the Jews in eastern Europe in the Middle Ages—Kiev as a center of culture—The Jewish colony in the Crimea—The Italian influence—Abraham Kirimi and his *Sefat Emet*—Moses of Kiev; his wandering life and literary and communal activity—The decline of the Kiev center.

Chapter Two: **JACOB POLLAK, MOSES ISSERLES, AND SOLOMON LURIA** / 21

The decline of the Kiev center—The role of Lemberg (Lvov) —The capital city of eastern Galicia—The first hostels of Torah in Poland—The economic situation of the Jews in Poland—The new metropolis of Jewish culture—Jacob Pollak, the founder of Talmudic academies in Poland—His manner of study—*Ḥilluk* and *pilpul* as unique rationalism—Shalom Shachna and his *yeshivah*—Moses Isserles (Rema) and his liter-

Contents

A Note on
Israel Zinberg

Dr. ISRAEL ZINBERG is widely regarded as one of the
foremost historians of Jewish literature. Born in Russia in 1873
and educated at various universities in Germany and Switzer-
land, he devoted more than twenty years to the writing, in
Yiddish, of his monumental *Di Geshikhte fun der Literatur bay
Yidn* (History of Jewish Literature). This work, published in
eight volumes in Vilna, 1929–1937, is a comprehensive and authoritative study of Jewish literary creativity in Europe from
its beginnings in tenth-century Spain to the end of the Haskalah period in nineteenth-century Russia. Based on a meticu-
lous study of all the relevant primary source material and
provided with full documentation, Zinberg's history is a nota-
ble exemplar of the tradition of modern Jewish scholarship
known as *die Wissenschaft des Judentums* (the Science of Judaism).

In addition to his *magnum opus*, Zinberg, who earned his
living as a chemical engineer, wrote numerous other valuable
monographs and articles on Jewish history and literature in
Russian, Hebrew, and Yiddish. In 1938, during the Stalinist
purges, he was arrested by the Soviet police and sentenced to
exile in Siberia. He died in a concentration camp hospital in
Vladivostok in that same year.

The reader who wishes a fuller introduction is invited to
consult the Translator's Introduction to Volume I of Zinberg's
History of Jewish Literature.

Foreword

In 1972 the Case Western Reserve University Press began publishing an English translation of Israel Zinberg's *History of Jewish Literature*. Zinberg, an engineer by profession, was a scholar by choice and inclination. In thirty years of intensive study in the great Jewish libraries of St. Petersburg (later Leningrad), he produced eight volumes in Yiddish portraying the course of literary creativity among the Jews beginning with the Golden Age of Spanish Jewry and continuing to the end of the last century. It was not until many years after Zinberg's death that a Hebrew translation was prepared and published in the State of Israel.

There has been no work of similar scope and magnitude in the English language, despite the fact that the Jewish reading public in Britain, South Africa, Canada, and the United States constitutes about half of the Jews in the world. Now, however, the Zinberg volumes have been beautifully translated into English by Dr. Bernard Martin, Abba Hillel Silver Professor of Jewish Studies and Chairman of the Department of Religion at Case Western Reserve University in Cleveland, Ohio. All the English-speaking lands are indebted to Professor Martin for his endeavor to make accessible a literary history such as Zinberg's, a history which depicts the intellectual strivings of the Jews, their aspirations, yearnings, and spiritual search in the medieval and modern worlds, in both of which they have played a not undistinguished role.

Special gratitude is due to the Press of Case Western Reserve University which inaugurated the challenging task of publishing this handsome and very important series of books. Each volume is an aesthetic as well as intellectual delight. The Case Western Reserve Press was aided in publication by a generous grant from the Memorial Foundation for Jewish Culture. The grant is, indeed, a memorial to the martyred Zinberg, who was arrested by the Soviet police in 1938 and deported to Siberia, where he died. We, for our part, are pleased with this opportunity to express our gratitude to the Memorial Foundation for the support which made possible the publication of the first three volumes.

Unfortunately, the economic difficulties from which many universities are now suffering has led to the dissolution of the Case Western Reserve Press and made it impossible for it to continue with the remaining nine volumes. That is why the Hebrew Union College—Jewish Institute of Religion, realizing the importance and cultural implications of this work, is cooperating with the Ktav Publishing House, Incorporated, in the publication of the remaining volumes.

The completion of this series will make available to the English-speaking world a magnificent account of the literary and cultural treasures created by the Jewish people during their millennial history.

Hebrew Union College—
Jewish Institute of Religion
Cincinnati, Ohio
January 1975

Alfred Gottschalk
President

Acknowledgments

The generous support of the Memorial Foundation for Jewish Culture, New York City, of the Morris and Bertha Treuhaft Memorial Fund, the Leonard, Faye, and Albert B. Ratner Philanthropic Fund, and Mr. and Mrs. John K. Powers, all of Cleveland, is gratefully acknowledged by publisher and translator alike. Without this generosity it would not have been possible for Israel Zinberg's monumental work to reach the new audience that it is hoped a translation into English will afford. The editor and translator wishes to express his appreciation to his friend Dr. Arthur J. Lelyveld, Rabbi of the Fairmount Temple of Cleveland and President (1966–1972) of the American Jewish Congress, for his aid in securing a grant from the Memorial Foundation for Jewish Culture for the publication of this work.

The translator also wishes to express his deep appreciation to Dr. Nathan Susskind, formerly Professor of German at the College of the City of New York and Visiting Professor of Yiddish at Yeshiva University, for his invaluable help in clarifying the meaning of many terms and concepts in Zinberg's Yiddish and Hebrew text. Responsibility for any errors of translation is, of course, the translator's.

It should be noted that Yiddish books with Hebrew titles are usually rendered according to the modern Sephardic pronunciation of Hebrew. In some cases the titles are also given in standard Yiddish transliteration.

A gift to my loyal friend
and life-companion—my wife.

Israel Zinberg

Transliteration of Hebrew Terms

א is not transliterated   ו = v (where not a vowel)   ל = l   פ = f

בּ = b   ז = z   מ = m   צ = tz

ב = v   ח = ḥ   נ = n   ק = k

גּ,ג = g   ט = t   ס = s   ר = r

דּ,ד = d   י = y   ע is not transliterated   שׁ = sh

ה = h   כּ = k   פּ = p   שׂ = s

כ = ch   תּ,ת = t

ָ = a   ֱ = e

ַ = a   ִ = i

ֹ , וֹ = o   ֵ = ei

ֻ , וּ = u   ֶ = e

short ָ = o   ֳ = o

יֵ = ei   ֲ = a

vocal *sheva* = e

silent *sheva* is not transliterated

Transliteration of Yiddish Terms

א	not transliterated	יִ	ey
אַ	a	יי	ay
אָ	o	כ	k
ב	b	כ,ך	kh
בֿ	v	ל	l
ג	g	מ,ם	m
ד	d	נ,ן	n
ה	h	ס	s
ו,וּ	u	ע	e
וו	v	פּ	p
וי	oy	פֿ,ף	f
ז	z	צ,ץ	ts
זש	zh	ק	k
ח	kh	ר	r
ט	t	שׁ	sh
טש	tsh. ch	שׂ	s
י	(consonant) y	ת	t
י	(vowel) i	ת	s

Abbreviations

JQR	*Jewish Quarterly Review*
JQR, n.s.	*Jewish Quarterly Review*, new series
MGWJ	*Monatsschrift für die Geschichte und Wissenschaft des Judentums*
PAAJR	*Proceedings of the American Academy for Jewish Research*
REJ	*Revue des Études Juives*
ZHB	*Zeitschrift für hebräische Bibliographie*

This volume is dedicated
to
Henry L. Schwartz
Far-visioned philanthropist
Distinguished American Jew

THE GERMAN-POLISH CULTURAL CENTER

BOOK ONE

CHAPTER ONE

The Center of Culture in Ancient Kiev;
ABRAHAM KIRIMI AND MOSES OF KIEV

The economic role of the Jews in eastern Europe in the Middle Ages
—Kiev as a center of culture—The Jewish colony in the Crimea—
The Italian influence—Abraham Kirimi and his *Sefat Emet*—Moses
of Kiev; his wandering life and literary and communal activity—The
decline of the Kiev center.

S IN western
Europe, so also
in the eastern
half of the con-
tinent, espe-
cially in the
broad land-
mass of which
the southern
provinces of
the Russian
empire con-
sisted in later
times, a sub-
stantial immi-
gration of Jews
appeared al-
ready in the
early Middle
Ages. In the
intensive commerce and close social relationships of northeast-
ern Europe and the Baltic regions with anterior Asia and the
lands adjoining the Black and Caspian seas, a very significant
role was played by the Jews in the land of the Chazars. As is
known, this country became at that time the most secure place
of refuge for Jews who were subjected to many persecutions
in neighboring lands. From Arabia, Persia, and distant Egypt
Jewish wanderers came to the country of the Chazars. The

immigration of Jews was especially large in the Crimean peninsula, which at that time was under the rule of the Chazar *chaghan*.[1] There the Jews who fled in droves from the "kingdom of Greece," the Byzantine empire, which persecuted its Jewish populace ruthlessly, settled.[2] At the end of the tenth century there were already populous Jewish communities on the Crimean shores of the Black Sea (Kaffa, Kerch, Chufut-Kale, etc.). This was also the case in the region of the Dnieper with its major center, Kiev, which at that time, after the commercial significance of the Chazar capital Itil declined, attained its zenith as the chief focus of the extensive transit trade between western Europe and the lands of anterior Asia. Along with this, the importance of the Jewish community of Kiev also increased greatly, for the largest role in the economic and industrial rise of the city on the Dnieper was played by the Jewish wholesale merchants, the world-engirdling Radanites,[3] who in the earlier period carried on their trade with the Far East across the wide sea-lanes. They would set sail on their own ships with merchandise from the west European harbors on the Mediterranean Sea and go as far as India, China, and Japan. Later, however, the newly risen Italian centers of the Levantine trade (Venice, Genoa, Pisa, Bari, and others) pushed out their competitors, the Radanites, from their sea-lanes, so that the latter had no alternative but to pursue their trade with the Far East over the more northerly route through the German and Slavic lands. The starting point of the Radanite trade was then formed by the Jewish communities of the Rhine cities of Mainz and Regensburg, and one of its major unloading stations was the city of Kiev on the Dnieper.[4]

With the economic and industrial importance of the Jewish community of Kiev grew its cultural role. It became and re-

1. On Jewish immigrants to the Crimea from Persia and Babylonia, see David Lechno's preface to *Siddur Ke-Minhag Kaffa* (*Ha-Karmel*, II, 344).

2. In 872 the Byzantine emperor Leo issued a decree that all the Jews dwelling in his land should be forcibly converted. The Arabic writer Ali ben Husain Abu'l-Hasan Al-Masudi relates in his *Murudj al-Dhahab* (in the French translation the work is called *Les prairies d'or*) that the Byzantine emperor Romanus I (919–944) "forced the Jews of his country to adopt the Christian faith and persecuted them severely . . . hence many Jews of Byzantium fled to the Chazars" (*op. cit.* in the French translation, II, 8–9).

3. The root of this name has not been completely established. For conjectures regarding it, see Simonsen in *REJ*, Vol. 54, 1907.

4. For a discussion of the Radanite trade and commerce with the Slavic lands see Schipper, *Virtshafts-Geshikhte Fun Di Yidn in Poiln*, Chapters 1, 2, 4, as well as his *Kultur-Geshikhte*, Chapter 1; J. Brutzkus in *Shriftn Far Ekonomik Un Statistik*, I, 69–75.

mained for a long time the chief center of culture of east European Jewry. Interesting in this respect is the well-known passage in Nestor's biography of the Russian priest Theodosius Pechersky in which there is a description of how the famous Christian hermit would frequently visit Jews at night and carry on long religious debates with them. While in the earlier Chazar period the Jews of Kiev were mainly under the cultural influence of Byzantine Jewry, the influence of the Jewish communities of western and central Europe now became dominant. The city on the Dnieper became the major unloading place not only for the material merchandise which the Radanites carried from the centers of the Rhine, but also for the spiritual treasures imported thence. The cultural threads binding the Jews of the Dnieper region with the *ḥachmei Lotir*, the intellectual centers of the Rhine, the Talmudic academies of Regensburg, Mainz, and the scholars of France, became ever stronger.[5] We have a reliable witness from that era, Moses Taku, a resident of the Rhine region, who tells us in his *Ketav Tamim*[6] how the famous Talmudic academy which Rabbi Jehudah Ḥasid founded in Regensburg used to obtain books from Babylonia through Russia. The Jews of the Dnieper region were accustomed to apply with important religious questions to the heads of the *yeshivot* of the Franco-German Rhine provinces.

"From our scholars and rabbis in Mainz, Worms and Speyer," enthusiastically declares the author of *Or Zarua*, "the Torah has been spread over the whole people of Israel, and according to their prescriptions have Jews acted since the communities in the Rhine provinces and throughout all of Germany, as well as in our kingdoms (i.e., in the Slavic lands), were established."[7]

To the famous *yeshivot* in the Rhine communities young men with a thirst for knowledge would also come from the Slavic lands. As a memorial of this intellectual influence, a certain number of handwritten copies of commentaries and other compositions by Franco-German scholars and rabbis of that era have come down to us. In these manuscripts, explanations in Slavic of difficult words are frequently found on the margin of the pages. It is clear that the copyists who came from Slavic

5. One must also take into account in this connection that after the terrible persecutions in the disturbed times of the first Crusades, the immigration of German Jews into the Slavic lands was also intensified.
6. See *Otzar Neḥmad*, III, 77.
7. *Or Zarua*, I, Responsum 662, 9.

countries, when transcribing important and popular works, would remove all the explanations and interpretations of difficult terms in German and French and exchange them for Slavic, a language more comprehensible to their countrymen.[8]

There is no doubt that for these handwritten copies we are indebted precisely to the above-mentioned young men who used to study Torah in the *yeshivot* located there. Some information about these students from the "land of Canaan" has even been preserved in medieval sources. A pupil of Rabbi Eleazar of Worms who wrote a commentary to the Pentateuch frequently quotes his teacher in it and in some passages refers to a certain "Rabbi Isaac of Russia"[9] who was probably also a pupil of Rabbi Eleazar. A Talmudic scholar of the second half of the twelfth century, Moses of Kiev, who used to send religious questions to the head of the academy in Baghdad, Samuel ben Ali,[10] was personally acquainted with the famous Tosafist Rabbenu Tam.[11] Thus, Moses of Kiev was a connecting link between the scholars of France and those of Babylonia. Some remnants of the literary activity of these Talmudic students from Slavic countries who used to go to western and central Europe to study Torah in the *yeshivot* there has even been preserved. In the library of the Vatican in Rome there is a manuscript entitled *Hiddushim Al Ha-Torah* that was written in Russia in 1094,[12] and in the Bodleian library at Oxford a manuscript of a commentary to the Torah has been preserved in which it is indicated that it was written in Russia in 1124.[13]

But the number of Talmudists in the region of the Dnieper was quite limited, and their literary work was of very slight value. In this connection, one must take account of the very low cultural level of the environment. The economic situation was also an extremely precarious one. The attacks of the nomadic tribes who would suddenly appear in great hosts out of the steppes and plunder the settled populace became ever more frequent. These were extremely unfavorable conditions for quiet cultural creativity. Indeed, we have some trustworthy witnesses from that time who relate how great the lack of

---

8. See M. Berlin, *Istoricheskie Sudbi Yevr. Naroda*, 170. It is quite possible, however, that some of these copyists came from the western Slavic provinces (Bohemia and others).
9. See *Kerem Hemed*, VII, 68.
10. See *MGWJ*, Vol. 39, p. 511.
11. See *Sefer Ha-Yashar*, No. 522.
12. See Harkavy, *Ha-Yehudim U-Sefat Ha-Slavim*, 10, No. 25.
13. See Steinschneider, *Hebräische Bibliographie*, XIII, 116

students and scholars in the communities of the Slavic countries was. In many communities the whole set of religious
functionaries consisted of a single individual; one and the same
person was rabbi, teacher, *ḥazzan*, or precentor of the congregation, etc.[14] And it would happen not infrequently that the
same "jack-of-all-trades" had very limited learning. In important religious questions the communities would therefore apply to recognized rabbis in western Europe.[15]

The situation of the long-settled communities in the Crimea
was no better. In their religious-cultural requirements they
were under the direct influence of Babylonia, from which the
immigrants who founded the oldest communities in the Crimea came.[16] Babylonia and Palestine also supplied the Crimean
communities with religious functionaries—rabbis, rabbinic
judges, and teachers of Torah. Of independent literary
creativity no information has come down to us, aside from a
few fragments of a handwritten prayerbook.[17] Definite ad-
vance in the cultural situation of the Jewish settlement is first
noticeable in the heyday of the Genovese colonies on the shores
of the Black Sea, especially after 1260, when the Genovese obtained from the Tatar Khan Oran-Timur the old port of Kaffa
(Feodosiya), which soon became the chief center of the Genovese colonies on the Black Sea. To be sure, the scholars Daniel
Chwolson and S. J. Fuenn attempted to show that the influence
of Italian Jews on the Jewish communities in the Crimea was
already discernible in the tenth century. Their conjecture,
however, rests on a single and very unfounded argument: they
believed that under the tombstone found in Chufut-Kale, on
which is inscribed the year 959 and the name Shabbetai Donnolo,[18] the well-known author of *Ḥakemani* was buried. But
there is no doubt that the author of *Ḥakemani*, who died considerably later than 959, has no relationship whatever to the tomb-

14. Interesting in this respect is the following passage of Rabbenu Tam's pupil Eliezer
    of Bohemia: "In most places in Poland, Russia, and Hungary there are no Torah
    scholars because of difficulties in which they live, and they engage for themselves
    a man of understanding wherever he may be found who serves them as leader in
    prayer, righteous teacher, and also as instructor for their children" (see Zunz,
    Gesammelte Schriften, III; *Responsa* of Rabbi Meir of Rothenburg, III, No. 112).
15. See for example *Maḥzor Vitry*, II, 243.
16. See David Lechno's introduction to *Maḥzor Minhag Kaffa* (Ha-Karmel, II, 344).
17. One such fragment is preserved in the first Firkovich Collection. In this manu-
    script there are several liturgical poems whose authors are not known from any
    other sources, e.g., Isaac ben Israel Sangari Rosh Yeshivah and Shelomoh (also
    Suliman) Alsingari. Apparently these authors lived there (see *Ha-Karmel*, II, 384).
18. On Donnolo, see Vol. II of our *History*, pp. 136–139.

stone of Chufut-Kale, and the cultural intercourse between the
Italian Jews and their brethren in the Crimea first began three
hundred years later, after the Genovese occupied Kaffa. We
know[19] that it was just in the second half of the thirteenth
century that the cultural flowering of the Jewish community
in Italy began, and the Jewish merchants who came to the
shores of the Black Sea brought with them not only material
goods but spiritual and cultural treasures as well. The diligent
Jewish copyists of Italy provided their brethren in the Crimea
generously with the best merchandise—books. The Jews of
Kaffa and Solchat obtained the possibility of becoming familiar
with the ideological currents that dominated Italian Jewish
circles. It is not at all accidental that from the year 1281 a handwritten copy of Abraham Ibn Ezra's commentary to the
Torah, which was composed in Italy and copied in Kaffa, has
been preserved.[20] Thanks to the cultural influence of the Italian communities, such an interesting personality as Abraham
Kirimi could arise as early as the first half of the fourteenth
century.

Of Abraham's life we know, unfortunately, virtually nothing. His name was forgotten for many generations, and only
in the nineteenth century was he saved from oblivion, thanks
to Abraham Firkovich. Firkovich found in the Crimea an entire work of Abraham's, a commentary to the Pentateuch entitled *Sefat Emet*. From the introduction[21] we learn that the author was born in the city of Eski-Krym (Solchat) and composed
the work in 1358 at the wish of his pupil, the Karaite Hezekiah
ben Ha-Nasi Elhanan. From the preface we also learn that the
author led an itinerant life and lived in poverty and distress.
Despite these difficult circumstances, Abraham managed to
obtain a many-sided and, for that time, thorough education. On
the basis of several references in *Sefat Emet*, it may be conjectured that his teacher was the then well-known scholar and
thinker Shemaryahu ben Elijah Ikriti of Negropont. Ikriti, like
Kalonymos ben Kalonymos, was for some time close to King
Robert of Naples, who was greatly interested in his exegetical
works. Born in Rome, Ikriti went as a child to the island of

19. See Vol. II, p. 181 ff.
20. See Vol. I, p. 158.
21. The introduction was published by Firkovich in *Ha-Karmel*, III, 53–54. The work
itself has still not been published, and the manuscript is in the Firkovich Collection. See our article in *Yevreyskaya Starina*, Vol. XI, "Avraam Krimski I Moisei
Kievski."

Crete, where his father served for a time as rabbi and *parnass*. The young Shemaryahu spent his *Lehrjahre* in Italy. There he obtained his education and in later years was in friendly correspondence with the Jewish community of Rome.[22] Of the great influence exercised by this Italian-educated scholar on Abraham Kirimi, testimony is provided by the fact that the latter quotes Ikriti's commentaries most eagerly and cites him as an authority in important questions.

Sefat Emet provides us very little information about the life of its author. But his personality and outlook on the world are quite clearly reflected in it. He was a man of wide-ranging knowledge with a keen, sober mind. Abraham Kirimi has very little use for "effusions of the soul" and poetic romanticism. To be sure, every *parashah* (weekly lection) and book of the Pentateuch in his commentary begins and ends with a two-line or four-line poem. But this is merely a matter of fashion; it is part of the style which the "chief of the commentators," Abraham Ibn Ezra, introduced. One must not look in Kirimi for stormy feeling, for outbursts of fervent enthusiasm. He is always calm and sedate. He recognizes only the logical, the clearly analytic idea or thought. In the course of his entire work, one cannot find a single allusion to popular legendry and mystical symbolism. He is concerned, above all, with the literal meaning, the interpretation of each individual word, its grammatical structure, and how logically to explain the given verse. He is very little interested, for example, in the fact that many commentators on the Pentateuch perceive in its first word, *bereshit* ("in the beginning") the deepest mysteries of the "work of creation." For him it is important merely to explain the philological peculiarity of this word. In the four rivers described as flowing around the garden that was the cradle of the human species, Abraham Kirimi seeks no allegories or mysterious allusions; he sees in them simply rivers and wishes to determine their geographical location. The author of *Sefat Emet* cannot pardon the famous commentator Rashi for having relied too much on Midrashim and legends. "Do not turn to Rashi's words," Kirimi declares; "his conclusions are not all by way of

22. When Shemaryahu Ikriti, because of difficult family circumstances, interrupted his large commentary to the Bible, the community of Rome inquired in a letter how the work was going and when he intended to finish it. Shemaryahu's reply was published by Abraham Geiger in *Otzar Nehmad*, II, 90–98. In the first Firkovich Collection under No. 518 is Shemaryahu Ikriti's tract *Hibbur Ish Ve-Ishto*.

literal interpretation."[23] Of all the commentators he prefers Ibn Ezra and the above-mentioned Shemaryahu Ikriti.[24] The supreme authority for Kirimi, however, is the "true scholar," Rabbi Moses ben Maimon,[25] and the rationalist spirit of *A Guide for the Perplexed* in fact hovers over his work. The author of *Sefat Emet* was firmly persuaded that the highest level of human perfection can be attained only in the realm of philosophical inquiry and, like Maimonides in his day, was convinced that "Thou shalt love the Lord" can only be a consequence of "Thou shalt know the Lord." Love for God can manifest itself only in seeking and understanding the great wisdom of His creation. Kirimi in places utilizes his rationalist standpoint with even more rigorous consistency than Maimonides. For this reason he very rarely employs the allegorical method in his commentary to the Pentateuch.[26] Even in the story of the serpent which seduced the mother of the human species he seeks no allusions or allegories whatever. He merely considers it necessary to express his doubts whether it is possible for a serpent to speak; it is common knowledge, after all, that only man is endowed with the living word.[27] It is also beyond doubt for him that whoever thinks that Balaam's ass actually obtained the power of speech all of a sudden "gropes in darkness."[28] The extraordinary and the remarkable, the miracles and wonders related in the Torah—these this strict rationalist endeavors to explain naturalistically, to explicate them according to common sense. Abraham Kirimi is not at all interested in the explanation that the rainbow is the great, miraculous symbol which God gave to mankind to signify that the sinful world would never again be punished by the all-destroying waters of a merciless flood. For him it is important only to familiarize the reader with what the *ḥachmei ha-meḥkar*, the natural scientists, say about the rainbow, according to what laws of nature the colorful phenomenon appears in the heavens when the rays of the sun strike the waterladen clouds. The same is true when Kirimi comes to the ten plagues with which

23. Ms. *Sefat Emet*, 78.
24. Abraham Kirimi very frequently cites "the sage, our teacher Shemaryahu, the son of the *parnass* Ikriti." See *Sefat Emet*, 9, 10, 11, 13, 14, 68, 79, *82ff.*
25. *Sefat Emet*, 65
26. Only in regard to Jacob's dream about the ladder with the angels ascending and descending on it does Kirimi agree with Maimonides that it must be understood as an allegorical parable (*Sefat Emet*, 40).
27. Ms. *Sefat Emet*, 9.
28. *Ibid.*, 223.

God punished the stubborn Pharaoh and his land. He relates in his commentary how the *ḥokerim* (scientific investigators) explain naturalistically the hail that fell on the earth and the thunder and lightning. The story of the patriarch Abraham and the three angels who come to visit him is declared by Kirimi simply a dream, and in this connection he refers to "the true scholar" Maimonides. He also explains the story of the bush that burned and was not consumed as a dream. And it is altogether in the spirit of Maimonides that he explicates the spirit of prophecy:

The prophets, when sent to the multitude, do not speak to it in philosophic language, do not adduce abstract arguments built on the foundation of intellectual, speculative thought, for the multitude would not understand this and their speech would have no effect. The multitude comprehends only what it touches with its hands, what it feels with its senses. Only selected individuals can grasp abstract ideas, philosophical theories. But the prophet speaks not merely to chosen persons; he must be recognized by the whole people, great and small.

Abraham Kirimi is not satisfied with all the explanations in the old sources of the meaning and etymology of the word *Pesaḥ* or of the meal with the *Pesaḥ* sacrifice, the central feature of the great festival of liberation in ancient times. He finds that all these explanations contradict each other, and he gives his own scientifically grounded one. He brings the Jewish festival into strict connection with the great spring festival that was celebrated in Egypt when the sun in the month of Nissan entered the constellation of Aries, the symbol of which is the lamb, the *"Pesaḥ* sacrifice."[29]

Kirimi also considers "foolishness" the idea so popular among Jews that God created the world in six days and rested on the seventh. Like Isaac Albalag,[30] he considers the "work of creation" an infinite, eternal, and everlasting creative act. And like the Sephardi Albalag, so the scholar from the Crimea had the courage to issue forth against one of the fundamental ideas hallowed by tradition among Jews and interpreted the statement of Genesis, *asher bara Elohim laasot* ("which God created and made"), in such a way that God is represented as creating the primordial powers which in the Torah bear the name *Elo-*

29. *Ibid.*, 83.
30. See Vol. III of our *History*, pp. 99–108

him, and these maintain the infinite process of creating and becoming.[31]

The most interesting thing in this connection is that a man with such liberal views was by no means regarded as a heretic in his milieu. This rationalist and freethinker was a rabbi and was so revered and beloved that his community for many generations preserved his memory with great reverence and blessed his name. In the Firkovich Collection we discovered an interesting document of the fifteenth century from which we learn that more than a hundred years after Abraham Kirimi's death the Crimean congregations would recall for blessing at their *Yizkor* or memorial service—together with "the great master, our teacher Moses ben Maimon" and "the sage, the master, our teacher, Abraham Ibn Ezra"—also "his excellency, our lord, the sage, the rabbi, our teacher and our master, Rabbi Abraham Kirimi." The Crimean Jews, we note, still remained so faithful even in the fifteenth century to the ideological spirit of their former "teacher and master" that, out of all the great savants and important figures of the Middle Ages, they had an attitude of special respect for the two foremost battlers for free, critical, speculative thought who were the actual guides of the author of *Sefat Emet.*

At that time, at the end of the fifteenth century, a scholar appears on the foreground of Jewish cultural life in the Crimea who came from abroad, from the principal center of the Jewish settlement in the Dnieper region—Kiev. This was Moses of Kiev or Moses Ha-Goleh II.

The importance of the Kiev center declined considerably for a time after the devastation it suffered at the hands of the victorious Tatar warriors. About the Jewish settlement before the period of decline we have very little information. We know only that at the beginning of the fourteenth century the community of Kiev used to obtain rabbis from distant Babylonia.[32] Gradually, when it was connected with Lithuania and Poland, Kiev began to revive. Its Jewish community also increased at that time. Kiev became "a city and mother in Israel" and in learned circles the expression "For from Kiev goes forth the Torah and the light of the Lord from Stardov" was commonly heard. In a letter that a Karaite, Solomon ben Abraham, sent from Kaffa to Kiev in 1481,[33] the correspondent notes: "I have

31. *Sefat Emet,* 7
32. *Ha-Karmel,* II, 407.
33. This letter is in the Firkovich Collection (no. 46), along with a whole pack of letters

long been told that in your communities, both the Karaite and the Rabbanite, there are many who devote themselves to science." Just at that time heading those in the community of Kiev "who seek knowledge and learning" was Rabbi Moses ben Jacob ben Moses Ha-Goleh, who acquired fame in the most varied literary realms—as Bible commentator, Talmudist, liturgical poet,[34] philologist and Kabbalist.

Thanks to his notes at the close of many *sidrot* (weekly pericopes) in his commentary to the Pentateuch, we know definitely the time when Moses of Kiev II was born. At the end of the *sidra* entitled *Emor* the author's birth is clearly indicated as having occurred in December 1448.[35] The place of his birth, however, is not definitely known. The Karaite scholars Elijah Bashyatzi and Caleb Afendopolo, who carried on a polemic with Moses Ha-Goleh, call him "Ashkenazi" and "Allemano"; this, however, is merely an indication that he was descended from Ashkenazic Jews. To be sure, Firkovich relates[36] that at the home of a certain Karaite named Isaac Uchsuz he saw a manuscript of Moses' above-mentioned commentary in which the author explicitly notes, "And I was born in the town of Shadov." This report, however, arouses strong doubts. First of all, there is considerable question whether in the first half of the fifteenth century the town of Shadov existed at all, for in the historical sources Shadov is first mentioned in the year 1539. Furthermore, it remains incomprehensible how it happened that one born in a castaway little town of distant Zamut should spend his *Lehrjahre* in the capital city of the Ottoman empire. We therefore conjecture that in the passage quoted by Firkovich it is not Shadov that is mentioned but the old Tarov of the Kiev region. It is not difficult to explain Firkovich's error

---

and documents from the Karaite communities in the Polish-Lithuanian provinces. The letter in question is even dated in the year 1381, but here we find Firkovich's hand. We have to do in this case with one of Firkovich's numerous forgeries. The forgery is here carried through in highly unskilled fashion. To the *resh* of the date *resh-mem-alef* Firkovich added a stroke, and thus the *resh* became a *kof*. The forger did not take into account one detail: the document was written in choice India ink but he remade the *resh* with ordinary ink which in time faded. Thus the forgery is easy to recognize.

34. See Zunz, *Literaturgeschichte*, 388. In the three-volume manuscript of the *Mahzor Minhag Kaffa* located in Leningrad in the library of the Society for the Dissemination of Enlightenment Among Jews there is also a liturgical poem with the acrostic *Ani Mosheh Ha-Goleh* (I, Moses the wanderer).

35. At the end of his commentary there is another indication of the same date. We quote from the manuscript of this commentary in the second Firkovich Collection.

36. *Ha-Karmel*, II, 39.

by the fact that in ancient manuscripts it is easy to take the Hebrew letter *tet* for *shin* and *resh* for *dalet*.

A sickly, emaciated person with abscesses on his body[37] but with a strong character and an enormous thirst for knowledge, the young Moses ben Jacob went to the great cultural center, the capital of the Ottomans—Constantinople. Besides studying Talmudic literature, he also diligently applied himself to general studies with Jewish scholars such as Abraham Tzarefati,[38] as well as with the well-known Karaite savant Elijah Bashyatzi.[39] At the age of twenty-four he was already renowned for his wide-ranging knowledge. He now had his own pupils, and from one of these, a handwritten copy of a cosmographic work which the pupil transcribed, as he himself indicates, for his teacher "Rabbi Moses ben Jacob of Russia" has been preserved.[40] Moses Ha-Goleh soon left Constantinople and settled in Kiev[41] where the Jewish community welcomed him with great honor. But he was not destined to lead a peaceful life. In 1482 the Tatars attacked Kiev, Moses lost all his fortune, and his children together with many other inhabitants were taken away as captives to the Crimea.[42] He himself, having been saved by some remarkable events, set out for Lithuania to collect the sum required for ransoming his captured children. But Moses was not satisfied with collecting money or ransoming his captives. With his aggressive nature, he could not pass up any suitable opportunity for argumentation, and when he visited Troki and Lutsk on his way he entered into disputations with the local Karaites. He also informed them that he

37. Elijah Bashyatzi refers to this in his letter to Moses Ha-Goleh. The letter is to be found among the above-mentioned documents preserved in the first Firkovich Collection, No. 44.

38. Apparently Moses ben Jacob married Abraham Tzarefati's daughter. In his unpublished *Otzar Neḥmad* (second Firkovich Collection, No. 3, p. 196) we read: "And my teacher, my father-in-law, Rabbi Abraham Ha-Tzarefati, may his memory be for blessing, welcomed me."

39. Bashyatzi points to this in his letter to the Karaite community in Lutsk: "Perhaps this man has forgotten the time that he was subordinate to me, when he studied astronomy with me" (first Firkovich Collection, No. 42).

40. The manuscript in question is in the library in Vienna. In it is an addendum indicating that it was completed in 1472. Abraham Epstein (*Ha-Eshkol*, IV, 149) refuses to believe that the person spoken of here is Moses Ha-Goleh since he was then only twenty-four years old. Epstein's doubts, however, are ungrounded, for Moses' contemporary and opponent in controversy, the Karaite scholar Caleb Afendopolo, also already had adult pupils at the age of twenty-four.

41. Berlin's conjecture (*op. cit.*, 193) that Moses Ha-Goleh spent some time in Palestine before settling in Kiev is very weakly grounded.

42. See Afendopolo's letter, published in *Hebräische Bibliographie*, XX, 122–124.

had prepared a polemic work against *Gan Eden*, a book on the commandments by their chief authority, the Karaite scholar Aaron ben Elijah. Caleb Afendopolo reports with clear strokes in his above-mentioned letter the tremendous sensation created by Moses' polemic in the Karaite circles. "When the two renowned Karaite communities (Lutsk and Troki) heard this," writes Afendopolo, "they trembled and suffered great anguish. Like true sages, they ardently wished to fulfill everything required of them. Above all, they wanted to obtain this work, but that was not possible because God brought it about that the manuscript was stolen and taken away to Kaffa."[43]

The Karaites of Lutsk realized that they could not refute the arguments of the skillful Rabbanite polemicist with their own powers, and so they applied to their brethren in Constantinople for aid. The first to come to their help was the well-known Elijah Bashyatzi. The sharply controversial tone in which Bashyatzi and his disciple Caleb Afendopolo[44] replied to their Rabbanite opponent testifies to the intense excitement Moses' polemic evoked.[45]

After Moses had succeeded in gathering the sum necessary to ransom his captives he returned to Kiev and there very diligently devoted himself to Torah. He wrote works on Hebrew grammar *(Sefer Ha-Dikduk)* and on the Jewish system of reckoning time *(Yesod Ha-Ibbur)*.[46]

But the years of peace did not last long. Suddenly and quite unexpectedly the community of Kiev and the entire Jewish settlement in Lithuania were stricken by a catastrophe. The grand duke Alexander Jagello issued a decree in 1495 expelling every Jew from all of Lithuania, as well as from the city of Kiev. Moses ben Jacob, along with the entire community, took up the wanderer's staff and years of homelessness began for him anew. Despite all the troubles and persecutions that the weak and sickly scholar had to endure, however, he did not forsake his beloved books or interrupt his literary activity even

43. Moses of Kiev wrote his polemic *Hassagot* on the margins of his copy of *Gan Eden*, which the Tartars plundered along with his entire library and later sold in Kaffa to the Jews residing there.

44. Copies of these documents are to be found in the first Firkovich Collection, Nos. 42, 44, 45.

45. In his old age, when Moses of Kiev wrote the introduction to his commentary *Otzar Nehmad*, he again entered into controversy with the Karaites and called them "ignorant men."

46. These works are mentioned by the author in his *Otzar Nehmad* (Parashah "Bereshit," p. 3; Parashah "Balak" and Parashah "Ha'azinu," p. 216).

in the years of exile and wandering. In the very year 1495, the year of the expulsion, when Moses of Kiev was transformed into Moses Ha-Goleh, he began a work of broad compass which characterizes most clearly the mood of its author in this period of persecution. We have noted that in his youth, spent in Constantinople, Moses devoted himself considerably to mathematics and other sciences. This was the heyday of the Constantinople community, when the influence of such men as Mordecai Comtino and their disciples was felt especially strongly. As was the case among all the "enlighteners" of Constantinople, so also for Moses of Kiev, Abraham Ibn Ezra was the foremost authority, and he had the greatest reverence for the memory of the "chief of the commentators." The young Moses, however, also had, in his years of study, opportunity to come into close contact with the bearers of the "true wisdom," with the "great scholars of Israel," as he himself puts it, who transmit the secrets of the mystical tradition entrusted to them from generation to generation, from the prophets on and even from the father of the prophets—Moses himself. The difficult experiences Moses of Kiev later lived through apparently considerably strengthened his mystical tendencies and moved him finally to undertake a work which he had long been contemplating. For Moses of Kiev the greatest authority in the realm of Kabbalist wisdom was the famous Bible-commentator Naḥmanides. He was firmly convinced that for this scholar of the thirteenth century all the mysteries of the Kabbalah were open and that in his work all the marvelous achievements to which the ancients, the Kabbalists of former generations, were privileged to attain in the realm of esoteric wisdom are preserved. In the least allusion, accidental word, or statement of Naḥmanides, Moses sought and found whole treasures of profound truths. To reveal and expound these truths of cosmic import, to preserve them for future generations—in this he saw the major task of his life, and to this end he decided to write a special work.[47] He realized his wish, however, only after the expulsion of 1495 in the "time of trouble for the lost sheep," as he notes in the poem of praise in which he celebrates Naḥmanides, the man "to whom the mysteries of the ten *sefirot* were transmitted."[48] This work is called *Shoshan Sodot* (Lily of Mysteries), because in it are discussed precisely the number of mysteries, six hundred fifty-six, which equals the numerical

47. See *Shoshan Sodot*, 43a (Koretz edition).
48. The poem is published at the beginning of *Shoshan Sodot*.

value of the word *shoshan* in *gematria*.[49] The author completed his work only many years later, for in one place (*Shoshan Sodot*, 73) the date 1509 is noted, and at the end of a handwritten copy which was in the possession of Jacob Reifmann it is indicated that the work was completed in 1511.[50]

It is worth noting that among the Kabbalist books which the author quotes in his work is *Sefer Ha-Kanah*,[51] and the author of this work (who is believed to be a contemporary of Moses of Kiev) is called in one place in *Shoshan Sodot* by the name Avigdor[52] and in another place Baal Ha-Giddur.[53] A special value for the history of Jewish mysticism pertains to another quotation that is introduced in *Shoshan Sodot*.[54] In the third volume[55] of the present work we discussed the teaching of the *Zohar* concerning the structure or form of man, through which the individual is created. "At the moment," the *Zohar* teaches,

when the soul unites with the body, the Holy One, Blessed be He, sends down to earth a form *(deyokna)* stamped with His seal. This form is present at the union of husband and wife and, if a man's eyes had the capacity, he would see it at their heads. The form has a human face and its image will be carried by the person who is to be born from the fertilized seed . . . It is this form that comes to us when we are born into the world, grows along with us, and accompanies us when we leave this world.[56]

"And this form," the *Zohar* adds, is a heavenly phenomenon." According to the *Zohar*, man's eye cannot see this form. But from a rather lengthy quotation in *Shoshan Sodot* we learn that in the circles of Abraham Abulafia's disciples the mystical idea developed that certain chosen persons, men of the holy spirit, are privileged to have disclosed before their eyes in moments of ecstasy their own ego, their heavenly form; and in this form they see the divine, the hidden and concealed. When a man

49. The last 193 sections are in fact a commentary to the *Sefer Yetzirah* and are therefore printed under a separate title-page, *Otzar Ha-Shem* (Koretz, 1779). The remainder was published only five years later.
50. *Ha-Karmel*, III, 208. On another manuscript with the same addendum, see Berlin, *op. cit.*, 195.
51. See Vol. III of our *History*, pp. 261–70.
52. *Shoshan Sodot*, 28b.
53. *Ibid.*, 24b.
54. *Ibid.*, 69b. The first person to note the significance of this quotation was the scholar of Kabbalah Gershom Scholem, *MGWJ*, 1930, 286–288.
55. pp. 48ff.
56. *Zohar*, III, 104, Parashah "Emor."

encounters his own ego as a separate form and penetrates into this form with the light of his eyes, he attains the level of the prophet, and in his form, his image, he sees divinity itself.

"There is a great mystery," we read in *Shoshan Sodot*,

in the expression, "Vast is the power of the prophets, who liken the form to its Creator." We have already attempted to explain this mystery according to our understanding, but I later found a special essay on this subject, and so I decided to introduce it here . . . And this is what is related in it: The enlightened sage Rabbi Nathan, may his memory be for blessing, thus explained to me: Know that the profound mystery of the prophet's revelation consists in the fact that he suddenly sees his own form standing before him. He then forgets his own ego, is separated from himself, and sees before him the form of his ego speaking to him and telling him what will take place in the future. It is of this mystery that the sages, may their memory be for blessing, say "Vast is the power of the prophets, who liken the form to its Creator." And the sage Rabbi Abraham ben Ezra said of prophecy, "He who hears is a man and he who speaks is a man." Another sage has written on this subject: "When I immersed myself in solitude it would happen that, through the power of 'combinations,' the light which I saw would go with me, as I have already mentioned in the book *Shaarei Tzedek*; but to see my own form standing before me—to this I was not privileged to attain, this I was not able to see." Still another sage writes the following: "I know quite definitely that I am neither a prophet nor the son of a prophet. The holy spirit does not rest upon me. I did not deserve this privilege. I was not sufficiently pure and refined for this, as it is said, 'I did not take off my coat and I did not wash my feet.' Yet heaven and earth are my witness, and those who are on high will confirm it, that once when I wrote down a profound mystical secret I suddenly saw my own form standing before me. My own ego departed from me, and I had to cease writing . . ." And to me also [i.e., the author of *Shoshan Sodot*], when I wrote this book and placed the vowels under the Ineffable Name, starry images in the form of the red glow at the setting of the sun appeared before my eyes. They confused me, and I had to interrupt my work. This happened to me several times in writing this composition.

In *Shoshan Sodot* numerous details that are extremely interesting from the ethnographic point of view are also to be found. The author reports, for example, as if it were common knowledge, that the luckiest number is the number 9. The ninth month is the luckiest month, the ninth day is the best day of the month, the ninth hour is an hour of blessing and joy, and whoever is born in the ninth year of the jubilee cycle in the ninth month on the ninth day of the month and in the ninth hour will certainly rise to royal estate.[57] He who sees a needle in a dream may be certain that his wife will bear him only girls, and he who dreams of a nail, his wife will bear only boys.[58]

Besides *Shoshan Sodot*, Moses Ha-Goleh also composed a whole series of mystical works which have not come down to us—among them a commentary to the Torah,[59] *Otzar Ha-Shem*,[60] *Shaarei Tzedek*,[61] and *Sefirot Elyonot*.[62]

It appears, however, that Moses Ha-Goleh was not born in the lucky ninth hour. He was not fated to have rest even in his old age. In 1506, when he found himself in the city of Lida in Lithuania, Tatars attacked the city, plundered everything and took many residents captive, among them himself. Moses was brought by the Tatars to Eski-Krym (Solchat). The Jews and Karaites living there at once fulfilled the commandment of "redeeming captives" and ransomed the scholar.[63]

Thus the Tatar warriors brought it about that Moses Ha-Goleh in his old age was cast into the birthplace of Abraham Kirimi. Because of the close connection between this city and the Italian communities, Moses found many books there which it had been difficult for him to obtain elsewhere. Only now did he consider the time propitious for realizing the wish he had cherished from his youth on: to write a work that would make Abraham Ibn Ezra's commentary to the Torah accessible and understandable to all. The famous scholar of Toledo was no less revered by Moses Ha-Goleh than was Naḥmanides, and he says of himself that he was "Abraham's slave and Moses' servant." This mystic and Kabbalist regarded it as his duty to show how greatly in error are those who have not properly immersed themselves in Ibn Ezra's views and wished, therefore, to assert that he denied the mysteries of the Kabbalah. For him, Abraham Ibn Ezra is one of the pillars supporting the whole structure of the "true wisdom." "The Kabbalah speaks with his mouth," says Moses of Ibn Ezra. In 1515 he completed

57. *Ibid.*, 24b.
58. *Ibid.*, 84b.
59. The author frequently mentions this work in his *Shoshan Sodot* (30, 43, 53, etc.), and also in *Otzar Neḥmad*.
60. Mentioned in *Shoshan Sodot*, 30, and in *Otzar Neḥmad*, Parashah "Aḥarei Mot."
61. See A. Epstein in *Ha-Eshkol*, IV, 150.
62. See *Shoshan Sodot*, 44a.
63. See Firkovich's report in *Ha-Karmel*, II, 39.

his well-known commentary to Ibn Ezra, *Otzar Neḥmad,*
which, however, has still not been published. The manuscript
is in the Firkovich Collection.

Shortly thereafter Moses Ha-Goleh settled in Kaffa where,
as guide of the community, he was destined to play an important cultural role. The community consisted of diverse groups.
Jews from various regions and lands came to Kaffa, and each
was attracted to his own countrymen. Thus, separate *Landsmannschaften* were formed. Each of these had its own prayer
service and conducted worship in its traditional fashion—the
Ashkenazic Rite, the Roman Rite, the Babylonian Rite, etc.
Controversies and arguments would also arise between the
various prayer groups. Thanks to his great authority, Moses
Ha-Goleh managed to bring all the *Landsmannschaften* into a
unified community, for which he composed a special order of
prayers that was known as *Minhag Kaffa* (Rite of Kaffa) and
accepted by all the Jews of the Crimea. To establish order in
communal life, the seventy-year-old Moses also composed special ordinances in 1518.[64] About two years later the unified
Jewish community of Kaffa brought its aged rabbi and guide,
the constant wanderer and exile, to his eternal rest.

64. Published in *Ha-Karmel*, III, 101.

CHAPTER TWO

Jacob Pollak, Moses Isserles, and Solomon Luria

The decline of the Kiev center—The role of Lemberg (Lvov)—The capital city of eastern Galicia—The first hostels of Torah in Poland—The economic situation of the Jews in Poland—The new metropolis of Jewish culture—Jacob Pollak, the founder of Talmudic academies in Poland—His manner of study—*Hilluk* and *pilpul* as unique rationalism—Shalom Shachna and his *yeshivah*—Moses Isserles (Rema) and his literary work—Isserles and Maimonides—Isserles' theological-philosophical work *Torat Ha-Olah*—Isserles as codifier—Solomon Luria (Maharshal) and his work.

HE EXPULSION from Kiev ordered in 1495 was, in fact, soon abrogated, and those who had been driven out quickly obtained leave to return to their former places. Nevertheless, the old cultural center did not regain its former strength, and that time marks the beginning of the intellectual decline of the Jewish community in Kiev. The place of Kiev was gradually taken in the Jewish cultural life of southern Russia by the chief center of eastern Galicia, the capital of "Red Russia"—Lemberg (Lvov). The flowering of the city was greatly facilitated by its advantageous location on the broad trade route that

connected the Ottoman empire with southern Russia and Poland, as well as by all the protective privileges and other important concessions it received from the Polish kings.[1] Lemberg
quickly became one of the major Jewish cultural centers in
Poland, a "city and mother in Israel," a "great city unto God,"
whose community is filled with "wise men and scribes," a true
"source of scholars and spring of understanding, a cornerstone
and foundation of the faith" (*She'elot U-Teshuvot Baḥ*, No. 72).

As early as the end of the fifteenth century there was a great
yeshivah in Lemberg that was renowned throughout the country. Heading it was Levi ben Isaac Kikenes. But it was not the
academy of Lemberg that was privileged to become the most
important center of Torah, the model and prototype of all the
other Talmudic academies of the whole land of Poland, but the
academy of the western center in Galicia, that of Cracow, with
its famous leader Jacob Pollak.

The first *yeshivot* in Poland were founded by immigrants
from Germany, Czechia, and Moravia, whose numbers began
to increase especially after the terrible years of the "Black
Death" and the frequent banishments of the Jews from the
German and Czech cities.[2] We have observed in one of the
previous volumes[3] that the literary creativity of the German
rabbis at that time consisted exclusively of magnifying the
stringency of laws and rules, in making ever stronger fences
and boundaries, in separating the Jewish community as much
as possible from the hostile external world. The leaders of the
generation saw before themselves a single task: to be faithful
guardians of the tradition of the fathers, to protect in all its
particulars the least custom of previous generations. These
tendencies were brought by the rabbis from Germany and
Bohemia into their new hostel of Torah. But in the new environment, under different social conditions, these assumed different forms, and the *Minhag Polin* (Polish Rite) to a certain
degree obtained a style at variance with the *Minhag Ashkenaz*
(German Rite). Because of the special socio-economic structure
and unique historical development of the Polish kingdom, the
Jewish populace for centuries had no less important a role in
the economic life of Poland and Lithuania than their ancestors

---

1. See Berlin, *Istoricheskie Sudbi Yevr. Naroda*, pp. 195–196.
2. For statistics on the growth of the Jewish population in Poland at the end of the
    Middle Ages, see Ignacy Schipper, *Kultur-Geshikhte Fun Di Yidn in Poiln*, 1926, pp.
    146–150; *idem, Istoriya Yevr. Nar.*, Vol. XI, pp. 106–110.
3. Vol. III, pp. 147ff.

had in the Rhine region before the Crusades. As the Franco-German Jews had done in their time, so now the Jews in Poland played a major role in the flowering of the cities and participated in all branches of commerce, industry, and crafts. The Polish kings eagerly employed Jewish lessees and tax-gatherers, through whose skillful hands all kinds of royal taxes and revenues were collected. As the bishops in the Rhineland cities had done in their day, so the wealthy land-owning nobility of Poland gladly engaged Jewish lessees and entrepreneurs. The noble lords were too indolent and frivolous to manage their own estates and to concern themselves with agricultural economy. This was done much better and more profitably by Jewish hands. As a result, the Jews in Poland and Lithuania, despite a stubborn competitive struggle with non-Jewish merchants and artisans,[4] managed until well into the sixteenth century to keep in complete force the general privileges and favorable statutes of the grand duke Vitovt and King Casimir IV. King Sigismund II even enlarged the rights of Jewish self-government. The rabbis and heads of the community obtained full administrative and juridical authority to adjudicate Jewish civil matters in an all-Jewish court, according to Jewish custom and Talmudic law. Even in the general Voyevoda court, when litigation between Jews and Christians was considered, Jewish "elders" *(seniores)* and representatives of the community also participated in the proceedings. According to the privileges of King Sigismund (1551), the Jewish populace had the right not only to elect rabbis and judges who conducted their spiritual and secular affairs, but the Jewish court headed by "Jewish doctors," i.e., rabbis, was also given the power to compel every member of the community to obey all its decisions, to excommunicate those adjudged guilty, and to apply to them all other modes of punishment, "according to Jewish law."

"An historical nation," the historian Simon Dubnow says of this,

with an altogether unique way of life, was distinguished by the Polish government as a social *class*, a distinct social group. While the Jews were a part of the urban populace, officially they did not belong to any of the general city groups . . . They formed a completely independent class of citizens with a separate self-government and their own judiciary. The Jewish community constituted a distinct community

4. The majority of the non-Jewish merchants and artisans were descended from German immigrants.

not only in the national-spiritual sense but also in the administrative-social sense; it was a separate Jewish city on the boundaries of the Christian city, with its own manner of life and its own religious, administrative, judicial, and social institutions.

Hence, at the time the Sephardic center of culture was destroyed and the Spanish and Portuguese exiles sought refuge on the shores of Africa and in the hospitable cities of the Ottoman empire, the Ashkenazim, the Jews who had come from German lands, created an important new center. Gradually another metropolis for the Jewish spirit, for the national culture, developed.

Closely associated with the communal autonomy and socio-legal position of the Jewish community in Poland is the direction in which the spiritual and intellectual creativity of Polish Jewry evolved. The relatively favorable economic situation created the atmosphere of broad-mindedness that is so important for spiritual-cultural evolution. This cultural rise, however, was a very one-sided one. It consisted almost exclusively in the flowering of Talmudic-rabbinic literature. But it must be remembered in this connection that the Talmud was for the Jewish communities of Poland not merely a sacred work which it was a religious duty to "study" for the sake of God, but also their *corpus juris*, their practical handbook in actual social life.

We have noted that, according to the general privileges granted by the royal government in Poland, the Jewish populace had its own court which judged "according to Jewish law," i.e., according to Talmudic law with all its hedges and ordinances, embracing all of religious, social, and family life. The Talmudic *corpus juris* extended its hegemony over the whole way of life of Polish-Lithuanian Jewry in perhaps even greater measure than over the Franco-German communities in the times of Rabbenu Gershom and Rashi. One must also bear in mind in this connection that since the times of Rashi and the Tosafists rabbinic literature had grown tremendously in compass.

This religio-legal literature, accumulated through many generations, ruled boundlessly over the minds of the Jewish community in Poland. Men sought in it not solutions to philosophical problems—"what is above and what is below," not an answer to the mysteries and enigmas of life, but principles and directions in the realm of practical problems and tasks. Only the scholar, one expert in the sea of the Talmud, could play a significant role in communal life, and had the potentiality of becoming a rabbi, a principal of a *yeshivah*, a member of a rabbinic court. Proficiency in all the tortuous and complex questions of Jewish law was also requisite for every member of the community who concerned himself with communal matters and took any part whatever in the autonomous Jewish government. To know how to "learn," to be a diligent student and pore night and day over the Talmud and rabbinic codes—this was the one assured way that led to power and honor, gave one the possibility of holding the most prominent positions in the self-government with its highest institution—the *Vaad*, the new incarnation of the ancient Sanhedrin which arose on Polish soil. It is therefore not surprising that in Poland, as in the days of the Geonim in Babylonia, Talmudic knowledge dominated the entire foreground of Jewish life. The Talmud and its commentaries and supplements ruled without restraint in the synagogues and houses of study, as well as at assemblies and in communal and private life. The rabbinic judge, the administrator, the community figure—all based themselves on the discussions of Abbaye and Rava. These were the focal point, the essence of the entire literary creativity of the Polish-Lithuanian Jews.

The actual founder of Talmudic scholarship and rabbinic learning in Poland was Jacob ben Joseph Pollak, the *baal ha-hillukim* (master of subtle distinctions).[5] In the biography of this famous dialectician there are many obscure, still unclarified blanks and contradictions. It has not even been definitely established from what country he came; only from his family name is it surmised that he was born in Poland. Pollak spent his youthful years in the famous *yeshivah* of Nuremberg whose guide and leader at that time was Rabbi Jacob Margolioth. From several allusions in his polemical writing[6] against the rabbi of Padua, Abraham Minz, it may be conjectured that Pollak spent some time in north Italy, where a very prominent role was played at that time by rabbis from the Germanic countries. At the beginning of the 1490's he was rabbi in Prague but soon had to leave the city (in 1492). Heinrich Graetz[7] and, following him, A. H. Weiss and others indicate that this came about as a result of the following cause. On account of a divorce question involving his young sister-in-law,

5. Born approximately 1460, died after 1532. The city in which Pollak spent his last years is not known (on this, see Wettstein, *Ha-Eshkol,* VI, 218–222).

6. See S. Wiener, *Pesak Ha-Herem*, pp. 12–16.

7. See his *Geschichte der Juden*, Vol. VIII, p. 58.

a fierce controversy erupted between him and many prominent rabbis. Pollak's opponents, chiefly Jehudah Minz and his
former teacher Jacob Margolioth, excommunicated him and he
therefore had to leave Prague. Meir Balaban, however, attempted to show on the basis of archival documents that the
divorce controversy occurred not in Prague but in Cracow and
not in 1492 but about ten years later.[8] The last assertion, however, is definitely inconsistent with the statement of Jehudah
Minz about the excommunication decree (*She'elot U-Teshuvot*,
No. 13) in which the date 1492 is explicitly given. Beyond this,
it has been established that one of the rabbis who excommunicated Pollak, his erstwhile teacher Jacob Margolioth, died no
later than 1493. One must therefore conclude that at the time
of the divorce controversy Pollak did, indeed, live in Prague,
but his young sister-in-law and also his mother-in-law, the
wealthy court-financier Rachel, lived in Cracow. It is beyond
doubt, however, that in 1495 Jacob Pollak was already residing
in Cracow, and in 1503 he was appointed by the king *Hochmeister*
or primate over all the Jews of the Polish kingdom. Because the
government, in doing this, had fiscal purposes in mind only,[9]
and because the chief rabbi was *appointed* by the state and not
chosen by the Jewish populace, the Jews perceived a threat to
their autonomy and received their new *Hochmeister* with great
hostility. To embarrass Pollak, the story of the divorce and the
excommunication was again revived by the disaffected Jews of
Cracow, and Pollak, in consequence of the quarrel that broke
out, had to leave the city for a time. Several years later (in 1509),
on the authority of a special royal letter of protection, he returned to Cracow. But the community had won its point; Pollak no longer occupied the position of chief rabbi. His wealthy
mother-in-law, however, gave him the wherewithal to establish a large Talmudic academy. Thanks to the energy and skill
of its head, this *yeshivah* became in a short time a true hostel
of Torah, and not for Poland alone. Jacob Pollak, the *baal ha-
hillukim* and great dialectician, brought it about that even in his
lifetime the following phenomenon, which is extremely important from the cultural-historical point of view, was discernible:
in the earlier period Talmudic students eager for knowledge
would go from Poland to Germany to study Torah in the
yeshivot there; but after Pollak founded his famous academy,[10]
the stream was reversed from west to east, and the brilliance

8. See *Yevreyskaya Starina*, 1912, p. 237.
9. See Schipper, *Kultur-Geshikhte*, pp. 138–139.
10. Pollak served as rector of this *yeshivah* until 1522. As a result of a sharp controversy

of the Polish Torah scholars obscured the reputation of the heads of the *yeshivot* in Germany. Pollak's importance, however, consists not merely in the fact that he established his great academy but mainly in the new mode of study that he fostered. With the name of Pollak, the *baal ha-ḥillukim*, the unique method of studying the Talmudic text, acute *pilpul* (dialectic or hairsplitting), in whose vesture rabbinic learning attained such a high level in the Polish lands, is closely associated.

Mystical currents and intimate experiences of effusion of the soul were absolutely alien to Pollak. A man with a sober, marvelously acute and analytical mind, he devoted all his rich intellectual powers to Talmudic discussion, to the sharp dialectic which he had inherited from the Tosafists and the later German rabbis but which he endowed with novel and unique forms. The most distinctive aspect of Pollak's dialectic is the *ḥilluk*, the analytic dissection: through keen, logical subtleties, to bring into close relationship the most varied, often even the most antithetical, matters. Not the law itself, not determining the real essence of this or that *halachah*, was the principal thing, but the mental activity, the keenness and ingenuity in interpreting the text. Of course, it was urged that these sharp and clever inventions made it significantly easier to obtain the correct rule and to render the most difficult, confused topics plain and clear.

The order of pilpulistic study proceeds in the following way: One takes various passages from the Gemara or the Midrash, pairs together two *halachot* or laws which at first glance have no relationship to each other; then, however, it is shown, with ingenious notions and tortuous explanations and subtleties, that the two laws are in close affinity and all contradictions are reconciled. Only now does a new stage commence: one proceeds to find logical inconsistencies in all the explanations and subtleties and, in order to reconcile *these* contradictions, seeks new explanations and devises new inventions. Alternatively, one takes a simple topic of the Gemara which is so clear and comprehensible that it does not elicit any doubts. The pilpulist, however, commences to find in this self-evident subject the vastest contradictions, endeavors to demonstrate this with numerous quotations from various Talmudic tractates, brings to

that broke out between him and the court surgeon Samuel, Pollak had to leave Cracow and settled in Palestine. See Wettstein, in *Ha-Shiloaḥ*, V, 542–543, and Balaban, *Yevreyskaya Starina*, 1912, p. 239.

the quotations the relevant explanations and conjectures of the scholars and codifiers, and therewith discloses with great acumen the enormous inconsistencies among the commentators themselves. And when the question is already so confused that it is literally impossible to find a solution, the pilpulist performs a new trick; suddenly he discloses that the contradictions are not contradictions at all and the confusion is not a confusion. He destroys, as if it were a simple spider-web, the whole ingenious tower which he himself had just constructed.

Again the slogan "The sovereignty of the intellect!" was raised. This rationalism, however, was of a very specific kind and with a special adjunct flavor. To be sure, only the intellectual, the sharply pointed, is recognized—but without the proper world-outlook, without the philosophical idea that might forge the rationalist elements into an organically whole structure. It is therefore not surprising that this unique, asexual rationalism, which was not fertilized with the seed and sap of creative powers, soon took on the pathological forms of fruitless sophistry. From a means which might facilitate obtaining the correct meaning of the text, it grew into an end in itself. Men devoted themselves wholeheartedly to *pilpul* not in order to attain the truth, or to obtain the correct essence of this or that law, or to enrich thought with real knowledge. The discussion itself, the trickery of mental tortuousness, of dialectic acrobatics—this alone attracted young minds, and in this they saw the whole substance of "studying Torah."

To be sure, in Jacob Pollak's lifetime the manner of studying fashioned by him had still not assumed these pathological forms. The immense scholarship of the head of the *yeshivah* of Cracow and his tremendous brilliance gained him a reputation as one of the greatest scholars, and he was honored with the title *Tzevi Yisrael Rosh Golat Yisrael* (the glory of Israel, the head of the Diaspora) whose "praise resounds from one end of the world to the other."[12]

It is quite characteristic of the celebrated *baal ha-ḥillukim* that he left no literary legacy out of fear that men would make of him a decisor and codifier. He was afraid that with his disciples and followers his written explanations and responsa might obtain the force of firmly established decisions, and this would weaken among them the desire to investigate and seek for themselves, with their own powers, the correct meaning of every rule and law. Each man must search on his own account

12. David Gans, *Tzemaḥ David*, II.

and decide about the meaning of every law as he himself sees fit—this was the slogan of the famed *baal ha-ḥillukim*, the great thinker and ingenious dialectician.

Pollak's pupil, Shalom Shachna ben Joseph, the rabbi and head of the *yeshivah* in Lublin who was appointed chief rabbi of all of Little Poland in 1541 by royal authority, adhered to this principle. He, like his teacher, did not publish any writings,[13] yet was renowned throughout all the Polish and German communities.[14] His academy attracted pupils "from one end of the world to the other,"[15] and from it the foremost rabbis of Poland and Lithuania came. In this academy Shalom Shachna's son-in-law, the famous Rabbi Moses ben Israel Isserles, better known under the acronym Rema, was also trained. Isserles, together with his relative and friend Rabbi Solomon Luria (Rashal or Maharshal), were the real founders of rabbinic literature in Poland. These two great scholars, the ornament and pride of old Polish Jewry, are also extremely interesting as persons. Indeed, in these richly endowed men we see most clearly the signs of decline and cultural backwardness which are discernible in the spiritual and intellectual life of Polish Jewry, even in the period of its first flowering.

Isserles was born in Cracow around 1520.[16] His father was *parnass* and head of the community[17] and gave his son the material requirements to establish, while still in his youth, a large *yeshivah* which quickly acquired a fine reputation and to which pupils from distant cities and countries were attracted.

Secular knowledge was not altogether foreign to Isserles, but he derived this knowledge not from his own environment but from the distant lands of Italy. One must bear in mind in this connection that Polish Jewry, as far as culture is concerned, was "a people dwelling alone." The higher nobility of Poland, which then belonged to the most cultured segment of European society, had only business contacts with the local Jews. Given the large role which the Dominicans and Jesuits played in Polish spiritual and intellectual life, the culture of Poland

13. Shalom Shachna's son Israel testifies that his father forbade the printing of his responsa and other writings (see the *Responsa* of Rabbi Moses Isserles, No. 25). See also the report of Shalom Shachna's pupil Ḥayyim ben Bezalel in the introduction to his *Vikkuaḥ Mayyim Ḥayyim*.

14. See *Tzemaḥ David*, I, 314.

15. Isserles, *Responsa*, No. 25.

16. Wettstein wishes to show that he was born only around 1530.

17. The young Isserles used to sign himself "Moses, the son of the distinguished teacher, the *parnass* and guide, Israel, long may he live."

had a markedly Catholic coloration. Rabbinic Judaism, therefore, saw in Polish culture, above all, the *Christian* culture that was hostile to it. The urban Christian populace, which regarded the Jews as their very undesirable competitors, could, given their bitter hatred, hardly arouse among the Jews the desire to draw close to their neighbors in the cultural realm. The Polish Jews, however, especially the community of Cracow, were in very close contact with Italy. The first splendid Hebrew printing presses were established in Italy and supplied the Polish settlement plentifully with books, even in later years when Poland had its own presses.[18] The Polish rabbis would apply especially frequently to the Italian rabbis with religious questions, and many young Jews went from Poland and Moravia to the land of the Renaissance to study Torah with the great rabbis living there who had come mainly from Germany.[19]

But it was not merely Judaic knowledge that Jewish youth sought in Italy. Many students who had obtained great competence in the Talmud in the Polish *yeshivot* would thereafter go to Italy (especially to Padua, whose university was renowned throughout the world) to study medicine. A certain number of Sephardic Jews, mainly doctors and pharmacists, also came to Poland through Italy. Some of these cultured "Spanish exiles" were physicians at the Polish royal court.[20] Isserles was on friendly terms with the court-physician Solomon Ashkenazi, who had emigrated from Italy to Cracow and later played an important political role at the court of the Turkish sultan. Isserles also had close contacts with several Italian communities. This is attested not only by his frequent correspondence with the famous Rabbi Meir (Maharam) of Padua, but also by the interesting point that he published his commentary to the Book of Esther, *Mehir Yayin*, in the Italian city of Cremona (1559).[21] The Jewish community of Cracow and its famous rabbi

18. The first Hebrew presses established in Poland were in Cracow (1530), Brisk (1546), and Lublin (1550). On the pioneering Hebrew presses in Poland, see H.D. Friedberg, *Toledot Ha-Defus Ha-Ivri Be-Polanya* (Antwerp, 1932); I. Rivkind, "Le-Toledot Ha-Defus Ha-Ivri Be-Polin," *Kiryat Sefer*, XI; *idem*, "Umbakante Krokever Drukn," *Bibliotek-Bukh*, Montreal, July 1934, 49–53.

19. See Vol. IV of our *History*, pp. 49ff. On the extensive cultural intercourse between the Polish and Italian communities testimony is incidentally provided by the following fact: In Cracow in 1590 a textbook entitled *Devek Tov* appeared in which the words of the Pentateuch are explained in both Yiddish and Italian.

20. See Balaban, *op. cit.*, *Yevreyskaya Starina*, 1912, p. 38.

21. Some scholars assert that Isserles studied for a time in Italian *yeshivot*. This, however, is not correct; Isserles was never in Italy.

and *yeshivah* head doubtless found themselves under definite Italian influence. This influence, however, was quite one-sided. The spirit and moods of the Renaissance era could little impress the famous pupil of the "uprooter of mountains" Shalom Shachna. In the domain of *pilpul* and dialectical acumen only one element—to be sure, a very important and valuable one—of the Italian Renaissance could find a powerful echo: the thirst for knowledge. But even this element here assumed highly peculiar and one-sided forms.

We have noted the rationalist tendencies discernible in the Talmudic academies of Jacob Pollak and his disciples. It should therefore occasion no surprise that the intellectually curious Moses Isserles, who had a definite inclination toward secular knowledge,[22] was more impressed by Aristotle's philosophical system, with which he became acquainted through Maimonides' work, than by anything else. Maimonides himself he called *ha-tayyar ha-gadol*, the great master who "comprehends all wisdoms."[23] *A Guide for the Perplexed* was, for him, the profoundest source of philosophical knowledge, and it is this book that he quotes most in his theological-philosophical work, *Torat Ha-Olah*. Following the pattern of the *Guide*, Isserles' *Torat Ha-Olah* is also divided into three parts, and many of its paragraphs begin with the notation, "Thus said the author of the *Guide*." *Torat Ha-Olah*, the only theological-philosophical work produced in Polish rabbinic literature in the course of the sixteenth and seventeenth centuries, created a great sensation in its time. It was celebrated in poems of praise,[24] and Isserles' renowned contemporary, Rabbi Solomon Luria, enthusiastically exclaimed, "From Moses (Maimonides) to Moses (Isserles) there arose none like Moses!" Even in modern times there has been a scholar who compared the author of *Torat Ha-Olah* with the author of *A Guide for the Perplexed* and asserted that "the spirit of Maimonides was revived in Moses Isserles."[25] It is unnecessary to say how far the author in question has here "exceeded the measure." However, it is extremely instructive to contrast and compare these two figures; only then does one see clearly the great distance in the realm of free philosophical-scientific thought between Spanish Jewry

22. Isserles had solid knowledge in the realm of astronomy and even wrote a commentary to Peurbach's *Theoreticae*. He also manifested a certain interest in historiography and wrote notes to Zacuto's *Yuḥasin*.
23. *Torat Ha-Olah*, 84b (we quote according to the first edition of 1570).
24. See the poem of praise printed at the beginning of the first edition.
25. See S. A. Horodetzky, *Le-Korot Ha-Rabbanut*, 1910, pp. 85–87.

of Maimonides' time and the Polish community of Isserles' generation. The *Guide,* in which Maimonides sets forth his religious-philosophic system, is a harmoniously complete structure; every part, every detail, is rationally fitted to the other. In this structure everything is clear and bright.[26] It is just the opposite, however, that one sees in *Torat Ha-Olah.* Here all is vague and diffuse. This is not a building, but a labyrinth in which everything is chaotically confused. The poor reader is carried over narrow, tortuous by-paths where gray, nebulous shadows grope in the darkness. Now faces appear that one might think are emissaries of the realm in which only cold, clear intellect prevails, but they immediately disappear, and strange, fantastic forms that revolve in a wild, magical dance come to the surface.

In the introduction it is indicated that the first part will be concerned with the architecture of the Temple—how the whole building, the altar and the vessels, looked. The other two parts will deal with the subject of sacrifices. These basic themes, however, are woven together with a frightful mixture of the most varied matters. In explaining the Biblical text Isserles attempts to utilize Maimonides' allegorical method, but this obtains with him the same naive, distorted forms that are to be found in the well-known apocryphal letter that Maimonides purportedly sent his son Abraham.[27] Of course, Isserles, like many others of that time, had not the slightest doubt that this letter was authentic and that the author of the *Guide* was also its author. He was firmly convinced that in the Temple and its vessels allusions to all the worlds and all the mysteries in the Torah are concealed, for the structure of the Temple is the mirror-image of the universal world-structure, of the entire cosmos.[28] "Know," he declares, "that every corner, every room, in the Temple is an allusion to profound ideas. Every gate is a symbol of a definite science or wisdom."[29] In every vessel and every article exalted matters and important mysteries are incorporated. The *menorah* or candelabrum is an allusion to the Torah. The olive oil is the scholars.[30] The flowers on the rods of the candelabrum are also a very profound mat-

26. See our *History,* Vol. I, p. 143.
27. See Vol. II, p. 110, Note 25.
28. *Torat Ha-Olah,* I, Chapters 2, 4.
29. *Ibid.,* I, Chapter 7, folio 12.
30. *Ibid.,* Chapter 16.

ter.[31] The eight garments of the high priest correspond to the eight commandments that were given man "before he sinned."[32] The laver is the symbol of prophecy; the incense an allusion to good deeds.[33] The curtain is the dividing wall between the human intellect and the "active intellect,"[34] etc.

All these overly subtle theories and notions are written up in stilted, cumbersome language that very frequently violates the most elementary principles of grammar.[35] The author of *Torat Ha-Olah* wishes to show, furthermore, that all the stories related in the Torah and most of its commandments and laws have one definite purpose: to demonstrate the "novelty of the world," to confirm that the universe was created in time. Belief in the "novelty of the world," Isserles asserts, is the "foundation of our Torah." And to this "foundation" testimony is provided by the Passover sacrifice and all the other sacrifices; even the manner of eating unleavened bread on the days of Passover—everything, must confirm the "novelty of the world" and show that it is not the heretics who maintain that the world is eternal who are right, but the Torah which tells of the creation of the world.[36] While the Kabbalists of Safed led by Isaac Luria transformed the Sabbath commandments into a marvelous mystery and Solomon Alkabetz sang his song of praise to the divine bride, "the Sabbath queen," the author of *Torat Ha-Olah* sought the logical implications of the Sabbath and came to the conclusion that "the chief intention of the Sabbath is to teach us the novelty or creation of the world."[37] Even in the custom of *Tashlich* Moses Isserles perceives an allusion to the creation of the world.

Quite in the spirit of Maimonides, Isserles quotes the words of a scholar that "he who has not enjoyed the pleasure that a man has when he manages to find an answer to the doubts to which his mind has given birth, has never in his life known true joy."[38] The human mind is compared by him to a burning torch that lights up the darkness. He believes that man's

31. *Ibid.*, Chapter 19.
32. *Ibid.*, Chapter 42.
33. *Ibid.*, Chapter 6, folio 42.
34. *Ibid.*, Chapter 26, folio 56.
35. Isserles himself frankly admits (*Responsa*, 7) that his style is quite unpolished and that he has only slight knowledge of grammar.
36. *Torat Ha-Olah*, III, Chapters 51, 53, 73.
37. *Ibid.*, Chapter 48, 60.
38. *Ibid.*, I, Chapter 6.

uniqueness consists in seeking and exploring the goal and purpose of being, and that his chief task is to clarify the essence
of everything through logical reason.[39] Isserles agrees with
Maimonides that the truly perfected man is one who, with the
aid of his intellect, has recognized the truth,[40] and that moral
perfection is only a stage to the supreme perfection—the perfection of the mind, thanks to which man obtains correct notions of divinity and of everything that exists.[41]

But this follower and admirer of Maimonides had very odd
notions of searching and knowing, of "perception of, and medi-
tation on, God." Raised in the arid, overly subtle atmosphere
of *pilpul*, Isserles saw in dialectical acrobatics and scholastic
ingenuities the surest way leading to the highest spiritual and
intellectual perfection. In this connection it is worth considering the chapters in the third part of *Torat Ha-Olah*[42] in which
the reasons why Moses hesitated so long and did not wish to
fulfil God's mission to Pharaoh are disclosed with keen *pilpul*.
The father of the prophets was thrown into deep doubts by the
seven arguments which the "heretics" and "deniers" set forth
against the creation of the world. Whereupon God Himself
entered into a long discussion with Moses in order "to refute
Aristotle's arguments" to the effect that the world is eternal.
God, Isserles insists, made use in this connection of Maimonides' strict proofs.[43] In a moment of dire need, when God did
not succeed in refuting one of Aristotle's arguments, He nullified it not with logical demonstrations but with a miracle that
He performed.[44] When Isserles speaks of the curses with which
the Torah threatens those who violate sexual morality he also
finds this an opportune time to demonstrate through *pilpul* that
the "father's wife" means the Torah from heaven, that "his
sister, his father's daughter" is prophecy,[45] etc.

In this respect Isserles's allegorical commentary to the Scroll
of Esther, *Mehir Yayin*, is also interesting. When an epidemic
of cholera broke out in Cracow in 1556 Isserles went to Szyd-
lowiec and there, to pass the time, wrote his commentary in

39. *Ibid.*, III, Chapter 7, folio 79.
40. *Ibid.*, Chapter 73, folio 173: "For he who has attained the truth is among the men
of excellence, and he who has not attained it is in the category of those who go
down to the pit of destruction."
41. *Torat Ha-Olah*, folio 79.
42. *Ibid.*, 104–108.
43. *Ibid.*, folio 108.
44. *Ibid.*, Chapter 46, 107b.
45. *Ibid.*, folio 106.

which the whole Book of Esther is transformed into a symbolic parable of man's life. The kingdom of Ahasuerus "from India to Cush" is man's life from the day of his birth to the day of his death, the golden dishes are an allusion to the desires of women, the seven eunuch chamberlains are man's basic powers, the king's two servants are the two cherubim at the gates of the Garden of Eden, Haman's wife is man's imagination, the Jew Mordecai is the human intellect, etc. At the end the author himself admits that the entire allegory, which is veiled in an ingenious web of *pilpul*, is merely intellectual play and by no means seriously intended.

Isserles does, indeed, quote Maimonides' *Guide for the Perplexed* at every turn in *Torat Ha-Olah*, but the two works are worlds apart. The author himself did not even notice this; the true spirit of the *Guide* was so alien to him that he naively believed that he was Maimonides' faithful disciple and his work a spiritual brother of the *Guide.* In this connection one must also take into consideration that in Isserles' generation the Kabbalah already dominated the minds of Jews. It permeated all of rabbinic creativity, the whole Jewish way of life, with its spirit. Isserles had the profoundest respect for the "wisdom of the Kabbalah." Kabbalah, after all, signifies not only mysticism but tradition, the heritage of the fathers. The men of the Kabbalah are guardians of great truths transmitted from mouth to mouth, from generation to generation, through the long chain which extends directly from Moses. Hence, the sober pilpulist Isserles, to whom mystical fervor and emotional enthusiasm were so alien, was also firmly convinced that "all the words of the Kabbalists are true"[46] and that the wisdom of the Kabbalah is "the true tree of life."[47] It did not even occur to him that the mystical Kabbalah and Aristotelian rationalism are two different worlds, two antithetical world-views. What mainly interested him in the Kabbalah was also the intellectual, the theoretical and logical, and he arrived at the conclusion that "all the sages intended one thing."[48] It is not by accident that Isserles so eagerly quotes the words of the Kabbalist Moses Botarel that "the wisdom of the Kabbalah and the wisdom of philosophy speak of one and the same thing, but with different words" (*Ibid.*, 75). Isserles himself concludes that

46. *Ibid.*, III, Chapter 4.
47. *Ibid.*, folio 77.
48. *Ibid.*, folio 72: *Kol ha-ḥachamim le-devarim aḥat* (?) *kivvenu.* Such grammatically awkward sentences are frequently encountered in Isserles' writings.

"it is known to everyone that the ways of the Kabbalah are essentially the ways of the true philosophers."[49]

Hence, Isserles' great indignation when he saw that, because the *Zohar* and other Kabbalist books were just then printed for the first time, many even of the common people began to study the Kabbalah is quite understandable. In the Kabbalah, too, Isserles saw above all *muskalot*, theoretical problems, a broad field for *pilpul* and intellectual exploits. Everything is thrown together by him in a mechanical mixture. Maimonides and Gersonides live quite peaceably in him alongside of Recanati, Hayyat and other Kabbalists. At one point he proceeds from Averroes' and Maimonides' views regarding the "intelligences"[50] and speaks at length of the universal role and significance of the "active intellect;" but along with this he concerns himself with *gematriot*[51] and believes firmly that through "combinations of letters," through joining the divine "names," a man may perform miracles and compel the planets to fulfill his will.[52] Now he argues, with Maimonides, that one who endeavors to fulfill the commandment "And thou shalt know the Lord" is closer to God than one who merely fasts and prays. At the same time, however, he expresses his great astonishment that Maimonides did not believe in the power of "combinations of letters" in view of the fact that the Kabbalists have, after all, the most assured knowledge of the marvelous and limitless power hidden in the "names" and their mysterious letters.[53]

Isserles frequently bases himself on the Kabbalists and believes with them in transmigration of souls and in the marvelous power concealed in "names" and numbers. He also wrote a commentary to the *Zohar*,[54] but neglected in it the most important point of the work, its ethical world-view, its teaching concerning the universal role of the human personality. Maimonides' rationalist teaching has its own pathos, the pathos of the convinced central idea, of militant thought. *A Guide for the Perplexed*, as well as its antipode, the mystical world of the *Zohar*, both have—each in its own way—their impressive power, their enormous drive, breaking through, persuading, and conquering. In the cold, sober *Torat Ha-Olah*, however,

49. *Ibid.*, folio 75.
50. *Ibid.*, I, Chapter 14.
51. *Ibid.*, Chapter 13; II, Chapter 6 ff.
52. *Ibid.*, Chapter 77, folio 163.
53. *Ibid.*, III, Chapter 4, folio 74.
54. It has remained in manuscript.

there is no spark of pathos; everything here is tediously inanimate and monotonously gray. There is in it much learning, rigorous piety, a wealth of subtle notions and *pilpul*, but the chief thing is lacking; there is no firm world-view, no proud flight of thought, eager for battle. The flame of the fervently believing heart, the trembling of the longing and questing soul is also missing. And if such a typical eclectic and epigone, who did not express a single independent philosophical idea, could pass in his generation as an original thinker and great expert in "external wisdoms," this is the best indication of how poor the Polish-German communities of that time were in the realm of secular knowledge.

The historical significance of Isserles, however, does not consist in his theological book of speculation. He became renowned as a codifier and author of keen legal responsa. We have already observed in the previous volume[55] that the Sephardic Joseph Karo was the classic representative of the tendency so clearly noticeable in the first generation of the Spanish exiles—not to presume to create new cultural values but to apply all energies to collecting and preserving with love and diligence the entire spiritual and religious heritage of previous generations, to systematize in the strictest order all the laws and rules with their further branches and interpretations. Karo labored a full twenty years on his monumental *Bet Yosef*, a compendium of all the laws and religious rules, assembled and ordered according to the pattern of Rabbi Jacob ben Asher's *Arbaah Turim*. In order that this compendium might be accessible to the Jewish masses, Karo composed his abridgment to *Bet Yosef*, the famous *Shulḥan Aruch*, in which are given in clear, simple statements, without discussion and in definitive form, all the laws and customs, following the same order as *Bet Yosef*.

Before the *Shulḥan Aruch* appeared, Moses Isserles had also come to the conclusion that it was necessary to create a popular collection of all the laws of Judaism. *Bet Yosef*, with its vast compass, did not satisfy him and he therefore himself wrote a commentary to *Arbaah Turim* and called it *Darchei Mosheh*.[56] Soon, however, the *Shulḥan Aruch*, which at once became extremely popular in the Sephardic communities, appeared. To be sure, the Ashkenazic rabbis were not entirely pleased with

55. See pp. 28ff.
56. Only the first two parts were published, and this many years after Isserles' death. The first part was printed in Fürth in 1760 and the second in Sulzbach in 1692.

the *Shulḥan Aruch,*[57] because the Sephardic Karo reckoned more with the authority of the Sephardic codifiers than of the Ashkenazic rabbis and in his decisions relied very little even on such great scholars as the French Tosafists. Karo, furthermore, took account mainly of the customs and way of life of the Sephardic communities and did not take into consideration the customs and order of the Ashkenazic Jews. So that the *Shulḥan Aruch* might truly become a work accessible to all and that the Polish communities might also be able to employ it in their religious practice, Moses Isserles made notes and comments on it and added many new paragraphs in which all the customs and laws which had entered into the life of the Polish Jews on the basis of the conditions prevalent in their midst are treated. This *Mappah* (Tablecloth) with which Isserles covered Karo's *Shulḥan Aruch* (Prepared Table) had a great role in the further development of rabbinic literature in Poland. Only thanks to Isserles' *Mappah* was the *Shulḥan Aruch* accepted also in the Polish-German communities as the authoritative code and guide in all religious and communal questions. The dominant place there, however, was occupied by the Ashkenazi, not the Sephardi, and where Isserles disagrees with the author of the *Shulḥan Aruch,* the law is according to Isserles.[58] Hence, in Poland the *Shulḥan Aruch* was printed only with Isserles' *Mappah,* and where there is a difference of opinion between the two codifiers, the publishers did not dilly-dally but threw out the corresponding passage in Karo. Thus, for example, the statement in which Karo declares that the custom of *Kapparot-shlogn* is a "foolish custom" was eliminated.

This joint work of the two great scholars, the Sephardi and the Ashkenazi, became in time the symbol, the incarnation, of rabbinic Judaism in its frozen and congealed forms. This compendium of laws and rules encompassed the entire life of the pious Jew like a thick net and gave strict supervision to his every step. Along with this, one must also take into considera-

57. For complaints against the *Shulḥan Aruch,* see Isserles' colleague Ḥayyim ben Bezalel, in the introduction to his *Vikkuaḥ Mayyim Ḥayyim* (Amsterdam, 1712); Rabbi Jehudah Loew of Prague, in his *Derech Ḥayyim* and *Derush Al Ha-Torah;* and many other rabbis of that age.

58. "Where there is a difference of opinion between the two great scholars of the *Shulḥan Aruch,*" writes Abraham Horowitz (of whom we shall speak later), "one must take greater account of Rabbi Moses Isserles' view." "In all the communities of Germany and Poland," writes Isaiah Horowitz, "it is already accepted that the decision is according to Rabbi Moses Isserles" (*Shenei Luḥot Ha-Berit,* Shaar Ha-Otiot).

tion that Isserles, in comparison with Karo, followed a strict interpretation of the law; his inclination was mainly to make the law more rigorous rather than more lenient. This is closely associated with the way Isserles maintains in his "notes" to the *Shulḥan Aruch.* For him, as for the major German rabbis, the accepted custom is considered the greatest authority of which one must take account. "No one may violate a custom," "a custom is not to be rejected"—such statements are repeated on numerous occasions by Isserles. "So they are accustomed to do"—this, for him, was the strongest argument. Since the German communities, which lived through many persecutions and expulsions in the course of generations, were extremely zealous, as we have several times observed, for the least custom and religious law, it is entirely understandable that the Ashkenazic decisor and codifier Isserles was also a strict constructionist in interpreting the religious precepts and prohibitions. The battlers for religious reform who, in the Haskalah period, issued forth so sharply against the heavy yoke that the *Shulḥan Aruch* imposed on the Jewish community were doubtless historically unjustified when they poured out all their wrath on the author of the *Mappah* and saw in him the symbol of obscurantism and the barbaric zealot who, with his severe rulings, made Jewish life so difficult and sad. Isserles, in fact, only expressed the moods prevalent in his environment. He did not create all the fences and restraints, all the strict customs which squeezed Jewish ghetto life like tongs. Indeed, we observe that wherever the custom, the expression of the popular will, is inclined to make the law more lenient, Isserles also becomes lenient and relies on the accepted custom. "The custom is to declare it fit for consumption" or "the custom is to be lenient," he notes in this connection. In consequence of the great reputation which Isserles obtained while still a young man, the most prominent rabbis would apply to him as the foremost authority in all important circumstances, and his Responsa[59] to all the difficult questions occupy a very important place in the rich responsa literature.

Of an altogether different stripe was the previously mentioned contemporary and close friend of Isserles, the famous Rabbi Solomon Luria, better known as Maharshal or Rashal. Luria was born in 1510 into a very prominent family tracing its genealogy back to Rabbi Solomon Yitzḥaki (Rashi). His

59. First published in 1640. We have employed the second edition published in Amsterdam in 1711.

birthplace has not been definitely ascertained. Some biographers indicate that he was born in Posen, others in Brest-Litovsk. It is known only that his teacher and guide was his grandfather, Isaac Klauber. In his youth Luria lived in Brest-Litovsk and other Lithuanian cities and around 1554 was elected rabbi in Ostrog, where he also founded his famous *yeshivah*. A short time later he was appointed chief rabbi of all Volhynia by royal decree. A man of obdurate will and strong character and also somewhat irascible, Luria acquired many enemies and opponents and, despite his great reputation as a scholar, had to lead a wanderer's life. He spent his last years in Lublin, where he died in 1573.

This Polish rabbi was endowed with the astute critical understanding of a first-rate scholar. Because he lived in a narrow, isolated environment, he employed his brilliant capacities only in the realm of *issur ve-heter* (what is forbidden and permitted in regard to food and related matters) and Talmudic questions.[60] In this limited field, however, he appears as an innovator and independent investigator. He was one of the first, perhaps indeed the first, to create the critical, scientific method of investigating the text of the Talmud and its commentaries. This profound and keen scholar laid down the way of precise understanding, of methodical inquiry into the complicated Talmudic text. In this connection, Luria manifests what was, for that time, quite extraordinary audaciousness, insofar as he is not at all carried away by the views and conclusions of the *Rishonim*, the rabbinical authorities of earlier generations. One of the later rabbis, the author of *Noda Be-Yehudah*, remarks with deep feeling: "Rabbi Solomon Luria had the courage to issue forth even against very great authorities, for he had the heart of a lion." Luria's slogan was "Back to the Talmud!" Only of the Talmud (the Babylonian and the Jerusalem) did he take account as the authoritative source for legal matters. In regard to all later commentators and codifiers he was quite independent, and not infrequently attacked them with extremely sharp strictures. Hence, he speaks with great mockery and contempt of those who blindly follow every author of previous generations and "cannot with their weak minds understand that the great scholars of former times could also be mistaken; they think everything that appears in an old manuscript is pure

---

60. Solomon Luria was also something of a liturgical poet, but his poems, *Zemirot Marshal* (1602), have very slight poetic value.

truth."[61] "To be sure," Luria adds sarcastically, "they, the codifiers, are indeed exalted, heavenly persons, but they explain and interpret like ordinary men. Hence, I give no more credence to one than the other . . . Only the Talmud is the arbitrator."[62]

Luria criticizes the rabbis and scholars of his generation even more sharply. In his day the number of *yeshivot* increased greatly in Poland, and their leaders were mainly disciples of the master of *pilpul*, Rabbi Shalom Shachna.[63] Luria, who was hostile to the method of *pilpul* which dominated these *yeshivot*, stresses the negative aspects of rabbinic culture in its first period of efflorescence in Poland. "Because of our many sins," he laments,

there are among us a great many who have *semichah* (rabbinic ordination) but very few good scholars. The number of the ignorant is growing. As soon as such a one obtains *semichah*, he makes himself great and gathers about himself young students, like the nobles who surround themselves with a whole retinue of servants . . . These are those who cannot comprehend any issue whatever in the Talmud or properly explain a *halachah*. . . . but these also rule over the community and over scholars, prohibit and permit, grant ordination to pupils who have not even studied with them but have given them payment and favors.[64]

Elsewhere Luria says, "There are rabbis who are extremely rigorous in interpretation of the law because they and their scribes profit from these rulings and their pockets are filled with money."[65]

Even more sharply than the author of *Vikkuaḥ Mayyim Ḥayyim* did Solomon Luria issue forth against the famed codifier of his day, Joseph Karo.[66] He could not pardon the latter's self-abasement before the authority of the *Rishonim*, the codifiers and scholars of previous generations, and therefore decided to compose a universal, exhaustive collection of all the

61. *Yam Shel Shelomoh*, the first introduction to the tractate *Ḥullin*.
62. *Ibid.*
63. The names of the rectors of the *yeshivot* in Poland and Belorussia of that era are listed in David Gans' *Tzemaḥ David*.
64. *Yam Shel Shelomoh*, Tractate *Bava Kama*, Ch. 8, No. 58.
65. *Ibid.*, Tractate *Kiddushin*, Ch. 2, No. 19.
66. On Luria's attacks on Joseph Karo, see Horodetzky, *Le-Korot Ha-Rabbanut*, p. 137, and Rav Tzair in *Ha-Shiloah*, V, 135. See also the second introduction to *Yam Shel Shelomoh*, Tractate *Ḥullin*.

halachot or laws, not basing himself on any of the codifiers but only on the sole source that he recognized—the Talmud. But Luria found that to utilize this single sure source, an enormously difficult task must first be executed—a critical examination of the accuracy of the Talmudic text. Until the first decades of the sixteenth century the Talmud circulated in various handwritten copies. The first printed editions, which appeared in Luria's youth, were carried through by men little suited for such responsible work; they did not even deem it necessary to correct the text by collating various manuscripts. Luria therefore believed it essential first to undertake the difficult and extremely time-consuming work of critically examining and emending the erroneous text, for he had concluded while still a young man that numerous contradictions and confusions in the old sources are to be explained by the fact that the Talmudic text had been corrupted by inept and careless copyists and that these errors had recently been magnified by printers and typesetters. There is no doubt that, thanks to the fine critical sense he manifested in this connection, the pious, orthodox Polish rabbi must be regarded as a predecessor of the "father of historical criticism," the free investigator and thinker Azariah dei Rossi. To recover the original, uncorrupted text when a sufficient number of ancient copies of the Talmud were not even at hand was a vastly difficult labor, and Luria's *Hochmat Shelomoh* is an extraordinary monument of rigorous, keen-minded, critical work and of immense scholarship. One must also take into consideration the respect Luria had for every word in the Talmud in order to understand the great caution with which he performed his critical work and how much effort the slightest textual change and emendation cost him.

The toilsome undertaking which Solomon Luria carried through in his *Hochmat Shelomoh* was only a prelude to his major work, *Yam Shel Shelomoh*, the abovementioned compendium of all the laws of the Talmud assembled in strictly systematic order and investigated and critically elucidated on the basis of the primary sources. Luria himself tells us of the thoroughness and depth with which he executed this work in his introductions to each individual tractate. He spent two entire years systematizing and explaining the laws in the first half of the tractate *Yevamot*, another year on the first two chapters in the tractate *Ketuvot*, and a half a year on only one chapter of the laws of *ḥalitzah*.[67] It is therefore not surprising that he did not manage to complete his monumental work but only to systematize and explain the laws of seven Talmudic tractates.[68]

The environment and the society, however, were, in a certain sense, stronger than the individual, even the brilliantly endowed individual. Solomon Luria does, indeed, display in his work the courage and acuteness of an independent critical investigator, but he could not tear himself out of the narrowly limited world-view of his surroundings. The *ḥochmot ḥitzoniyyot* (secular sciences) are considered by him the source of heresy and threatening destruction. "There is no heresy and ruin like their wisdom," he writes indignantly to his colleague, Moses Isserles.

Isserles, the compromiser and eclectic, was convinced that all the sciences and the entire philosophy possessed by the European peoples were borrowed from the Jews and drawn from the sacred Torah. Luria, however, refused to follow this compromise. There is no wisdom beyond the Torah; everything outside it is heresy—this was his slogan and credo. He cannot pardon Isserles for the fact that the latter, dealing with a certain matter in one of his responsa, relied on an argument of Aristotle's. "Like a knife cutting into living flesh," he writes in his angry reply,

have your words wounded me. You have surrounded me with whole packs of sciences, but mainly with secular sciences . . . You always mention the gentile Aristotle, and the true wisdom, our Torah, is veiled in sackcloth. She laments that her children forsake her . . . When I saw how you hold on to the wisdom of the gentile Aristotle, I cried out: Woe is me, that my eyes see and my ears hear that the best and the loveliest is hidden in the words of this unclean one, and the sages of Israel endeavor—God forbid—to adorn our sacred Torah with these words.[69]

Solomon Luria had an attitude of coldness and covert indignation toward Maimonides and his followers,[70] because they

---

67. *Yam Shel Shelomo*, Introduction to Tractate *Yevamot*.
68. *Bava Kamma, Yevamot, Betzah, Kiddushin, Gittin, Ketuvot*, and *Ḥullin*.
69. Isserles, *Responsa*, No. 6.
70. See the first introduction in *Yam Shel Shelomoh* to the Tractate *Ḥullin*. Luria also issues forth strongly against the free-thinking Abraham Ibn Ezra.

had devoted themselves so greatly to Aristotle's philosophy and to the secular sciences. Against them he sets up, as the ideal, the orthodox and pious sages of France, Rashi and Rabbenu Tam.

Like Isserles, Luria has the profoundest respect for popular customs. "The custom is not to be changed but followed," he frequently repeats and even notes that at times "a custom nullifies a law." But the punctilious Luria could not be satisfied with customs which, in his view, violate the bounds of strict piety and may destroy the restraints of modesty and chastity. Hence, he was a determined opponent of the cheerful games and pastimes with which the young would spend their leisure. He complained especially of dances in which boys and girls participated together. "When men and women sit together at a wedding," he declares, "one may not recite the blessing 'For joy is in His habitation,' for at that hour there is no joy before the Holy One, blessed be He, in His habitation."

CHAPTER THREE

Disciples of Isserles and Commentators on the Shulḥan Aruch

Echoes and after-effects of the Renaissance era—The aprocryphal letter of Aristotle—Twilight—David Gans and his *Tzemaḥ David*—Abraham Horowitz as rationalist—The rationalist as penitent—Horowitz as author of *Berit Avraham* and *Yesh Noḥalin*—Mordecai Jaffe as eclectic—The reactionary moods and their causes—Rabbi Solomon Edels and Rabbi Meir of Lublin—The commentators on the *Shulḥan Aruch:* Joel Sirkes (*Baḥ*), Joshua Falk (*Sema*), and Shabbetai Kohen (*Shach*)—The shadowy aspects of rabbinic literature in Poland —The overly subtle *pilpul*.

 E OBSERVED in the previous chapter that in the second half of the sixteenth century in Poland, especially in the *yeshivah* of Cracow headed by Rabbi Moses Isserles, the influence of medieval religious philosophy was still felt. The irascible Rabbi Solomon Luria complains strongly of Isserles in his letter quoted above: "I have myself seen how in the prayerbooks of the students at the *yeshivah* the prayer of Aristotle is written, and for this the negligence of so great a man as yourself is responsible, for you yourself mingle Aristotle's words with the living words of God."[1]

1. Isserles, *Responsa*, No. 6

This great "sin" of the Talmudic students, who had Aristotle's letter inscribed in their prayerbooks, shows most clearly what a weak resonance philosophical ideas obtained in Moses Isserles' *yeshivah* and in what naive forms they found expression there. The prayer of Aristotle to which Solomon Luria alludes is undoubtedly the well-known legendary letter which Aristotle is supposed to have sent to his pupil, Alexander of Macedon.[2] In this letter the famous Greek thinker becomes a penitent. He regrets the views he had previously expressed in his works, because some "sage of the sages of Israel" had a discussion with him and showed him that the opinions he had uttered were false. Aristotle's error consisted in believing that truth can be attained only in the purely rationalist way, through intellectual inquiry. But now, thanks to the "sage of the sages of Israel," he knows that man can attain the truth only with the aid of divine revelation. "If I could assemble all my works that are scattered over the whole world," Aristotle further admits, "I would burn all and not leave one of them, so that they might not lead others astray." This letter of "repentance" made Aristotle acceptable in the eyes of the pious Talmudic students. They forgave him his "heretical doctrine" that the world is eternal because in his old age, thanks to the "sage of the sages of Israel," he repented.

In any case, Moses Isserles' *yeshivah* was the only one that had a certain number of scholars who were more or less competent in "the external wisdoms," or secular sciences. These few men, who refused to lock themselves up entirely in the "four cubits of the law," are extremely interesting for the period in question, because in them are reflected most clearly the contemporary twilight moods in the light of the last rays of the Renaissance which were about to set and would soon be covered by the shadows of the growing reaction.

We shall here pause on only three of these interesting personalities, all disciples of Moses Isserles. A special place among them is occupied by David ben Solomon Gans, the only representative of secular knowledge in his milieu, the only scholar who had the courage to concern himself not with rabbinic responsa and religious laws but with scientific matters. Born in a small Westphalian community (in Lippstadt in 1541), Gans was educated in German Talmudic academies (at Bonn and

2. See Gedaliah Ibn Yahya, *Shalshelet Ha-kabbalah.*

Frankfurt) and then came to Cracow to study with Moses Isserles. He later reported the great influence Isserles had on him.[3] In his lectures and explanations Isserles would frequently base himself on arguments from various sciences, such as astronomy, mathematics, and philosophy; this aroused in Gans, who was eager for knowledge, a strong desire for these "external wisdoms."

Not about the men of *ḥillukim*, the great masters in the realm of *pilpul*, did the youthful David Gans dream, but of Euclid, Ptolemy, and Copernicus. For some time, while living in the town of Nordheim, he occupied himself especially with Euclid's mathematics.[4] After settling in Prague in 1564, he devoted himself intensively to astronomy, worked in the local observatory, and in this way had occasion to become acquainted with the famous scientists Kepler and Tycho Brahe. Especially for Tycho Brahe he made extracts of the Hebrew reworking of the famous Alphonsine Tables.[5] He was also in correspondence with the well-known astronomer Johann Müller (Regiomontanus). Gans' work *Neḥmad Ve-Naim*, on astronomy and mathematical geography,[6] is the mature result of his scientific activities. In the introduction the author gives a historical overview of the development of these sciences. But it was not because of these scientific works that he became known throughout Israel. It was his historical chronicle, the universally known *Tzemaḥ David*,[7] which made him famous. Moses Isserles, who himself provided Abraham Zacuto's *Yuḥasin* with necessary notes and addenda, also strengthened in his pupil who hungered for knowledge a desire to occupy himself with history. To arouse interest in historical events among the masses of the people, Gans decided to produce a popularly written chronicle of Jewish and general history. In the preface to his book he writes: "I do not here intend to become well known and obtain great honor; after all, anyone can write such a purely compiled work. I have not written my book for sages and scholars filled with Torah, but for ordinary householders and young people." In the introduction to the second part, the author notes: "I

---

3. See the preface to *Neḥmad Ve-Naim*, where Gans mentions his teacher in Cracow with keen gratitude: "The pious man, my master and teacher who nourished and raised me, Rabbi Moses Isserles."

4. See *Tzemaḥ David*, I, 52 (we quote according to the Warsaw edition of 1878).

5. See the preface to *Neḥmad Ve-Naim*.

6. Published in Jessnitz, 1743, by Joel ben Yekutiel of Glogau. Gans' other mathematical works, *Meor Ha-Katan*, *Migdal David*, and others, were eventually lost.

7. Completed in 1592.

wrote my book for a generation wearied by grievous exile. My desire is to rejoice the saddened souls of plain householders who obtain their morsel of bread with great trouble and toil. Let them, after their painful anxieties and labor, forget their cares as they read the interesting events of former and later times."

In the first part of his work Gans presents, in brief notes written according to chronological order, an overview of the major events and significant personalities in Jewish history from the Biblical period to 1592.[8] In the second part he gives a general overview of world history from the ancient kings of Babylonia to the emperor Leopold who ruled in his own time. In putting together the second part, Gans employed the chronicles of Cyriak Spangenberg, Laurentius Faustus, Hubertus Holzius, Georg Cassino, Martin Borisk and others. The author himself, in noting this in the preface to the second part, deems it necessary to defend himself for employing alien sources deriving from non-Jews.

I foresee that many will complain of my using foreign, non-Jewish writers and relating here, in the second part of my work, wars and other things which are in their eyes secular matters, for they think that such vain words may not in any case be read on the holy Sabbath day. I will not enter into any long defense here. Let my protection and support be the great scholars in Israel, the Jewish religious thinkers, who used to take from Aristotle and other philosophers everything that had a proper kernel and discarded the husk.

Gans observes, in this connection, that previous Jewish historians, such as Abraham Zacuto, Joseph Ha-Kohen, and others, also utilized foreign sources. He is certain that this is "for the sake of heaven," for such historical chronicles may, after all, be extremely useful, since from all the stories and events described in them one sees very clearly "how vast is God's providence over his faithful sheep; when great and powerful kings and states were destroyed, so that not even any memory of them remained, God, blessed be He, sheltered the people of Israel under His wings and did not permit them to be consumed."

It is characteristic of our author that, among accounts of various political events and wars, he considers it necessary especially to stress the immense importance of Gutenberg's

8. Gans also wrote a special treatise on the Ten Tribes (*Tzemaḥ David*, I, 19). This work, however, has not been preserved.

·◦❧{ *48* }❧◦·

great invention, the printing-press.[9] But the ardent admirer of the printing-press is also an extremely pious and God-fearing Jew. He therefore deems it essential to note all the epidemics, troubles, and afflictions, such as floods, earthquakes, and various signs that have appeared in the heavens; for these, he asserts, are tokens and harbingers of coming oppressions and trials. Here appear most clearly the contradictory moods and tendencies that are so characteristic of the twilight period, of the time of the parting of ways and spiritual crisis. An excellent astronomer, Gans knew quite well the circumstances under which eclipses of the sun and moon occur, and he tells of this at considerable length in his *Neḥmad Ve-Naim*. Nevertheless, he feels obliged at once to add: "It cannot, however, be in any way denied that eclipses proclaim the tidings of evil decrees, as the sages of the Talmud long ago pointed out."[10] The same is true in regard to earthquakes. Gans knew very well that there are "those" who explain earthquakes in an altogether natural fashion. "We, however," he adds, "know from the mouth of the prophets that an earthquake is a manifestation of God's wrath."

When Gans mentions "those" who explain earthquakes naturalistically, he points to Azariah dei Rossi,[11] whose work is quoted most in *Tzemaḥ David*. Gans here finds himself in a certain embarrassment. He reckons chronology in his work, as was the custom among Jews, from the creation of the world. But he had diligently studied dei Rossi's *Meor Enayim*, in which it is thoroughly demonstrated that the Jewish system of reckoning time is built on very weak foundations.[12] The scientifically competent Gans can appreciate the weighty arguments of dei Rossi, and he must admit that the latter has established his thesis "with common sense and good reason" and that it is extremely difficult to refute his arguments. But dei Rossi's thesis is inconsistent with the tradition of the fathers; hence, it *must* be refuted, it *must* be shown that his arguments are not arguments, that his proofs are not proofs. The pious Gans undertakes this thankless task and, indeed, immediately indicates what he intends thereby: "The purpose of my words is to urge that we do not need to follow new theories, but to hold

9. "There is no other invention of such great benefit to all the inhabitants of the world, and nothing is comparable to it in value among all the sciences and inventions from the time God created man on earth."
10. *Neḥmad Ve-Naim*, Gate Eleven, No. 297.
11. *Tzemaḥ David*, II, 187.
12. See our *History*, Vol. IV, p. 109.

fast to that which our fathers have left us as a legacy. The tradition and the customs of our fathers is a Torah for us, and we will remain faithful to it throughout all generations unto eternity. It will not depart from our mouths and from the mouths of our children and the mouths of our children's children forever."[13]

"Let us not seek new things"—for the sake of this slogan, which for many generations dominated the entire German-Polish community, David Gans, the competent student of Copernicus' new astronomical system and the good friend of the great Kepler, nevertheless held with iron tenacity to the Ptolemaic astronomy which Copernicus had just ruthlessly undermined. He assures his readers that the Ptolemaic system will remain valid "in the present day and to the end of all generations."

Thus did the power of *kabbalat avot*, the tradition of the previous generations, destroy, in the reaction that was constantly intensified at the end of the sixteenth century,[14] even the smallest shoots of free speculative thought. Especially interesting in this respect are the transformations which another pupil of Moses Isserles, Abraham Sheftels[15] or Abraham Halevi Horowitz,[16] went through in the course of his literary activity.

Very little is known to us of Horowitz's life. We know only that his father Sheftel (Shabbetai) ben Isaiah was a rabbinic judge in Prague, where Abraham spent his youth. From several remarks in his *Yesh Noḥalin*, which he wrote in his old age, it may be conjectured that Abraham Sheftels in his young manhood lived a free and lusty life and did not despise the "bitter drop." "This day I remember my sins," writes the aged Horowitz; "I used at times to stumble in the matter of intoxication, and because I was often drunk in youth I was not always careful in this condition to remove myself from sin." From Prague the young Horowitz moved to the new Jewish cultural center, Cracow, to study Torah in the famous *yeshivah* of Rabbi Moses Isserles. Isserles, the ardent follower of Maimonides, aroused in his intellectually curious pupil a great desire for

13. *Tzemaḥ David*, I, 25–26; II, 77.
14. See our *History*, Vol. IV, pp. 115ff.
15. He is mentioned quite frequently under this name by his son's contemporary and good friend, Joseph Juspa of Nördlingen, the author of *Yosif Ometz*.
16. This interesting personality was first critically explored by the historian S. P. Rabinowitch in *Yevreyskaya Starina*, 1911. See also S. A. Horodetzky's article in the same journal, 1913, 146–158.

books of speculation, but the pupil went considerably further than his master, With great enthusiasm he immersed himself in medieval Jewish religious philosophy, and his first work, *Ḥesed Le-Avraham*,[17] was a commentary to Maimonides' *Shemoneh Perakim* and to Samuel Ibn Tibbon's introduction to *Shemoneh Perakim*. In this commentary, which Horowitz wrote, as he himself notes in the introduction, in a clear, popular form "for the benefit of men and young students who are not accustomed to walking in the ways of speculation," the author frequently repeats the typically Maimonidean notion that even the received text of the sacred books must be based on the foundations of philosophical investigation. Shortly afterwards Horowitz left Cracow and settled in Posen. Here in 1559 he issued a tract[18] which undoubtedly has a cultural-historical significance, for it acquaints us with the ideological moods which even at that time already had followers among certain strata of the Jewish youth.

From this tract we learn, first of all, that even before the young Horowitz went away to study in the *yeshivah* of Cracow there was an obdurate struggle among the students in the *yeshivah* of Prague between the "orthodox" and the "freethinking" elements. At the head of the orthodox group was a young zealot named Joseph. A great scholar in the Talmud, he was, in addition, an ardent Kabbalist and believed fully that the prophet Elijah himself came to visit him at night. He was a fierce opponent of "secular sciences," declared Maimonides a "complete heretic," and warned the students of the *yeshivah* that they should not dare read *A Guide for the Perplexed*, because it is filled with heresy. The young zealot complained strongly, however, not only of Maimonides but even of such orthodox, pious scholars as Rabbi Solomon ben Adret, Rabbi Isaac Arama and Rabbi Isaac Abravanel, because these maintained that some of the Talmudic *aggadot* or legends must be considered merely allegorical parables and not be interpreted literally.[19]

17. Written in the middle of the 1550's and first published in 1577.
18. This work was not preserved in full. P. Bloch found only a part of the tract in Gaster's collection of manuscripts and published it as an anonymous fragment (since the beginning and the end were missing) in *MGWJ*, 1903. S. P. Rabinowitch, in the article mentioned above, was the first to show that this is a fragment of Horowitz's polemic work.
19. This pious Kabbalist later went to Palestine and settled in Safed where he became one of Rabbi Isaac Luria's associates. In Palestine he was known by the name Joseph Ashkenazi and acquired a great reputation not only as a Kabbalist but also

Leading the "freethinkers" in the Prague *yeshivah* was Abraham Sheftels, who used to carry on constant debates with the opponent of the secular sciences, Joseph. Several years later the disputants met again in Posen, where the Kabbalist Joseph, together with his father-in-law Aaron, who had just been appointed district rabbi of Great Poland and become head of the *yeshivah* in Posen, returned almost at the same time (in 1557) as Abraham Sheftels.[20] Joseph deemed it necessary to carry on his battle against philosophy and books of speculation also in the capital city of Great Poland and further influenced his father-in-law to summon up all his energy and cooperate in the holy war. Rabbi Aaron was an extremely pious man with an altogether unique outlook. It is worth noting that in one of the sermons he preached in the synagogue he announced that in the present generation the sorcerers have lost all their power, because Ashmedai, the king of the demons, died not long ago and his place has been taken by a new king and the sorcerers have still not understood "what his nature is" and with what sort of incantations one can approach him.[21] Under the influence of his zealous son-in-law, Rabbi Aaron issued forth on the Great Sabbath of the year 1559 with a fiery sermon against the secular sciences *(ḥochmot ḥitzoniyyot).* He urged upon his congregation that one must occupy himself day and night only with the Talmud and its commentaries and supplements.

All other books belong to the "books of Homer" of which the Talmud says that they "may not be read" and ought to be thrown into the fire. One must also not spend too much time on the twenty-four books of the Bible.[22] Rabbi Aaron even saw God's just punishment in the fact that in 1554, at the command of Pope Paul IV, copies of the Talmud had been burned in most Italian cities. This was a punishment for the fact that three years earlier, in 1551, such a heretical work as Maimonides' *Guide for the Perplexed* had been published in Venice.[23]

This sermon enraged the "freethinkers" of Posen. They refused to forgive the old rabbi for undertaking to insult his and their teacher and guide, Maimonides. Abraham Sheftels came forward with his tract in response to Rabbi Aaron's ser-

---

as an outstanding expositor of the Mishnah. He was reverently called the "great Tanna." See David Conforte, *Kore Ha-Dorot,* 36b (we quote according to the Venice edition); Kaufmann, *MGWJ,* 1898, 38.

20. See *Tzemaḥ David,* I, 56 (Warsaw edition, 1878).
21. *MGWJ,* 1903, 278.
22. *Ibid.,* 167.
23. *Ibid.,* 346.

mon. The tract is written in an extremely sharp and, in places, rather crude tone. The rabbi and his son-in-law are frequently complimented with such epithets as fool, wicked man, ass, filthy mind, etc. These invectives cannot, however, diminish the literary value of this battle document. A belligerent temperament, a wrathful impetuousness and passionate tone, are clearly felt in it. The bitter sarcasm and brilliant style of the work remind one in places of the talented satirist who wrote *Alilot Devarim.*[24] Like the latter, Abraham Sheftels disliked insinuations and half words and openly and freely expressed "heretical" thoughts such as could hardly have been expected from a pupil in a pious Polish *yeshivah.* The rabbi of Posen had again stirred up the old question: May one occupy himself with secular knowledge outside the Talmud? Rabbi Aaron, as we have seen, answered this question quite definitely: No, it is forbidden to read books on the "external wisdoms." Abraham Sheftels issues forth with the same decisiveness with his reply: We cannot get along with the Talmud alone. It is written in the Torah, "For it is your wisdom and your understanding in the eyes of the nations." Merely with scholarship "in all chambers of the Talmud," he declares sarcastically, we will not pass in the eyes of the nations of the world as a wise and understanding people. On the contrary, the Talmud, with its theories and homilies, is a mockery and laughter in the eyes of the nations.[25] And we know very well from experience that even in religious disputations only the *baalei ha-ḥochmot,* the masters of wisdom, those who are proficient in various sciences, triumph.[26] Horowitz refuses to be content with the pious compromisers who seek authorization to occupy oneself with the "external wisdoms" at the time of twilight, in the free moments of the period between day and night. He speaks frequently of equal rights, maintaining that secular studies deserve no less attention than study of the Talmud. "Every study, every branch of knowledge," he declares, "demands a great deal of toil and trouble, whether it be the Bible, the Talmud, or any of the other sciences. Every man is obliged to perfect himself in these as much as possible, and whoever does not fulfill this obligation will have to give account for it in the future."[27]

Horowitz's highest ideal is Maimonides. In him he sees the

24. See our History, Vol. III, pp. 271–77.
25. *MGWJ*, 1903, 263.
26. *Ibid.*
27. *Ibid.*, 268.

proud battler for philosophical thought. Hence, he pours out all his wrath on the rabbi of Posen and his son-in-law who permitted themselves to charge Maimonides with heresy. Like owls and bats that cannot bear the light of the sun's rays, Horowitz indignantly exclaims, so you blind fools, who believe in every idiocy and madness, cannot bear the light of Maimonides' wisdom. You have the presumption to declare as a book of pure heresy his *Guide for the Perplexed*—the faithful pointer of the way, the wondrous medicine which heals all poisonous wounds and liberates one from all spiritual and intellectual doubts! This book has a peerless capacity for refreshing man's languishing soul, enlightening his mind, and raising him above the vanities of life. It liberates him from superstition and encourages him to destroy all the idols and false gods and to raise himself to the level of true perfection. And you undertake to declare such a book noxious? You, obscure men, cannot forgive Maimonides for the bitter truth that he expressed in his day about such foolish and ignorant rabbis as you are.[28] Against the great scholar in Israel, against the godly man *(ha-ish ha-elohi)* Rabbi Moses ben Maimon, undertake to come forward such petty, ignorant men as tell the people from the pulpit wild, foolish tales that Ashmedai the king of the demons has died, and because the sorcerers are still not familiar with his successor, they can now have no power! Laugh at him, all you men of understanding, make him a mockery and scorn! Declare openly whether such a man is fit to be a judge presiding over an entire country. Is this not the greatest shame for the whole land?[29]

Abraham Horowitz writes further:

And a man of such poverty of understanding has the impudence to explain to his congregation that the "decree" concerning the burning of the Talmud which took place not long ago in Italy is a punishment for the fact that *A Guide for the Perplexed* was printed in Venice several years before. Does this foolish rabbi not know that two hundred years ago[30] the Talmud was also burned in masses? This was in France shortly after the *Guide for the Perplexed* was consumed at the stake as a result of the denunciation of fanatical, ignorant rabbis, like the present rabbi of Posen. Forty days after the *Guide* was burned, volumes of the Talmud were put to the torch in the very same place,

28. *Ibid.*, 268–270.
29. *Ibid.*, 278
30. In fact it was three hundred years earlier.

and the ashes of the *Guide's* pages were mingled with the ashes of the Talmud . . .[31]

The previously mentioned satirist, the author of *Alilot Deva-rim*, and his associates fought for a lost cause,[32] but they battled courageously to the end in the firm belief that they were struggling for the truth and that their ideal was the only valid one. Another fate was appointed for their follower who carried on the struggle under Maimonides' flag a hundred years later. The Sephardic community had already been destroyed. In Italy the rays of the Renaissance had been covered by the thick clouds of the Catholic Counter-Reformation, which also choked the reforming tendencies in Poland. Under the cold breath of the intensified reaction, Abraham Horowitz also eventually repented. He himself destroyed what he had earlier built. A stormy battler for free thought in his youth, he became in his old age a pious teacher of morality who preached repentance and mystical asceticism. In his youth he wrote his rationalist commentary *Ḥesed Le-Avraham*. In his old age (1602) he regretted it and considered it necessary to re-write his commentary in a completely new fashion. In the introduction he promptly announces that in the first version, written in his younger years, there are many things that "are not according to the truth but according to imagination." In the commentary itself he constantly repeats *mea culpa* and points out to the reader that in the first version "I interpreted this very differently" but this was false: "Remove the first version; as I have written here, so is the principle."[33] The militant lampoonist became in time a humble and modest man. "I am dust and ashes"—with these words he begins his ascetic and pious book of ethical instruction, *Berit Avraham*. "I know the truth," Horowitz further writes in his introduction, "that every man is destined to give reckoning and account before God, and so I thought in my heart: What shall I do and what shall I answer when the day comes and I will have to stand before the true judge? I then heard in the depths of my soul the warning words: Mortal man, enough sleeping! Arise and enter God's house!"

The whole work, which consists of thirteen chapters, is per-

31. *MGWJ*, 1903, 346–47.
32. See our *History*, Vol. III, pp. 271–77.
33. The second version of *Ḥesed Le-Avraham* is printed in all Talmud editions together with *Shemoneh Perakim*.

meated with one fundamental idea—repentance. "With repentance we shall obtain merit and live and inherit the life of the world to come!" the author exclaims. Repentance is,the final goal of all man's goals. It is the acme of human perfection. The work ends with a series of prayers and supplications, "new as well as old," and a tremendously long litany of confession *(ashamnu be-aruch)*. All these prayers and supplications, as well as the commentary to them, that are given in *Berit Avraham*, testify to the profound moods of penitence and regret which the erstwhile rationalist and freethinker experienced.

Horowitz's later works, *Emek Ha-Berachah*[34] (on the benedictions connected with the enjoyment of food or drink) and *Yesh Noḥalin*, which was popular for generations, are saturated with the same penitent moods. *Yesh Noḥalin* is a kind of testament which the aged Horowitz left for his children and in which he gives them ethical instruction and teaches them how to follow the right path and not stumble. It is extremely difficult to recognize in this book, written in such a humble, ascetic tone, the former militant lampoonist. All of man's thought and action, the aged Horowitz tells his children, should be permeated with one idea—to serve God, to strive toward the goal of sanctifying life. "The whole world with all its clamor, with all its deeds, its glory and greatness," declares Horowitz, "is foolish and vain beside the service of God." Every limb in man must be an agent for serving God: "the ears must receive the word of the sacred Torah; the eyes must turn to heaven; the lips must be pure in order that they may teach the ignorant, reprove the wicked, and console the downcast; the feet must walk in God's way and go to aid the needy, hasten to the synagogue three times a day, arrive among the first and depart among the last."

One must serve God, Horowitz repeatedly insists, not out of fear of punishment. "You shall not occupy yourself with the commandments in order to obtain a reward, or remove yourself from sin out of fear of punishment, but you shall serve God out of love." Man must sanctify and purify life, as it is written in the Torah: "Ye shall be holy." A person must spend as much time as possible in solitude. For the sake of God he ought not to utter profane words, for this is "the ugliest of all qualities." He should flee from controversy and not bear hatred toward anyone, "for hatred prevents one from doing good." "Take care not to anger a gentile, for he is vengeful and wrath burns everlastingly in him." "Be of the humble, for humility is the

---

34. First published in 1597 with marginal comments by his son Isaiah Horowitz.

greatest virtue; it is even more important than wisdom." "Love one another," Horowitz concludes his testament, "and let peace prevail among you."

No less typical is the third and, incidentally, most important of the three pupils of Rabbi Moses Isserles mentioned above— Rabbi Mordecai ben Abraham Jaffe. Whereas Horowitz's world-outlook changed in the course of years, in Jaffe one can observe at the same time a mixture of the most varied conceptions and moods.

Mordecai Jaffe was born in 1530 in Prague into a very prominent family. His father Abraham was a great scholar and respected communal leader. Some historians conclude that he is to be identified with the *Hofjude* or court Jew Abraham Bohemus, whom numerous historical sources mention as "prefect" and tax collector over all the Jewish communities in Poland.[36] Already as a boy Mordecai Jaffe manifested extremely brilliant capacities, and his father sent him to the major center of Torah of that time, Poland. There the young Jaffe spent several years in the *yeshivot* of the great scholars Rabbi Solomon Luria and Rabbi Moses Isserles. Isserles had an especially strong influence on Mordecai Jaffe, arousing in his intellectually curious pupil interest in philosophical problems. Shortly after Jaffe returned to his home and there established a large *yeshivah*, a time of trouble began for the Jews in Bohemia. By a decree of 1561 all Jews had to leave Prague. Jaffe then went to Italy where he devoted himself intensively not only to rabbinic literature but also to "external wisdoms"—philosophy and mathematics. From Italy he went to Lithuania. In 1572 he was rabbi in Grodno and from there came to Lublin. At that time his name already resounded throughout the Jewish world and he was recognized as a great scholar and spiritual leader of all of Polish Jewry. In Lublin Jaffe's organizational abilities manifested themselves in their full splendor. Thanks to his energetic activity, the national-communal role of the *Vaad Arba Aratzot* (Council of Four Lands), whose meetings were held in Lublin at the time of the great fairs, increased greatly. Mordecai Jaffe's signature leads those of all the thirty rabbis who subscribed to the well-known ordinance of 1590 "that no rabbi shall receive rabbinic office for money (given) before or after, or through other conditions that bring monetary profit."[37] Jaffe later oc-

---

36. See *Yevreyskaya Starina*, 1912, 355.
37. See the Yaraslov proclamation of 1640 published in Harkavy's *Hadashim Gam Yeshanim*, No. 3, 17.

cupied the rabbinic office in Kremenets (Volhynia) for a short period, and in 1592 was invited to be rabbi in his native city of Prague. As a seventy-year-old he went to Posen, where he died in 1612 in the eighty-second year of his life.

In rabbinic literature Mordecai Jaffe attained a vast reputation with his five-volume *Levushim,*[38] a collection embracing the whole of rabbinic law, with all its rules and decisions. This work, which appeared in three editions in the author's own lifetime, contended for some decades with the *Shulḥan Aruch* for the dominant place as the code of rabbinic practice, and it was difficult to decide which of them would prevail and remain the universally recognized law-book and guide in ritual-religious life. The *Shulḥan Aruch* finally won out, despite the fact that Jaffe's *Levushim* is written in clearer language and the material is better arranged.[39]

Mordecai Jaffe's literary activity, however, was not limited to laws and religious rules. Like his teacher Moses Isserles, who wrote notes to *A Guide for the Perplexed* and the speculative work *Torat Ha-Olah,* Jaffe also composed a commentary to the *Guide* and to Maimonides' work on the laws of sanctifying the new moon *(Levush Or Yekarot).* He also wrote a work, *Levush Eder Ha-Yakar,* on astronomical calculations and the Jewish mode of reckoning time. The intellectual decline of that period is clearly noticeable, however, in the literary activity of this great scholar. Jaffe was quite tolerant of the "external wisdoms" and philosophical speculation, by which he understood only Aristotle's teaching—and that in the vesture which it obtained in Maimonides' *Guide.* But he considered it necessary to set forth the following two conditions: first, one may look only into such books of speculation as are altogether free of heretical ideas, and second, only those who are already well versed in the Talmud and are clear about all the laws and commandments may concern themselves with "external wisdoms."[40]

Along with this, Jaffe regards it as essential to emphasize the profound abyss that separates the "external wisdoms" from the sacred Torah, for the compass of all the sciences is, after all, extremely limited and nothing new can be devised in this

---

38. The title is characteristic of the style of that era. Since his name was Mordecai and in the scroll of Esther it is written, "And Mordecai went out in the dress *(levush)* of royalty," Jaffe clothed all ten works that he composed with the title *Levush.* Hence he is known in rabbinic literature by the name Baal Ha-Levushim.

39. On this, see the work of Rav Tzair in *Ha-Shiloah,* VI, 129–136.

40. See *Levush Ateret Zahav,* Chapter 246, No. 4.

realm, while the Torah is as deep as the sea and has no boundaries or shores. Quite characteristic is the following passage:

The sages of Israel occupy themselves with the wisdom of the Torah and prophecy, which is wider than the world and deeper than the sea. It is impossible to grasp its mysteries, to fathom its depth, for from every letter and jot or tittle one can expound heaps upon heaps of laws, as, indeed, is written in Scripture: "Man knoweth not the price thereof." Even the greatest sages cannot learn all its secrets, and if they were to live eternally, their wisdom would certainly grow each day but they would still never reach the end of the mysteries of the Torah, for its wisdom has no limit. But the wise men of the nations of the world know only the seven wisdoms, the product of the limited human mind. These wisdoms or sciences were thought out by the sages and great men of Greece. It is therefore not difficult to explore this realm in its length and breadth, and no matter how much the scholar may afterwards rummage and search, he will no longer be able to find anything new there (*Levush Techelet*, Ch. 224, Sec. 7).

In these lines the contempt for European science which was so characteristic of the most backward period in the Jewish ghetto—from the end of the sixteenth century to the middle of the eighteenth—appears very clearly.

Mordecai Jaffe stood at the crossroads, on the boundary of two eras. Hence, it is not surprising that he was a typical eclectic, without a clear and firmly established position. A competent mathematician and admirer of Maimonides, Jaffe also believed in magic, demons and incantations; every Saturday night, after the end of the Sabbath, he considered it necessary to recite a special formula filled with "names" and incantations. Like his teacher Moses Isserles, Jaffe tried to explain the essence of the spirit of prophecy rationally, but he was also an ardent follower of the "esoteric wisdom,"[41] wrote a commentary on the works of the Kabbalist Menaḥem Recanati, and discussed in his *Levushim* theosophical-mystical problems such as the ten *sefirot*, transmigration of souls, and many others.[42]

We have observed that the famous "triad"—the three great rabbis, Shalom Shachna, Solomon Luria and Moses Isserles— laid the foundations of rabbinic scholarship in the new Jewish

41. He was familiarized with the mysteries of the Kabbalah by the Kabbalist Mattathias ben Solomon Delacrut.
42. For a discussion of Mordecai Jaffe, see Rav Tzair, *op. cit.*; S. Urison in *Yevreyskaya Starina*, 1912, 353–369; and Horodetzky, *Le-Korot Ha-Rabbanut*, 1911, pp. 145–174.

cultural center in Poland. In considering Isserles' three disciples, we noted that young men eager for knowledge would come from Bohemia, Germany and other countries to the Polish Talmudic academies which were everywhere recognized as the major seats of Torah. From the furthest lands men would apply to Poland, as to the highest tribunal, in regard to the most important matters and the most difficult religious-judicial questions, relying on the great authority of the rabbis and scholars there. As these rabbis decided, so it was; their word had the authority of a legislative court.[43] All of Poland was filled with Talmudic academies.[44] Every father hoped and dreamed that his son would be a great scholar in Israel, a rabbi or head of a *yeshivah.*

"In all the dispersions of Israel," relates the chronicler Nathan Hannover of the period before the massacres of 1648,

study of Torah was nowhere so widespread as in Poland. Every community had its Talmudic academies. The head of the *yeshivah* was paid generously so that he might be able to devote himself to it entirely, heart and soul, without extraneous worries. The whole year through he would not cross the threshold of the academy except to go to the synagogue, but would sit and study Torah day and night. The students of the *yeshivah* were also maintained by the community, and each would receive a fixed stipend every week. Every student would be given at least two boys to teach so that he might accustom himself to transmit to others what he himself had learned and become proficient in *pilpul.* Meals were provided for the students from the community charity fund or from the communal soup kitchen. A community of fifty householders would support no less than thirty Talmudic students. Each student, with his two boys whom he taught, would live with a householder. Even if the student obtained his requirements from the community, the householder would nevertheless feed him at his table like his own son . . . In the whole land of Poland there was hardly a single home where Torah was not studied. Either the master of the house himself, or his son, or his son-in-law, or a student who took his meals in his home, was a scholar. Often all of them together were students and scholars. . . . For this reason every community was rich in students. If, for example, there were in a community fifty householders, there were around twenty scholars who were crowned with the honorary title *morenu* (our teacher) or *ḥaver* (associate or colleague). Above all of them was the *rosh yeshivah,*

43. See Solomon Luria, *Responsa*, No. 33; Moses Isserles, *Responsa*, Nos. 11, 15, 55, 65.
44. The chronicler Nathan Hannover of Zaslav relates that hundreds of rectors of Talmudic academies *(roshei yeshivot)* would come together at the fairs.

the principal of the academy. All the scholars deferred to him and would come to him at the *yeshivah* to do him honor."[45]

One must bear in mind in this connection that in the second half of the sixteenth century the autonomy of the Jewish communities was legally confirmed through a series of royal decrees and resolutions of the Sejm. Rabbinic literature and Talmudic law therefore obtained the utmost practical importance. The Jewish court, recognized by the government and vested with broad powers, carried out its binding decisions and verdicts not only in religious questions but also in monetary cases and various communal and family matters.[46] To study Torah day and night, to be well versed in the Talmud and codes, was not only a manifestation of piety, of great devotion to the commandments wherewith one purchases life in the world-to-come; it was also the most assured way which led to influence in communal life, gave one the possibility of attaining the highest degrees of power and honor in the community: to become a rabbi, a principal of a *yeshivah*, a president of a court, a *parnass*.

At the same time (around the beginning of the seventeenth century) the last remnants of free speculative thought disappeared from Polish Jewry and interest in philosophy and "external wisdoms" was entirely extinguished. External causes also contributed to this effect. Precisely at that time, when the Jagellonian dynasty disappeared from the stage of history, the Catholic reaction was strengthened in Poland and, along with it, hatred of the Jews on the part of the enlarged urban populace, which regarded them as the most threatening competitors in the economic realm, was magnified. The fact that reactionary tendencies became ever stronger in Jewish social circles contributed not a little to the same result. The wider the barrier separating the Jewish ghetto from the external world grew, the narrower and more backward became the intellectual atmosphere that dominated the Jewish society of Poland. The intelligentsia, its keenest minds, were concerned exclu-

45. *Yeven Metzulah*, pp. 60–61 (we quote according to the Cracow edition of 1895).
46. *Yeven Metzulah*, 47: "The legal establishment in Poland was as it had been before the destruction of the Temple in Jerusalem, when they established courts in every city . . . and the leaders *(parnassim)* of the four lands were like the Sanhedrin in the Chamber of Hewn Stone, and they had the authority to judge every Jew in the kingdom of Poland and to make restraints, institute ordinances, and punish a man as they saw fit; and every difficult matter was brought to them for their judgment."

sively with the laws of the Talmud and displayed all their acumen in ingenious *pilpul.* The overly subtle mental activity, the exclusive love for the intellectual and the keen, which ruled unrestrictedly in the Polish *yeshivot* of that era, created the soil for the growth of a narrowly utilitarian pragmatism. Contempt for secular knowledge and science developed there not only out of religious motives, out of fear of heresy; the Jewish youth also saw in the "external wisdoms" nothing but foolish pastimes which could be of no use in practical life under the conditions of that age.

All this brought it about that in the first half of the seventeenth century the Talmudic students and scholars no longer possessed the slightest knowledge of the "wisdoms of the peoples of the world," and when in the second decade of the century the intellectually acute Joseph Solomon Delmedigo[47] came to Poland, he was not a little amazed on seeing the hatred and contempt Jews there had for philosophy and secular knowledge in general.

While the aged Mordecai Jaffe, who grew up in the earlier period and was educated in the *yeshivah* of Moses Isserles, still displayed a certain interest in religious philosophy and secular knowledge, the younger students and scholars of his generation already devoted themselves heart and soul exclusively to Talmudic studies. Among the Torah scholars who occupied the foremost place in the Polish rabbinate at the threshold of the seventeenth century, only the famous Rabbi Samuel Eliezer Edels[48] (known under the acronym Maharsha) had some knowledge of religious philosophy and expressed the idea that mathematics and astronomy might be useful for study of the Torah. He also deemed it necessary to note the danger that the method of *pilpul,* which dominated the contemporary Polish academies, could involve, and openly declared that the *ḥillukim* (divisions or analyses), with their "*pilpul* of vanity, remove one from the truth and do not produce the desired result."[49] Edels himself, however, also employed his rich capacities chiefly in honing the minds of the *yeshivah* students through sharp contrasts created by pairing together various texts and through clever ideas and ingenuities intended to rec-

47. See our *History,* Vol. IV, pp. 155ff.
48. Edels was born in Cracow in 1555 and at the age of twenty was already the rector of a *yeshivah,* for the founding of which the financial resources had been provided by his mother-in-law Edel. Later he served as rabbi in Chelm and Lublin. Edels spent his last days in Ostrog where he died in 1631.
49. *Ḥiddushei Aggadot, Bava Metzia,* 85.

oncile the contradictions that emerged. A man with a marvelously sharp mind, Edels obtained a reputation as an excellent dialectician with his *Ḥiddushei Halachot*, subtle explanations of Talmudic laws. This commentary, which soon became one of the major subjects of study in the academies, is written very profoundly and laconically and, moreover, in difficult language. It is therefore not surprising that a "bit of Maharsha" became a synonym for an extremely difficult matter or keen dialectic. Edels' commentary to the aggadic part of the Talmud, *Ḥiddushei Aggadot*, in which religious-philosophical views that are of little originality are interwoven with mystical ideas from the Kabbalah, was less successful in obtaining renown for him.

One other interesting point must be noted in Edel's work—the social motif. Edels complains very frequently of the social injustices and moral corruption of his time. He reproaches the people of his milieu with the charge that, out of greed and love for luxury, numerous evils and injustices are committed. Men who have grown rich in a very dishonest way become communal leaders. They appoint as rabbi whomever they wish, and rabbinic posts are sold for money.

Quite typical of that time is Edel's contemporary, Rabbi Meir (Maharam) of Lublin.[50] His elemental force, his entire *raison d'être*, was Talmudic dialectic or *pilpul*. Here he was a tremendously brilliant figure, and everything outside this realm he disparaged as the dust of the earth. He read his sharply pointed *ḥillukim* before a great host of pupils, and wrote keen *novellae* to the most difficult tractates of the Talmud and published them under the title *Meir Einei Ḥachamim*.[51] His responsa were renowned in the rabbinic world. Of the "philosophy" of the great scholar, the following point may give some testimony. In one of his responsa he discusses at length the difficult question: What is the law regarding a married woman who has had sexual intercourse with a demon who at first appeared to her in the form of her own husband and the second time disguised himself as a Polish nobleman?[52] To be an ingenious swimmer over the "sea" of the Talmud, to mani-

50. Born in Lublin in 1558. From 1582 to 1586 he was *rosh yeshivah* in his native city and later occupied a similar position in Cracow. In 1595 he was elected chief rabbi of Lemberg. In consequence of a controversy that broke out between him and the local *rosh yeshivah* Joshua Falk, Meir had to leave Lemberg. In 1613 he was invited to serve as rabbi and *rosh yeshivah* in his native city and died there in 1616.
51. The title contains an allusion to his name Meir.
52. Meir of Lublin, *Responsa*, No. 116.

fest great resourcefulness in mental inventions and sharply pointed notions—this was the greatest ideal, the fondest goal of life for this extremely arrogant and smug Talmudic scholar. He regarded the men of the *Shulḥan Aruch*, Joseph Karo and Moses Isserles, with contempt. He refused to rely on these codifers, for they manifested relatively little sharp *pilpul.*[53]

The *Shulḥan Aruch* had many other opponents among the contemporary scholars besides Rabbi Meir of Lublin. Some of the rabbis found that the *Shulḥan Aruch* was not a true compendium, since numerous essential laws are lacking in it. Others, again, considered it a great defect that in the *Shulḥan Aruch* only the definitive law is given but the pertinent literature is not cited. One of the *Shulḥan Aruch's* severest critics was Rabbi Meir's townsman, the famous Joel ben Samuel Sirkes, better known by an acronym derived from the initials of his major work, *Bayyit Ḥadash,* as "the Baḥ."[54] This distinguished scholar, one of the foremost rabbis Poland had in the seventeenth century, perceived in philosophy the source of heresy and was persuaded that it was the seductive "strange woman" about whom King Solomon admonished so severely in the Book of Proverbs and of whom he predicted that "all who come to her will not return."[55] He could not forgive the Italian rabbi, Jehudah Minz, for permitting the holding of masquerades during the days of Purim for the sake of "the joy of the festival." The pious Joel Sirkes complains strongly of the very popular custom following which "people disguise themselves in strange clothes during the days of Purim, men in women's clothing and women in men's," and that "no one protests against this practice." "Even worse," complains Sirkes, "is the fact that people put masks on their faces so that they will not be recognized . . . This must not be permitted—either on Purim or at weddings."[56]

We have observed that Sirkes was also an opponent of the *Shulḥan Aruch.* He believed this book unworthy of becoming the definitive code among Jews. Hence, he wrote a new commentary to Jaocb ben Asher's *Arbaah Turim* under the title *Bayyit Ḥadash,* hoping that this "new building" would be the necessary and proper one that would replace the *Shulḥan Aruch.*

53. *Ibid.,* No. 11.
54. Born in Lublin in 1561, he was rabbi in Pruzhany, Lublin, Medzibozh, Cracow, and Brisk. He died in Cracow in 1640.
55. Sirkes (Baḥ), *Responsa,* Vol. I, No. 4. Sirkes' two-volume *Responsa* contain extremely valuable material on the Jewish way of life in Poland and Lithuania.
56. *Bayyit Ḥadash* to *Yoreh Deah,* No. 188.

Sirkes' work[57] has, indeed, great virtues and elicited strong admiration in the world of rabbinic scholarship. But it did not attain its chief goal—to displace the collection of Karo and Isserles. Despite the obdurate battle of many respected rabbis and scholars, the authority of the *Shulḥan Aruch* continued to grow, and it was gradually recognized as the major practical handbook for religious-civil law in all Jewish juridical institutions and as the code with which the rabbis, judges, and communal leaders *(parnassim)* had to reckon.

A pupil of Rabbi Meir of Lublin, the acute rector of the Talmudic academy in Cracow, Rabbi Joshua Hoeschel ben Joseph,[58] points out in his well-known responsa, *Penei Yehoshua*, that among the "sages of the lands of Poland" the custom already is that everything written in the *Shulḥan Aruch* may no longer be changed, just as is the case with the Torah itself.[59] The law-book of Karo and Isserles was explored and studied with no less diligence than the Talmud, and the foremost rabbis of the first half of the seventeenth century acquired renown with their commentaries to the *Shulḥan Aruch*. The rabbi of Lublin, Joshua Falk Ha-Kohen, who was president of the Council of Four Lands after Mordecai Jaffe, is famed in rabbinic literature under the name "the Sema," the first letters of his brilliant commentary to the *Shulḥan Aruch* entitled *Sefer Meirat Einayim*.[60] The rabbi of Ostrog, Rabbi David ben Samuel Halevi,[61] who at the time of the persecutions of 1648 fled to Moravia and later settled in Lemberg, also became known as "the Taz" from the initial letters of his work, *Turei Zahav*, a commentary to the *Shulḥan Aruch*.[62] The Sema and the Taz supplied all the omissions and defects which the critics discovered in the *Shulḥan Aruch*. The entire discussion concerning

57. For a discussion of it, see Rav Tzair, *op. cit., Ha-Shiloaḥ*, VI, 319–321.
58. Born in Vilna in 1578, died in Cracow in 1648. Joshua Hoeschel acquired renown with his work *Meginei Shelomoh* in which he attempts to dispose of all of the contradictions the Tosafists found in Rashi.
59. *Penei Yehoshua*, II, No. 50.
60. On Falk's work, see Rav Tzair in *Ha-Shiloaḥ*, VI, 233–238. A cultural-historical interest also pertains to Falk's *Kuntras* which contains the ordinances that he instituted in the Council of Four Lands in 1607 regarding the prohibition against taking usury and various other prohibitions. The work was first published in 1692.
61. Born in Ludmir (Vladimir-Volynski) in 1586; died in Lemberg in 1667.
62. The commentary to *Yoreh Deah* was published in 1646. The remaining parts were published after Halevi's deah. When the news of the messianic claimant Shabbetai Tzevi reached Lemberg, the aged Halevi dispatched his son and stepson as emissaries to Turkey, and these brought him from Shabbetai Tzevi a handwritten letter with a gift, a silk shirt.

each individual law and all the sources and indices necessary thereto were generously provided by Falk and Halevi in their commentaries.

As great as the authority of the Sema and the Taz in rabbinic literature was, these men were far surpassed by a younger exponent of the *Shulḥan Aruch*, the famous Shabbetai ben Meir Ha-Kohen.[63] Shabbetai was a splendidly gifted man with a remarkably keen, analytic mind and an enormous capacity for work. While still quite young, he systematically explored the entire Talmudic and rabbinic literature[64] with great assiduity, and at the age of twenty-four published his famed commentary on the ritual part of the *Shulḥan Aruch (Yoreh Deah)* under the title *Siftei Kohen.*[65] In this work the rabbinic literature of Polish Jewry attained its highest brilliance. In the case of every problem which he discusses, Shabbetai introduces with marvelous acumen and scholarship all the views which the codifiers and scholars before him had expressed regarding the law in question and compares all the rebuttals, contradictions, and controversies with the theories and arguments. Finally comes the conclusion, the result attained through dialectical skill and rigorous logic: his own definitive verdict and decision. Written with no less brilliance and mastery is Shabbetai's commentary to the second part of the *Shulḥan Aruch,* "Ḥoshen Mishpat." The young scholar with his gigantic intellect overshadowed all his predecessors and was recognized in later generations as the foremost authority in the extensive realm of Talmudic law.

Shabbetai Ha-Kohen's work had one additional virtue which was extremely rare in contemporary rabbinic literature. Most of the scholars in Poland wrote in a crude, unpolished and often (as we have already noted in the case of the author of *Torat Ha-Olah*) even corrupted and grammatically defective language. In this particular Shabbetai is an exception. He was

---

63. Born in 1621 in Vilna. His father Meir Kohen Ashkenazi acquired fame with his responsa *Gevurat Anashim.* At the time of the massacres of 1648 Shabbetai Ha-Kohen fled to Prague and served for a time as rabbi in Dresnitz (Moravia) and afterwards in Holesov (Holleschau), where he died at the age of forty-two in 1663. For a discussion of him, see S. J. Fuenn, *Kiryah Ne'emanah,* pp 74–78, where Kohen's letter to the Christian Hebraist Valentini Widrich of Leipzig, with whom he was friendly, is given; Graetz, *Geschichte der Juden* (Hebrew translation), Vol. VIII, pp. 114–115.

64. He himself tells of this in the introduction to his *Siftei Kohen* (Amsterdam edition, 1756).

65. Known by the acronym *Shach.*

an excellent stylist, and later, in discussing the memoir and lamentation literature which the terrors of the persecutions of 1648 elicited, we shall have occasion to speak of the stylistically lovely elegiac works of the great Talmudic scholar.

It is highly characteristic of that period, however, that even this man, who was so richly endowed in literary respects, also refused to recognize any intellectual occupation besides *pilpul* and *novellae* in the law, and sought to show that a father is obliged to study only the Pentateuch with his son and not the other Biblical books, because such is the custom among Jews, and "the custom of Israel is Torah."[66]

Even in the heyday of rabbinic literature in Poland, the darker sides of this literature clearly manifested themselves. The exclusive interest in the overly-pointed intellectual, the bookish racking of brains in the religious realm, the arid hair-splitting regarding the least custom and commandment—all this created a favorable atmosphere for the rootage and growth of the principle that the most important and essential thing in matters of faith is *learning* itself, the investigation and explanation of the laws and customs in all their details. The more congealed and rigid the forms and vestment of rabbinic literature became, the more did *pilpul* and the overly subtle suck out and suffocate the juices of the organic and vital. Unconsciously, without at all wishing it, the deeply pious rabbinism of Poland brought it about that, in the moral realm, inner feelings were displaced by purely mechanical custom and the fresh, living field of the "duties of the heart," as they were called by Baḥya Ibn Pakuda, was transformed into the arid, fruitless desert of automatic, formal "duties of the limbs." Sharply pointed, mind-splitting scholastic as the product of the method of *ḥillukim* which had flowered in Poland—this was an end in itself, a unique kind of "art for art's sake." As once, among the extreme left-wing rationalists of Maimonides' school, verses from the Bible and stories of the Torah were transformed into commentaries on Aristotle's theses and principles, so the masters of *pilpul* and *ḥillukim* in the Polish *yeshivot* utilized the text of Holy Scripture as weapons in their ingenious battles to sharpen the mind, to make the logical idea more acute, to manifest ever greater perfection in the realm of

66. *Siftei Kohen, Yoreh Deah, Hilchot Melamedim*, No. 245: "And I say that the custom of Israel is Torah . . . and a father is not obliged to teach his son the Bible when they study the Talmud."

brilliant scholarship. It is therefore not surprising that precisely in the rabbinic world itself—to be sure, mainly in the German-Moravian lands—many recognized the great danger inherent in this tendency. These promply declared a fierce war against it. Of this in the next chapter.

CHAPTER FOUR

Custumals;
THE MAHARAL OF PRAGUE, EPHRAIM OF LUNTSHITZ, AND YOM-TOV HELLER

Books of *minhagim* (custumals)—Joseph Juspa of Nördlingen and his *Yosif Ometz*—Yozpa Shammash and his *Minhagim De-Kehillah Kedoshah Virmisa*—The Maharal of Prague as hero of popular legends; the Maharal as scholar; his attacks on Azariah dei Rossi—the Maharal's world-outlook—The Torah as the foundation of the world—The mystery of the national community; "My son, my firstborn Israel" —The mission of the chosen people—The Maharal's battle against *pilpul;* his proposal for reforming the education of children—The Maharal's fellow-battlers—The preacher Ephraim of Luntshitz— The Maharal's disciple and follower, Rabbi Yom-Tov Lipmann Heller—An "untimely figure"—Joseph ben Isaac Halevi; a Maimunist as critic of Maimonides—Yom Tov Heller as scholar and exponent of the Mishnah—His memoirs, *Megillat Eivah.*

E HAVE noted that in the Polish *yeshivot* every law or custom served primarily as material that might be utilized for clever scholarship and ingenious dialectic. But in Germany at that time a different phenomenon is to be discerned. The communities there did not lead as calm and secure a life as did the Polish communities. The frequent persecutions and expulsions strengthened their desire to preserve the customs of their fathers as faithfully and strongly as possible, to make them beloved by their generation and their children through heartfelt ethical instruction. Hence we observe that, as had been the case earlier in the fifteenth century,[1] so in the sixteenth and seventeenth centuries as well, a unique literature of books of *minhagim* (customs), in which the practices mainly of older communities such as Speyer, Worms, Regensburg, Frankfurt-am-Main, etc. are described, was produced. These custumals have a significant cultural-historical value, for in them numerous details of the contemporary way of life are preserved. We shall here dwell on two of them which describe the customs of the ancient communities of Frankfurt-am-Main and Worms.

Joseph Juspa ben Phineas Seligmann Nördlingen, chief rabbinic judge in Frankfurt-am-Main, in 1630 completed his *Yosif Ometz*,[2] in which he gives an account of all the laws and customs "which are carried out through the year," from the beginning of Sivan to the end of Adar, and "in special detail all the customs of the holy community of Frankfurt-am-Main." The author began the work at the threshold of the seventeenth century and wrote it in the course of several decades. He himself stresses in the introduction that he composed his work not for scholars but for plain people. Hence it is written quite simply, without scholarly pretensions, in the gentle, sincere tone of a book of moral instruction. "Every custom of our fathers is Torah," the pious author writes.[3] As he familiarizes us with the "customs of the holy community of Frankfurt-am-Main," we learn interesting particulars of its way of life. The author tells us not merely of such details as that many "men of good works" would put on gloves before going to sleep so that they might not touch the naked body with their hands during the night (p. 37), or that the external garment worn on the Sabbath was sewn with a closed sleeve on the right side so that one might not forget when going out into the street and violate the prohibition against carrying anything on the Sabbath (*ibid.*, p. 72); he also acquaints us thoroughly with all kinds of drinks and dishes that our ancestors used to enjoy (*ibid.*, pp. 51–52). Joseph Juspa tells us further how it was the custom at

1. See the third volume of our *History*.
2. First published in Frankfurt-am-Main in 1722. We have employed this first edition.
3. *Yosif Ometz*, 72.

that time before a wedding to fete the bride and groom on two consecutive Sabbaths before the wedding. The first Sabbath was called *der kleiner Spinholz* and the second *der grosser Spinholz* (p. 83). To welcome the Sabbath Jews would sprinkle the synagogue with spices, and in order "to add to the sacred from the profane" they would begin welcoming the Sabbath when it was still broad daylight. To draw out the Sabbath meal into the night or at least until the setting of the sun (*ibid.*, p. 74) and, along with this, not to speak any profane words, Joseph Juspa composed a rather long "Shir Ḥadash Le-Lel Shabbat" (A New Song for the Night of the Sabbath) in which he celebrates the great importance of the Sabbath candles. Because this commandment was obligatory upon the Jewish woman, the author translated each Hebrew verse into Judaeo-German or Yiddish rhymed lines.[4]

We also find in *Yosif Ometz* interesting details about the disabilities of the Jews in Germany. "If a Jew walks through the gentile streets," the author complains, "they cry after him 'dog' or other such insulting epithets and throw dirt and stones at him" (*ibid.*, p. 109). On the first day of Rosh Hashanah, the author further relates, it was the custom to go to a pool or to the river Main to observe the ceremony of *Tashlich*. But as a result of the work of Satan, at the gate of the city leading to the river a soldiers' guard was placed; these were "men of war" who did not allow any Jews through. The Frankfurt Jews therefore had to conduct the *Tashlich* ceremony not at the Main but at the rampart of the city where, through a narrow ditch, the waste water with all the filth of the city flowed. The author could not bear this and agreed with the leaders of the community to attempt to win the favor of the "guardians of the gate" through much wine, with the thought that if this were done for several years, it might be hoped that "the ancient custom would be restored" (*ibid.*, 121). The author also provides[5] many fascinating details about the rising of the Frankfurt Christian mob against the Jews in 1614, which is described in the well-known *Megillat Vintz*.

The observations of the author of *Yosif Ometz* on how necessary it is that every Jew become familiar with the laws and prayers of martyrdom, for every son of Israel must be prepared to give up his life, are extremely touching. For greater effect, he notes in his custumal the "laws of the benediction to be

4. The song was composed by Joseph Nördlingen in 1596.
5. *Yosif Ometz*, 85, 119, 135–136.

recited by one who sanctifies the Name" (i.e., a martyr) which he copied from the "manuscript" of the famous *shtadlan* or communal intercessor, Joselman of Rosheim (*ibid.*, 58–59). Along with this, the author speaks with genuine feeling of the importance of faith and trust. One may and must, he repeats over and over again, live in faith and believe in God's great miracles, for without miracles no Israelite can endure all the dangers that surround him at every step. And Joseph Nördlingen also introduces interesting details from the life of the Jews in the time of war (the Thirty Years War), indicating the miracles which they experienced and thanks to which they survived (*ibid.*, 166–167).

Even more interesting is the custumal of Worms composed by the local sexton, Jephthah Joseph Yozpa ben Naphtali Herz Levi of the family Minzpach, in the name of the community. Unfortunately, we know very few details of the life of this extraordinary man. Born in 1604 in Fürth, he came, as he relates,[6] to Worms in 1623 to study in the *yeshivah* of Rabbi Elijah Loans and then spent his entire life in Worms. In 1648 he was appointed sexton and trustee of the local community and held this position until his death in 1678. In this pious and God-fearing sexton there was a poetic nature. The old, melancholy city of Worms, with its medieval mysteries and marvelous legends, attracted him with their poetic magic, and he felt impelled to write down for future generations all the stories and mystical legends that lurked in the shadows of the city walls and of the narrow, crooked streets of the Jewish ghetto. Thus was created *Maaseh Nissim*, the sexton's collection of legends, of which we shall speak at length only in the next volume, for the original Hebrew text of this collection was apparently not preserved[7] and only the Yiddish translation, published by the author's son Eliezer in 1696, became known and popular.

Not only the legends of former times, however, were precious to the sexton of Worms but also the actual, palpable life which unfolded before his pious eyes. The customs, the way of life of the community—these, too, received his attention, and he described them in 1648 in his other book, *Minhagim De-Kehillah Kedoshah Virmisa* (Customs of the Holy Community of

6. See *Maaseh Nissim*, No. 2.
7. Benjacob asserts that the Hebrew text was published during the author's lifetime (in 1662). However, no bibliographer has ever actually seen the work, and Benjacob's report is not confirmed by anyone else.

Worms).[8] It is not the law, the religio-legal aspect of these customs, that mainly interests the sexton Yozpa. Not this does he consider it important to note down for future generations, but the way of life itself, in which he senses the palpitation and breath of vitality, the simple poetic grace of collective power and joy in life. When, for example, Joseph Nördlingen, the author of *Yosif Ometz*, dwells on the "laws of Purim," he considers it important first of all to admonish that the Scroll of Esther must be "written properly, according to the entire law" (*ibid.*, 133). In speaking of the custom of "changing garments," he admonishes that one must not, for the sake of Heaven, violate the prohibition against *shaatnez* (mixing garments of two different species of cloth), for this is a prohibition explicitly stated in the Torah (*ibid.*, 135). The sexton Yozpa writes here in a very different fashion. He is interested, first of all, not in the law, but in the "Purim play," the manner in which the Jewish youth rejoiced on the happy days of Purim, and he gives us in his "book of customs" the following colorful portrait:

The Sabbath after Purim, quite early in the morning, the young men go into a house that is distant from the synagogue and there put on the Sabbath outer garments which are called *seiti mantil*.[9] Everyone wears a mitre on his head, as is the custom, but not as a mark of sorrow. Leaving the house they march in pairs, one next to the other, and at their head strides a boy, a servant of theirs, who is called *knell-gabbai*. This *knell-gabbai* is dressed in jester's clothes, dances, and plays all kinds of foolish tricks. Before the young men walk the *gabbaim*, and each of these carries a staff with illustrations on it. After the *gabbaim* comes the whole pack of young men. So the entire group strides with great jubilation until it comes to the synagogue. In the synagogue the young men seat themselves on the platform. Although during the rest of the year the householders sit on the platform, when this Sabbath comes, they leave it to make room for the young men. And when the *ḥazzan* or cantor begins the prayer "Magen Avot," the young men leave the platform and enter the "city" where the president of the court *(av bet din)* sits, and the president of the court places his hands on the head of every young man and blesses him, just as the children are blessed at the inauguration of the Sabbath . . . After-

8.   Unfortunately this work has not been published to the present day. Large extracts were given by M. Güdemann in his well known work and by A. Epstein in the ...*ufmann-Gedenkbuch*, 1900, pp. 288–317. The entire work in manuscript consists of a hundred and sixty-five folios in quarto.

9.   This is the cloak with the sewed-up right sleeve which the author of *Yosif Ometz*, as we have previously noted, describes (*op. cit.*, 72).

wards the young men go to the women's synagogue. If they wish, they go there through the so-called "Jewish Gate"[10] and come to the "city" of the wife of the rabbi, or president of the court. And the rabbi's wife places her hand on the head of every young man and blesses him. Afterwards they march around among the rows of seats in the women's synagogue and go out. The *gabbaim* always lead the procession, and the young men go in and out only behind them. At the morning service on the Sabbath the *gabbaim* wrap themselves in their prayer-shawls, like the householders, and when the verses of the Psalms are chanted, they go to every householder who is supposed to receive an honor, for example, to the one who on the Sabbath is to be called to the rolling up of the Torah, or to the elevation of the Torah, etc., and ask him to forego his honor this time, for it has been firmly established that each year on this day all the honors shall be distributed among the young men. And so they go also to the *gabbai tzedakah* (the treasurer in charge of charity) and ask him to forego the honors which are to be sold on that day. In the same way they come also to the *parnass ḥodesh* (parnass of the month) and ask him to forego the *Segen*, for the *Segen* also belongs on that Sabbath to the young men. And even if one or another [of the householders] should be stubborn and refuse to forego [his honors], the young men pay no attention and take all the honors, even the *Segen*, against that person's will. And even if someone is ritually obligated to be called to the Torah that day, for example, one whose wife had just risen from childbirth and he has come to the synagogue for the first time, or one who has *Jahrzeit* (the commemoration of the anniversary of a parent's death) that day, the young men are not required to call him to the Torah unless he gives them at least a measure of wine. If he does give it to them, they are obliged to call him to the Torah. But one who must recite the prayer for escaping harm *(Gomel)*, the young men are in no case obliged to call up, for he can recite this prayer some other time. In short, on this Sabbath the young men are the most important! Custom is stronger than law, and the young men are at the head. One of the young men's *gabbaim* takes *Segen* and calls the other youths to the Torah. Only the rabbi receives the seventh summons to the Torah. All the other honors are also distributed among the young men by the *gabbaim*. The honor of rolling up the first scroll of the Torah comes to the rabbi.[11] There is still another custom that creates a great privilege for the youths. The *parnassim* are obliged to give the young men a promissory note in which the amount of wine each individual householder is to grant them is written down: which one a half measure, which a whole, and which two or three—all according to the wealth of each householder and according to the number of the young men. And every householder is obliged to give as much as is

10. The gate through which the godmother brings in the male child for circumcision.
11. It is not altogether clear here whether the official community rabbi or the "Purim rabbi" is meant.

written down for him on the note. If he does not give willingly, they compel him until he satisfies the young men. It is also permitted to take a security pledge on what is coming to them without special authorization from the rabbi and the community. This note is put together by the *hegmon parnass (Judenbischof)* and the *parnass hodesh,* and both of them affix their signatures to the note as attestation.

After Purim the young men are invited to the homes of several prominent householders. There they participate in the Purim banquet. The young men bring with them much of the wine which they have received on the note and drink and rejoice, one day in one householder's home and the next day in another's. These banquets are optional. None of the householders is compelled to invite the young men home and arrange a banquet for them, but whoever wishes to fulfill this *mitzvah* (commandment) and to rejoice with the young men studying Torah—it is well with him. On Purim the young men sew around the hats they wear a little garland which they call *Kränzchen mit Fliederlach* (garland of elder blossoms). They do not remove these garlands from their hats as long as they still have some of the wine they receive on the note.

The report Yozpa gives us concerning the banquet which the two "bridegrooms"—the "groom of the Torah" and the "groom of *Bereshit*"—prepare on Simhat Torah is no less interesting. Here the amiable Yozpa provides us with such a lively and vivid picture of the Jewish way of life in the seventeenth century that it is worth quoting the passage in its entirely:

On Hoshannah Rabbah they already prepare the tables and the *Brauthaus* for the banquets which the "groom of the Torah" and the "groom of *Bereshit*" will give on Simhat Torah . . . On Simhat Torah, after the morning meal, the sexton's boy calls out through the streets: "Lead the bride and groom to the *Brauthaus!*" Then the groom of the Torah with his good friends and relatives, as well as the groom of *Bereshit*, go to the *Brauthaus* and carry with them many fine fruits to set on the table and also to throw through the windows to the children who stand around the house and very happily catch the fruit. Two of the *gabbai tzedakah* also bring their lovely fruits and set them on the tables. A Christian woman who witnessed this joy was so pleased by it that before her death she stipulated in her will that the garden she owned not far from the Jewish cemetery was to be given to the Jewish community, on condition that each year the fruits of this garden be used to decorate the tables at the banquet of Simhat Torah and be thrown as a gift to the children who rejoice around the *Brauthaus*. I who write these lines saw this with my own eyes and ate these fruits, and not long ago, during the war, this garden was destroyed. It was from it that the fruits which the two *gabbai tzedakah* used to bring into the *Brauthaus* came, but since the garden has been destroyed, the *gabbai tzedakah* bring their own fruits, and such is the custom to the present day. The "grooms" and those who accompany them seat themselves at the table, all the rabbis also come in honor of the Torah, as do practically all the householders of the city. Some sit, some stand around the table. Whoever has a keg of wine in his cellar brings a full jug with him. The "grooms" also bring along a good deal of wine so that there will be no lack of drink. All eat fruit, drink wine, and rejoice. In the courtyard in front of the *Brauthaus* they arrange a great fire and a half hour later, when the fire is burning well, the president of the court, together with the rabbis and the "grooms" and other householders, come out, and all witness this rejoicing. The householders dance around the fire and play all kinds of games. Frequently the president of the court also comes to them and participates in the games around the fire in honor of the Torah. So they spend the time until the afternoon service, and they also drink wine at the fire. The "grooms" provide the wine. The wood for the fire is provided by the sexton, and the "grooms" pay him for it.[13]

Such customs, which are extremely interesting for cultural history, were, however, preserved only in the German lands, not in Poland. This was not merely because the German communities, especially in the Rhine provinces, were considerably older than the Polish; a much greater role was played in Poland by the one-sided pilpulist and rationalist tendency that we noted in the previous chapter. The students of the Polish *yeshivot* were interested only in the intellectual and keen, the sharp-witted and scholastic. To be sure, among the Jewish scholars in Poland there were also men of feeling like the sexton and trustee of Worms who refused to content themselves with acute *ḥillukim*, because they were attracted to the popular and interested mainly in the spiritual needs of the common people, the "members of the multitude," as the author of *Yosif Ometz* puts it. These men concluded that they must go to the people and create in the language comprehensible to them—Yiddish. Hence, we shall speak of these only in a later part of our history. But in the rabbinic literature of that era also monitory voices were heard pointing publicly to the danger which the way of study prevalent in the Polish-German *yeshivot* at the end of the sixteenth century might entail. To be sure, the battle against *pilpul* began "outside the land," not in Poland itself but in the German-Moravian lands, and the major role in this "war for a religious cause" was played by the great scholar of the

13. *Minhagim De-Kehillah Kedoshah Virmisa*, 312–13.

generation, the famed rabbi of Prague, Rabbi Jehudah Loew ben Bezalel, better known as the Maharal of Prague.

The Maharal is undoubtedly the most interesting and original personality among the Ashkenazic rabbis of the sixteenth and seventeenth centuries,[14] and not without reason did *"der hohe Rabbi Loew,"* as he was called by his generation, become the favorite hero of popular imagination, which wove around his name a colorful crown of the most marvelous legends. To this day, the legend survives that in the attic of the old synagogue of Prague lies the *golem* which the Maharal kneaded out of clay and which, with the aid of the Ineffable Name, he made into a living creature who served him as a loyal emissary and performer of his will at every critical moment when the community or all Israel was in great danger. Not too long ago the Maharal's *golem* was "revived," and the gifted contemporary poet H. Leivick chose him, together with his creator *der hohe Rabbi Loew*, as the central figures of his masterpiece, *Der Golem*. In *der hohe Rabbi Loew* the people saw not merely the great scholar but also the faithful friend and protector. The popular legend of how the great Emperor Rudolph summoned the rabbi of Prague to Vienna, closeted himself with him, and for hours carried on a discussion with him is known to all. What they spoke of has remained undisclosed. It has merely been conjectured that the rabbi and emperor carried on a learned discussion about astronomy and alchemy.[15]

The renowned rabbi of Prague was, indeed, somewhat proficient in the "external wisdoms." He had a certain knowledge of mathematics and astronomy, was familiar with medieval religious philosophy, and emotively says of Maimonides that he was filled with wisdom like the sea.[16] In his numerous works he frequently notes that one ought to be proficient in astronomy, mathematics and the other natural sciences, for they are the stages leading to the peaks of the "wisdom of the Torah."[17] "One ought also to study the sciences of the nations of the world," says the Maharal, "because these are also of God ... especially the sciences that explain the nature and order of the world. It is certainly obligatory to study these, for through

14. Rabbi Loew was born in the 1520's and died in 1609.
15. A masterly portrayal of the meeting between the emperor Rudolph and Rabbi Loew is given by the talented novelist Max Brod in his novel *Tycho Brahes Weg zu Gott* (1916).
17. See *Netivot Olam*, "Netiv Ha-Torah," Chapter 14.

them one learns to understand the Creator."[18] But this great
scholar who, more than all the other German rabbis of that era,
was versed in secular knowledge, also remained faithful to the
outlook of his age. He, too, had the greatest fear of free, critical
thought which refuses to rely blindly on the tradition of the
fathers. In this he saw the most dangerous heresy and arrogant
desecration of God's name. For the sake of God, the pious
Maharal admonishes, one must guard against relying on the
views of the sages of the nations of the world when these in any
way contradict our faith or the sages of the Talmud. One must
remove himself from these views as from the most pernicious
heresy, for the sages of Israel drew their knowledge from the
only sure source, "from the mouth of prophecy and the mouth
of Moses." They are the loyal bearers of the sacred tradition,
and every word of theirs is a living well of wisdom.[19] As a
competent student of astronomy, the Maharal was quite familiar with the epoch-making discoveries of Copernicus.[20] But he
had no doubt that correct knowledge of the movement of the
sun and the moon can be found only among the Jews, for, as
he points out with naive simplicity, "the sages of Israel have
received a teaching from Moses at Sinai which God transmitted to him, and He alone can know the truth."[21]

Now, one can imagine the great indignation, mingled with
fear, that seized the pious Maharal when he read Azariah dei
Rossi's *Meor Einayim*, which had recently appeared in Italy.
How is this?—to have the arrogance to declare openly and
publicly that our sages were not proficient in certain scientific
branches and that many of their statements cannot be taken
seriously but must be understood as poetic and rhetorical
flourishes? To declare the Jewish mode of reckoning time,
which is based on the tradition of our ancients, false and ungrounded? And not one of the scholars of the nations of the
world is it, but an Israelite, one of the "seed of Abraham," who
permits himself such heresy? Shall a son "of our generation,
that is so poor in knowledge," the Maharal scolds, have the
impudence to issue forth against our ancient authorities,
"against our holy men who lived thousands of years earlier,"

18. *Ibid.*
19. *Ibid.* See also *Be'er Ha-Golab*, 13, 90, 100 (we quote according to the Warsaw edition
    of 1873).
20. See *Netivot Olam*, "Netiv Ha-Torah," Chapter 14, p. 24.
21. *Ibid.*

and does he undertake, along with this, to rely on foreign authorities? And to think that such heretical views, which deserve "to be burned by fire," are printed openly and without hindrance![22] For the Maharal it was clear that a man who could allow himself to issue forth with this kind of work is not only a "heretic," but also a "fool and speaker of slander." How could the shepherds of Israel, he wonders, permit dei Rossi's heretical work to see the light of day?[23] He hopes that the people of Israel "which clings faithfully to God and His Torah" will carry out his strict decree concerning this sinful book and wipe out the memory of it. "Let it be known among all the children of Israel," he exclaims emotively, "that his work is filled with heresy, and every pious Jew must guard himself not only from reading *Meor Einayim* but even from holding it in his hands."[24]

It is interesting that the Maharal, when attacking *Meor Einayim* with such burning wrath, nowhere calls the author by name. He is only mentioned as "one of our people." He also believes that Aristotle does not deserve to have his name mentioned,[25] for the Greek philosopher taught that the world is eternal and that everything happens according to strict, ineluctable laws and thereby denies the miracles of the Torah.

The Maharal's literary legacy has a significant interest for every objective historian of culture. When one reads his words attentively, an altogether unique world is revealed in its full compass. This world is narrow and limited. Bestial cruelty and bitter hatred from the outside separated German Jewry through a high and firm wall from its environment. In this ghetto-world, with its locked and barred gates, everything was retarded and old-fashioned. Here doors and windows were closed so that no ray of free speculative thought might penetrate. Here the boundless rule of the tradition of the fathers, of the firmly established custom which the "ancients," the earlier generations, left as a legacy, obtained. And yet a unique magic lies in this old-fashioned world-view which appears so clearly in the literary legacy of *der hohe Rabbi Loew*. He impresses one forcibly with his moral power, with his sincere feeling and harmonious integrity. This straitly bounded, mel-

22. *Be'er Ha-Golah*, 91.
23. Apparently the battle which the Italian rabbis waged against dei Rossi's work was unknown to Rabbi Loew.
24. See *Be'er Ha-Golah*. pp. 90–101.
25. See the introduction to *Gevurot Ha-Shem*.

ancholy and dark world is permeated with a single desire, a single demand—upward, to the heights, to the truth, the only universal truth!

The Maharal speaks with great indignation of "those philo-sophizers,"[26] those who are devoted to the world of ideas of the Greek thinkers and attempt to interpret the Biblical text in accord with it and to prove all the miracles recounted in Scripture naturalistically by way of reason. "Only our sages," he insists, "understood the profound truth that miracles can-not be explained through man's ordinary reason, for they are the result of a completely different kind of lawfulness and regularity than the everyday phenomena of nature." One must know and remember, he frequently asserts, that there are two kinds of regularity, which must not be confused if one does not wish to grope about in a labyrinth of contra-dictions. Beyond the natural regularity that governs the ev-eryday and usual phenomena of nature, there is another—the universal and superterrestrial—and it is to this latter order of regularity that the phenomena we call miracles belong.[27] It is clear, the Maharal concludes, that miracles cannot be ex-plained by common, practical sense, the kind of thinking that is suited to explicating the ordinary phenomena of nature. Not in practical knowledge, not in perfecting the human rea-son, does the supreme bliss, therefore, consist; this must be sought in another realm, the realm of *faith*. Not with the lim-ited human mind but only through faith can man draw close to God, "for faith," the Maharal many times reiterates,[28] "is cleaving to Him." But even "cleaving," the sweet and tender palpitation with which faith fills the human heart—even this divine gift is not given to man in total perfection. This is merely the potentiality for, or the possibility of, perfection; only when it is embodied in action, in doing, and in the will to fulfill the divine commandments, does the potentiality be-come actuality and does man attain the highest level of per-fection.[29] To observe the commandments of the Torah, the

26. When Rabbi Loew speaks of the Jewish "philosophizers," he dwells especially on Gersonides (see the long introduction to *Gevurot Ha-Shem*).
27. See the introduction to *Gevurot Ha-Shem*. The Maharal here incidentally touches on the question of the "separate intelligences" and speaks mockingly of the opin-ion of the "seekers" and "philosophers" who assure us that the sun and moon are living intelligences. "Do not believe in this," he admonishes the reader, "for it is utter folly."
28. *Tiferet Yisrael*, 138. See also *Gevurot Ha-Shem*, Chapters 9 and 11.
29. See *Tiferet Yisrael*, Chapters 2–3, 7ff.

Maharal repeats on numerous occasions, is the golden stairway which raises man to supreme beatitude.[30]

The Maharal speaks with contempt and sarcasm of the rationalists who see the summit of perfection in sharpening the mind, in delving into the thought-world of speculation. They believe that through immersing oneself in *muskalot* (abstract ideas) the immortal essence is born in the mortal and accidental; on the basis of this they conclude that only the intellect of the thinker and scholar who unites with the "active intellect" through his searching and investigation in the world of ideas is immortal. "All this," the Maharal cries out, "is pure folly!"[31] "The rationalists," he further declares, "who follow the ways of the 'philosophers' cannot at all understand how through commandments of action, through practical, physical deeds, man can attain the stages of eternal beatitude and supreme perfection."[32] With their narrowly limited common sense "they have not stood in the secrets of the Lord;" they cannot grasp the divine mystery and do not understand that the commandments of the Torah are constructed not according to the laws of human reason but out of divine reason, and that they rest not on the foundations of the laws of nature but on a regularity of a much higher degree.

The rationalists wish to explain the *mitzvot* or commandments of the Torah in a purely utilitarian way, to measure them with the yardstick of usefulness and harmfulness. They endeavor to show the reason for each individual commandment rationally and naturalistically, "as if the Torah were a book like other books of remedies or books about nature." They cannot comprehend that in a purely utilitarian way, from the standpoint of usefulness and harmfulness, one cannot explain the reasons of the commandments, for the Torah is, after all, not built on the laws of nature but on the divine mind. Not to benefit man, not to endow him with this world and the life of the world to come, were the commandments given, but as a strict yoke and decree, as a divine command.[33] For the

---

30. *Ibid.*, Chapter 4.
31. *Ibid.*, 23.
32. *Ibid.*, Ch. 6.
33. *Ibid.*, Ch. 6: "The commandments of the Torah are not to benefit man but to serve as a yoke . . . The divine commander has imposed them on us like a king who imposes decrees on his people." See also *Netzaḥ Yisrael*, 20a: "For it is quite impossible to say that the giving of the Torah was for the sake of Israel, in order to bring them to good in this world and to the life of the world to come . . . for the giving of the Torah is a yoke upon Israel . . . This was not for the sake of Israel's good

Torah was not given out of mercy, and the world does not stand on mercy. God did not create the world in order to do good and bring utility, but everything is "a decree of judgment," the inevitable result of the rigorous divine order which is pure righteousness.[34] To be sure, the Maharal adds, it is written in the Torah: "To do all these statutes, that it may be well with us." But this does not mean that God gave us the commandments in order to benefit us. He commanded them to us *ke-melech ha-gozer,* "as a king who decrees." It is true that all the commandments God laid upon the Jews bring us good and happiness as soon as we fulfill them; from God only the perfectly good and just can come, for all His deeds are, after all, the absolute good. But there can be no talk here of sympathy or compassion, for everything is rigorous law, the command of the divine will which is absolute justice.[35]

The major point distinguishing the Torah from speculation, from the various sciences, the Maharal several times repeats, is the fact that in the latter the purely *ethical,* the principle of justice, is lacking. Not proficiency in the natural sciences, not knowledge and familiarity with the movements of the planets and the nature of the four basic elements, he points out, can therefore bring us close to God and endow us with eternal bliss. This can be effected only through studying the Torah and its commandments, for the Torah is embodied justice. And what can so bring us near to God as justice? God, blessed be He, is universal justice itself.[36] The Torah cannot be anything other than the supreme prototype of righteousness and justice, for it is the revelation of God's wisdom, the manifestation of the highest, transcendant lawfulness. Its basic principle is the absolute, divine goodness.[37] The Torah is, in the Maharal's understanding, the foundation-stone of the world, the "law and order of the world." Without it the whole cosmos would lapse into chaos.[38] It is eternal, one, integral and indivisible in its oneness, for, the Maharal reiterates a number of times, only that which is one and integral has the fullness of perfection.[39] Because the

---

but as a decree, like a king who issues his decrees to his servants to place a burden on them" (we quote according to the Prague edition of 1599).

34. *Tiferet Yisrael,* Chapter 6, p. 17.
35. *Ibid.*
36. *Ibid.,* Chapter 11; *Netivot Olam,* "Netiv Ha-Torah," Chapter 9.
37. *Tiferet Yisrael,* Chapter 20. See also *Netivot Olam,* Chapter 1.
38. *Netzaḥ Yisrael,* 20. See also *Tiferet Yisrael.*
39. *Gevurot Ha-Shem:* "For all that is single is everything . . . the divided is a

Torah is the supreme revelation of divine wisdom, he who wishes to devote himself to it heart and soul must remove himself entirely from the world, forget all pleasures and corporeal matters, just as it is written, "This is the law: when a man dies in the tent . . ."[40] The Maharal, the rabbi and preacher, however, deems it necessary immediately to point out that one must not think that the Torah was given only for the chosen few, "for the great sages." The Torah is free and open; in its simplicity and wholeness it belongs to all alike.[41]

"The Torah was given to all," the Maharal declares on numerous occasions; but not every soul is fit to receive the divine wisdom which the Torah revealed to the world. Rabbi Loew, to be sure, notes that by the term *re'acha* (your neighbor) the Torah means everyone who observes the seven commandments of the sons of Noah,[42] but he insists a number of times that not all men have similar souls, nor is the entire human species permeated in like measure with the feeling of divine holiness. Not among all nations did the souls of their members attain such a morally exalted level that they could accomplish "all the divine deeds that are the commandments of the Torah." To this one must be suited from birth. There must be a spiritual affinity, so that the soul intuitively strives and yearns for this. The only people with the definite potentiality, with the related "divine soul" which feels itself intimately associated with the incarnate divine wisdom, the sacred Torah, is the people of Israel.[43] In this consists its chosenness, its predestined mission.

We find in the Maharal numerous poetically written pages in which he marvels at the wondrous mystery inherent in the national community, which lives in the multiplicity of each individual but always retains its oneness and integrity, for "outside oneness there is no perfection."[44] The people of Israel, he asserts, is not a part of society as a whole; it is a single and unique nation which has no analogue. And, indeed, in its oneness lies its universal wholeness, for only that which is one is

---

material thing." *Netzah Yisrael*, 140: "For everything perfect is single and the one is perfect, for perfection does not apply to the thing that is not one but divided."

40. See *Derush Al Ha-Torah*, 13; *Netivot Olam*, 11.
41. *Netivot Olam*, 10. See also the introduction to *Tiferet Yisrael*.
42. See *Be'er Ha-Golah*, 104.
43. See *Tiferet Yisrael*, Chapter 1; *Gevurot Ha-Shem*, last chapter.
44. Cf. above.

everything.[45] Even though the people of Israel has sinned, it remains "the son of the king" who bears the stamp of his father's perfection. Of it God has said, "My son, My firstborn, Israel." Israel is the embodiment or incarnation of divinity on earth.[46] In the Maharal's theological conception is reflected in a very unique way the old concept of tri-unity concerning God the Creator, the divine wisdom or Torah, and His "appointed" one—"My son, My firstborn, Israel," who is as eternal as the Torah.[47] The Torah and Israel complement one another; they were predestined for each other. In this affinity, this predestination, which binds the Torah to the people of Israel from eternity, Rabbi Loew perceives the profound meaning of the ancient Talmudic legend which relates that when God wished to give the Torah to the Jews at Mount Sinai, "He held the mountain over them like a tub, so that they would accept the Torah," threatening that otherwise the mountain would bury them underneath itself. For the bond between the Torah and its appointed one, the people of Israel, was a necessity, a result of the supreme universal lawfulness or regularity.[48] But, Rabbi Loew insists (and here it is possible that the influence of Ḥasdai Crescas is discernible), the people of Israel did not accept the Torah commanded by God out of compulsion. It was, indeed, a necessity, since it was the consequence of the predetermined divine will and with it were associated the harmony and perfection of the world; nevertheless, the people of Israel did this out of free will, because its "divine soul" felt its affinity to the "destined"—the divine Torah.[49] Truly free, in the Maharal's view, is the profound believer, the man all of whose thought and action is directed to the only living source from which the heavenly daughter, the human soul, draws her sustenance.[50]

The bond between the people of Israel and its "destined," the Torah, is the revelation of genuine human freedom in the world. Here appears very clearly in the Maharal's religious outlook the idea that occupies such an honored place in Chris-

---

45. *Gevurot Ha-Shem: Aval Yisrael einam ḥelek kelal, ki bem yeḥidah she-lo timtza od kemotah, she-im atta motze kemotah haitah ha-ummah ha-zot ḥelek . . . aval attah she-hi yeḥidah hi ba-kol, she-kol mi she-hu yaḥid hu ba-kol.*

46. See *Gevurot Ha-Shem*, Chapter 39; *Netzaḥ Yisrael*, Chapter 13.

47. *Tiferet Yisrael*, Chapter 1; "The Torah was created before the creation of the natural world, and Israel was also created before the natural world."

48. *Ibid.*, Chapter 32.

49. *Ibid.*

50. See *Gevurot Ha-Shem*, Chapter 9.

tian theology—the idea of the man-God. But the man-God does not here reveal himself in the form of a mortal, of a single human person, but as an entire community, as a national society. The Jewish nation, God's "son and firstborn"—this is the man-God in whom the whole human species, the entire cosmos, obtained its appointed form, its goal and purpose. Along with this, Rabbi Loew determinedly attacks those who hold Maimonides' view that the angels are at a much higher level of perfection than man and man's highest manifestation, the Jewish people.[51] The angels, says he, are appointed only to carry out specific tasks, but the people of Israel is God's son, and as such reveals His greatness and proclaims His glory and splendor. Indeed, for this reason God bears the name of Israel and says, "I am the Lord, your God," not "I am the Lord, the God of the angels."[52]

Here we touch upon an important point that is very characteristic of the Maharal's outlook. We alluded, in the introduction to our history to the lovely Biblical legend which relates that the Creator brought before Adam, the man who had just come into being, all the creatures that swarm on the dry land, in the air and in the sea, in order that he might give them names; and with the name which the man gave it does each creature *live*. This legend finds its complement in the beautiful Talmudic legend which relates that after God created man out of clay, the angels asked complainingly, "What is his character? Of what use is this creature?" The Holy One Blessed be He thereupon said to them, "The wisdom of this creature created out of clay is greater than yours." Then, to prove it, God brought before the angels all the beasts and birds so that the angels might tell "what their character is" and designate each with a name. But to the angels, who roam constantly in the celestial heights, the earth and its inhabitants were foreign; hence they could not appraise the earthly creatures and certainly could not give them names. God then brought the creatures before Adam, who immediately said, "This beast shall bear the name ox, this one camel, this one donkey, etc." God then asked the man, "And what is My name?" "For You," the man answered, "the name *Adonai* (Lord) is proper, because You are the Lord of all." The Holy One Blessed be He then said, "Let it be so. I am He with whose name man has designated Me!"

51. *Gevurot Ha-Shem*, Chapter 44.
52. *Ibid.*

In this *midrash*, the Maharal further explains, is hidden one of the profoundest "mysteries of the Torah and secrets of wisdom," for, he insists, man is the *ikkar ha-metziut* (main point of existence). He is the measure of all values, the central point in the orb of the world, and everything that exists is appraised according to the form it receives in man's sight, according to the name with which man designates it.[53]

But the Maharal goes still further. Even the Creator of the universe manifests Himself to the world under the name and under the concepts with which man has clothed Him. The Creator reveals Himself as "the God of Israel" and is disclosed in the form in which man grasps Him.[54]

We encounter here in the world-outlook of Rabbi Loew the unique theological anthropomorphism that is so characteristic of the *Zohar*, in which man is regarded as the absolute *Ein Sof* (Infinite) in limited, personified forms, or, more simply expressed, as the earthly, material bearer of divinity.

In the Maharal's view, man is the "main point of existence," and the crown of the human species is "My son, My firstborn, Israel." The difficult question then arises with all its tragic contradictions: how is it that the "divine son," the destined one of the Torah, the "unique" and "chosen" people, languishes in bitter exile? The sixteenth century rabbi of Prague was, after all, a witness of so many persecutions and oppressions which Jews had to endure in that era and speaks with moving pathos of the terrible sufferings and degradations in which the "offspring of Jacob, the holy seed," live. "How can words of consolation be of help here?," he exclaims.[55] Nevertheless, he teaches, one must not lose courage. Such is the order of the world. Through fire gold is refined and freed of dross. All the afflictions and punishments have made the people of Israel harder than steel and saved it from destruction. The chosen people must suffer because it is of a different world. It is a bearer of higher laws that are inconsistent with the material laws of nature, and its fate will also be shared by the redeemer of the world, the king Messiah. "There is no end to the sufferings of the Messiah," for the earthly world with its material laws of nature "opposes the divine word," refuses to recognize the exalted and divine.[56] "Because the people of Israel is the

53. *Tiferet Yisrael*, Chapter 33.
54. *Ibid.*
55. *Netzaḥ Yisrael*, Chapter 44.
56. *Ibid.*, p. 45a.

foundation of the world," Rabbi Loew insists, "it must be dispersed over the whole world and its country must be the entire earth."[57] To be spread over the whole earth and withal to remain "a people dwelling alone"—this, the Maharal, the son of the isolated medieval ghetto, deems it essential to repeat many times. The Jewish people, he indicates, must live an altogether separate life and not come into close contact with the nations of the world; otherwise it will lose its uniqueness and no longer be the "one and whole" people. Not without reason did our sages point out that the Jews were redeemed from slavery in Egypt for their merit in not having assimilated with the surrounding populace, not adopting their language, or their names, or their mode of dress.[58] The Jews in relation to other peoples, the Maharal further notes, are like fire with water: as long as fire is separated from the water, its flame burns brightly, but as soon as fire comes into contact with water, its flame is extinguished and darkness swallows the light.[59]

Hence Rabbi Loew issues forth decisively against those who are lenient in regard to regulations governing the relationship between Jews and the surrounding populace. He complains strongly, for example, of those who believe that the prohibition against the "wine of idolators" has lost its validity because there is no longer reason to fear that Christian people "now pour libations to idols".[60] One must, he teaches, separate himself as much as possible from the external world. "Follow the ways of our fathers, devote yourself heart and soul to the study of the Torah with its commandments and all the details of the commandments and the details of the details."[61] The Torah should be studied, the Maharal notes in this connection, not in isolation but in fellowship, together with others.[62] Only in friendly discussion or debate of souls having an affinity for each other is the truth born. "The Torah is acquired only in fellowship," he several times reiterates. He knew very well, however, that in the method of study characterized by *pilpul* and *ḥillukim*, which then dominated the Polish and German

---

57. *Ibid.*, p. 57.
58. *Gevurot Ha-Shem*, Chapter 43.
59. *Netzaḥ Yisrael*, p. 37
60. *Derush Al Ha-Torah*, 46
61. *Tiferet Yisrael*, end of Chapter 13.
62. *Derech Ḥayyim*, 107b: "For when a man is alone he does not receive the Torah . . . if he studies the Torah by himself he is foolish" (we quote according to the first Cracow edition).

yeshivot, "studying in fellowship" could not lead to "the disclosure of truth." It only strengthened tremendously among the Talmudic students the desire for casuistic, overly subtle convolutions, performed to dazzle one another with sharp notions and ingenious inventions. For the real meaning and true content of the matter or law under discussion, there was, in all this, little concern. Hence Rabbi Loew, having the temperament of the genuine reprover and battler, issued forth with all his energy against the contemporary system of education and set himself the task of completely reforming the Jewish youth's mode of study. This problem of reforming the educational system, along with a very keen critique of the method of *pilpul*, is especially treated by the Maharal in the introduction to his *Netivot Olam* and in his well-known *Derush Al Ha-Torah* which he published in 1593. But he considers this question so important that he returns to it in almost all his other numerous works as well. His battle against the contemporary order of study undoubtedly has a cultural-historical significance, for through it we learn interesting details about the way of life in the elementary schools and Talmudic academies of that era.

"From the day that I came to understanding," the Maharal relates in the introduction to his *Derush Al Ha-Torah*,

I have observed carefully and seen how badly our generation carries on the conduct of Torah and study. I said to myself: "This is not the way which our fathers and the holy men of former times followed; the difference is so vast that there can be no comparison." Therefore some years ago I strengthened myself like a lion and desired to make improvements in this realm according to my understanding. But I did not succeed in this, for the sons of our generation declare, "We will follow the many." Not long ago I made a new attempt and addressed a summons to the lands of Poland and Russia, asking them to make the necessary improvements in this area. But once again I accomplished nothing. Nevertheless, I do not withdraw from the enterprise or lose courage. I shall hope that my words of instruction will yet be heard and reach attentive and pious hearts . . . If I thereby succeed in bringing aid to one out of a thousand or leading him on the right way, I will take no account of the thousand fools who stop up their ears and avert their eyes . . .

The method of *pilpul* which the Talmudic sages utilized, the Maharal further says in his *Derush Al Ha-Torah*, was not at all "empty or vain ingenuity." It was really an important means of obtaining in dialectical fashion the correct content or essence of each law—not as is the case with our present pilpul-

ists, "who make a fraud out of the Torah of our God." They
call this "words of sharpness." Certainly they are "stabbing
words," words that spear and tear the hearts of those who
listen to them. Quite consciously and deliberately they pervert
and falsify a given section of the Talmud for the sole purpose
of exhibiting the feat of sharp ingenuities. This brings it about
that the ways of Torah are lost, for those who thirst with their
whole heart for true knowledge say: Of what avail can all these
trickeries and dazzling works be? They therefore remove
themselves from our *yeshivot*, where only young men who are
devoid of knowledge and whose desire is not the Torah remain.[63]

"Woe for the shame and disgrace," Rabbi Loew exclaims
elsewhere,[64]

that our generation differs from all others! The honor of the Torah,
its glory and splendor, have disappeared in it, and we are all naked,
without knowledge—and this for the sake of *hillukim* and *pilpul!*
. . . Let them not say that *pilpul* sharpens minds; it only makes one
foolish and ignorant. We see to what this "sharpening" has brought
us . . . If the students in their early years and at the beginning studied
the plain meaning of the Talmudic text, the learning of their childhood would remain with them and they would at least know several
tractates, but now they know nothing—and this because they immediately begin with *Tosafot*, even before they have obtained any
notion whatever of the Talmudic text itself . . . One cannot, after all,
make the same demands of small children and adults. Among us,
however, men refuse to know anything of this. And if you try to
argue with a father and give him to understand that he should first
teach the "principle of the law" to his child and not immediately
confuse his mind with *Tosafot*, this will seem to him as if you were
saying that he should not teach his son at all. For the father thinks
only of glory . . . Do not believe that everyone who can ask questions
on a matter, who is an "uprooter of mountains" and a keen practi-
tioner of *pilpul*, is already a master of Torah. No, he is not a master
of Torah but only of *pilpul!* And where there is no real knowledge
of Torah, there also reverence of God is lacking . . . Know, all you
students of Torah who sit in the *yeshivot*, if all the seas were ink, they
would not suffice to describe the tremendous ruin this method of
study has wrought—this method which has brought it about that in
countries where there were once such great scholars as Rashi, Rabbenu Tam, and the Tosafists, now, because of our many sins, the
Torah has been entirely forgotten and both Torah and deeds have

63. *Derush Al Ha-Torah*, 33.
64. *Netivot Olam*, Chapter 5.

been taken away from them . . . If only one out of a thousand realized how great the danger is, this would be some consolation to me. But no one sees and wishes to understand. Therefore my heart grieves and my eyes weep . . .[65]

In the later chapters of this work, the Maharal again touches upon the crucial question of educating children.

All children go to the teacher to learn Torah, but there is great apprehension that with the barbaric order of study prevalent among us, this can only bring harm. On studying the Bible and the Mishnah no emphasis at all is placed, and the study of the Gemara is also conducted in such a way that it can have no good result. As the child comes to his teacher without any knowledge of Sacred Scripture, so he goes away from him. The Mishnah, which is, after all, the foundation and chief element in the study of Torah, is also not studied, and so the children remain with nothing. With their own hands, they make themselves miserable. They wish to fly into the highest heavens and fall ever lower, and no arguments whatever are of any avail. The teacher thinks only of himself, and the father, with his slight understanding, wishes that his son should learn the entire Torah in a brief period. His son is still a little boy, and he already sends him to distant places to draw Torah from deep wells. All these dreams, however, run off like water, and it is well if the child at least brings back with him the little Torah with which he went away, so enormous is the number of the ruined ones whom the absurd order of learning has crippled for life.[66]

But Rabbi Loew was not content merely with sharply criticizing the contemporary order of study. In many of his works[67] he also pointed out the way to improve the education of children and, along with this, always insisted that he was not here proposing new reforms. He desired only a return to the right way which the ancients, the sages of the Talmud, followed.

The ancients, declared the Maharal, led school children on the correct way to a definite goal. The present generation has lost this way. It wishes to construct a new building, not giving thought first to the necessary foundation and proper cornerstones for it. In former generations, the order of study was carried on according to a definite plan. At the age of five the child was introduced to the study of the Pentateuch, at the age

65. *Ibid.*
66. *Netivot Olam*, "Netiv Ha-Torah," Chapter 10.
67. See *Tiferet Yisrael*, Chapter 56, pp. 110–111: *Gur Aryeh* (Commentary on the Torah), V, 6, 7: *Derush Al Ha-Torah*, 36–37; *Derech Hayyim*, IV, 6.

of ten to the Mishnah, and only at the age of fifteen to the Gemara. He was conducted from the simple to the difficult, and only after he had become familiar in his early years with the foundation of our faith was he able to proceed to further study, to the Mishnah which is the living root out of which the mighty tree of Talmudic literature grew. Thus did our sages proceed in former times. Quite different is the custom today in our lands. The fools in our generations do everything topsy-turvy. The Pentateuch is studied with the children in a strange, barbaric way. Every week they begin to study the *sidra* (pericope assigned for reading in the synagogue that week) with the child. But because the young child cannot learn the entire *sidra*, they stop in the middle and the next week immediately proceed to the next *sidra*. Thus the child learns only tornout fragments without any connection and finally knows not a single *sidra* in its entirety. If someone attempts to demonstrate how absurd such an order is and that another way ought to be sought, he at once receives the answer: "As all are accustomed to do, so do we also." And when the child who has learned nothing reaches the age of six or seven, they at once begin studying the Gemara with him. Even in maturer years, it is more difficult to grasp the Talmudic text if one has not previously acquainted himself thoroughly with the Mishnah, especially in childhood. But our teachers and guides refuse to understand any such thing. Even this, however, is too little for them. As soon as the boy has become somewhat at home in the Talmudic text, they begin to stuff him with *Tosafot* which he, with his childish mind, is not at all capable of understanding. If at least they would stop with *Tosafot*. But they climb still further and stuff the little boy's head with *pilpul* and *ḥillukim*. He wastes his powers and best years with crazy, foolish questions, with tortuous theories and crooked notions which dissolve like spider webs, and he remains naked and bare, without accurate information and true knowledge.[68] Can such a thing be allowed to continue in the tents of Israel—to accustom children to falsehood and the spirit of mendacity? To waste years only on sharpening the mind? But even this is not true. It is not with crooked subtleties and wild inventions that one can sharpen the mind so that it may easily grasp the truth. On the contrary, through tortuous *pilpul* the mind is no longer capable of thinking clearly and logically. But our Torah is the Torah of truth, and your *pilpul* obscures the truth and merely

---

68. See *Gur Aryeh*, 205b (we quote according to the first edition, Prague, 1578).

spreads falsehood and lying. Rabbi Loew angrily cries out, "Better that you should become artisans, carpenters and hewers of wood; demonstrate your art and mastery in these things. Here, in artisanry and handwork, mastery and ingenuity can be of the greatest utility. Here artistry is the way of truth, the way which our Torah follows. But your trickeries in sharpening the intellect are pure lies, and falsehood and truth are, after all, in total opposition to each other."[69]

In this way, the Maharal complains, children grow up among us void of information, without thorough knowledge of the Bible, the Mishnah and the Gemara. The students of the *yeshivot* themselves, however, do not understand this. They adapt themselves to the taste of those who supply them with all their needs. Should a young man's entire sum of knowledge consist merely of *pilpul* and pointed subtleties, the ignorant multitude nevertheless believes that this is the profoundest wisdom, and the young man sees in this his best goal, the right way to make a career for himself. For he thinks to himself: I will thereby acquire a name among those who will provide me with all good things and will ingratiate myself with rich people, obtain a practical, business-like wife, and no longer know of any cares.[70]

To fight against this corrupt order of study, the Maharal established numerous societies for the study of the Mishnah.[71] These propagandized for the reforms he projected—reforms which consisted essentially in restoring the old order of study practiced by the sages of the Talmud: first, teaching the Bible to the children and only then, when they are already versed in it, passing on to the Mishnah and the Gemara.

But all my trouble, Rabbi Loew laments, has been in vain. There are always men who sin and make others sin, whose whole intention in study of Torah is merely self-aggrandizement and search for glory. They persuade the common people: It is better for your son to devote himself as much as possible to the *pilpul* of the Gemara, for thereby he will acquire fame, become a great scholar in Israel, and with his glory illuminate you and your whole household.[72] And the simple householder allows himself to be led astray through these flattering words.

69. *Tiferet Yisrael*, p. 110.
70. *See Gur Aryeh*, 205–206.
71. That he not only proposed but himself actually founded such societies or fellowships is attested by his disciple Rabbi Ephraim of Luntshitz (*Ammudei Shesh*, 28) and the author of *Tosafot Yom Tov*, of whom we shall speak presently.
72. See *Derush Al Ha-Torah*, 34.

He believes in truth that the study of the Mishnah is too simple and elementary, that genuine keenness can be demonstrated only in *pilpul* and *ḥillukim*.

Thus even so great a scholar and one with such vast authority as the Maharal could not swim successfully against the stream and carry through his projected reforms in the order of education for children. He did not succeed, despite the fact that he was not alone in the battle that had begun but had some capable co-workers. His chief collaborator was the popular preacher, Ephraim ben Aaron of Luntshitz.[73] Ephraim spent his youth in Yaroslav,[74] then was principal of the *yeshivah* in Lemberg. From 1604 on he was rabbi and principal of the *yeshivah* in Prague, where he died in 1619. Ephraim of Luntshitz is known as the author of numerous works: a commentary to Rashi, *Keli Yakar*, which was published at the expense of the *Vaad* (Council of Four Lands),[75] and books of ethical instruction, namely, *Ir Ha-Gibborim* and the very popular *Olelot Efrayim*, in which numerous legends and stories from the Midrashim are employed with intimate tenderness. His comprehensive work *Rivevot Efrayim*, homilies on the Pentateuch, has remained in manuscript.[76]

Ephraim gained special renown as a brilliant preacher. He preached sermons not only in Lemberg and Prague, where he spent his years; he would also travel to the famous commercial fairs at Lublin where the Council of Four Lands held its sessions, and there, before the assemblage of the rabbis of Poland and leaders of the communities, give his fiery sermons of reproof.[77] With his sharp words of admonition, Ephraim made many enemies.[78] Since he published some of his sermons in a special collection entitled *Ammudei Shesh*,[79] we may learn from them that the "important people," the rabbis and heads of the communities, were indeed compelled to listen to very unpleas-

---

73. He frequently calls himself by the double name Solomon Ephraim. The first of these names was given to him only in his later years, when he was dangerously ill.
74. See the preface to *Olelot Efrayim*.
75. See the preface to *Keli Yakar*.
76. See *Olelot Efrayim*, 28 (we quote according to the Vilna edition of 1877).
77. See the introduction to *Ammudei Shesh*.
78. He refers to his enemies and persecutors in the introduction to *Ammudei Shesh*.
79. Ephraim relates that in 1607, when an epidemic broke out in Prague, he and many other inhabitants of the city fled and settled in the little town of Bishitz, four miles from Prague. There he had a good deal of leisure, which he employed to write down some of his sermons and prepare them for publication. *Ammudei Shesh* first appeared in 1617.

ant words from the militant and forthright preacher. When
Ephraim, for example, introduces the statement of the
Gemara, "The words of the Torah are not fulfilled except by
men who are humble, like Moses and Abraham," and that
wisdom is "found most among those who are small and lowly
in their own sight," he at once adds:

But among the Torah students of our generation the quality of
humility is not to be found at all. On the contrary, nowhere in the
world are there men so proud and arrogant as they. He who knows
anything at all of the Torah believes that there is no one like him, and
let him only imagine that you have somehow touched his puffed-up
honor, and he will consider nothing but will revenge himself more
than the primordial serpent. Each believes himself greater than the
whole world, and none of these scholars of the generation is willing
to recognize another. Each insults the other, speaks every possible
evil of him, endeavors to show that the other is an ignoramus, a base
man who understands and knows nothing. He alone is the wise man,
the great man, and all others are nothing . . . And how vast is his joy
when he hears something evil spoken of another scholar. He perceives in the other his competitor whom he must degrade and make
a mockery and a scorn.[80]

These qualities of pathological arrogance and envy so prevalent among the scholars of his generation derive, according to
the author of *Olelot Efrayim,* in a certain measure from the
abnormal method of study dominating the elementary schools
and *yeshivot.* With the same indignation and almost in the same
style as the Maharal, Ephraim of Luntshitz speaks of the absurd method of teaching the Pentateuch to the children. The
child, he complains, is still so young that he cannot understand
anything, but they already begin to teach him the Pentateuch,
and that not in order but in separate fragments—this week
several verses from *Bereshit,* the next week from *Noaḥ,* etc.
Also, in these verses the child is taught only the meaning of the
words but not the connection between the verses, which would
make it possible for him at least to obtain some notion of what
it is all about. The Pentateuch is employed here only as a little
textbook to learn the language, just like all other textbooks.
Thus they mechanically drill into the child the meaning of the
individual words, but of the content of the Torah, of its laws
and teachings, he has no conception. And with such wretched
information, the child immediately passes over to the study of

80. *Ammudei Shesh,* Chapter 5, 6a, and the last chapter.

the Gemara. Here also they begin with tractates that are not at all suited to his understanding, e.g., *Eruvin* and *Ḥullin*. Is it to be wondered, then, that all this quickly evaporates from the child's memory, and from his years of study in school there remain only vague, unsystematic bits of information, but not the essential familiarity with the commandments and the moral teaching of the Talmudic sages? Responsible for all this is the foolish pride of the fathers, who desire that their children manifest their great keenness as quickly as possible, so that people might marvel at their acute minds which, when they are still very young, grasp the most difficult *Tosafot* and sharpest *ḥilluk* and already understand ingeniously the secret of "making an elephant pass through the eye of a needle with *pilpul*." The main point in learning among us, Ephraim adds bitterly, is the honing of the mind with "the *pilpul* of vanity and chaos" that is called by us *ḥilluk*. It is literally scandalous to see how a rabbi, an aged man and long a dweller in a *yeshivah*, who is recognized and accepted in the entire region, performs tricks, discloses tremendous *ḥiddushim* (novellae), and pretends that such is the literal meaning of the Gemara, when he himself knows that all this is falsehood and vanity, that he merely dazzles his own and others' eyes. Has there ever in the world been such a delusion, that men should spend days and years in absurd ingenuities which are pure falsehood—and all this for the sake of empty pride, to obtain a reputation as a clever man and uprooter of mountains?

To be sure, the preacher of Luntshitz adds, having in mind the aged Maharal, I know very well that at the present time also there are "a few, the remnant of the generation," who would like very much to topple this order of study, but they cannot accomplish this, for they are "lost by reason of their fewness" in the face of the great number of rabbis who mislead the multitude and assure it that *pilpul* is the "chief thing in the Torah." The multitude allows itself to be persuaded, and so things remain as they are. Ephraim relates further how he himself used to carry on long discussions with the "great sages of the generation in our land" about annulling "the learning of sharpness and *pilpul* which is called *ḥilluk*." But it was of no avail, for these "sages of the generation" perceive in *pilpul* the most effective means of obtaining honor and office, occupying the most prestigious positions as brilliant *yeshivah* heads. All their arguments about the importance of *pilpul*, however, have no foundation. We see clearly that in Palestine, for instance, and other lands where Jews do not concern themselves with false *pilpul*, the scholars are expert "in all the sciences and all the codes," for they do not waste their years in vain foolishness, as is the case among us.

To save the young, Ephraim of Luntshitz insists, we must reform the order of study. The reform that he proposes is, in all details, similar to the order of learning which the Maharal, on whom he in fact bases himself, had proposed. Rabbi Loew, as we have observed, had no success in his battle for the new method of study, but in one particular he did have great good fortune: he raised up a disciple, an excellent scholar who continued what his teacher had struggled for all his life. When Ephraim notes the great importance of the Maharal's ordinance concerning societies for the study of the Mishnah, since the Mishnah is the major foundation of rabbinic Judaism, he adds: "Especially now the Maharal's desire that men study the Mishnah every day is very easy to fulfill, since Rabbi Yom-Tov Heller has written his commentary to the Mishnah which is so easily comprehensible to all."[81]

Rabbi Yom-Tov ben Nathan Heller was the most gifted among the aged Rabbi Jehudah Loew's pupils. Born in Wallerstein (Bavaria) in 1579, he came when he was still quite young to the *yeshivah* in Prague and at the age of eighteen was already a rabbinic judge in that city. The youthful judge, however, was not only extremely well versed in the sea of the Talmud; he also had quite extensive knowledge of the "external wisdoms." He composed an astronomical work, *Derush Ḥiddush Ha-Levanah*, and was a competent mathematician. At the age of nineteen he wrote a commentary to Jedaiah Ha-Penini's *Beḥinat Olam* and a scientific work on Samuel Archevolti's well-known philological book, *Arugat Ha-Bosem*.[82] In his preface to Joseph ben Isaac Halevi's grammar, *Siaḥ Yitzḥak*, Heller laments that in his generation there is so little concern with philology.

It is possible that Heller's interest in secular knowledge was aroused by the aged Maharal, but it is beyond doubt that the greatest influence in this respect came to the young Heller from a unique personality with whom he became acquainted when he was a rabbinic judge in Prague. This man's name was Joseph ben Isaac Halevi. The only thing that we know about him is that he came originally from Lithuania. Strange and unnoticed, he passed quickly before his generation and then

81. *Ammudei Shesh*, "Musar Ammud Ha-Torah."
82. See our *History*, Vol. IV, p. 129

disappeared like a shadow and was forgotten, for he belonged
to those tragic figures whose bitter fate brings it about that
they are not born at the right time. They wander, lonely and
sad—these "untimely" figures. No one knows or understands
them. They roam with deep sorrow in their hearts, for they
know that their rich spiritual powers go to waste uselessly, and
their fate is loneliness and oblivion.

We do not know who Halevi was or with whom he studied
Torah. It has only been ascertained that when he was quite
young, he was already a man of extensive scholarship with a
profound knowledge of the Jewish religious philosophy of the
Middle Ages. As a young man he left his home and settled in
Prague where he used to read books of speculation with young
people, mainly Maimonides' *Guide for the Perplexed*. In 1611 he
published his *Givat Ha-Moreh* in Prague, and both the publisher and Ephraim of Luntshitz in his note of approval[83] marvel at the comprehensive knowledge of the young author. At
that time, when the dominion of *pilpul* was boundless and all
minds were absorbed in study of the Talmud, the young Lithuanian gave his total attention to purely philosophical problems. He was not interested in the laws of what is prohibited
and forbidden in food and related matters but in the teachings
of Aristotle and Averroes, not in the codifiers and commentators on the Talmud but in *A Guide for the Perplexed*. The author
of *Givat Ha-Moreh* does, indeed, stress the vast significance of
Maimonides and his philosophical work, but he is not carried
away and points out that Maimonides is no more than human
and occasionally commits logical errors.

Systematically, calmly, and with great learning Joseph ben
Isaac analyzes Maimonides' attempt to ground philosophically
the existence of the First Cause that is free of the least semblance of matter and corporeality, and comes to the conclusion
that this attempt failed.[84] The young author incidentally dis-

83. Ephraim writes in this note: "This announces to all that there has come here to
the holy community of Prague a young man, Rabbi Joseph ben Isaac Segal (Halevi)
... From the time he began to disseminate his theories and to teach others wisdom
in philosophical matters and speculation in divinity, his nature has been known
—that he has a name and memorial in the sciences mentioned above, to the point
that great scholars of our community who have heard him and learned from him
the *Guide for the Perplexed* and scientific matters mentioned above give testimony
about him ... He is a new vessel filled with old wine."
84. In the introduction to *Givat Ha-Moreh* he writes: "Our intention in this short essay
is to disclose the defects in the theory of the sage Rabbi Moses ben Maimon on the
establishment of the existence of the one, non-material First Cause." The author
incidentally notes that he is not satisfied by the arguments which Ḥasdai Crescas

closes quite keenly the error Maimonides commits when he wishes to dispose of the profound contradictions between the outlook of those who take the position that the world was created in time and those who hold the Aristotelian view that the world is eternal and that matter has existed everlastingly. But let my readers not think, Joseph ben Isaac Halevi admonishes, that I intend through my criticism to diminish their desire to familiarize themselves with this work. On the contrary, I especially insist on its true greatness and immense value, and I am highly indignant at the fools who in their time had the presumption to declare the *Guide* a pernicious and dangerous book. I have criticized a few of Maimonides' assumptions not because they are more weakly grounded than the assumptions of our other scholars but precisely for the opposite reason. The defects of the other Jewish scholars can be easily perceived by anyone interested in philosophical problems, but to expose the failings of such a profound thinker as Maimonides is extremely difficult.[85]

Joseph ben Isaac divides into four categories those who believe that one ought to remove himself from Maimonides' *Guide*. To the first category belong those who consider it a heretical book that ought to be condemned to burning because its basic assumptions are taken from the Greek philosopher who maintains that the world is eternal. The second category consists of men who call themselves "sages of the Kabbalah" but are in fact very far from the Kabbalah, or tradition of the fathers; they oppose the *Guide* only by reason of their slight understanding. The third category are theologians and scholars who refuse to know of anything beside the Talmud and think that only those who pore day and night over the Gemara attain true perfection and merit the world-to-come. These men, Joseph ben Isaac adds, do not understand that for true perfection, general knowledge is also essential; if they understood wherein man's bliss and perfection consisted, it would be clear to them that Maimonides' *Guide* is indeed the best pointer of the way for one who strives for the supreme goal.[86] To the fourth category, according to the author, belong those who recognize the great value of the *Guide* but are so small in their own estimation that they think no common mortal can fathom the tremendous profundities of this book of speculation deal-

---

puts forth against Maimonides in regard to this question (*ibid.*, 26b).
85. *Ibid.*, 29b
86. *Ibid.*, 30b

ing with such exalted matters. These men, he adds, must understand that the author of this work was not an angel but a man, like each one of us, and what a man has produced other men can also understand, for all come from one human source.[87]

There is no doubt that this fourth category was extremely miniscule in size, and the third group swallowed it up entirely. Apparently the author of *Givat Ha-Moreh* himself understood this. He soon became convinced that he had no one listening to him, that his voice found no echo, and that he was like a solitary tree in the wilderness. He made another attempt and two years later published his work *Ketonet Passim*.[88] After this, however, he lapsed into total silence. In time this scholar was so thoroughly forgotten that even such an eminent savant in Hebrew literature as Abraham Geiger, when he encountered in Joseph Solomon Delmedigo mention of *Givat Ha-Moreh*, confessed that he had no idea who the author of this work was.[89]

One of Joseph ben Isaac's very few followers and admirers was Rabbi Yom-Tov Heller. He candidly admits[90] that the young scholar from Lithuania familiarized him with philosophical matters, and when the latter wished to publish his *Givat Ha-Moreh* Heller added his annotations to the work.

As the Maharal's faithful disciple, Heller was also a determined opponent of the method of *pilpul* which ruled in the *yeshivot*, and indeed it was under the influence of his famous master and teacher that he devoted all his attention to the "foundation stone of the whole Talmudic literature," the Mishnah. As Solomon Luria in his day set forth the Talmud as the basic source of the *halachah* or law, so Heller declares the Mishnah to be such a fundamental source. In order best to adapt such an ancient collection as the Mishnah to this role, Heller composed his famous commentary, *Tosafot Yom Tov* (first published, together with the text of the Mishnah, in Prague, 1614–1617). However, because after the close of the Mishnah the *halachah* grew greatly and it was no longer possible to ground in, and associate many customs and decisions with, the text of the Mishnah, Yom-Tov Heller composed, as an addition

---

87. *Ibid.*
88. The book is extremely rare, and no more than two or three copies of it have been preserved. We have not managed to examine it.
89. Geiger, *Melo Chofnajim*, 75.
90. In his *haskamah* to *Givat Ha-Moreh*.

to his first work, a double commentary, *Leḥem Ḥamudot* and *Maadanei Melech*, to the *Hilchot Ha-Rosh* of the famous codifier Asher ben Yeḥiel. Heller's commentaries are written in clear and elegant language. Everything in them is grounded logically and lucidly with exemplary simplicity. Despite the fact that Heller's clear style was so little suited to the taste of that time, he was quickly recognized as one of the foremost authorities in ritual questions. Not without reason, however, does he declare himself to be a friend and disciple of Joseph ben Isaac, the author of *Givat Ha-Moreh*. He has the courage to express at times quite "heretical" ideas. He speaks, for example, with enthusiasm of Azariah dei Rossi's *Meor Einayim*, of which his own teacher had declared that it should be condemned to burning. In his commentary to the Mishnah he does not agree in places with the explanations of the sages of the Talmud. In a note to one *mishnah* he declares publicly: "The sages of the Talmud here give another explanation, but since the law is not thereby changed, we have the right to teach the meaning as we understand it."

A special place among Yom-Tov Heller's works[91] is occupied by his *Megillat Eivah*, in which he described the catastrophe he lived through during the Thirty Years War. As chief rabbi from 1627 on of all the communities of the province of Bohemia, Heller was also president of the commission that was required annually to collect the considerable sum of forty thousand *gulden* imposed on the Jewish populace of Bohemia as an extraordinary war tax. The sum was sent annually to Vienna. In collecting the tax, however, certain controversies, as might be expected, arose. There were men who, out of personal motives, complained to the imperial treasury that the system by which the commission allocated the war tax among the various communities was unjust. The plaintiffs, however, were not satisfied with this. Some of them denounced the chief rabbi before the emperor to the effect that in one of his works (*Maadanei Melech*) he permitted himself to blaspheme the Christian faith. On the basis of this denunciation, Rabbi Yom-Tov Heller was summoned in 1629 to Vienna, and upon his arrival was imprisoned by imperial order in a cell with hardened criminals. Among other charges lodged against him, the rabbi of Prague was accused of the grievous sin of praising in his work the

91. A complete roster of Yom-Tov Heller's published works, as well as of those that have remained in manuscript, is given by Israel Halpern in *Kiryat Sefer*, VII, 140–148.

Talmud which had, after all, been burned as a harmful book at the command of the Pope. As a blasphemer of Christianity, he was threatened with the death penalty. In consequence of the intervention of the Jewish community of Vienna, the death penalty was exchanged for a fine of ten thousand *gulden,* and Heller was forbidden to occupy a rabbinic post in any community whatever in all the provinces of the Austrian crown. He then settled in Poland (in 1631), was for a brief time rabbi in Nemirov, and later (in 1634) was appointed chief rabbi of Vladimir, Volhynia. In the years spent in Volhynia Heller devoted himself greatly to communal matters and frequently appeared at the Council of the Four Lands as the representative of the communities of Volhynia. He carried on an especially stubborn battle against an ancient "plague" in Jewish communal life—the fact that officials would sell the rabbinic office for money, and in this way unfit persons not infrequently obtained coveted rabbinic positions. Despite all obstacles, he carried through in the Council of the Four Lands a renewal of the prohibition, "with decrees and excommunications," that no one should dare purchase a rabbinic post.[92]

In the last years of his life[93] Yom-Tov Heller was chief rabbi of Cracow. It is these final twenty-five years of his life, from the time of the denunciation in Prague until he settled in Cracow, that he describes in his *Megillat Eivah,* which he first wrote in Yiddish and later himself translated into Hebrew.[94] These memoirs, written in a calm, epic tone, are important not only as the most reliable source for the biography of the author; they also have both a literary and a historical value. Heller's autobiography is extremely rich in interesting details portraying Jewish life in the era of the Thirty Years War, as well as the relationships between the Jewish communities and those who represented them with the external power, with the higher and lower imperial officials.

92. *Megillat Eivah,* 36–38 (we quote according to the Vienna edition of 1862).
93. He died in 1654.
94. The Yiddish manuscript was in the hands of the well known preacher A. Jellinek (see *Le-Korot Ha-Gezerot,* I, 25).

CHAPTER FIVE

Lurianic Mysticism in Poland:
ISAIAH HOROWITZ

Disputations about the Talmud—The Maharal's apologetic work
Be'er Ha-Golah—Rationalist currents in Poland—Isaac Troki and his
Ḥizzuk Emunah—The growth of reaction at the beginning of the
seventeenth century—Jewish mystical currents of that period—The
mystic and pilpulist, Nathan Spira—Isaiah Horowitz and his literary
work—The doctrine of asceticism and the "hallowed" life—*Shenei
Luḥot Ha-Berit* and its significance

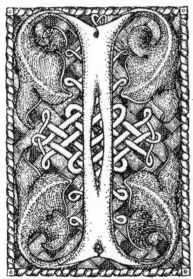 N HIS *Megillat Eivah* Yom-Tov
Heller relates how, in defend-
ing himself in court against the
charge of having blasphemed
Christianity, he had occasion to
carry on a full discussion about
the Talmud and its alleged
"harmfulness." We have noted[1]
that the Italian humanists, who
so eagerly studied Hebrew and
the literature of the Kabbalah
with the aid of Jewish scholars,
nevertheless deemed it necessary to publish works attacking
Judaism. The literary battle
against Judaism was carried on,
however, much more inten-
sively in Germany. The Reformation, to be sure, aroused particular interest in the Hebrew language, but the initiator of the
movement, Martin Luther, issued forth in extremely hostile
fashion against the "mendacious" Jews with their "stony,
diabolically iron hearts." He wished thereby to show how unjustified the Catholics who charged that he was favorably disposed toward the Jews were.

Along with great interest and reverence for the Bible, en-
mity toward those who preserved the original of the Book with

1. See Vol. IV of our *History*, p. 55.

such self-sacrifice was manifested most clearly in Germany. With the success of the Reformation movement, polemics against the Jews were greatly strengthened. It was said that they falsely interpret the text of the "Old Testament" because they are blinded by the "mendacious" Talmud which, as is known, is full of barbaric superstitions and bitter hatred for Christianity. The oppressed and beaten Jews of Germany did not dare enter into disputations with their opponents, as the Italian Jews had fearlessly done in their day. When the well-known *shtadlan* Joselman of Rosheim requested permission of the city council of Strasbourg to reply to Luther's attacks, his request was denied. With fear and trembling, in an extremely cautious and low-keyed tone, Jews undertook to reply to the charges issued against the "mendacious" Talmud. In this "defense" literature the Maharal's *Be'er Ha-Golah* must be given special mention.

The Maharal indicates in his apologetic work that all the charges with which the opponents of the Talmud attack it focus chiefly on the following seven points: (1) In the Mishnah and Gemara there are laws and ordinances without foundation in the Torah, or Law of Moses, in which it is explicitly warned, "You shall not add, and you shall not diminish." (2) In the Talmud numerous laws of the Torah are interpreted in extremely false fashion. (3) The Talmud does not take account of the clear meaning of the Biblical text and interprets it as it pleases. (4) Many Talmudic stories and legends are full of blasphemy. (5) The Talmud contains many foolish and tasteless old wives' tales. (6) The sages of the Talmud were ignorant in the natural sciences. (7) The sages of the Talmud treated non-Jews illegally and cruelly. The Maharal attempts merely to acquit the Talmud of these charges. He could only carry on a weak campaign of defense and did not dare himself become the aggressor and step forward proudly in the role of accuser. In this respect the situation in Poland at that time was more favorable.

The religious tumult which the Reformation provoked in the second half of the sixteenth century produced in Poland a whole series of rationalist sects with distinctly anti-Catholic views. Some of these, for example, the Socinians and Anti-Trinitarians, who denied the dogma of the Trinity and rejected the divine nature of Christ, were in definite affinity with the theology of Judaism. The Catholic priests exploited this and declared these sects "Judaizing" or "half-Jewish." To purge themselves of such a "grievous" charge, the theoreticians and leaders of the sects discovered that the best method was to declare war against the "false" Jewish faith, to attack it with tracts and lampoons, and to summon Jewish theologians and rabbis to religious disputations. In this respect the Socinian Nicolaus Paruta, the chief leader of the Anti-Trinitarians Simon Budny, who translated the Hebrew Bible and the Gospels into Polish (Nieswicz, 1572), and the theologian of Lublin Martin Chekhovich obtained special renown. The Jewish side was not silent, either. Against Chekhovich's *Razmowia Christianski*, thirteen dialogues in which he assails the dogmas of Judaism and carries on a disputation with the Jews about their inimical attitude towards Christ and his teaching, Naḥman Jacob of Belshytz issued forth with his polemical work *Odpiss na dialogi Czechowicza* (1581). This work is now extremely rare.[2] We have not had the opportunity to read it and do not even definitely know whether its author was a Jew or possibly a Karaite.[3] In any case, this "reply" made a very slight impression. Chekhovich even came forth in the same year with a counter-document, but the work of Jacob of Belshytz was quickly forgotten. Soon after Jacob, however, a considerably stronger opponent appeared whose battle against the Christian theologians undoubtedly occupies one of the most brilliant pages in the polemic literature of the sixteenth century. This was Isaac ben Abraham of Troki, author of the famous *Ḥizzuk Emunah*.

We noted earlier[4] that the distinguished scholar Joseph Solomon Delmedigo, during the years that he spent in Lithuania, made friends mainly among the local Karaites. He justified this with the contention that in Poland men of secular culture were to be encountered only among the Karaites, while the Jews wished to know nothing besides the Talmud. That the cultured author of *Elim* was not unjustified is confirmed by the fact that it was precisely among the Karaites that a polemicist with such wide-ranging knowledge as the author of *Ḥizzuk Emunah* was found at that time. Isaac ben Abraham was born in Troki in 1533. Well trained in Latin and Polish, he studied Christian theological literature thoroughly and, when still quite young, had occasion to carry on religious disputations

2. Several fragments of Belshytz's polemic work are given by Abraham Geiger in his *Gesammelte Schriften*, III, 191, 213, and by Dubnow, *Istoria Yevreyev*, III, 137 [*Die Weltgeschichte des jüdischen Volkes*, VI, 366.]
3. The historian Meir Balaban even doubts that the polemicist Jacob Belshytz ever existed.
4. Vol. IV, p. 157.

with Catholic and Protestant theologians.[5] Later he had frequent opportunity to issue forth against the followers of the Socinians, the Anti-Trinitarians, and other sects.

"When I was young," he relates in the introduction to his work, "I was frequently in the courts of the nobles and royal counsellors. I became familiar with their works, listened to their words, and became convinced that they were extremely ignorant and that all their arguments and the questions they put forth in their disputations only demonstrate how little they understand the text of the Bible."

The religious debates, relates the author, were conducted in a very peaceful fashion and did not at all hinder consequent friendly relationships between the opponents. This indicates how tactfully and tolerantly the Polish clergy and the secular officials behaved at that time in their disputations with the Karaite scholar, who was an extremely serious and keen opponent. In connection with this one must take into consideration that Isaac Troki's position was especially favorable by reason of the very fact that he was a Karaite. In polemics with him one could not employ the stock arguments about the "mendacious inventions" of the Talmud and its "impudent attacks" on Christianity. Isaac Troki was very remote from *pilpul* and casuist acrobatics. He sought interpretations that were in accord with common sense and was especially interested in thoroughly exploring the Biblical text. It must be admitted that among the rabbis of that era it is difficult to find anyone who knew the language of the Bible so well and was as excellent a stylist as the author of *Ḥizzuk Emunah*. Isaac's style was as pure and lucid as his thought. To be sure, his outlook was extremely limited. He was firmly convinced, for example, that the entire Book of Psalms was composed by King David.[6] He apparently had no idea that there is such a place as America, despite the fact that he lived about a hundred years after Columbus. All this, however, could not prevent him from carrying on his disputations with the theologians and sectarians with great success. A man with a clear and coldly sober mind to which mystical emotions and the feeling of enthusiasm were completely alien, Isaac approached the text of the Gospels with a sharp, analytic scalpel and laid bare with ruthless logic all its

5. Preface to *Ḥizzuk Emunah:* "I debated with cardinals (*hegmonim*) and the chief officials of the lands."
6. *Ḥizzuk Emunah,* Part i, Ch. 40 (we quote according to the edition of 1865).

contradictions and inconsistencies.[7] With his great learning, it
was not at all difficult for him to show that the Christian dogma
of the immaculate conception and the doctrine of the inno-
cently crucified God who was resurrected were extremely
widespread among the peoples of the ancient Orient and that
the Christians adopted them from these.[8] He stresses the fact
that there are numerous passages in the Gospels which show
most clearly that neither Jesus himself nor those close to him
regarded him as God's son, but the authors of the Gospels only
attempt—and this quite awkwardly, with one contradicting
the other—to demonstrate that he was descended from the
royal house of David.[9] When Isaac criticizes the dogma of the
Trinity, he also makes use of the arguments of the Anti-
Trinitarians and quotes quite frequently the works of the
previously mentioned Chekhovich, Budny, and Nicolaus
Paruta.[10]

Calmly and quietly Isaac Troki reveals how illogical and
historically false are all the interpretations the Christian
theologians make of certain verses in the books of the Hebrew
prophets in order to ground Christian dogmas. With caustic
sarcasm he speaks of the complaints on the part of the Christian theologians that the Jews mistranslate the text of the Bible.
In any case, Isaac declares, it is not they, the Christian theologians, who should speak of this. Step by step, with numerous
quotations, he shows how frivolously and ignorantly the authors of the Gospels dealt with the Biblical text, how clumsily
they would tear chopped-up phrases out of context, reverse
their true meaning, and thus obtain support for their theses.[11]
All this, however, was still too little, Isaac Troki adds. These
"ignorant and untruthful men" not only distorted and incor-
rectly explained the text; they deliberately falsified it, and out
of petty, partisan motives, fabricated quotations that are nowhere to be found in the Bible. Very frequently they place
falsified quotations in the mouth of Jesus himself. Among
them, for example, it appears that Jesus says to his disciples:
"You have heard it said, 'You shall love your neighbor and hate
your enemy.' "[12] They indicate that this verse is to be found in

7. *Ibid.*, pp. 44, 226.
8. *Ibid.*, p. 29.
9. *Ibid.*, pp. 285, 288, 313.
10. *Ibid.*, pp. 86, 91, 96, 173, 321ff.
11. *Ibid.*, pp. 187, 194, 221ff.
12. Matthew 5:43.

the Book of Leviticus (Chapter 19, verses 17–18). But this is something that never was. Leviticus merely says, "You shall not hate your brother in your heart . . . You shall not take vengenance or bear a grudge against the children of your people." They make Jesus forget that in the Torah it is written, "And you shall love your neighbor as yourself." According to the evangelist,[13] Jesus declares, "I give unto you a new law: You shall love one another." It is true, Isaac sarcastically adds, the Gospel does in fact set forth a new law: "Do good to those that hate you, bless those who curse you, and if a man strike you on one cheek, turn the other to him also."[14] But do Christians observe this commandment? And the apostles themselves —did they fulfill it? When the high priest Ananias ordered the apostle Paul beaten, did Paul not cry out in great wrath, "God will smite you!"? And did not Jesus himself declare: "Think not that I have come to bring peace on earth; I came not to bring peace but a sword."[15] Jesus cried out, "Father, forgive them, for they know not what they do."[16] Why, then, do you persecute us Jews with such rabid hatred? Why do you avenge yourselves so cruelly upon us? Jesus explicitly stated that he did not come to destroy the law, and that as long as heaven and earth endure not a single jot or tittle of the law would pass away. But you have abrogated the laws of the Torah of Moses. Not only Jesus and his apostles, but even their followers, observed for generations one of the major commandments of the Torah—Sabbath rest. Why, then, do you not observe the commandments of the Sabbath? You violate not only the law of Moses but the Gospel as well, and you do not fulfill the commandments Jesus laid upon you. Jesus said, "Sell all you have and give it to the poor." It is in no way noticeable that you Christians observe this commandment.[17] And Isaac Troki proceeds to point out with numerous examples how greatly the Christian church has removed itself from the teaching of the Gospels.

It must be admitted, however, that Isaac Troki's very matter-of-fact and logically grounded critique is, at times, too partial. With genuine brilliance and with the sharpened vision of the careful opponent, he does, indeed, manage to expose all the

13. John 13:34.
14. Luke 6:27–29.
15. Matthew 10:24.
16. Luke 23:34.
17. *Hizzuk Emunah*, p. 281: "I have never seen any Christian doing so."

weak points and logical inconsistencies in the text of the Gospels. A man of sober common sense, however, not infrequently becomes short-sighted and unjust when he tries to employ, in questions of ethics and inward experiences, the criteria of arid rationalism and strict consistency. The wondrously beautiful story in the Gospel of the woman taken in adultery and the Pharisees, whom Jesus addresses with his marvelous, simple, but shattering words, "He that is without sin among you, let him be the first to cast a stone at her," arouses in our Karaite scholar pious wrath: How, then?—This is not according to the law; it is explicitly stated, "And you shall remove the evil from your midst." These defects, however, did not weaken the massive power of Isaac Troki's sharp criticism. Its weak aspects were perhaps felt, but in the state of scientific investigation of that time men could not disclose these and fight against them.

Only in his old age did Isaac Troki decide to write down all the conclusions of the religious disputations he used to carry on and to systematize then in one collection, so that this might further serve as a weapon, a *ḥizzuk emunah* (strengthening of faith). This work, to which he therefore gave the title *Ḥizzuk Emunah*, was completed not long before his death. Only the register of quotations and the index which the author intended to add at the end remained unfinished, and these were compiled by his pupil, Joseph ben Mordecai Malinovski,[18] who also wrote an introduction to the work. Jews could not even think of publishing such a sharply anti-Christian polemical work at that time; hence, it was quickly circulated in numerous handwritten copies, not only among Karaites but also in rabbinic circles, where people had no idea that the work came from a Karaite author.[19] The tone in which *Ḥizzuk Emunah* was written contributed not a little to this. Isaac Troki everywhere speaks in the name of all Israel, of "the Israelite nation." "We Jews" he writes, "are persecuted and oppressed." Elsewhere he says, "With the Jewish people the happiness of the whole world is bound up," etc.

In no place is any hostility whatever to the Talmud and the Rabbanites discernible. To be sure, one point in *Ḥizzuk Emunah* necessarily made a very odd impression on the Jewish reader of that time. The author nowhere refers to the sages of

18. Malinovski acquired a reputation among the Karaites as a liturgical poet and compiler of religious anthologies (*Minhagim* and *Kitzur Inyan Ha-Shebitah*).

19. The well known rabbi of the seventeenth century Yair Bacharach mentions Isaac ben Abraham Troki among the most important rabbinic authorities.

the Talmud and introduces no quotations from Talmudic literature. This seemed so strange and unnatural that some persons immediately undertook to "improve" *Ḥizzuk Emunah* in this respect. In copying the work various additions were made. Statements of the Talmudic sages were added to the author's arguments in order to strengthen their force.[20] One such handwritten copy, in which, incidentally, the date 1615,[21] when Isaac Troki had long been dead, is given, came eventually into the hands of the well-known German Hebraist Johann Christoph Wagenseil, who published the work (1681), together with a Latin translation, in his comprehensive collection *Tela Ignea Satanae*. Wagenseil did this in order, as he himself indicates, "that Christians might have the opportunity of refuting this work which may have the effect of increasing the delusion of the Jews even more." But the pious German professor was greatly mistaken. By publishing Isaac Troki's work he did not weaken the "delusion" of the Jews but gave an effective weapon into the hands of the "heretics" and "enemies of Christianity." The printed *Ḥizzuk Emunah* created an enormous sensation and numerous heretical rationalists, such as Voltaire and the French Encyclopedists, made use of Wagenseil's Latin translation[22] in their obdurate battle against the dogmatic teaching of the Church. "The most determined opponents of the (Christian) Church," declares Voltaire, "did not cite any arguments that are not to be found in the *Ḥizzuk Emunah* of Rabbin Isaac."[23]

When Isaac Troki speaks of the cruel persecutions which the Jews had to suffer in various Christian countries, he gratefully mentions his own native country, "whose rulers and princes behave with justice and mercy and do not oppress the Jews living in their land."[24] At the end of the sixteenth century, however, the situation of the Jews in Poland deteriorated sig-

20. See *Ḥizzuk Emunah*, 43, 53, 162, 250, 257.
21. *Ibid.*, 250, 257. In the library in Leningrad of the Society for the Promotion of Enlightenment Among Jews there was a manuscript of *Ḥizzuk Emunah* in which, in the passages in question [Chapters 42 and 43], the correct date 1593 is given.
22. *Ḥizzuk Emunah*, together with the Latin translation, was reprinted in 1705. In 1717 a German translation appeared. In 1851 one in English, and in 1865 a new German translation by D. Deutsch, together with a corrected Hebrew text, were published. There are also Yiddish and Spanish translations.
23. *Mélanges*, Vol. 3, p. 344: "Il a rassemblé toutes le difficultés que les incrédules ont prodiguées depuis . . . Enfin les incrédules de plus determinés n'ont presque rien allegués qui ne sont dans ce 'Rempart de la foi' du rabbin Isaac" (quoted according to A. Geiger, *op. cit.*, 211).
24. *Ḥizzuk Emunah*, 273.

nificantly. The reform tendencies in Polish society were violently suffocated by the Catholic reaction. The Jesuits became increasingly dominant, and they made it their purpose to persecute in the cruelest fashion not only the evangelical Christians and Socinians but also the "blasphemers of Christ," the Jews, and to make of them pariahs without any rights. Under the influence of the general reaction and the deterioration of the social situation, the strict, orthodox tendencies in the Jewish milieu, as we have already noted, were also strengthened. Mystical currents, too, became ever more prominent. In this connection, however, one must bear in mind the great difference between mysticism as a world-outlook and the wisdom of the Kabbalah as a doctrine based on tradition and recognized for generations. The Kabbalist teaching, which was hallowed through the tradition of the fathers and revered because of the firm belief that its genealogy goes back directly to Moses himself, was regarded at that time as the greatest authority. Everyone acknowledged it, even those sober, "common sense" natures to whom the soul's mystical drive, the sweet palpitation of ecstasy and spiritual effusion, were completely alien. All the Polish rabbis of the sixteenth century had an attitude of supreme reverence for the wisdom of the Kabbalah. This was true both of Rabbi Moses Isserles who was interested in philosophical problems and of Rabbi Solomon Luria who regarded Aristotle "the Greek" with such animosity. Rabbi Mordecai Jaffe, the author of the *Levushim*, studied the "esoteric wisdom" with the Italian mystic Mattityahu Delacrut[25] and wrote a commentary on Menahem Recanati; and the well-known codifer Rabbi Joel Sirkes declared that whoever does not believe in the wisdom of the Kabbalah is a "denier" and deserves excommunication.[26] All these, however, were merely codifers, great scholars and brilliant masters in the realm of Talmud, not mystics. But at the threshold of the seventeenth century new currents began to appear. To this, as we have already observed, external circumstances contributed not a little.

Under the boundless dominion of the Jesuits, Jews came increasingly to be tried on the blood libel. Hostility toward them assumed ever more clearly the form of a mass movement. In Vilna the burghers carried on an actual pogrom against the Jews because they regarded them as their most threatening

---

25. The well known editor and commentator of Joseph Gikatilla's mystical works.
26. Sirkes, *Responsa*, No. 4.

competitors. In Posen also the Christian mob often attacked
the Jewish neighborhoods. The frequent ritual murder trials,
with their barbaric cruelty, were reminiscent of the Spanish
Inquisition. In Polish literature, too, anti-Jewish propaganda
became ever stronger. The clerical writers—Moyetzki, Slesh-
kowski, Michinski, and others—circulated among the people
venomous tracts and lampoons, full of falsehoods and libels
against the Jews and Judaism.[27]

Just at that time the Lurianic practical Kabbalah, which was
so thoroughly permeated with messianic yearning and hope,
penetrated into Poland through Italy. To souls terrified by
troubles and persecutions, the lovely dream of speedy redemption, when the whole world would become entirely worthy
and purified, when the sparks of good would be liberated from
the "shells" of evil and the long-awaited redeemer appear, revealed itself in all its splendor. This messianic Kabbalah soon
found many ardent followers among the Polish Jews. One of
the first important representatives of this tendency was the
Cracow *rosh yeshivah*, Nathan Nata ben Solomon Spira.

Born in 1585 into a prominent rabbinic family,[28] Nathan
Spira was renowned as a prodigy when he was still quite
young. "My father," his son Solomon declares with great feeling, "was endowed with marvelous capacities and had a memory the like of which is not to be found."[29] Of the great reputation he attained as a scholar in the Talmud and rabbinic
literature, testimony is provided by the fact that at the age of
thirty-two he was invited to Cracow as principal of the Talmudic academy in the place of the deceased Moses Margolioth.
But Nathan Spira was far more interested in the "esoteric
wisdom," the "holy" *Zohar* and Isaac Luria's Kabbalah, than in
the wisdom of the Talmud. His son Solomon relates in his
above-mentioned introduction how Spira used to rise at midnight and, with heart-rending weeping, lament the destruction
of the holy city and the fact that Israel and the *Shechinah*
wander in exile. With bitter tears he would pray that redemption might come speedily and the fallen tent of David be raised
up. Once, at midnight, the prophet Elijah appeared to him and
proclaimed that the ministering angels sing paeans before God

27. See Dubnow, *op. cit.*, III, 115–117.
28. His grandfather Rabbi Nathan Nata Ashkenazi was rabbi of Grodno and acquired
    a reputation with his compositions *Melo Shearim* and *Imrei Shefer*.
29. Preface to *Megalleh Amukkot Va-Ethanan* (we quote according to the first edition of
    1637).

with the melodies which he, Nathan, employs when he mourns the destruction of the Temple and the exile of the *Shechinah.*[30]

Nathan Spira acquired fame chiefly as a Kabbalist. On every Sabbath and festival he would preach profound sermons on the mysteries concealed in the letters of the Torah,[31] and the most important of his works are his two Kabbalist books bearing the joint title *Megalleh Amukkot.* But Spira was a very unique Kabbalist, a Kabbalist who was also a pilpulist. As a mystic, he undoubtedly experienced sweet and painful moments of mystical ardor, of transcendence of corporeality. From childhood on, however, he lived in the atmosphere of overly subtle casuistry, breathed the air of arid debate and cold, calculated reflection. It is therefore no surprise that he was so enchanted by the Talmudic *midrash* which relates that Moses, upon receiving the Torah, "studied it and forgot it;" as much as he learned of it, he at once forgot "until God endowed him with the great gift of *pilpul,*" for "through *pilpul* Moses glorified the Torah."[32]

Indeed, the scholar of Cracow saturated the entire Lurianic Kabbalah with the spirit of intellectualist *pilpul.* The imagination of this mystic lacked both zest and scope; the cold breath of excessively subtle and arid scholasticism hovered over it like a leaden pall. "Nathan Spira," says the historian Dubnow, "applied to the Kabbalah the method of Talmudic *pilpul* and thereby produced a dialectical mysticism which had as remote a relationship to theosophy as the subtleties of the masters of *pilpul* in the Talmudic academies had to purely scientific thought."[33] Anyone who takes Spira's *Megalleh Amukkot Va-Ethanan* in hand must agree with this harsh verdict. No matter where the reader opens this composition, he at once feels surrounded by a thick forest of mystical word-confusion, of obscure symbolic notions lacking substance. The *parashah* or pericope *Va-Ethanan*, the prayer of Moses in which he beseeches God to allow him to see with his own eyes the land for which he had yearned so long, the land of his people "which is beyond the Jordan," is interpreted by the Kabbalist Spira in 252 ways,

30. See also Ephraim Margolioth's introduction to *Megallah Amukkot Al Ha-Torah* (we quote according to the Lublin edition of 1901).
31. His son Solomon writes in the introduction in question: "God gave him the tongue of the learned to preach on Sabbath and festivals words of truth and righteousness, choice fruit and spices, sweet and sharp explanations with deep mysteries of accents, letters, and vowels, words that no ear had ever heard preached before."
32. *Megallah Amukkot Al Ha-Torah*, "Parashah Lech Lecha," 16 (according to the Lublin edition of 1901).
33. Dubnow, *op. cit.*, 136.

and it is in this that the whole work consists. Moreover, the work remained fragmentary; Spira had intended to interpret *Va-Ethanan* in fully a thousand ways, but death intervened in his forty-eighth year[34] and he did not manage to complete his labors. A no less painful impression is made by Spira's other comprehensive work, his mystical commentary to the Pentateuch entitled *Megalleh Amukkot Al Ha-Torah*. In it we encounter all the elements of Luria's Kabbalah—the doctrine of the "perfected world," of *ibbur* or "impregnation of souls," of original sin, of the *tzinorot* or channels, etc. But Spira "reveals" very little; there is not one new idea or a single vivid, colorful picture in his work. He merely "demonstrates" the correctness of Luria's ideas with his "iron" proofs, which consist of a frightful confusion, of a web of words interwoven with all kinds of *gematriot* and numbers—numbers without end. The mystery of *gematria* is transformed by this Kabbalist into an ingenious play of *pilpul*, and his work swarms so abundantly with the most difficult and mind-boggling calculations that one begins at times to imagine that he has before him not a text of Kabbalah but an account book.

Another mystic of that generation, however, managed to rend this dusty web of *pilpul*. This was Isaiah Horowitz, the son of the previously mentioned Abraham Horowitz. Born at the beginning of the 1570's, Isaiah, like his father, was educated in Cracow. There he studied Torah with Rabbi Solomon ben Leibush and with the famous *rosh yeshivah*, Rabbi Meir, the Maharam of Lublin. When he was still quite young, Isaiah Horowitz had acquired such a reputation in the rabbinic world that he already played a prominent role in the communal life of Polish Jewry. His name is included among the thirty rabbinic signatories to the decision adopted in 1590 to the effect that no one should dare purchase a rabbinic post. In the same year his father, Abraham Horowitz, proposed to him that he look over the manuscript of his book of ethical instruction, *Emek Berachah*, and also permitted him to add his own comments and supplements. In these supplements of the still very young Isaiah, the mystic who everywhere perceives profound divine secrets is already discernible. To many of the commandments and precepts Isaiah Horowitz adds his comment: "He who has entered into the garden knows that here one of the deep mysteries of the Torah is concealed."

The young Isaiah Horowitz held the position of rabbi and

34. Spira died in 1683.

rosh yeshivah in various cities in Volhynia. Later, in 1606, he was invited to become rabbi of the ancient community of Frankfurt-am-Main, but after the expulsion of 1614 returned to his native city, Prague. As head of the Talmudic academy he had a great reputation. His school attracted pupils from various provinces, and many of them were supplied by him with all their needs. "At his table," his son Sheftel relates, "no fewer than eighty persons ever sat down, and the finest dishes were served, both on weekdays and on the Sabbath and festivals."[35] All this, however, provided little satisfaction to the mystically-minded Isaiah Horowitz. His fondest dream was to settle in "the land of life," in the center of the world, Jerusalem, and to "kiss the dust" of the holy city of Safed where "three divine men"—the "angel of the Lord of hosts" Joseph Karo, Rabbi Moses Cordovero, and Rabbi Isaac Luria—once lived. In 1621 Isaiah Horowitz left Prague and set out for Jerusalem, where he was received with great honor.[36] Thanks to the cooperation of Rabbi Ḥayyim Vital's son Samuel, Isaiah Horowitz managed to become familiar with the manuscripts which revealed to him all the mysteries of Luria's Kabbalah. Gaining familiarity with this mystical world, Horowitz completed in 1623 the monumental work which he had begun in Prague, *Shenei Luḥot Ha-Berit*, better known under the acronym *Shelah*, and wrote his commentary to the prayerbook, *Shaar Ha-Shamayim*. Horowitz's years of peace and quiet in Jerusalem did not, however, last long. In 1625, at the command of the local Turkish pasha, he and fifteen other rabbis were arrested and, without being charged with any offense, imprisoned. The intention was to obtain from the Jewish community a large sum of money as ransom. Horowitz, however, managed to escape from prison and settled in Safed. He died in 1629 and was buried in Tiberias.

His major work, *Shenei Luḥot Ha-Berit*, was first published by his son Sheftel in Amsterdam in the 1640's. The structure of

35. See the preface to *Vavei Ha-Ammudim*.
36. Horowitz's description of contemporary life in Jerusalem is interesting: "Jerusalem, despite the fact that the destruction in it is great, is even now the joy of the world. There is peace and tranquility in it. The finest foods and best wines are to be found in it, also geese and hens, as in Prague, not to speak of all kinds of fruits and grapes. The number of the Sephardim increases daily. They now amount to more than five hundred families and they build large houses there. This is undoubtedly a sign of approaching redemption. May it be speedily, in our days, Amen. Soon, with God's help, you will hear that the Ashkenazic community there is also increased and strengthened, for I know that many are traveling here."

this work is exceedingly confusing. *Shenei Luḥot Ha-Berit* (The Two Tablets of the Covenant)—these are "the two Torot," the Written Torah and the Oral Torah, but they are really one Torah. The material of each *luaḥ* or tablet is divided by our author into three parts: (1) *Ner Mitzvah*, which deals with the observance of the commandments and all the laws associated therewith; (2) *Torah Or*, the mysteries hidden in the commandments; and (3) *Tochaḥot Musar*, ethical instruction. This material from both *luḥot* or tablets is mixed together, interwoven in various "gates," "paragraphs," and "houses." Despite its lack of system, *Shenei Luḥot Ha-Berit* is one of the most remarkable works produced in that era. To be sure, along with fine moral maxims and profound philosophical-theological ideas, the work abounds with extremely naive, purely medieval superstitions. Yet in the many hundreds of folio pages a marvelous integrity is discernible. The tone is very earnest and yet extremely tender, and everything is permeated with mystical fervor and breathes enthusiasm.

In the introduction the author at once declares that he is an ardent devotee of the "true wisdom": "I intend merely to disclose a very small amount that I have received from writers and books following the paths of the *Zohar*, especially from the sacred works of Rabbi Meir Ibn Gabbai, Rabbi Moses Cordovero and the holy, godly Rabbi Isaac Luria, may his memory be for a blessing." To be sure, Isaiah Horowitz is not only a Kabbalist but also a rabbi and *rosh yeshivah* who was educated in the spirit of the Polish Talmudic schools and the commentaries on the *Shulḥan Aruch*. He himself proclaims, "We are of the strictest constructionists in interpreting the law." But he infused all these laws and severities with the spirit of mysticism and, following Isaac Luria, transformed every commandment into a mystery, perceived in every precept a multi-significant symbol, a holy secret that "no mortal can fathom, even if he were to live thousands of years."[37] It is, however, not only in the commandments and laws that a mysterious power inheres, but even in the letters; they also are symbols of cosmic phenomena. Not merely the Torah but the text of the Talmud, Horowitz asserts, consists of divine "names" alone. "Whoever has had the privilege of fathoming these secrets of the Kabbalah knows what marvelous things are concealed in the sayings of the Talmudic sages." Even in the legends, stories and parables of the Talmud Isaiah Horowitz sees "great and won-

37. *Shenei Luḥot Ha-Berit*, "Toledot Adam."

drous mysteries." All ethical matters, all obligations that a man
has to other men and to God, are based, according to Horowitz,
on two foundations—love and holiness. "A man must not bear
hatred in his heart toward any other man," the author of *Shenei
Luḥot Ha-Berit* teaches. "You must not accuse your neighbor in
thought or word or deed." "It is written in the Torah, 'And
thou shalt love thy neighbor as thyself': this means that whatever is dear and precious to you, you must also do to your
neighbor." "If anyone has sinned against you, forgive him at
once, for the whole community is like one body. Would you
punish one hand with the other if the former had caused pain
to any limb?"[38] The entire world rests on the principle of "And
thou shalt love thy neighbor," for, Horowitz teaches, through
his love for another a man comes to the love of God, because
both loves are merged in the divine unity.[39] And as far as
serving God is concerned, he constantly reiterates, this can be
done only with love. God must be loved not out of desire for
reward nor out of fear of punishment, but only out of "inner
love," out of "great longing and yearning, with deep, tender
love for God,"[40] so that a man "may unite himself and be
merged with Him in vast, thirsting, and eternal love."[41] In this,
Horowitz several times repeats, consists the goal and purpose
of man—that he raise himself to his divine prototype and become, as it were, like Him.

In full consonance with the world-view of the *Zohar*, Horowitz constantly stresses the supremely important role of man
in the cosmos.[42] The world, he declares, was created for the
sake of man. Man is of a higher degree than the angel, for the
angel was created entirely good. His good deeds are not sanctified through the effort of free will; he does only good because
he cannot do evil. Man's deeds, however, are a consequence of
the hard struggle which the good impulse carries on with the
evil impulse within him. Only through grievous suffering and
obdurate struggle does his will finally attain the high level.
Hence, he serves as a pattern for the angel; the angel yearns for
him. The angels do not know of achievement, of the process
of perfection. They are always at rest. Not without reason does
the prophet (Isaiah 6:2) say "the seraphim were standing."

38. *Shaar Ha-Otiot*, "Ot Bet."
39. *Ibid.*
40. *Asarah Maamarot*, "Ha-Maamar Ha-Shelishi."
41. *Shenei Luḥot Ha-Berit*, "Toledot Adam."
42. *Ibid.* "How fearful is man—his creation, his image, his form, his learning, and his
    end—for all is in the highest heights."

They do not struggle; they stand in one place. Quite different, however, is man. He is not a "stander" but a "traveler." He is in perpetual movement from stage to stage, from one level to another. Man, with his deeds, with his drive toward the good, also influences the "upper worlds," for he is, after all, stamped with the seal of the Holy One, blessed be He. This seal binds man to God, as it were, "as with a hanging chain whose last links dragging on the earth influence the links that are on high."

In full agreement with the philosophy of the Kabbalah, Horowitz also rejects the dualism of good and evil. He attacks Gersonides and "his faction" who took the position that only good derives from the divine nature and evil has an independent existence. Primordially, says Horowitz, everything was good, and the space of the world was filled with unobscured light. Evil existed only potentially; but through his "sin" in allowing himself to be led astray by the serpent, man transformed evil from a potentiality into an actual existent. Through this injury, through the obscuring of the divine light, spirit was transformed into matter, into *kelipah* (shell). As a result of the "sin" of Adam, good was mingled with evil. But this disrupted harmony may be restored by man. Through a pure, sanctified life man can again raise the gross *kelipot* to their radiant source and transform evil into its opposite, into the source of good.[43] Then the reign of "all good" and "all light" will once more begin. Man must think of this and remember it throughout his life. He must hallow life, hallow everything around himself; he must illuminate the earthly and crude with the divine light. "My children," Isaiah Horowitz teaches, "always, day and night, think of increasing holiness and of nearness to God." Man is to hallow every act, every limb. He must regard his ten fingers as a symbol of the ten *sefirot*, his heart as the embodiment of the "Holy of Holies," etc. His every step, all his acting and thinking, is to be hallowed with the idea of divinity, so that he may be privileged to attain the level of "God's tent" in which He rests.

Typical in this respect is the way the ascetic Horowitz regards sexual intercourse between man and wife. The codifiers deal with the matter of marriage only as a positive commandment: "Increase and multiply." But Horowitz here steps forth not as a codifier but as a mystic. In full consonance with the

---

43. *Ibid., Shaar Bet Yisrael,* "Bet David." "For then the evil brings about the great good, for it is not the case that the evil is annulled, but it is changed into good."

men of the Kabbalah, he perceives in the union between man and wife a profound ethical symbol: through sexual union man attains the supreme, divine harmony. The erotic drive, the primal source of being and becoming, is purified by Horowitz and enveloped in a garment of sanctity.

"There is no holiness among all the holinesses like the holiness of the union of man and wife," the author of *Shenei Luḥot Ha-Berit* emotively exclaims. Sexual union is a reflection of the great mystery—the union of the *sefirot* called *Yesod, Tiferet,* and *Malchut*. And Horowitz speaks at length of the secret of the "union of man and wife" and explains in mystical fashion the statements of the Talmudic sages that "he who has no wife is not a man" and "everyone who lives without a woman, lives without good, without joy, without blessing."[44] Even the matter of eating and drinking is considered a mystery by Horowitz. Man must regard himself, when eating, as "being in the place of the priest," the food he eats as "being in the place of the sacrifice," and the table as taking "the place of the altar." But at an even more exalted level than eating and drinking is fasting. Fasting, declares Horowitz, sanctifies man; in refraining from food he offers himself as a sacrifice.

Horowitz's monumental work is thoroughly saturated with the severe, ascetic spirit of Isaac Luria's Kabbalah. The supreme degree of perfection, according to *Shenei Luḥot Ha-Berit,* is attained through solitude. The only way that purifies and hallows man is repentance. The initial letters of the word *teshuvah* (repentance), the author further explains, represent the Hebrew words for fasting, sackcloth, ashes, weeping, and lamentation. A Jew may not laugh, Isaiah Horowitz teaches, as long as the people of Israel and, with it the *Shechinah,* is in exile. Like the Maharal, Horowitz dwells on the difficult question: Why are the sufferings of the chosen and unique people, whose name God Himself bears, so vast?—Through sufferings comes redemption. Sufferings purify one from the *kelipot* or "shells," from evil. In this Horowitz perceives the great mission of the Jewish people, the redemptive power of its grievous sufferings. In tender words he speaks of the martyr's way of the Jewish people, of "this little lamb among wolves which is exposed to the sword, hunger, slavery, and shame." And he comforts the people, promising that its suffering will effect the redemption and bring the "end" near. Soon, soon the Messiah, the redeemer, will come. He will liberate "his people from the yoke

44. *Shaar Ha-Otiot,* 101–103 (we quote according to the first Amsterdam edition).

of the nations," justice will rule the world, and "the Lord shall be One and His Name One!"

Horowitz did not create a new system. He was merely a follower and popularizer of the Lurianic mystical ideas which the "lion's cubs" disseminated. But the dreaming mystic of the banks of the Nile obtained in this Polish-German rabbi an enthusiastic disciple and agent who marvelously understood how to adapt his doctrine to the inner, spiritual world of Polish Jewry. Horowitz found the appropriate tone, the tender language in which to express so clearly the hopes, dreams, and beliefs in which the ghetto of that time, surrounded by a fiery circle of hostility and contempt, lived. It is therefore not surprising that when the great misfortune came and Polish-Ukrainian Jewry in the bloody years of Chmielnitzki drank the cup of suffering and affliction to the dregs, *Shenei Luḥot Ha-Berit* became the favorite book of the people. In it grieved and afflicted hearts sought and found consolation and salve for their painful wounds. With love and gratitude they merged the name of the author with the title of his book, and in the memory of later generations the "holy Shelah" remained one of the most precious friends and teachers.

CHAPTER SIX

The Massacres of 1648 and Their Echo in Literature

The massacres of 1648 and their echo in literature—The memoirs of Nathan Hannover, Samuel Feivish Feitel, Shabbetai Ha-Kohen, Abraham Ashkenazi, Meir of Sczebrszyn and Gabriel Schussburg—The laments and elegies of Shabbetai Ha-Kohen, Yom-Tov Heller, Sheftel Horowitz, Moses Narol and others—The intellectual decline of Polish Jewry.

REMENDOUS HOPES were placed on the year 1648. In the "holy" *Zohar* it was predicted that in year *Zot* the redemption would come and "every man would return to his patrimony."[1] All waited impatiently.[2] And now the long-anticipated year was here, and what arrived was not redemption but enormous destruction and terrible misfortune. Bogdan

---

1. See our *History*, Vol. V, p. 138.
2. Shabbetai Ha-Kohen laments in his *Megillat Eifah*: "In the year [5] 408, of which I thought that in it [the letters of the Hebrew word for "it," *zot*, also amount to 408] Aaron would come into the innermost place of the sanctuary, my lyre was turned into mourning and my joy into sorrow." And Sheftel Horowitz, the son of Isaiah Horowitz, emphasizes in his well known elegy:
    In the year that is numbered 5408
    I believed that I would go out free.

Chmielnitzki's bands of Cossacks scourged Jewish communities with fire and sword, and in that frightful year more Jewish victims fell than in the time of the Crusades and the Black Death. Around seven hundred Jewish communities were destroyed, and hundreds of thousands of persons perished under the knife of the murderers or succumbed as victims of the epidemics which then broke out.[3] Like the Crusades in their age, so the persecutions of 1648 called forth an entire literature consisting chiefly of memoirs and elegies. The literary value of these sad memorials of the bloody year of terror is quite varied. Among the memoirs of that time are to be found, for example, such works as the *Tit Ha-Yaven*[4] of Samuel Feivish Feitel who lists in a dry, protocol-like tone 262 communities which Chmielnitzki's henchmen destroyed and notes, in addition, the number of victims in each community. Such *hazkarot neshamot* (memorials of souls) have a certain historical significance but their literary value is slight. However, some historical chronicles of that time which carry the stamp of genuine literary creativity have also been preserved; there is no doubt that their authors possessed the keen eye of the careful observer and the pen of the gifted writer. Among these the most important place is occupied by Nathan Hannover's *Yeven Metzulah*.

Nathan's father, Moses Ashkenazi, lived in Ostrog, and it is very likely that Nathan was born there.[5] He studied Torah first with his father and later in the famous *yeshivah* of Ostrog. While still a youth, he became especially interested in the "esoteric wisdom", with which the well known Kabbalist, Samson Ostropoler, who later perished at the hands of Chmielnitzki's bands in Polonnoye, familiarized him. Hannover's strong inclination toward the Kabbalah is already to be observed in his sermon "Taamei Sukkah," preached in 1646 in

3. The historical sources do not agree on the number of the victims. Some of the elegies of the "persecutions of 1648" speak of "more than three hundred" Jewish communities destroyed (*Le-Korot Ha-Gezerot*, I, 9). Nathan Nata Hannover notes the number as seven hundred (*Yeven Metzulah*, 10). The author of *Tzaar Bat Rabbim* who relies on "important communal records" relates that no fewer than 744 communities suffered (*ibid.*, 14). Rabbi Mordecai of Kremsier estimates the number of those who perished as approximately 120,000 (*Le-Korot Ha-Gezerot*, III, 25). The author of *Tit Ha-Yaven*, however, estimates the number of victims as much higher —670,000.

4. First published in Venice (1655). Thereafter reprinted in Gurland's *Le-Korot Ha-Gezerot*, V, and again reprinted, with additions, in David Kahana's supplement to *Le-Korot Ha-Gezerot*, pp. 18–28.

5. For a discussion of Hannover's life and literary activities see Dr. I. Israelsohn's work in *Historishe Shriftn*, I, 1–26.

Cracow. In this sermon he explained all the statements of the Talmudic sages that have any relationship to the matter of the *sukkah* by way of mystery and allusion. Nathan lived through the persecutions of 1648 in Zaslav, the birth-place of his wife. His father perished at the time of the massacre, but he managed to escape with his family. He then spent some time in Germany, where he supported his family by giving sermons in various cities.[6] After protracted wanderings he managed to arrive in Italy. In 1652 he found himself in Venice and a year later obtained the post of rabbi at Livorno (Leghorn) where he became friendly with Hayyim Vital's pupil, the Kabbalist Hayyim Kohen, who gave him a close familiarity with the Kabbalah of Rabbi Isaac Luria. Nathan himself relates[7] how he became acquainted with the Kabbalist Nathan Spira, who had just come from Palestine, and both of them traveled to Venice, where they met the Kabbalists Samuel Aboab and Moses Zacuto, with whom Hannover became intimate friends.[8]

Surrounded by Kabbalist friends and immersed in the secrets of the hidden wisdom, Hannover spent several quiet years and devoted himself to literary work with great assiduity. Of the mystical works he wrote, only his *Shaarei Tziyyon*, a collection of prayers for fast days, festivals, etc. with a Kabbalist content, has enduring cultural-historical value.[9] An ardent follower of Isaac Luria, Hannover included in his collection numerous prayers of the "lion's cubs"—Hayyim Vital, Hayyim Kohen, and other Kabbalists of Safed.[10] "The compositions of Nathan Hannover," writes Dr. Israelsohn, "became very popular and beloved among the people. Some of his prayers passed over into the contemporary prayer books and are still used to the present day. So, for example, thanks to him, *tikkun hatzot* (midnight prayers for the end of the exile and the restoration of Israel)—a custom which had theretofore been practiced only in several Italian communities—became widespread. From there it also passed into our prayer books. The prayer "Ribbono Shel Olam," recited after removing the

6. He collected most of these sermons in his still unpublished work *Neta Sha'ashuim.*
7. In the preface to his collection of prayers *Shaarei Tziyyon* (Prague, 1662; afterwards reprinted a number of times). The preface is to be found only in the first edition.
8. In the preface to *Shaarei Tziyyon* Hannover writes: "A man like me, my intimate companion, my friend and my comrade, the chief rabbi and faithful Kabbalist, Rabbi Moses Zacuto."
9. *Shaarei Tziyyon,* the author relates in the preface, is the fifth part of a large mystical work that he projected in five parts, corresponding to the "five *partzofim.*"
10. See our *History,* Vol. V, pp. 66ff.

scrolls of the Torah from the ark, and "Yehi Ratzon," said after the Priestly Blessing, are also taken from this collection and have been incorporated into the prayer book."[11]

As a result of this collection of prayers, Hannover became known and beloved among the masses of the people. He acquired fame, however, not only in his own day but in later generations with his classic historical work, *Yeven Metzulah* (published in Venice in 1653), in which he describes the terrible events of the bloody years 1648–1652.[12] This rabbi and Kabbalist possessed something that was extremely rare at that time—a broad historical world-outlook which gave him the capacity to evaluate quite objectively the events he describes in his chronicle. Before proceeding to the bloody deeds of the Cossack bands, he provides an extremely melancholy portrait of the grievous economic and religious-national situation in which the serf population of Little Russia lived under the despotic rule of the Polish magnates and nobles. He also stresses the sorry role played in the exploitation of the Little Russian peasants by the Jewish lessees of estates. Typical is the close of his introduction: "The poor masses of Little Russians were so degraded that almost all nations—even that which is trodden by all peoples—ruled over them."[13]

In clear and sharp features he describes the bloody massacres which destroyed the oldest Jewish communities in Ostrog, Nemirov, and Tulchyn. Quietly and calmly, without high-flown rhetorical flourishes or pathetic cries of woe, Hannover tells of the horrible events that took place in the Ukraine. He relates for future generations how

the skin was flayed from men who were still alive and their flesh thrown to dogs; the hands and feet of others were hacked off, and over their still quivering bodies wagons were driven and the horses trampled them with their feet. Grievous wounds were inflicted on men, but they were deliberately not pierced through on the spot; they were cast into the streets so that they might struggle with death in horrible agony for a time. Many were buried alive. Little children were killed at their mothers' breasts; they were chopped and cut up like fish ... or they were run through with spears, roasted over the fire, and then offered freshly roasted to their mothers. Pregnant women had their bellies torn open, their still unborn children were thrown into

11. *op. cit.*, p. 18.
12. Of Hannover's important philological work *Safah Berurah* (a dictionary in four languages) we shall speak in a later part.
13. *Yeven Metzulah*, 6 (we quote according to the Cracow edition of 1895).

their faces, and into the ripped-open bellies live cats were sewn, and the hands of the women were cut off so that the miserable victims would not be able to remove the scratching cats . . . In other places bridges were made of Jewish children, and then they rode over them with loaded wagons or threw them into wells and covered them with earth . . . There is no terrible death that our brethren did not suffer there . . .[14]

Filled with dramatic power is Hannover's description of the destruction of the community of Tulchyn. The local Polish *szlachta* or nobility decided to hand over their courageous Jewish fellow-battlers to the enemy in order thereby to save themselves. The Jews, who learned of the plot betimes, made plans to fall on the Poles, who were less numerous then they. "Then," relates Hannover,

the head of the *yeshivah* Rabbi Aaron arose and called out, "Listen, my brethren! We are in exile among foreign peoples. If you attack the *szlachta*, other countries will soon become aware of it, and they will —God forbid—avenge themselves upon our brethren there. If this is a decree from heaven, we must accept it in love and trust God's mercy. How are we better then our brethren in Nemirov?"

Our chronicler relates further how the Cossacks took away from the Jews of Tulchyn their goods and possessions and then locked up the entire Jewish populace in a garden. There were three rabbis there, who warned the people to be prepared to die as martyrs and that none of them should dare deny the religion of his fathers. All then cried out, "Hear, O Israel, the Lord our God, the Lord is One! As He is the One and only One in your hearts, so is He also in our hearts!" For three days the Jews were locked up. Then a herald came to them from the Cossacks with a banner in his hand, fixed its staff in the ground, and called aloud, "Whoever is willing to accept the Christian faith will remain alive!" No one answered. Three times the herald called out, and all were silent. Then the Cossacks entered and, with barbaric cruelty, killed everyone, including the three rabbis.[15]

To make the destruction that fell upon the Jews of the Ukraine still clearer for the reader, Hannover presents in the last pages of his work a vivid picture of Jewish spiritual and cultural life in Poland on the eve of the catastrophe. His por-

14. *Ibid.*, 15–16.
15. *Ibid.*, 24–25.

trayal of the contemporary *yeshivot* with their methods of study, the various charitable institutions, the autonomous courts, the assemblies of the *Vaad*, etc. make it one of the most important and valuable documents acquainting us with the way of life of the Polish Jews in the first half of the seventeenth century.

While Hannover was still living,[16] one Moses ben Abraham translated his *Yeven Metzulah* into Yiddish and published the translation in Amsterdam in 1655. In the eighteenth century (1738) a new Yiddish translation of the chronicle appeared, and in the nineteenth century the work was also translated into French, German, and Russian.

Hannover's chronicle is written in a simple and clear prose style, without rhetoric or flourishes. Completely different in style is the chronicle of another great figure of that generation who lived through the terrible destruction—*Megillat Eifah* of the renowned author of *Siftei Kohen*, Shabbetai Ha-Kohen.[17] *Megillat Eifah* is written in the form of a summons to all Jews throughout the world. Shabbetai describes the great misfortune that struck Polish Jewry and proposes that the twentieth day of Sivan, the day designated in the memorial books as a day of sorrow in memory of the martyrs in Blois,[18] henceforth be set aside as a "day of fasting, mourning and lamentation" and that in all communities the victims of the massacres of 1648 and 1649 should be mourned on it.[19] His summons is written in rhymed prose, and the brilliant dialectician and "uprooter of mountains" here proves himself a superb stylist and master of language. Filled with emotive power, for example, is the description in *Megillat Eifah* of the destruction of the community of Homel.

The bands surrounded them [the Jewish populace of Homel] in a narrow circle, took away all their possessions, left everyone naked and bare . . . and like sheep before slaughter they huddled the misera-

16. The spirited chronicler was not destined to live his last few years in peace. A constant wanderer, Hannover in the 1670's moved from Moldavia to Ungarisch Brod (in Moravia), and there served as a rabbinic judge and preacher. During the war between Turkey and Austria the enemy broke into Ungarisch Brod (July 14, 1683) and massacred the entire Jewish community. Nathan Nata Hannover also perished at the enemy's hands (see *MGWJ*, Vol. 37, 272–274).

17. See above, pp. 66ff.

18. See our work, Vol. II, p. 23.

19. Shabbetai Ha-Kohen's proposal was accepted at a meeting of the *Vaad Arba Ha-Aratzot* (see *Le-Korot Ha-Gezerot*, 1892, 55).

ble ones together—dumb, terrified, cast down. The vile men then said to the Jews in a peaceable tone: 'Why should you perish and allow yourselves to be slaughtered like cattle for the sake of your God, who has mercilessly poured out all His wrath upon you? Better for you to serve our gods. Then we shall all be one people together. We shall let you go free, restore your fortunes to you, and you will live like the rich lords' . . . But the faithful children of the holy seed, who are forever slain for the sake of God's name, renounced the pleasures of the world. Old and young, boys and girls, men and little children—all cried their bitter cry to the exalted God who dwells on high: 'Thou only God, Thou king of all worlds, for the sake of Thy holy name do we give up our lives. We will not serve strange gods!' And they confessed to each other, justified the judgment that had come upon them, and with great weeping recited lamentations . . . Then the vile men fell upon them with great anger and ruthlessly slew young and old, sons and daughter, all without exception . . .[20]

While Hannover's chronicle is written in the calm, quiet tone of a memoirist, in *Megillat Eifah* pathetic outcries in which bitter pain and the longing, unsatisfied demand for vengeance break through are frequently heard. When Shabbetai Ha-Kohen relates how in one city Chmielnitzki's bands "threw fifteen hundred Jewish children into pits and while they were still alive covered them with earth, and from beneath the still moving earth the childish voices were heard," he breaks off in the middle and hurls his wrathful cry: "O God, wilt Thou be silent and allow this, Thou God in heaven?"

In this respect two other chronicles of that time are highly characteristic—*Tzaar Bat Rabbim* of Abraham ben Samuel Ashkenazi and *Tzok Ha-Ittim* of Meir ben Samuel of Sczebr-szyn.[21] The value of these chronicles, which, like *Megillat Eifah*, are also written in rhymed prose, is not merely historical; they are also interesting from the literary point of view. Especially fascinating in this respect is Abraham Ashkenazi's chronicle which has the subtitle, "A Lamentation Over Poland."[22] Every paragraph begins with a verse from the Biblical Book of

---

20. The author of *Tzok Ha-Ittim*, when describing the destruction of the community of Homel, particularly stresses the role of Rabbi Eliezer.
21. *Tzok Ha-Ittim* was first published in Cracow in 1650. Six years later a shameless plagiarist, Joshua ben David of Lemberg, reprinted the work in Venice under his own name. See H. J. Gurland, *Le-Korot Ha-Gezerot*, III, 7.
22. The author intended, apparently, to publish his work in Venice. Testimony to this is provided by the poem of the well known Kabbalist and poet Moses Zacuto which is to be found immediately after the title-page. For some unknown reason, however, the work was not printed in its own day, and only in modern times did H. J. Gurland first publish it in his *Le-Korot Ha-Gezerot*, II.

Lamentations. Then comes the description of the terrible events in the Ukraine. But the description is carried through not in the calm tone of a chronicler; this is a pure cry of lamentation, filled with pain and terror, a bitter weeping over the destruction of Polish Jewry—a weeping constantly interrupted by wrathful cries and insistent demands of the Almighty, the God of Israel, that He fulfill His judgment and repay the blood-thirsty enemy for his terrible deeds.

"O God fearful and exalted," the chronicler exclaims,

Thou hearest the cries of woe! Thou wilt avenge Thyself on the vile men who spread the scrolls of the Torah over the streets, trampled them in the dirt and turned the synagogues into stables . . . Remember that the blood that has been shed cries to the heavens! Or can the innocent blood spilled by men be forgotten? Is it possible that Thou hast forsaken and forgotten us forever? . . . Behold, dogs and swine tear the limbs of slaughtered children who have not been given burial. Pregnant women have had their bellies ripped open. Trembling children were torn in two, their heads smashed against the stones . . . All the caves and pits are filled to overflowing with slain Jewish sons and daughters. The skin was flayed from Jewish maidens, their limbs were cruelly torn, they were thrown bound into water. Take vengeance, O God, who dost accept the cries of the oppressed! Take vengeance for the innocent and pure little doves! Cursed be the bloody murderers! Let them be pursued and plagued to eternity, despised and persecuted by the flame of Thy wrath

The author thereupon begins again to recount the terrible deeds that occurred in the communities of the Ukraine. He tells of a miserable father into whose hands the bloody executioners forcibly pressed a knife and with the fathers' hand severed the neck of his son. He tells of a sexton who guarded his sanctuary, his synagogue, with its scrolls of the Torah from the bandits, and the latter laughingly tore him limb from limb and then cut him up into four parts and hung these in the corners of the synagogue. He tells how women and girls were raped before the eyes of their husbands and fathers, how the necks of children were cut through and the murderers with satanic laughter inquired of their parents whether the slaughter was performed in the ritually proper way or not. All these descriptions are accompanied by the author with wrathful outcries: "Thou Lord God, terrible and fearful, pour out Thy wrath on those who blaspheme Thee, take vengeance on these venomous serpents, avenge Thyself for the perished martyrs who sacrificed themselves for Thy names's sake!"

Like Ashkenazi in his *Tzaar Bat Rabbim*, so another chronicler of that time wove into his sorrowful history texts from the Biblical Book of Lamentations. This was Gabriel ben Joshua Schussburg in his *Petah Teshuvah*.[23] This work is written in the form of a commentary on the Book of Lamentations, but it is a very unique commentary. Life itself, the bloody years 1648–49, wrote this commentary to the Biblical text, and every verse is illustrated by the author through the horrible events in the Ukraine. The barbaric Cossack bands were so insatiable in their murders that every chronicle of that time provides new and heart-rending details. Schussburg's chronicle is also rich in such details and, despite the fact that it is written in a dry, protocol-like style, it makes an enormously powerful impression.

As did the days of the Crusades, so the terrors of the persecutions of 1648 and 1649 called forth a literature of *kinot* (dirges or lamentations) and *selihot* (penitential prayers). "The Muses of terror and misfortune," as Leopold Zunz puts it, inspired the rabbis and scholars who lived through the bloody events in the Ukraine to lamentations and liturgical poetry. The famous author of *Tosafot Yom Tov* wrote his heart-felt "El Male Rahamim" and in his well-known supplication "Eleh Ezkereh" described in shattering images the terrible events that occurred when "dead bodies rolled around over fields and forests and did not receive burial, and living persons were buried in pits and graves." Supplications and lamentations were also written by the son of Rabbi Isaiah Horowitz, Sheftel Horowitz,[24] the rabbi of Posen, and many other rabbis—among them Shabbetai Ha-Kohen who mourned the destruction of the hundreds of communities not only in his *Megillat Eifah* but also in numerous laments.

As in the chronicles of that age, so also in these lamentations and supplications the voice of protest and unstilled vengeance is frequently heard. Samuel Halevi, the author of the supplication "Allele Et Ezkor Ha-Tzarah Ha-Gedolah,"[25] in which he mourns the destruction of Nemirov and Tulchyn, calls out complainingly to God:

23. First published in Amsterdam in 1651; reprinted in the last section of *Le-Korot Ha-Gezerot*, 1892, 30–54.
24. E.g., the well known *selihah* "Shavti Be-Veit Adonai" (reprinted in *Le-Korot Ha-Gezerot*, III, 19–24).
25. Reprinted in *Le-Korot Ha-Gezerot*, V.

Thou hast seen the agony of Thy children and not
   looked down from on high;
Thou hast removed grace and mercy from Thy people.

The author of *Mizbaḥ Yaakov* and *Kol Yaakov*, Rabbi Jacob
Koppel Margolioth, who himself miraculously survived, concludes his lovely elegy "Al Eleh Ani Bochiah" with the summons to God:

Take revenge for the blood of Thy servants;
O Lord God of vengeance, come forth!

But these heartfelt lamentations mourn not only the victims
who perished in terrible agony but also the desecration of the
Torah and the great cultural desolation—the fact that the major center of Jewish learning was ruined. "The lamp of the
commandment and the light of the Torah have been extinguished," mourns Rabbi Margolioth in the lamentation "Al
Harugei Ḥachmei Polanya," "and sit in the darkness in shame.
A pillar of fire once shone in the congregation of Israel. Who
now will reveal the mysteries of the Torah?"[26]

Especially characteristics in this respect is the *bakkashah*
(supplication) of Rabbi Moses ben Eliezer Ha-Kohen (Katz) of
Narol. His father, a nephew of the author of *Reshit Hochmah*
(Elijah de Vidas), came to Poland from Safed to publish his
uncle's book of moral instruction and remained in Poland
throughout his life. His youngest son Moses, who studied with
the famous Rabbi Samuel Edels, was not only a Talmudic
scholar but also devoted himself extensively to mathematics
and medicine. Moses Katz was rabbi in the town of Narol in
Volhynia when Chmielnitzki's bands destroyed the entire
community. Only the rabbi managed to escape with his family.
He reached Germany and from there was invited to occupy the
post of rabbi and teacher in Metz.[27] There he composed his
bakkashah[28] in which he laments the great destruction of Polish
Jewry:

26. *Ibid.*
27. See *Le-Korot Ha-Gezerot*, III, 8–14, where all the sources for Moses Katz's biography
    are presented.
28. The *bakkashah* was first printed in 1659, and reprinted in *Le-Korot Ha-Gezerot*, III,
    14–17.

O delicate Poland, thou chosen one in Torah and knowledge, there has been none like thee since the people went into exile. Now thou art wasted and homeless, forgotten and forsaken! There all the shepherds of the people were accustomed to assemble, there the foundations of the faith were wont to be established, there the laws and statutes for the entire people used to be studied. To whom shall I now liken thee, O land of Poland? Where are the *yeshivot* with their scholars? Who will now explain the laws, who will reveal the mysteries of the Torah, who will conduct us over the depths of the wisdom of the Talmud? The house of Jacob has become ashes, God's holy ark has been taken away from us . . . !

THE GERMAN-POLISH CULTURAL CENTER

BOOK TWO

CHAPTER ONE

The Period of Intellectual Decline

Economic and intellectual regress—The noxious influence of the way of pilpul on the preachers—The preachers' guide, Leket Yosef; its tasteless and corrupt style—The opponents of pilpul, Berechiah Berach Spira and Yair Ḥayyim Bacharach—Jonathan ben Joseph and his Yeshuah Be-Yisrael—The learned doctor, Tobias Cohn, and his Maaseh Tuviyyah—David Nieto, Jehudah Briel, Avi'ad Sar-Shalom Basilea, and Solomon Hanau—Shabbetai Bass, Yeḥiel Heilprin and Isaac Lampronti.

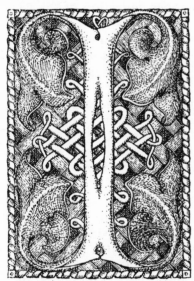N THE previous chapter we noted that most of the elegies and supplications produced after the bloody catastrophe are permeated with the bitter feeling that the Jewry of Poland can no longer heal its grievous wounds and that the Polish seat of Torah, the most important center of Jewish knowledge, is now destroyed forever. To be sure, the fear was not altogether justified. Poland continued to be the major Jewish center, but indeed, a half-ruined center, and for a whole century could not regain its erstwhile strength. The decline of the country itself, the pathological process of corrosion which consumed the feudal-clerical Polish kingdom in ever greater measure, contributed not a little to this. The decade 1648–1657 produced enormous destruction both in social and cultural respects. When the refugees returned to their wasted homes, they found themselves in an extremely difficult situation. After the decade of wars the entire land reflected a fearful picture of decline and devastation. The process of destruction which seized the kingdom with its

backward and decrepit order was felt most painfully by the unprotected and ravaged Jewish community.

The foundations of the Jewish self-government were shattered, and it had lost its former glory. The debts of the impoverished communities increased fearfully. Ever more frequently they had to buy off the church and the Jesuits because of numerous persecutions and all kinds of libels. To liquidate these debts the communal taxes grew ever larger, and since it was extremely difficult to collect these taxes from the greatly impoverished populace, the community council had to adopt the harshest measures. Gradually, as the decay of the state-organism progressed, the governing council of the Jewish community was transformed into a true oligarchy, which brutally employed its power to oppress and exploit the masses of the people in shameless fashion. The masses, who felt the burden of the tremendous taxes with special intensity, began to carry on a struggle against the leaders of the community with their unjust allocations and their improper collection of the royal and communal imposts.

In this stubborn battle of the people against the wealthy communal leaders, who had influence at the court of the lord and were powerful among the nobles and royal officials, the rabbis occupied an indefinite and ambiguous position. Some of them genuinely sided with the common people and frequently protested against the unjust deeds of the community leaders. These rabbis had, because of this, to suffer a great deal from the men of power and monied aristocracy who would persecute them strongly for their "rebelliousness,"[1] Mainly, however, the rabbis were in league with the magnates and community leaders and thereby evoked the resentment of the common people. It would also not infrequently happen that a struggle broke out between both privileged groups—between the intellectual aristocracy, the rabbis, on the one hand, and the communal leaders and financial aristocrats, on the other. Each group wished to have complete authority in communal matters.

All this brought it about that the rabbinate and the rabbis gradually lost their erstwhile glory and respect in the eyes of the masses of the people. Along with this the intellectual atmosphere of the rabbinic world also became narrower and more stifling. To be sure, in Lithuania and Crown Poland the rabbinate retained its solid position even after the persecutions of

1. See Bershadski, *Litovskiye Yevreyi,* 21–22.

1648, for the Cossack wars had not caused such destruction in these territories as in the Ukraine; but in them also intellectual decline and impoverishment is strongly discernible. Even in the most brillant realm of Polish-Jewish culture, rabbinic-Talmudic literature, the spirit of original creativity was virtually extinguished, and the generation following the persecution of 1648 did not produce a single famous rabbinic figure comparable with the great scholars of earlier generations. The work of the most prominent and respected rabbis of that time consisted of whole mountains of notes and supplements to the *Shulḥan Aruch*, which was already recognized at that time as the definitive code, the Urim and Tummim in the field of Jewish law and statute. Moses Rivkes of Vilna wrote his *Be'er Ha-Golah*, Abraham Abele Gumbiner his *Magen Avraham*, Hillel bar Naphtali Herz his *Bet Hillel*, etc. When a rabbi of the second half of the seventeenth century, Aaron Samuel Koidonover, insisted to such an extent on his own opinion that he refused to rely blindly on the authority of the *Shulḥan Aruch* and its keen commentators, the "Taz" and the "Shach," he employed his own brilliance only in writing pointed notes to *Kodashim*, the laws of the sacrifices and the Temple ritual, which were already only "Messianic laws," without any practical import.

Given this intellectual poverty and crippling of thought, the pernicious forms which the method of *pilpul* and *ḥillukim* assumed in the Polish-Jewish world of study manifested themselves even more sharply. The outlandish spinning of ingenious but distorted ideas and subtleties did not in fact help to sharpen the mind but rather to ruin and stultify the intellectual capacities of the individual. With this sophistry of the worst kind, logic and common sense were turned upside down, and the simple and the natural obtained crude and distorted forms, as in a crooked mirror. Literary style, appreciation for the artistic, polished word, never fell so lamentably low as in that twilight period of decline. But *pilpul* dominated not the Talmudic academies only; it also ruled the pulpit of the synagogue. Not the scholar alone sought to dazzle people with his clever notions; the preacher endeavored to do the same. The latter did not set himself the task of teaching the people morality and proper conduct but sought rather to display his great learning and to show with what brilliance he could resolve the most difficult questions and reconcile the most confusing contradictions. This way was followed not only by the common preachers but by the great scholars of that era. For example, in the collection of sermons *Tiferet Ha-Gershuni* of such a respected rabbinic authority as Gershon Ashkenazi (died 1693), one can find numerous piquant examples of precisely this kind of clumsy, pilpulistic preaching.

At that time even special handbooks for preachers with ready-made pilpulistic subtleties and indications of how they are to be utilized were produced. Characteristic in this respect is the handbook of Joseph ben Mordecai Ginzburg of Brest-Litovsk, *Leket Yosef*, which appeared in Prague in 1689. Its topics are organized alphabetically, mainly according to the names of important Biblical personalities. On every theme the author has ready-made a whole collection of overly subtle, absurd questions, and along with these no less "brilliant" answers are provided. All this is so barbarically strange and totally inconsistent not only with the scientific method of thinking but with plain common sense that the reader begins to think he has before him a kind of Purim parody or satirical caricature. Unfortunately, this is not a parody but a handbook and guide for preachers. To the second edition of *Leket Yosef* (published in Offenbach, 1716) was added at the end a special section *Sugyot Ha-Talmud*, with principles and indications of how one must split hairs in the subtle analyses of the rabbis *(ḥillukei de-rabbanan)* "to sharpen the delightful young men." The principles which the author of *Leket Yosef* offers "the delightful young men" surpass considerably all the anecdotes told about the scholastic disputations in which the Christian theologians of former ages were so ingeniously expert. Laws and rules, moral instruction and ethical statements, the Biblical books themselves—all are here utilized as a means for the play of *pilpul*, for hocus-pocus and swindlery.

These handbooks of *pilpul* are also typical from the point of view of their form and style, more correctly, of their formlessness and lack of style. In this "valley of dry bones," where every living sentiment has died out and every breath of inquiring thought has been extinguished, everything is diffuse and nebulous. We have here a kind of tedious mixture of unclear words and sounds, which cast a heavy gloom over the reader.

But, along with this, one must note that even in this benighted period there were a few rabbis and preachers who fought against the distorted *pilpul* and its corrupting influence. Among these battlers the most honored place is occupied by the well known preacher of Cracow, Berechiah Berach Spira. "Among us," Berechiah laments in the preface to the second volume of his collection of sermons, *Zera Berach*,

have appeared false preachers, little foxes who do great harm . . .
They concern themselves only with deception and hocus-pocus, and
spend their time in vain cleverness and dazzlement, in pairing *midrashim* and statements of the rabbis which are as remote from one
another as east from west and between which there is no connection
whatsoever . . . These swindlers and tricksters only mislead people
with their lies and falsehoods, and they make themselves great and
have the impudence to declare that the *Rishonim*, the teachers and
preachers of former generations, did not understand the meaning of
the Torah . . . One can no longer be silent. It is right and proper to
become zealous for God and His sacred Law and seek to overthrow
this mendacious learning whereby they falsify the Torah. This kind
of study ought to be forbidden much more than the study of philosophy and the secular sciences, which was banned in the days of Rabbi
Solomon ben Adret and Rabbi Asher ben Yeḥiel.

"We have seen with our own eyes," further complains the
author of *Zera Berach*,[2]

how after this "confused learning" began to dominate our lands,
great darkness and confusion came into the world. Troubles in
hosts, one destruction after another, one misfortune after another,
came upon us. Rivers of blood flowed, and bodies were not
brought to burial. Entire communities were destroyed. How
many great scholars were condemned to bizarre and terrible
deaths! How many synagogues and houses of study were destroyed and scrolls of the Torah ripped into shreds! Thousands
upon thousands of Jewish souls perished. We were many, but
now only a few remain. It is impossible to recount what struck us
—and all this is punishment for our sins . . ."

The well known rabbi of the age, Yair Ḥayyim ben Samson
Bacharach,[3] issued forth no less sharply against *pilpul* and
ḥillukim. The epidemic of *pilpul* was so great at that time that
some preachers had the audacity to introduce into their sermons quotations that never existed; they would then proceed
to explain these fabricated and difficult matters with all kinds
of dialectical subtleties and thereby show off their cleverness.
Bacharach attacked one of this type of preachers, Aaron Teomim, who later served as rabbi in Cracow, in a work[4] in which

2. We quote according to the Amsterdam edition of 1730.
3. Born in 1639, died in Worms in 1702.
4. Because Teomim later perished tragically in Cracow in an assault by bandits (see
   Ir Ha-Tzedek, 132), Bacharach decided not to publish his polemical work, and even
   made a note about this on the manuscript. Bacharach's work was first published
   in modern times by A. Jellinek in *Bikkurim*, I, 4–26.

he points out the great harmfulness of the method of *pilpul* and how corruptingly it affects the young. Bacharach addresses the same problem in his responsa, *Ḥavvot Yair,*[5] in which he sets forth a complete program of more normal education for children. To be sure, he is not here an innovator; he merely repeats the thought of his great-grandfather, the famous Rabbi Jehudah Loew ben Bezalel (the Maharal of Prague). However, Bacharach's responsa reflect very clearly how impoverished and retarded the world outlook even of this most respected rabbi of that era was. When the author stresses how important it is for the young to study the *Shulḥan Aruch,* he adds:

According to what I have heard, in earlier generations Jews in their youth used to study the *Akedah,* the *Ikkarim,* the *Kuzari,* and their like . . . The present generations, which remove themselves from these studies, do well, for it is good and seemly for us and our children that we believe in everything commanded us, without any speculation whatever. I have spoken of this at greater length elsewhere.[6]

One must take into consideration in this connection that the author of *Ḥavvot Yair* was himself somewhat familiar with medieval Jewish speculative literature and also had a certain knowledge of the secular sciences, mainly mathematics and astronomy. Very interesting in this respect is a section in *Ḥavvot Yair* (No. 129). One of his correspondents applied to him, as an expert in astronomy and mathematics, with a rather difficult scientific problem. Bacharach relates at length in his reply that he wasted a great deal of time in his youth on these studies; he even wrote works on astronomy, but finally became persuaded that his knowledge in this realm was very slight and consequently burned his mathematical works.[7] One must remember, in this connection, that he derived his astronomical knowledge exclusively from medieval Jewish sources. He still lived in the world of the ancient Ptolemy and believed that the sun revolves around the earth which obviously remains firmly fixed in one place, as is written in Scripture: "it standeth forever." Hence, in his astronomical calculations he ran up against insoluble difficulties[8] which had long before been re-

5. Nos. 123, 152.
6. *Ḥavvot Yair,* No. 123, folio 116b.
7. *Ibid.*
8. *Ibid.* "And I am ignorant of knowledge and have not human understanding, and all the books and writers expert in this science would not suffice to enlighten me on the truth of the matter, so that my mind should be at rest."

solved by the brilliant discoveries of Kepler, Copernicus, and Galileo.

Another rabbi of that time, Jonathan ben Joseph of Ruzhany,[9] found himself in a similar situation. From his youth on he was attracted by the "science of reckoning" and, with the aid of medieval Hebrew handbooks, obtained solid knowledge in mathematics and astronomy. He was grieved by the fact that these sciences were now at such a low level among Jews, whereas in former generations they had flourished. When Rabbi Jonathan fled in 1710 from his native city in Lithuania, where an epidemic had broken out, he took a vow that if he survived he would set himself the task of spreading knowledge of astronomy among Jews. He fulfilled this vow about ten years later (in 1720) when he published, with numerous drawings and illustrations, his astronomical work, *Yeshuah Be-Yisrael*, a commentary on Maimonides' *Hilchot Kiddush Ha-Hodesh*. He also wrote a commentary to Abraham bar Hiyya's *Tzurat Ha-Aretz* and first published the Hebrew translation of Johann de Sacrobosco's astronomical work, *Liber de Sphaera Mundi*. But this diligent and intellectually curious scholar also had no conception whatever of the revolution that had taken place in the field of his favorite science, as a result of the brilliant investigators of the sixteenth and seventeenth centuries. Separated by a solid wall of hatred and contempt, the inhabitants of the German-Polish ghetto were cut off from the European intellectual and scientific life of their era. Like Honi the Circle-Drawer of the Talmud, these men, buried alive, lived off the crumbs of knowledge remaining as a legacy from former and happier generations.

A fortunate exception in this respect is the cultured doctor, Tobias ben Moses Cohn,[10] the author of *Maaseh Tuviyyah*, who managed to break through the narrow walls of the ghetto. His father, the well known rabbi of Narol,[11] as we have noted above, fled to Germany after the destruction of the community of Narol. From there he went to assume a rabbinic post in Metz, where four years later (1652) his son Tobias was born. When he was eight years old Tobias was orphaned and, together with his elder brother, set out for Poland, where the

9. Jonathan ben Joseph was the grandson of Jacob Koppelman, the author of *Ohel Yaakov* (a commentary to Joseph Albo's *Ikkarim*). See the preface to *Yeshuah Be-Yisrael*, 1720.

10. A special monograph on this scholar was published by Dr. A. Levinson (*Tuviyyah Ha-Rofe Ve-Sifro Maaseh Tuviyyah*, 1924).

11. See above, p. 135.

families of his parents lived. In Poland the young orphan became thoroughly acquainted with Talmudic literature, but this did not satisfy him.

Tobias himself relates: "I saw the great poverty and the exile and the constant wars in the land, and the incessant troubles, one misfortune after another, one destruction after another, and I thought to myself: What have I to do here? One must go as far away as possible." He was drawn to that science in which his father and grandfather had been trained, medicine, and decided to go to Italy to study it there. One must bear in mind that not only in the times of Rabbi Moses Isserles but later as well, the Polish Jews had frequent contacts with the communities of northern Italy. Even in the seventeenth and eighteenth centuries, despite their constantly growing intellectual isolation and the hostility of the Polish Jews toward the secular sciences, an exception was made for one science—the science of healing. Not infrequently young men from the Polish *yeshivot* would go to Padua to study medicine.[12] Jan Warchal, who studied the archives of the University of Padua, noted down the names of several scores of Jewish young people who came from Poland to study medicine there.[13] The frequent protests on the part of Christian citizens and the denunciations which certain Christian doctors, such as Slesczkowski, Schultz, and their like, issued against their Jewish colleagues with the intent that Jewish doctors be forbidden to practice among Christians did not always succeed. Many Jewish doctors were trusted and accepted in the most prominent Christian circles. The doctor and head of the Jewish community council of Lemberg, Simḥah Menaḥem, was for a time court-physician to King John Sobieski. The doctor of Vilna, Aaron Gordon, who at the end of the seventeenth century studied medicine at Padua, was also a court physician. To Padua also came Tobias Cohn after he had studied medicine for a while in a German university. Cohn returned to Poland as a trained physician and there engaged in

12. The regular intercourse between the Polish and Italian communities is attested by the fact that in 1590 there appeared at Cracow a book entitled *Devek Tov* in which the words of the Bible, arranged in alphabetical order, are explained in Judeo-German and in *Italian*. Also in 1653 Nathan Hannover published a similar handbook, entitled *Safah Berurah*, in which the Biblical words are translated in Judeo-German, Latin, and Italian.

13. See Jan Warchal, "Zydzi polscy na uniwersytecie padewskim," *Kwartalnik Zydów w Polsce*, 1913, III, 37–72. See also Balaban's above-mentioned article; Graetz, *Geschichte der Juden* (Rabinowitch's Hebrew translation), VII, 325–326; and S. Fuenn, *Kiryah Ne'emanah*, 104, 113.

medical practice. The Christian doctors, however, were not pleased with the competition of their Jewish colleague and began to persecute him strongly. In disgust Tobias left Poland and settled in Turkey, first in Adrianople and later in Constantinople, where he found support from the famous diplomat and physician Israel Kunian. Apparently through the latter's aid, Tobias was appointed physician at the court of Sultan Ahmed III. In Constantinople in 1701 he also completed his valuable work, *Maaseh Tuviyyah*, a kind of encyclopedia of metaphysics, theology, astronomy, medicine and other sciences.[14]

Tobias had conceived this work while still in his student years, when he and his friend Gabriel, the only two Jews at the university of Frankfurt-am-Oder, had to suffer much from their Christian colleagues who used to mock them and their people. "In the religious debates which they would carry on with us," relates Tobias,

they would set forth as the clearest proof that God has withdrawn from the Jewish people, our ignorance and enormous backwardness in all realms of science. I then took a vow and determined that, as soon as I had obtained my goal, I would know of no rest or sleep until, with God's help, I would produce a work embracing all the sciences. Let our traducers see and be persuaded that not only among them are all sciences to be found.

In the very first chapter of his work Tobias Cohn complains that among Jews in recent times the desire for speculation, for searching out and investigating the truth, has been entirely extinguished. Jews rely completely on the tradition of the fathers which has been received through inheritance, whereas our Torah has commanded that one must not only believe but also search out "the existence of God blessed be He." To the pious reader of the German-Polish ghetto who was steeped in barbaric superstition and firmly believed in all kinds of destroying spirits and demons, in Kabbalist "combinations of letters" and amulets, in the incantations and formulas of miracle-workers and sorcerers, the author of *Maaseh Tuviyyah* endeavors to give more rational concepts about the nature of angels,[15] the matter of reward and punishment,[16] etc. To the students of the Polish and German *yeshivot* who know so well that on every statement of the Talmudic sages, even a simple

14. First published in Venice in 1707.
15. *Maaseh Tuviyyah*, Part One, *Maamar* Two, Chapter 2.
16. *Ibid.*, *Maamar* Five, Chapter 3.

aphorism or ingenious parable, whole mountains of theories and subtleties have been constructed, Tobias Cohn openly declares that even the commandments of the Torah were not firmly established for eternity but need to be modified according to the demands of the time and the changes that occur among the "receivers and bearers of the Torah."[17] A man of sober common sense, Cohn mocked with biting sarcasm those who are mired in superstition, believe in all kinds of old wives' tales, and tremble before evil spirits and sorcerers. "There is not," the author of *Maaseh Tuviyyah* exclaims bitterly, "another land like Poland, in which men devote themselves so much to demons, amulets, incantations, combinations of names, and all kinds of dreams."[18] Elsewhere[19] he says, "I am not interested in mysteries; I am concerned only with the natural and the regular." When he mentions the belief in the coming of the Messiah, Cohn deems it necessary to dwell at length on the troubles which the messiahs have produced among Jews, and provides in this connection a (from the historical point of view) very important overview of the Shabbetai Tzevi movement.[20]

Cohn also wages his strenuous battle against superstition and false notions in the second part of his work, in which he gives a special treatment of medical problems. He calls the particular attention of the reader to the fact that the greatest obstacle in curing the sick is superstition and foolishness whereby men rely on charlatans, exorcisers, and miracle-workers who treat all diseases with incantations, amulets, and formulas. "Medicine," says Tobias Cohn in the preface to this part, "is a very simple science in the eyes of all these charlatans, but it is a very difficult science for the knowledgeable doctor." Highly interesting in this respect is the eighth chapter, in which Cohn presents his theory of the causes that produce the well-known ringworm disease. "In this chapter," the author begins, "I will speak for my friends and brethren in Poland of the cruel disease so common in this land." Cohn introduces all the views that had been expressed before him about this sickness. There were such "experts" as saw in ringworm some-

17. *Ibid., Maamar* Three, Chapter 3: "So the divine commandments need to be changed according to the times . . . From this you may learn that the divine religion, even though it is not changed in all respects, may be changed in one part from a prohibition to a permission and from a permission to a prohibition, according to the changes of the receivers and bearers of the Torah."
18. *Ibid.*, Part Two, Chapter 8.
19. *Ibid.*, Chapter 5.
20. *Ibid, Maamar* Six.

thing brought on by sorcerers and demons. But the author of *Maaseh Tuviyyah* declares on the basis of his long practice in Poland among the poor that this disease comes from the filth and non-hygienic conditions in which these people live.[21]

But the force of old ideas and the tradition of the fathers dominated the Jewish ghetto so powerfully that even such a sober scientist as Tobias Cohn refused to acknowledge the cogent proofs of the natural scientists when these were too sharply inconsistent with a dictum of Holy Scripture. In the chapters in which he speaks of astronomy he acquaints the reader with the system of Copernicus and points out that "at present many peoples agree with this view," but he himself concludes that the Copernican theory must be considered false, because it is in total contradiction with many verses of the Bible. Hence, he declares the brilliant founder of modern astronomy "the first-born of Satan." Taking into consideration the lucid and sober style of the author of *Maaseh Tuviyyah*, it is difficult to believe that this was merely an ingenious feint, a clown's grimace, of the kind that those Mohicans of the Renaissance era, Leo de Modena and Joseph Solomon Delmedigo, employed so frequently in their day. Indeed, we find not only a son of the German-Polish ghetto but even cultured representatives of other Jewish communities in western Europe of that period of regress manifesting their hostile attitude to critical and free investigative thought. Highly typical in this respect is Tobias Cohn's contemporary and colleague, the head of the London Sephardic community, the rabbi and preacher David Nieto.

Born in Venice in 1654, Nieto studied medicine in Italy, then served for a time as a rabbinic judge in Livorno (Leghorn), at the same time practicing medicine. In 1702 he assumed the rabbinic office in the Sephardic community of London, where he died in 1728. Nieto was a man of broad, many-faceted knowledge. Familiar with a number of European languages, he displayed great interest in philosophy, mathematics, astronomy and philology. Secular and theological studies, art, poetry[22]— everything fascinated this intellectually curious *ḥacham* of London. But this very versatility of his aroused a certain suspi-

21. Cohn first wrote his essay on ringworm disease in Latin and gave a lecture on the subject at a session of the medical faculty in Padua. At the end of his work Cohn provides a brief but valuable dictionary of medical and technical terms in three languages-Latin, Hebrew, and Turkish.
22. Nieto himself wrote poems quite fluently. Several of them were published in Paperna's *Kol Ugav*, 1–2, 78.

cion among the orthodox; they felt that he was somewhat
overly familiar with the secular sciences. It happened that in
one of his sermons Nieto dwelt on the concepts of God and
nature, on the connection between the Creator and the universe. The pious heads of the community detected in this a
dangerous heresy. They suspected that their *hacham* was inclined toward Spinoza's philosophical system.[23] On this matter
a controversy erupted, and they applied to the foremost rabbinic authority of that time, Tzevi Ashkenazi (Hacham Tzevi)
to arbitrate the question. Only because Tzevi Ashkenazi declared that he saw no heresy in Nieto's sermon[24] did the controversy come to an end and the *hacham* remain the leader of
the community.

This adds a special interest to the ideas Nieto expressed in
his well known work *Matteh Dan* (published in London in 1714)
on the relationship between faith and secular knowledge. This
polemical work, which attempts to defend the Oral Torah
against the attacks of the Karaites, bears the subtitle *Kuzari
Helek Sheni* (*Kuzari*, Part Two) and consequently is written like
Jehudah Halevi's work, in the form of five discussions between
a Jewish sage (*haver*) and the king of the Chazars. To be sure,
the structure of Nieto's *Matteh Dan* is greatly inferior to Halevi's masterpiece. The Castilian poet based himself in his *Kuzari*
on an actual historical fact. With Nieto, however, the narrative
is extremely artificial. It tells of a Jewish scholar setting out on
a ship from Venice in the year 1710. On the way a terrible storm
broke out. The ship reached the shores of the land of the
Chazars (this in the year 1710!), and as soon as the king of
Chazars learned that such a great Jewish scholar was in his
land, he invited him to visit and entered into long conversations with him about significant philosophical-religious problems. In the fourth discussion the cultured Nieto speaks at
length of the great importance of the secular sciences and endeavors to show that the sages of the Talmud also devoted
themselves extensively to such sciences and considered them
extremely useful in studying the Torah. But Nieto believes it
essential immediately to emphasize that one can employ these
sciences only so long as they do not contradict the faith. "The
theories of the sages of the gentiles that are inconsistent with
our Written or Oral Torah," the author of *Matteh Dan* con-

23. See Graetz (Rabinowitch's Hebrew translation), VIII, 371, 598. See also *Kol Ugav*,
    78.
24. See Hacham Tzevi's *Responsa*, No. 18.

cludes, "these 'thou shalt utterly detest and abhor, for it is a cursed thing.' "[25] Like Tobias Cohn, David Nieto also rejects Copernicus' teaching about the movement of the earth because this contradicts the well-known Biblical verse, "Sun, stand thou still upon Gibeon."

In this respect the Italian Nieto is typical of his age, of that time of twilight when inquiring thought became so timorous, and heavy, dark shadows covered the Jewish quarter not only in Poland and Germany but also in the land where the Renaissance had once taken place. Even the most cultured men—and there were a certain number of these in the Italian ghetto—were afraid of free criticism and of independent investigative thought. Worth mentioning as an example is the philosophically educated rabbi of Mantua, Jehudah Leon Briel (born around 1643, died in 1722). A determined opponent of the Shabbetai Tzevi movement, Briel took an active part in the struggle against the imposter and schemer, Nehemiah Ḥayon.[26] In his pamphlet, *Ha-Tzad Tzevi*, Ḥayon reproaches the rabbi of Mantua for not being at all competent in mystical literature but only in the "study of Latin and philosophy." Among Briel's other sins, Ḥayon mentions that he shaves his beard and has never married, thereby violating a positive commandment of the Torah.[27] And this "philosopher" and specialist in "the study of Latin," who translated Seneca's letters into Hebrew and composed several philological and polemical works,[28] refused not only to read but even to take into his hands Gersonides' *Milḥamot Adonai*, on the ground that the pious author of *Akedat Yitzḥak*, Isaac Arama, testified of Gersonides that his book contains many heretical ideas.[29]

Even more typical in this respect is Briel's pupil, Aviad Sar-Shalom Basilea. Born into a well-to-do family, Basilea received a comprehensive education. In his youth he assiduously studied astronomy and mathematics,[30] and was familiar not

25. *Matteh Dan*, 59b.
26. See Briel's letter published in *Inyenei Shabbetai Tzevi*.
27. See Graetz (Rabinowitch's Hebrew translation), VIII, 605–606.
28. These works remained in manuscript. In the Asiatic Museum in Leningrad there is a manuscript (of 1708) written in Briel's own hand—a commentary on the Book of Daniel and notes to several other Biblical books. On the margins of the manuscript a later hand wrote various notes in Italian. The manuscript consists of ninety-six pages, with only the end missing.
29. *Emunat Ḥachamim*, Chapter 11.
30. *Ibid.*, 2b: "In my youth I studied natural science and the science of the stars until I gained a reputation among the gentiles in these areas."

only with medieval but also with the new Cartesian philosophy.[31] In his later years, however, he became an ardent follower of the "esoteric wisdom"[32] and a determined opponent of philosophy, in which he perceived a great danger for religion.[33] Like the pious Joel Sirkes,[34] so Basilea also concluded that "all who come to her will not return."[35] He could not forgive Abraham Ibn Ezra for the free, critical ideas he expressed in regard to the redaction of the Pentateuch.[36] Basilea also declared the commentators to Maimonides' *Guide for the Perplexed* "those who make many to sin," and the profound Moses Narboni is for him not only a "complete heretic" but a "fool of utmost folly."[37] In Gersonides he sees the man who "fights against God," and the author of *Meor Einayim*, Azariah dei Rossi, he does not even wish to mention by name, "because all his words incline to heresy, for his intent was to drive us away from God and to remove us from His Torah."[38] Even in Jedaiah Ha-Penini's *Beḥinat Olam* this zealot detected heresy that must be uprooted,[39] and he complained strongly of the rabbi of Ancona, Samson Morpurgo, because the latter had in his youth (1704) published Jedaiah's poem with a new commentary *(Etz Ha-Daat)*. "He who printed this work," angrily exclaims the author of *Emunat Ḥachamim*, "will have to render account for it."[40]

Given such attitudes, it is easy to imagine in what a difficult situation the few men of that era who were not disposed to follow blindly in the trodden way of the tradition of the fathers and who made the slightest attempt to adopt a critical attitude toward the authorities of earlier generations found themselves.

31. *Ibid.*, 4b.
32. Interesting are the arguments with which he endeavors to show that the *Zohar* is indeed an ancient work (*Ibid.*, Chapter 25). Basilea himself wrote mystical commentaries, and in Baron Günzburg's collection there was the following manuscript (No. 687): *Sodot Ve-Kavvanot Ha-Shofar Ve-Od, She-Shalaḥ Aviad Sar-Shalom Le-Rabbi Avraham Segre* (1701).
33. *Emunat Ḥachamim*, 29b.
34. See above, p. 64.
35. *Emunat Ḥachamim*, 27b, 38a.
36. *Ibid.*, 10a.
37. *Ibid.*, 19a.
38. *Ibid.*, 38a.
39. *Ibid.*, 15b, 27a.
40. *Ibid.*, 16a (we quote according to the first edition, 1730). Apparently the sharp tone in which *Emunat Ḥachamim* was written brought it about that Aviad's friend, Gad de Laquila, after becoming familiar with the work in manuscript, begged the author not to publish it.

In this respect the difficult life-path of the philologist Solomon Zalman Hanau is highly instructive. Born in Hanau in 1687, Solomon manifested while still in his youth a special interest in that branch of science which did not attract the least attention in the German-Polish *yeshivot*, namely, philology and Hebrew grammar. While still a boy he studied through all the old Jewish grammarians and philologists, and at the age of twenty issued his own work, a Hebrew grammar entitled *Binyan Shelomoh* (1708). In the second introduction the young author complains that the grammar of the language of the Bible is so neglected. Young Jews concern themselves with *pilpul*, show off their cleverness and expertise in Talmudic literature, but they have no conception of what grammar is and cannot read through a single prayer, a single sentence even, without grammatical errors.[41] These courageous swimmers over the "sea" of the Talmud, the author of *Binyan Shelomoh* further complains, consider it improper to concern themselves with grammar, which they do not even regard as a real discipline. With youthful smugness the author asserts that in his work he has corrected numerous mistakes of the older grammarians.

The tone of the young author is indeed a rather strong one, even polemically sharp in places. That a young man should issue forth with such self-assurance against anciently recognized authorities, that he should dare to catch Abraham Ibn Ezra, Rabbi David Kimhi, and Isaac Abravanel in errors—this reflected an unheard-of impudence and literally smacked of "wantonness." Along with this, the following point is interesting. In the third preface to his work Solomon Hanau mocks Abravanel because the latter complains of Jeremiah that the prophet was not properly familiar with the principles of grammar. To be sure Hanau here defends the prophet; nevertheless, the contemptuous tone that he adopted toward such a great scholar as the pious Abravanel greatly enraged the leaders of the community in Frankfurt where Hanau's book was published. As soon as his *Binyan Shelomoh* came off the press, they decided to burn the book, on the ground that it might bring others to the impudence of mocking recognized authorities. However, in consequence of the fact that the highly respected son-in-law of the famous David Oppenheim took up Hanau's cause, the decree was nullified, but only on condition that at

41. *Binyan Shelomoh*, second introduction: "And the children of Israel know nothing of the grammar of the holy language. They read the Bible every Sabbath and New Moon and they cannot read a single verse without error."

the end of his work the author write an apology in which he would beg forgiveness of all the great scholars whose honor he had impugned. The apology did, indeed, save the book from being burned, but it did not save the author from all kinds of persecutions. Despite his extensive knowledge and great capacities, Hanau could not obtain any position and supported himself by giving Hebrew lectures[42] and selling copies of his grammar. When, some time later, he sharply criticized one Azriel and his son Elijah of Vilna for their poor edition of the prayer-book, these considered it necessary in their polemic first of all to remind their critic of the "sin of his youth"—the fact that he had had the presumption to attack great scholars. Hanau therefore discusses once again in the preface to his later work, *Shaarei Torah*, the question that had become so tragic for himself: whether it is permitted to criticize the views of acknowledged authorities. In this connection he ventures to express the (for that time) heretical idea that it is allowed everyone to seek and investigate the truth, and that he may, in doing this, not rely blindly on the views of recognized authorities, for these also are no more than human and can commit errors.[43] With this Hanau again aroused the anger of the pious leaders of the generation, and the fanatical Jacob Emden Ashkenazi called him "the rash and confused one."[44]

The extent to which the congealed thought of German-Polish Jewry of that age regarded with suspicion and hostility everything that was not completely according to long-established order is best attested by another scholarly work of that period. This is the bibliographical handbook, *Siftei Yeshenim*, of Shabbetai ben Joseph Bass. As a fourteen-year-old boy,[45] Shabbetai lost his parents, who perished in the slaughter of the Jews in his native city of Kalisch in 1655. The orphan then went to Prague where, thanks to his magnificent bass voice, he was

42. According to the report of a contemporary of his, Hanau was a lecturer in Hebrew at several universities in Holland (see *ZHB*, 1904, 94).
43. Hanau writes: "Surely I did this in the integrity of my heart and with cleanness of hands, in that I sometimes criticized some author of the authors of previous generations, for it is Torah, and it is permitted to everyone to seek and inquire after the truth. And it is written in the responsa *Havvot Yair* that it is allowable to write about any author of the ancients who was mistaken, for an author is also human and does not escape error. Furthermore, it is not proper to hide the truth."
44. His reply to Emden's attacks were published by Hanau at the end of his grammar *Tzohar Ha-Tevah* (1733), which was very popular in its day and was reprinted a number of times.
45. Shabbetai Bass was born in 1641 and died in Krotoschin in 1718.

immediately taken on as a singer in the famous Altneuschul. Richly talented, the young singer devoted all his free time to scientific studies. In 1669 Bass reprinted Moses Sertel's well-known glossary of the Bible, *Be'er Mosheb*,[46] which he accompanied with an extensive introduction wherein he set forth in simple, clear fashion the principles of Hebrew grammar. Later he also published his own commentary to Rashi. But he acquired fame in a very different realm. In the course of the years 1674–1680 Bass made a journey through Poland, Germany, and Holland, stopping for a rather long period in all the important Jewish cultural centers of that era. In 1679 he settled in Amsterdam, where he effectively utilized the rich library of Moses d'Aguilar, a member of the Sephardic community. This gave him the opportunity to complete in 1680 his fundamental bibliographical work, *Siftei Yeshenim*, which he had already conceived in Prague. In this work, thanks to which Bass has been recognized as the father of Hebrew bibliography, are noted 2400 works (2200 Hebraica and over 160 Judaica), listed alphabetically by their titles. With every work the name of the author, the format, the place and year of publication, and also in brief the content of the work is given.

Most of the works noted here had been held by Bass in his own hands; the rest he described relying on Buxtorf and Bartolocci. Bass divided all the Jewish literary works known to him into two groups—Biblical and post-Biblical, and each of these two groups he further subdivided into ten sections. As a supplement to his bibliographical catalogue Bass presents an index of names, in which among the authors noted are the Tannaim, Amoraim, Sevoraim and Geonim. The introduction to *Siftei Yeshenim* also has a cultural-historical value. Shabbetai Bass knew very well the suspicion with which his generation regarded every new thing, all that is outside the common and anciently established order. He therefore considered it essential to emphasize that a bibliographical handbook can in no way be injurious to faith. Quite the contrary; it may be extremely useful and bring men to reverence of God. In this connection he even relies on a great scholar, the "holy Shelah," the pious Isaiah Horowitz. As an opponent of *pilpul* and *ḥillukim*, Bass also put forth in this introduction proposals to reform the order of education of children, and again this time relied on an authority, Isaiah Horowitz's son Rabbi Sheftel,

---

46. *Be'er Mosheb* will be discussed further in a later part of our *History*.

who set as a model before the Ashkenazim, the German-Polish Jews, the schools and academies of the Sephardic community in Amsterdam.[47]

Only in later generations did the Jewish world learn properly to appreciate the "father" of Hebrew bibliography. In the Christian world of scholarship, however, Shabbetai Bass became well known as soon as his *Siftei Yeshenim* appeared. The bibliographical work of Bassista (so Bass was called among the Christians) was translated into German and Latin and served as the foundation of Wolf's large-volumed *Bibliotheca Hebraea*.

In ideological affinity with *Siftei Yeshenim* is the work of the rabbi and *rosh yeshivah* of Minsk, Yeḥiel ben Solomon Heilprin.[48] Like Bass, Heilprin was also an opponent of the method of *pilpul*. Himself a great scholar in Talmudic literature, he gave all his attention to that study which least interested the Polish *yeshivot*—historiography and historical investigation. His life's-work, on which he labored for decades, *Seder Ha-Dorot*, consists of three parts: (1) *Yemot Olam*, the order of the generations from ancient times to the second half of the seventeenth century (in this the author made use of the historical works of Abraham Zacuto, Gedaliah Ibn Yaḥya, and David Gans); (2) *Seder Tannaim Ve-Amoraim*, the order of the Talmudic teachers; and (3) *Shemot Ha-Sefarim Veha-Meḥabberim*, the names of the books and authors of the post-Talmudic era (here the author relies mainly on *Siftei Yeshenim*). The most valuable part of the work is the second, in which Heilprin systematizes and illuminates in very competent fashion all the confused and frequently contradictory information about the creators of the Talmud, the Tannaim and the Amoraim. But such works were of little interest to Heilprin's generation, which was absorbed in *pilpul*, and *Seder Ha-Dorot*, which was completed in 1725, was first published in 1768 when Heilprin had already long been in his grave.

Many years after its author's death another major work of that era appeared—*Paḥad Yitzḥak*, a Talmudic encyclopedia composed by the physician, rabbi and *rosh yeshivah* of Ferrara, Isaac Lampronti.[49] While still a student at the University of Padua, Lampronti conceived his monumental work on which

47. On Shabbetai Bass's Yiddish work *Derech Eretz*, see Volume Seven of our *History*.
48. Born approximately 1666, died in 1746. For a discussion of Heilprin's life, see N. Maskileison in his edition of *Seder Ha-Dorot*, 1878–1882.
49. Born in 1679, died in 1756. For biographical details see *Divrei Fi Ḥacham Ḥen*, 131–137, and the preface to *Paḥad Yitzḥak* (1885 edition).

he labored all his life. In the author's lifetime only the first two volumes (from the letter *alef* to the letter *dalet*) appeared. The further volumes began to come off the press only in 1796, and the work appeared in complete form only in modern times (in 1887). *Paḥad Yitzḥak* is distinguished by the same virtues as well as the same defects as Heilprin's work: enormous diligence and great scholarship, but weak structure and insufficient critical, scientific exploration of the collected material. The value of Lampronti's encyclopedia is increased by the fact that the author introduced many important documents by prominent persons.

CHAPTER TWO

Ethical Literature

The growth of messianic-mystical tendencies—Jehudah Ḥasid of Shedletz and his followers—Preacher-mystics and ethical literature —Hirsh Koidonover and his *Kav Ha-Yashar*—The ascetic and melancholy character of *Kav Ha-Yashar*—Elijah Ha-Kohen and his *Shevet Musar*—The gracious God and sinful man—The "calculators of the end" and mystical sectarians—The struggle of the rabbis against the covert Sabbatians.

E HAVE observed how arid *pilpul* with its clever *ḥillukim* and overly sharp mental ingenuities became a self-sufficient goal, an independent and immense structure the bricks for which were provided very assiduously by the keenest minds of Polish Jewry. This "*pilpul* for the sake of *pilpul*," the cold, calculated, and sharply intellectual notions regarding "things of the heart," i.e., ethical-religious matters, could not, however, satisfy men with sensitive hearts and believing, longing souls. In the atmosphere of dry *pilpul*, vain pedantry, and congealed routine, these men yearned for the living source of fervent belief and religious sentiment. We have noted how powerfully these dreaming souls were attracted by the hidden depths of the *ḥochmat ha-nistar* (esoteric wisdom) and how in this environment *Shenei Luḥot Ha-Berit*, the classic work of its type, in which the ideas of the "holy Ari," Rabbi Isaac Luria, are so enthusiastically promoted, was produced. The severely ascetic Lurianic Kabbalah with its mystical spirit permeated the entire rabbinic world and emerged ever more clearly as the most important factor in the spiritual and intellectual life of Polish Jewry.

Terrifying stories about the punishments that await men in hell, transmigration of the soul, all kinds of destroying spirits, incantations and amulets with wonderful "names," and "combinations of letters" that create and destroy whole worlds, ruled unrestrainedly over the popular imagination. Because the real world became for the Jew a vale of sorrow, of terrible sufferings and endless degradations, he created for himself another world—a world of mystical dreams and fantastic visions. And this world, the mystical-fantastic world, assumed in the eyes of the residents of the ghetto more real and concrete shapes than the actual world. Nevertheless, this imaginary world was a mirror and reflection of the melancholy reality. The number of bitter enemies and adversaries of the Jewish population grew ever greater. The Catholic clergy and the urban crafts and guilds ruthlessly persecuted the Jews at every step, and simultaneously the imagination of the people, veiled in a mystical haze, created countless hosts of destroyers and evil spirits lurking for man everywhere and ready to destroy him forever. If a man forgets himself even only for a moment and allows himself to be led astray by the evil inclination, he is already lost, and the terrible punishment of hell awaits him. One moment of pleasure is repayed with endless affliction and suffering. Men with tender, sensitive, and trembling souls endeavored to remove themselves as far as possible from the sinful present world, led an ascetic life, and mortified their bodies with fasting and flogging, in order thereby to overcome the power of the *kelipot* (shells) and hasten the "end," the redemption of the world.

Ever more melancholy and desperate became the atmosphere in the Jewish ghetto. After the great catastrophe occurred and wild bands of Cossacks destroyed hundreds of communities on their bloody march, one thought became ever sharper and more insistent in the consciousness of the people, frozen in deathly terror: it is not possible to go on living this way; something must happen and put an end to the intolerable sufferings of the people. The great misfortunes which have occurred—these are the *ḥevlei ha-mashiaḥ*, the "pangs of the

Messiah." This basic idea dominated the consciousness of the people and injected the salve of hope into grieved hearts. Men calculated and discovered that *ḥevlei ha-mashiaḥ* is equivalent in *gematria* to the Hebrew letters for 1648, and that the name of the leader of the Cossack bands, Chmil (Bogdan Chmielnitzki) is the *notrikon* for *ḥevlei mashiaḥ yavo la-olam* (the pangs of the Messiah will come to the world).[1] And when the proud cry of the mystic of Smyrna, "I, your Messiah, Shabbetai Tzevi!" was heard throughout the Diaspora, it evoked immense jubilation in the Polish communities. "The Jews," relates the Ukrainian writer of that time Galatovski, "triumphed; some abandoned their homes and property, neglected their affairs, and declared that the Messiah would soon come and bring them on a cloud to Jerusalem. Others fasted entire days and did not give even small children anything to eat. Some bathed in winter in ice-holes, reciting newly composed prayers while doing so."[2]

But the glorious hope was not fulfilled, and the messianic movement came to a tragic end. The sultan of Turkey threw the expected Messiah into prison, where he became a Moslem. The widespread national-political movement which this extraordinary man had called forth could not, however, be completely destroyed. In various places in Poland appeared fervent mystics who summoned and admonished the people to fast and repent all the more, for the redemption would soon come. A particularly strong sensation was created by Jehudah Ḥasid of Shedletz.[3] A rigorous ascetic and ardent adherent of the practical Kabbalah, Jehudah Ḥasid firmly believed that soon the great wonders would appear. He established a special order of *Ḥasidim* (pious ones) who wished to bring on the "end" through fasting and mortification of the flesh. Jehudah Ḥasid wandered from city to city and, in the synagogues and houses of study, with a scroll of the Torah in his hands, summoned the people to penitence and heartfelt prayer in fiery sermons. His addresses made a powerful impression on the people. The number of the *Ḥasidim* grew constantly, and in the year 1700 a host of a thousand persons led by Jehudah Ḥasid set out for Palestine, there to welcome the long-awaited redeemer with pomp and ceremony. Many of the *Ḥasidim* perished on the

1. See *Le-Korot Ha-Gezerot*, II, 27.
2. Dubnow, *op. cit.*, Vol. 3 [*Weltgeschichte*, VII, p. 60]. On the deputation which the Taz sent to Shabbetai Tzevi, see above, p. 65, Note 62.
3. For a discussion of Jehudah Ḥasid, see David Kahana in *Kenesset Yisrael*, I, 775–784; Graetz (Rabinowitch's Hebrew translation), VIII, 358, 583–584.

way, and those who arrived in Jerusalem were tragically disappointed. The redeemer did not come, Jehudah Ḥasid soon died, and his followers, having no means of livelihood, returned to Europe and dispersed over various countries.[4]

It is clear that men with restless souls and longing hearts could not be completely satisfied by arid *pilpul* with all its subtleties and clever, dialectical notions. Hence, it is quite natural that besides the religious, rabbinic-scholastic writings, a literature of ethical instruction veiled in mysticism also developed. Along with the pilpulistic preachers discussed above, for whom the handbook *Leket Yosef* was produced,[5] there also appeared preachers of an entirely different kind, mystical preachers whose Urim and Tummim were the mysterious *Kitvei Ha-Ari*, the Kabbalist manuscripts of Rabbi Isaac Luria and his disciples, full of "secrets of eternity," of divine revelations. With enormous enthusiasm these preachers disseminated Luria's ideas, clothed in "tales of wonders," in fearful accounts of torments of the grave, of transmigrations of souls, of destroying spirits, of the terrible punishment awaiting the wicked in hell and the glorious reward prepared for the righteous in heaven. But men were not content merely with sermons. At the same time special books of moral instruction which were extremely popular were also produced. In order that this ethical literature might reach the masses of the people, it was written in both Hebrew and Yiddish. We shall discuss it at greater length in a later volume of our work. Here we shall dwell only on one of the most typical ethical books of this type which was, indeed, written in both languages—*Kav Ha-Yashar* by Tzevi Hirsh ben Samuel Koidonover.[6]

Basically *Kav Ha-Yashar* is not an original or independent work. The author himself indicates in the introduction that he made extensive use of the work of his teacher, the rabbi of Minsk, Joseph ben Jehudah, and that a number of chapters "are really his words," i.e., were taken verbatim from Joseph's book, which was entitled *Yesod Yosef*.[7] *Yesod Yosef*, composed at the end of the 1680's,[8] did not, however, enjoy good fortune; for

4. Some of Jehudah Ḥasid's followers, disappointed in their hopes, converted to Islam, and several went over to Christianity.
5. See above, p. 138.
6. The Hebrew text first appeared in 1705, the Yiddish translation in 1724.
7. For a further discussion of the question of the extent to which the author of *Kav Ha-Yashar* drew from *Yesod Yosef*, see the work of I. Sosis in *Tsaytshrift*, I, 15–24.
8. In the preface to the first edition of *Yesod Yosef*, which appeared in Shklov in 1785,

almost a hundred years it remained in manuscript, unknown and forgotten. But the work of Joseph ben Jehudah's pupil, Koidonover's *Kav Ha-Yashar*, became one of the most beloved books of ethical instruction among the Jewish people.

Tzevi Hirsh Koidonover was born in Vilna. His father, Aaron Samuel, acquired a considerable reputation in the rabbinic world with his Talmudic writings. Of Tzevi Hirsh's life in Vilna we have very little information. We know only that as a result of some denunciation or slander he, together with his family, was imprisoned for all of four years. As far as may be surmised from several phrases in the introduction to *Kav Ha-Yashar*, his misfortune was brought about by the leaders of the Vilna community, whom he calls "men of horns" and "violent persons." In the preface to his father's book *Tiferet Shemuel*, which he published in Frankfort in 1696, Tzevi Hirsh indicates that the man chiefly guilty of the denunciation which brought him such distress was a certain Ben Zion Hort. Koidonover repaid his four years of imprisonment by presenting in his work a frightful portrait of the communal leaders and officials, depicting how they oppress the masses of the people and, like leeches, suck the blood and marrow of the impoverished multitude. One cannot suspect the author of having here given, out of hatred, a highly prejudiced portrait and of having employed overly somber colors, for precisely the chapter in which Koidonover portrays the behavior of the community leaders of the time was copied almost verbatim from his teacher's *Yesod Yosef*. Since this passage has a definite cultural-historical interest, we quote it here in its entirety:

Like the cloud which disperses and disappears, like the wind that is carried away and returns no more, so is the ruler and leader who does not conduct himself as befits a guide in Israel and does not assume the burden of the children of Israel. He perishes and departs suddenly from the world, and no memory remains of his children. In this net many leaders are caught, on account of their arrogance and lordliness and the fact that they cast excessive fear upon the people—and this not for the sake of God's name. They enjoy all pleasures and delights and do not help the people with the taxes and levies. They lighten the tax burden for themselves and increase it as much as possible for others. When it comes to honor and glory, they take their share first. Their faces are always florid, fat, and healthy, for they

---

the editor notes: "And it is now close to a hundred years that this book has remained in manuscript and has not yet been printed."

indulge in all the pleasures their hearts desire. In other peoples' troubles they take no part; they are not moved by their sufferings. And God's assembly, the children of Abraham, Isaac and Jacob, are crushed and degraded. They go about naked and barefoot because of the taxes through which the agents and servants of the community despoil them. These come into their homes cruelly, seize and plunder whatever they find, and see to it that the owners are left naked and bare. They take away even their clothing, even their prayer-shawls, and sell these for paltry sums, so that nothing remains to them except the straw in their beds. In the season of cold and rain they shiver, and the householder and his wife and children each weep in a separate corner. But if the leaders helped pay the taxes, the burden would not be so great on the average householder and on the poor people. There is, however, an even greater sin: the leaders eat and drink from communal charity funds, and from these present dowries and wedding gifts to their sons and daughters. And this money is always from the taxes that have been robbed and from the labor of the hands of Jews. Before each such *parnass* and leader a herald goes forth and exclaims: 'This is he who eats the flesh and blood of the holy people of Israel! He robs poor persons, orphans and widows!' And the herald curses him with many curses, and his prayer is not heard. May God, blessed be He, preserve us from this punishment.[9]

After Koidonover was released from prison, he decided to move away from Vilna, and at the end of the seventeenth century was living in Frankfort, where in 1705 he published his book of moral instruction, which he had completed while still in Vilna.[10]

In no other popular work is the stifling and oppressive atmosphere of the Jewish ghetto of the seventeenth and eighteenth centuries felt with such leaden heaviness as in Tzevi Hirsh Koidonover's *Kav Ha-Yashar. Yesod Yosef,* for example, from which Koidonover drew so extensively, utters admonitions to penitence, gives ethical instruction to the people, and pleads with them to follow the right path and fulfill God's commandments. But *Kav Ha-Yasher* does not plead; it demands with indignation and wrath, it casts fear on the reader, it wishes to terrorize him with the frightful agonies of hell, so that he will follow the right way out of fear. "O mortal man," the author exclaims in the very first chapter, "if you knew how many

9. *Kav Ha-Yashar*, Chapter 9: *Yesod Yosef*, Chapter 9, p. 7.
10. In the preface to *Kav Ha-Yashar*, where the author relates how he fled from his home naked and in distress, he adds: "And there remained nothing with me except this book of mine written to benefit the many."

demons of the *sitra aḥara* (other side) lurk for every drop of blood in man's heart, you would at once devote yourself to the service of God with your whole soul and body." When the author of *Kav Ha-Yashar* warns about false oaths, he immediately threatens: "Wicked Lilith, the mother of the demons, who, because of our numerous sins, arouses so many evil decrees against Israel, is always in the house in which there are false oaths. She lives in that house and slays little children, God forbid! And in the room or in the city in which there are false oaths there is usually poverty."[11]

The entire work literally swarms with all kinds of demons, scoffers, and destroying spirits. In it the most precise information about all their deeds and diabolical inventions is presented. With great learning it lists how many thousands of spirits place themselves on the nail of a woman's finger and what power all kinds of sorcerers and evil spirits obtain over men for the least sin. Lilith has under her 480 hosts of destroying spirits, corresponding to the numerical value of the name Lilith, and her comrade Maḥlat has subject to her 478 hosts, corresponding to the numerical value of Maḥlat.[12] When Koidonover wishes to show the grievous punishment that awaits a person who is miserly and does not give charity, he relates a long story of a certain rich man who was a great miser and tells how the man came into the power of the destroying spirits and was saved only as a result of the fact that he repented betimes and undertook to donate large sums to charity.[13]

The popular legends related by the author of *Kav Ha-Yashar* as real events have a certain ethnographic as well as cultural-historical interest. Hence, we present one of them here by way of illustration: In 1681–1682 evil spirits appeared in a stone wall standing in a large street in Posen. First they occupied the cellar, whereupon the cellar was locked and no one dared enter it. Once a certain young man did attempt to go into the cellar; a quarter of an hour later he was found dead on the threshold. A short time after the death of the young man the destroying spirits began to appear in the "hall" of the wall, and when the members of the household began cooking the noonday meal in the oven, the spirits would drag out the pots and pour ashes

11. *Kav Ha-Yashar*, Chapter 56.
12. *Ibid.*, Chapter 68.
13. *Ibid.*, Chapter 25.

and mud into the food. Gradually the destroying spirits became stronger, occupied one room after another in which people lived, and gave the inhabitants no rest. They would tear off the lamps from the brackets and hurl them to the ground and overturn all the other vessels and objects. They did not harass the people themselves but so embittered their lives with their pranks that the people had to abandon the dwelling, and there was great mourning in the holy community of Posen. The community thereupon took counsel to devise some means of expelling the evil ones. They tried all sorts of things, but nothing availed. Then they sent a special messenger to the famous *baal shem* ("master of the name" or miracle worker) called Rabbi Joel of the holy community of Zamosc. As soon as the *baal shem* came, he commenced to adjure the destroying spirits with holy names, demanding that they explain why they had settled in a house where people live; according to the law, destroying spirits may not settle in an inhabited residence but only in a place of filth or a waste place. The destroying spirits explained that this house specifically belonged to them and that they could prove it by the law of the Torah. They were even prepared to go to legal proceedings in the rabbinic court of the city of Posen. The *baal shem*, Rabbi Joel, and the judges thereupon sat down in the court chamber. They heard a voice from one of the destroying spirits but saw no form or figure. The voice argued that once a certain Jew had lived in this house, which had belonged to him. This Jew was a goldsmith, and he cohabited with a female demon and by her had "strange children, children who are corrupters." The goldsmith was married and also had children by his human wife, but he especially loved the female demon and his soul was bound to hers. He would even frequently have to interrupt his prayers, leave the synagogue, and go do the bidding of his demon lover. Once, on the festival of Pesaḥ, the goldsmith was sitting and conducting the *seder*, as is the custom among Jews in all the dispersions of Israel. In the middle of the banquet he rose from the table and went to the lavatory. His wife pretended not to know or observe anything, but in a while quietly went to see why he tarried so long. She looked into the lavatory through a crack and saw a beautiful, bright chamber and in the center of it a table laden with gold and silver vessels. Near it was a magnificently decorated bed. On the bed lay a marvelously beautiful woman naked, and lying with her was her husband the goldsmith. In terror the woman returned to the room. A quarter of an hour later her husband came back. She did not say a word

to him but the very next day went to the rabbi, the great
scholar Rabbi Sheftel, and told him everything. The rabbi at
once summoned the goldsmith, and the latter confessed that he
was living with one who was not of the seed of man. The rabbi
thereupon wrote an amulet with holy "names" for the goldsmith. In the power of this amulet the goldsmith had to leave
the strange woman who derived from the destroying spirits.
Before his death, the female demon came to him and wept
before him for his abandonment of her and her children. She
embraced and kissed him until he agreed to give her and her
children a portion of his estate, promising her the basement of
the wall. Then the wars of 1648–1658 began in Poland. During
that time the goldsmith and his heirs died. He now had no heirs
except the children of the female demon. They were the goldsmith's legatees and the wall belonged to them by law. To the
arguments of the destroying spirits the previous residents of
the wall, however, replied that they had purchased their dwelling from the goldsmith. Moreover, demons cannot be considered the seed of the children of men, and their mother, the
female demon, had coerced the goldsmith into living with her.
The court decided that the destroying spirits were unjustified
and have no portion in the wall, for their place is in the desert,
not in an inhabited locality. After this verdict Rabbi Joel again
adjured the destroying spirits, and they had to leave the house.
They were even compelled to abandon the cellar and departed
into the forests and deserts. The author of *Kav Ha-Yashar* adds
that here you have the best proof of what a great sin it is when
a man copulates with Lilith or with a female demon of those
classes which Maḥlat rules.[14]

When a distinguished Jewish scholar relates such "actual
events," one must not be at all surprised that the common
people believed in all kinds of old wives' tales and attempted
to increase their paltry income with the aid of magic and the
formulas of sorcerers and exorcisers. The naive author of *Kav
Ha-Yashar*, however, complains of this, declaring it sinful and
contrary to the sacred Torah. "Men," he laments, "have come
to be of so little faith . . . that it is very common among brainy
persons (shopkeepers, tavern owners, and the like) that when
they see their livelihood diminished, they refuse to accept this
with love as a decree and perform all kinds of magic so that

14. *Ibid.*, Chapter 69. We shall discuss the sources of this story in the next volume of
our work.

their income might be restored to them. This is a grievous sin."[15]

It is quite understandable that the indignant and ascetically minded author of *Kav Ha-Yashar* has the greatest hostility toward all secular knowledge whatsoever, and in general for everything smacking of the external European world. A certain cultural-historical value pertains to the passage in *Kav Ha-Yashar* in which the pious author complains that "there are now many people who let their small children learn to speak French." The term "many people" is doubtless an exaggeration; nevertheless, there is no question but that the pious moralist here touches on a definite and real fact. The Jewish communities in Germany and Poland of that age were, indeed, deeply pious, and the *Shulḥan Aruch*, along with the Kabbalah of Rabbi Isaac Luria, ruled unrestrainedly over their minds. Nevertheless, in cultural respects (not to speak of inner social contradictions) the contemporary Jewish community was not entirely monolithic. There was a certain group, albeit a rather small one, whose special social situation compelled it to be somewhat more lenient in regard to the laws of the *Shulḥan Aruch* and at times to bend certain religious customs. This consisted of the *Hofjuden*, the bankers and tax farmers, who used to lease or purchase certain royal taxes and revenues. These wealthy Jews, who had social intercourse with the Christian nobility and were frequent guests at the princely and noble courts, gradually became more "worldly" and obtained, at least externally, a more European appearance. One must take into consideration in this connection that in the courts of the German princes and nobles of the seventeenth and eighteenth centuries French culture and the French language were extremely fashionable. The same was true in Poland. Especially after John Sobieski, who married a Frenchwoman, was elected king of Poland in 1674, the language of France became even more stylish among the Polish nobility. All this contributed to the fact that among certain very wealthy Jewish tax-farming and banking families French and, with it, the external vesture of European culture also penetrated.

Against this "desecration of God's name" the author of *Kav Ha-Yashar* issues forth with severe complaints.

15. *Ibid.*, Chapter 28. This passage is to be found in virtually the same words in *Yesod Yosef*, Chapter 57, 27b.

In the present generation I have seen many persons who have become licentious, who do not conduct themselves like the whole people and go about dressed like the gentiles. In addition, they shave their beards and thereby violate five negative precepts, for in a man's beard there are five edges, as the Gemara counts them, and for each edge one violates a separate negative commandment. Furthermore, as a result of these things one frequently does not know whether or not a man is a Jew, and when he is asked his name he calls himself by a gentile name. It also happens at times that he travels with some nobles on a journey to a distant place where he is not recognized and people do not know whether he is a Jew. He then stumbles by eating ritually forbidden food and drinking the wine of idolaters, for one transgression draws another in its train. And it is not enough that he brings evil on himself and his soul; he also causes evil for the community of Israel, for such a man delays the redemption by the fact that he exchanges his name for a gentile one. Therefore, those who do so will suffer grievous punishment. One of the merits for which the Israelites were liberated from Egypt was that they did not change their language. At present, however, I have seen a great stumbling-block among the majority of the land, in the fact that, because of our many sins, numerous people do not behave rightly. It is established among us that a man ought to teach everything to his sons when they are small in Hebrew, so that the son shall be accustomed to speak the holy tongue in holiness. In recent times, however, there have been men who have allowed their little children to speak French or other languages. And when the son grows up, his father takes no care that he attend the house of study, but his chief concern is that he go to school to learn the languages of the gentiles. It is established among us that the Sanhedrin knew all the seventy languages, but they learned these languages only secondarily; the principal thing among them was to study the Torah. Now, however, Jews do precisely the opposite: the chief thing is to learn French and other languages of the gentiles, and only occasionally to occupy oneself with the study of Torah. For this they will suffer great punishment.[16]

Another book of ethical instruction which appeared shortly after Tzevi Hirsh Koidonover's work was no less popular among the masses than *Kav Ha-Yashar*. This book was entitled *Shevet Musar* and was composed not in Poland or Germany but in the distant birthplace of Shabbetai Tzevi, Smyrna. Its author, Elijah ben Abraham Ha-Kohen,[17] who was a rabbinic

16. *Ibid.*, Chapter 82. It is interesting that Koidonover's younger contemporary Rabbi Jacob Emden also complains that the wealthy Jews teach their children French. He finds that this study, especially when along with it the youngsters occupy themselves with music, leads to frivolity and obscenity.

17. He died in his old age in 1729.

judge and preacher in Smyrna, wrote many books (sermons, *novellae* to the Talmud, and the like) but acquired fame only with his *Shevet Musar*. Published in Constantinople in 1712, it soon became so popular throughout the Jewish world that, as early as 1726, it was printed in Vilna in Yiddish translation.[18] In this way it became accessible to the broadest strata of the people. The judge of Smyrna was by nature a great optimist; he believed with perfect faith that man is born to enjoy much happiness, for the Creator is, after all, a God full of mercy and of boundless grace. Hence, Elijah ben Abraham Ha-Kohen speaks with intense anger of the heretics and deniers who urge that man was created so that "vengeance might be taken on him."[19] God in His great compassion has fashioned man in His divine image, and it lies within man's choice "to strengthen himself through his deeds to arrive at a level higher than that of the angels."[20] Happy is the fate of man, for he has been given the capacity to sanctify and raise to the supreme levels everything around him, all the pleasures of the world. The best wines and foods, the most beautiful palaces, the splendid fields, the lovely song of birds—everything can be lifted by man to the supreme state of a praise and paean to God.[21]

In this spirit a unique debate is described by the author of *Shevet Musar* between man and the earth[22] and between the soul and the body—a debate which forcibly reminds one of the conversation Saint Francis carried on with his "brother ass," as he calls the sinful body. Man argues with the earth and charges that all troubles come from it. With its enormous cruelty it transforms the loveliest splendor into rottenness and ugliness. The best spices it turns into stench and loathesomeness; the most joyous, laughing colors it covers with filth and corruption. To this the earth replies calmly and quietly that she, the mother of all living things, was created by God holy

18. On the title-page of the Yiddish translation appears the following statement: "My beloved masters, men and women, inspect this beautiful work, for we have translated this worthy and important book into Yiddish. We hope that it will greatly please God and the world, for it leads man in God's way and adorns him for the world-to-come. You may well believe me that until now the world has never had a book such as *Shevet Musar*. So run and buy the pleasant book, and do not spare your money, for if you will read it, you will not regret it. Thereby we will merit having the Messiah lead us into the land of Israel. Amen. Selah" (we quote according to the Shklov edition of 1797).

19. *Shevet Musar*, Chapter 2.

20. *Ibid.*, Chapter 2, 7a. (We quote according to the Yiddish translation, Shklov, 1797).

21. *Ibid.*, Chapter 3.

22. *Ibid.*, Chapter 15.

and pure. It is man with his sinful life who has brought a curse
upon her. Men themselves, through their impure deeds, "destroy themselves and make themselves abhorrent." Man is responsible for all the evil in the world. "In short," the earth
concludes, "man with his own hand brings about life or death
for himself."[23] The sinfulness of man is great, but greater still
is God's grace, and as soon as man begins to repent, his sins are
forgotten. The tears of repentance wash them away. "Repentance has no end or limit," the author of *Shevet Musar* exclaims.[24]
The rabbinic judge of Smyrna becomes the inspired poet of
repentance. He himself composes prayers of penitence,[25] and
also introduces into this book prayers by Rabbenu Baḥya,
Jehudah Ḥasid, David Ibn Abi Zimra and others, to soften the
heart of the reader, to arouse in him the desire for repentance.

But the author is not content with this. After all, man's heart
is stubborn, and so he desires to subdue it with the same means
that the author of *Kav Ha-Yashar* so eagerly employed—the rod
of fear and terror. Not without reason did the *dayyan* of
Smyrna entitle his book *Shevet Musar* (The Rod of Instruction).
"In order that the reader may tremble and be afraid,"[26] "in
order to inflame and frighten hearts,"[27] as he puts it, Elijah ben
Abraham Ha-Kohen overwhelms men with the terror of punishment in hell and portrays in gruesome images the hell above
and the hell below and the horrible afflictions awaiting the
sinful man who has not repented. "Woe to him," threatens the
author, "who does not think of the sufferings that await him;
woe to him who does not remember that he is like a shadow
on the earth; woe to him who forgets the fearful image of the
angel of death; woe to him who does not remember the agony
of the torments of the grave; woe to him who does not think
of the day of judgment and the verdict of hell; woe to him who
does not remember the terrible deaths and the transmigrations
of the soul . . ."[28]

Elijah ben Abraham does not tire of describing in minutest
detail the dark chambers of hell with their sinful inhabitants.[29]
"Hell below," he relates,

23. The debate between man and the earth is to be found only in the Hebrew text.
    In the Yiddish translation there is no mention of it. We quote according to the
    Jerusalem edition of 1863, p. 39.
24. *Shevet Musar*, Chapter 19, 50a.
25. *Ibid.*, Chapters 7, 18, 21, 29, 31, etc.
26. *Ibid.*, 69a.
27. *Ibid.*, 68b.
28. *Ibid.*, Chapters 4, 8, 10.
29. *Ibid.*, Chapters 9, 26.

is large and wide and occupies tens of thousands of miles, and in it are individual compartments by the thousands, one more terrible than the other, and there all the wicked are punished, each according to his deeds. The fire wherewith the wicked are burned is sixty times stronger then the fire on earth . . . There are coals that are as large as mountains and valleys, and through hell flow rivers of pitch and sulphur springing out of the depths of the abyss. In it are all kinds of monstrous and ugly destroying spirits that inflict punishment on the wicked. And all these hosts of destroying spirits were, in fact, created by the sinful deeds of the wicked, as the sages of the Talmud declare: "He who violates one commandment has obtained for himself one accuser." Besides these destroying spirits there are thousands of others that were appointed to punish sinners after hell was fashioned. The sufferings and afflictions wherewith the wicked are punished are extremely diverse: some are strung up and the destroyers throttle them; some have their eyes gouged out; some are hanged by the neck—each according to the magnitude of his sin.[30]

The author of *Shevet Musar* introduces countless "credible and reliable stories" recounting the horrible punishments men have received for each individual transgression, how sinful souls roam around in "the world of confusion" and suffer the most fearful transmogrifications.

Let the wise man be terrified and the understanding man be frightened when he lifts his eyes toward the heavens and when he searches all four sides of the world, which are a journey of five hundred years distant from each other. Here the sinful soul will have to fly to and fro, from one end of the world to the other, just as a bird flies in the air and tries to ascend toward the heavens but cannot do so, for it is cast down from above and its wings are made heavy, to throw it to the earth. And when there is a soul whose sins bear heavily upon it, it will be hurled in a sling-shot, just as a stone is thrown from one end of the world to the other. From the depth of the earth it will be thrown up to the skies and then allowed to fall again.[31]

In total antithesis to all these sad images, the author then portrays in vivid colors the pleasures in heaven awaiting the righteous and those who have repented betimes.[32]

Like the author of *Kav Ha-Yashar*, so Elijah ben Abraham Ha-Kohen is extremely hostile toward secular knowledge. In the deepest chambers of hell he locks, along with the slander-

30. *Ibid.*, Chapter 26, folio 68a.
31. Yiddish translation, Shklov edition, 76a.
32. *Ibid.*, Chapter 26.

ers, "the heretics and deniers."[33] "The greatest fools are those who think they will become wise from external books," he declares.[34] "One who desires to study external wisdoms will have his ear closed, so that it will not hear," we further read.[35] "One who wishes to have good pupils should not allow them to read 'external books.' "[36] "One who desires to save many souls, let him not have mercy on heretics and deniers, for he who has mercy on a wicked man is cruel."[37] "He who wishes to write a scroll of the Torah should erase and burn heretical books."[38]

Another characteristic feature is worth noting. As great as the reverence of the author of *Shevet Musar* for the "holy Ari" (Rabbi Isaac Luria) was, he nevertheless manifested a definite coldness towards messianic mysticism. "He who desires to bring the redemption near should remove it from his mind, for it will come when least expected." This statement may give some support to Heinrich Graetz's conjecture that the author of *Shevet Musar* is the Elijah Ha-Kohen who composed the polemical tract *Sefer Merivat Kohen* directed against the Sabbatian, Abraham Cardozo.[39]

Just at that time the struggle against all who drew upon themselves the least suspicion that they were followers of Shabbetai Tzevi was especially strengthened. This was connected with the fact that among the mystics and *Ḥasidim*, with all their asceticism and frequent fasting and mortification of the flesh, an opposite tendency became ever more clearly noticeable, precisely under the influence of Shabbetai Tzevi's ideas: liberation from the rabbinic severities and prohibitions in the realm of ritual and ethics. And these two antithetical tendencies—the most rigorous asceticism and moral profligacy—were not infrequently braided together in one confused skein. Leading the previously mentioned *Ḥasidim* was, along with Jehudah Ḥasid, his collaborator, Ḥayyim Malach, who spent a long time among the Sabbatian circles in Salonika. This Malach (the word means "angel," but his opponents called him Satan) used to assert that just as Moses sojourned forty days in

33. *Ibid.*, folio 68.
34. *Ibid.*, Chapter 6, folio 14.
35. *Ibid.*, folio 22.
36. *Ibid.*
37. *Ibid.*
38. *Ibid.*
39. *Sefer Merivat Kohen* was written in 1707, and several supplements were added to it by a certain Yom Tov Romano Ibn Pakudah.

the heavens and then returned to earth, so Shabbetai Tzevi would come back forty years after his death and complete the redemption.[40] When Malach returned from Turkey to Poland he began, as a devoted follower of Shabbetai Tzevi's doctrine, energetically to promote the idea that, in order to become hallowed and completely subjugate the *kelipot* or shells, one must first go through the forty-nine gates of uncleanness, for evil is, after all, the source of good. The highest and truest levels of purity can only be attained by the soul that has descended into the depths of filth and tasted the poisonous liquid of black sin.

Thus in Poland—mainly in Galicia and Podolia, which were close to Turkey and the major center of the Sabbatian sect, Salonika—whole groups of sectarians began to form. The people soon crowned them with the epithet "Shabsay-Tzvinikes" or, more briefly "Shebsin." Pathological mystical fantasies, messianic hopes, and dark superstitions were interwoven among these sectarians with a vague protest against the heavy yoke of the *Shulḥan Aruch* and a half-elemental hunger for revival and liberation. In this stifling, unhealthy atmosphere, searching but crippled thought became powerlessly confused in a labyrinth of contradictions and lost any clear understanding of good and evil, of what is permitted and what forbidden. Naturally, one must be extremely cautious in considering the information provided by such bitter opponents of everything bearing the least hint of Sabbatian "heresy" as the fanatical Jacob Emden; nevertheless, it is beyond doubt that the mystical sectarians of Ḥayyim Malach's school would frequently allow themselves deeds contrary not only to the rabbinic codes but also to the principles of European ethics.

In 1713 one of the covert Sabbatian propagandists, the adventurer Nehemiah Ḥayon, agitated the entire rabbinic world with his composition *Oz Le-Elohim*, in which he spoke at length in mystical, allusive language of God's tri-unity. Soon a sharp conflict erupted in which the leaders of the two parties were the rabbis of both the Sephardic and Ashkenazic communities of Amsterdam, Solomon Ayllon and Tzevi Ashkenazi, the latter better known as Ḥacham Tzevi.

---

40. Rumors were even noised about that Ḥayyim Malach and his associates used to carry on symbolic rites of worship with dancing around a wooden image of Shabbetai Tzevi (Jacob Emden, *Torat Ha-Kenaot*, 57).

During the years 1713–1714 both sides issued a whole series of tracts, summons and proclamations[41] in which Ashkenazic, Sephardic, and Italian rabbis participated. It became apparent that Nehemiah Ḥayon had numerous followers spread over different lands. The rabbis perceived a threat to Judaism in the "heretical" ideas disseminated by the covert "Shabsay-Tzevi-nikes" and determined to take the severest measures. In the summer of 1722 a conference of rabbis, delegated from various communities, took place in Lemberg, and there, with sounds of rams' horns and snuffed-out black candles, all the followers of Shabbetai Tzevi's doctrine who would not, by a specific time, declare that they recanted and were returning in penitence with a perfect heart were excommunicated. These harsh measures, however, had slight success, and three years later the rabbis considered it necessary once again to issue forth against the "Shebsin" with the ancient weapon of the ban. The persecutions, however, could not destroy the "malignant leprosy," the sectarian groups with their "blasphemous" ideas.

In that restless time one of the loveliest but also most tragic personalities of Jewry in the eighteenth century, the poet and mystic Moses Ḥayyim Luzzatto, appeared on the scene.

41. Part of this polemic literature is published in Jacob Emden's *Torat Ha-Kenaot*, and also in the collection *Inyenei Shabbetai Tzevi*, 117–138.

CHAPTER THREE

Moses Ḥayyim Luzzatto

Moses Ḥayyim Luzzatto as poet and mystic—His poem *Yam Ve-Yabeshet*—His new poetic forms—His biblical drama *Maaseh Shimshon* and dramatic idyll *Migdal Oz*—The poets Samson Modon and Abraham ben Shabbetai of Zante—Luzzatto as mystic—His messianic-mystical works—Luzzatto under the ban—His later literary work—The significance of his allegorical drama *La-Yesharim Tehillah*—The poet's unexpected death.

 HE GREATEST misfortune for a gifted poet is to be born in a twilight era of decline, to breathe throughout his life the suffocating atmosphere of a hazy environment veiled in shadows. And the more colorful and vivid the poet's gift, the more tragic his fate. It was under the burden of such a bitter fate that the poet Moses Ḥayyim Luzzatto lived and worked.

Luzzatto's childhood passed happily and brightly. Born in 1707 into a wealthy merchant family in Padua, he received the most careful education. His teachers were the well-known Talmudist, Isaiah Bassani, and the highly cultured rabbi of Padua, Isaac Ḥayyim Kohen de Cantarini, who was renowned as a skillful physician. Besides the Bible, Talmud, and rabbinic literature, the young Luzzatto also diligently studied natural sciences and several European languages—of the ancient ones, Greek and Latin, and of the modern, Italian and French. At the age of sixteen he was already extremely well versed in the Talmud, and in the codes and laws of what is permitted and forbidden in the matter of food and related topics he had no less knowledge then the most eminent rabbis of that time. But the arid Talmudic material did not satisfy the young Luzzatto. He was attracted to another world—the magical world of poetry and literary creation.

Luzzatto displayed his bent for poetry when still quite young. In the elegy[1] in which the fifteen-year-old poet mourns the death of his teacher Isaac Kohen Cantarini signs of his significant literary gifts are already quite clearly discernible. In this youthful poem Luzzatto shows himself a master of poetic forms, one who understands the art of forging tender sentiments into supple, resonant verses.

How fully the young Luzzatto had already mastered the language of the Bible at that time is best demonstrated by his philological work *Leshon Limmudim*, composed at the age of seventeen in 1724. In clear and elegant fashion the young author tells the reader how the modern theoretical-scientific study of the poetic art developed on the foundations of ancient Roman rhetoric. The principles of European style and sentence construction are illustrated with numerous quotations from the Bible. Luzzatto shows in this connection a remarkable feeling for the unique qualities of the Hebrew language, which had long since died on the lips of the people but had nevertheless not ceased to be the major vehicle of the living national culture. For the Hebrew reader of that era it was literally a revelation when the seventeen-year-old author endeavored to explain that language develops not according to the principles of grammar but, on the contrary, that grammar is first constructed in consonance with the forms that the living language assumes in its natural growth and development. When we see that this feeling is lacking among the Hebrew grammarians, this is because they have lost a sense of the Biblical tongue as a living language.[2] That the poet himself genuinely experienced the vital source of Hebrew is magnificently shown in a lovely poem which he composed at that time. At first glance, this poem

1. Published in *Otzar Ha-Safrut*, IV, 158–163.
2. *Leshon Limmudim*, 21 (we quote according to the first Mantua edition, 1727).

appears to be a simple "occasional song"; it is a wedding poem that the poet sent as a gift to a friend of his. Epithalamia were, in that era, quite fashionable among the Italian Jews. In this respect they imitated their Christian neighbors, among whom a special wedding literature, called *nozze*, was produced. "At that time," Mordecai Ghirondi of Padua relates,[3] "everyone who could write verses at all used to compose wedding songs in honor of his friends."[4] Almost every intelligent young man was something of a connoisseur of poetry. Even in guides for letter-writing one could find not only models of elegant style but also principles and instructions on how to write poems.[5] Against this flood of songs, this plague of poetry-writing without a spark of talent, Luzzatto's contemporary, the gifted poet Samson Kohen Modon, poured out his wrath in his sonnet "El Har Zemirot,"[6] in which he portrays with caustic irony how all kinds of talentless nonentities attempt to climb the mountain of song (Parnassus). They merely trample all restraints and besmirch the living spring of poetry. "Those who do not understand how to speak a word nevertheless attempt to sing songs. How wise it would be for them to be silent."

The level of technical proficiency in the construction of verses attained at that time in Italy in Jewish intellectual circles is best attested by the literary activity of Luzzatto's and Modon's contemporary, the physician Abraham ben Shabbetai Kohen of Zante. The good doctor had a great weakness for writing poetry. He reworked the entire Book of Psalms into verse, as well as the medieval liturgical poem, *Perek Shirah*,[7] in which all the birds and beasts become envious of the "sweet singer of Israel" and, in the style of the Psalms, sing a hymn of praise to the Creator. Abraham published this paraphrase in Venice in 1710 under the title *Kehunat Avraham*.[8] Before the text a whole series of eulogies by the author's friends is printed. In stilted octaves and sonnets, all these friends marvel at the great achievements and poetic merits of the author. For his part, Abraham, to show what sort of fellow he was at poetry-writing, replied to each song of praise with a poem written in the

---

3. *Toledot Gedolei Yisrael*, 18.
4. See also Paperna's *Kol Ugav*, 79.
5. See, for instance, the guide for letter-writing entitled *Megillat Sefer*, printed in Cremona, 1566.
6. Published in Modon's collection of sonnets, *Kol Musar* (Mantua, 1725). This collection was reprinted in 1845, but is nevertheless a bibliographical rarity.
7. Mendele Mocher Seforim reworked *Perek Shirah* into verses in Yiddish.
8. The last part of *Kehunat Avraham* appeared in print only at the end of 1725.

same verse-construction and with the same rhymes as the song itself. *Kehunat Avraham* takes up several hundred pages, but the reader will not find in this sea of facile verses a single one in which not merely a skillful hand but genuine poetic sentiment is discernible.

Just when the last pages of *Kehunat Avraham* came off the press, the young Luzzatto presented to his friend Isaac Marini, on the day of his marriage to the beautiful Judith Italia, his epithalamion *Yam Ve-Yabeshet.*[9] Under the magic of splendid poetic talent, a simple wedding gift is transformed into a magnificent poem that occupies a prominent place in the history of the development of poetic forms in Hebrew literature. Luzzatto skillfully utilizes the play on words inherent in the name of the bridal pair (Marini signifies the sea, and Italia, the land or firmament). He portrays in his poem the mighty struggle between the two elements. Ardent passion, however, makes peace between them, and they are united in sweet embraces. Everything is new and unusual in this wedding song. It is the first poetic work in Hebrew literature in which the exclusive influence of ancient, classical literature and of the Italian Renaissance is clearly noticeable. To be sure, the brothers Frances,[10] especially the younger, not infrequently utilized Italian poetic forms. Immanuel Frances wrote not only tercets and sonnets but also sestets, octaves, and canzoni.[11] He employed Greek mythology, quoted Virgil,[12] and introduced entire verses of Torquato Tasso and other Italian poets.[13] Nevertheless, in all his work, in the images he employed, even in the meter and rhyme of the verses, the exclusive influence of the medieval Hebrew poets of the Spanish-Arabic period is felt. Only the young Luzzatto had the courage to rebel against the ancient, established style. He refused to follow the trodden paths of the famous Andalusian poets; he rejected their poetic forms with their oppressive burden of Arabic meter. The youthful stormer also declined to acknowledge the unconditional rule of rhyme. Like a spring freshet from the mountain tops, the clear, unrhymed verse flows free and unhindered in *Yam Ve-Yabeshet.* Luzzatto is not fond of mosaic art; he rejects

9. First published in *He-Ḥalutz*, II, 106–116; separately printed in 1873.
10. See the previous volume, 168ff.
11. See *Metek Sefataim*, 13, 48, 52, 54, etc.
12. *Ibid.*, 11.
13. *Ibid.*, 17.

the popular *musiv*[14] style, for he is not content with the lifeless treasures that have come down through inheritance. For him the language of the Bible is a living, bubbling spring from which he draws generously. The poet of *Yam Ve-Yabeshet* considers the Biblical word not a congealed stream of lava but a supple, plastic material out of which he can create ever new forms.

At the time the young seventeen-year-old poet composed his *Yam Va-Yabeshet* he also made a courageous attempt to produce a historical drama. When he wrote his *Leshon Limmudim,* in which he familiarizes the reader with the various poetic forms, Luzzatto could not provide any example whatever of a modern Hebrew drama. He then decided to fill this vacant corner in the temple of Hebrew poetry himself and produced his three-act Biblical drama, *Maaseh Shimshon.*[15] Here also the poet sought novel, purely European forms and created his own style. Luzzatto remained faithful to the Biblical theme but also wove into his dramatic work the allegorical elements that were so popular on the Italian stage. Allegorical personalities—the gods of Love (*Amor*), Duplicity, Avarice—figure in *Maaseh Shimshon* together with Biblical personages. The drama is written in free verse but every scene ends, as in Shakespeare's plays, with a rhymed stanza. The immaturity of the author is still discernible in the construction of the drama as well as in the characterization; nevertheless, in this youthful work the master hand of a brilliant poet is already felt. Especially remarkable in this work is the language, rich in forms and imagery. It is very close to Biblical, yet original and unique. In the young Luzzatto not the least hint of blind subjection to the "canon," the Biblical word—as we observe this in the later era of the Meassefim—is noticeable. With him it is only the verbal construction material that is Biblical, but the structure of the sentences, the plastic images, and the musical rhythm of the verse are all modern European.

The "Psalm" book composed by Luzzatto shortly after *Maaseh Shimshon* (in 1726) alone is written completely in the spirit and style of the Bible. Here the poet remained faithful to his Biblical model, even in regard to the number of chapters. In

14. For a discussion of the *musiv* style, see Volume I, pp. 173–176.
15. Until relatively recent times Luzzatto's youthful drama was known only through the fragments that Joseph Almanzi published in his work on Luzzatto. *Maaseh Shimshon* was published in full by S. Ginsburg in 1927 in Tel Aviv.

places he manages to approximate the marvelous beauty of the original. Nevertheless, this work remains nothing more than an imitation and does not reach the level of original, independent creation.

A year later Luzzatto returned to the drama-form and wrote the idyllic play in four acts entitled *Midgal Oz* or *Tummat Yesharim*.[16] Here it is no longer the ancient Biblical forms that serve the poet as a model but the Italian pastoral dramas, with their classical prototype, Guarini's famous *Pastor Fido*.

The plot of *Migdal Oz* is not especially interesting. It relates how on top of a mountain a tremendously strong tower with a lovely garden on its roof had been standing from ancient times. No mortal could ever penetrate it, for its walls were smooth and firm, without gates and doors. The king proclaimed throughout the land that to the man who would manage to enter the tower and ascend to the garden he would give his lovely daughter, Shelomit, in marriage. Once upon a time a prince from a foreign land named Shalom rode by, saw the marvelous and mysterious tower, inspected it from all sides, and decided to enter it. For a long time he wandered around it seeking a way into the inner chambers until he found a cave hidden under stones overgrown with grass which led into the tower. There he noticed a door, climbed up to the garden, and then went on his way; the king's proclamation was unknown to him. After this, the narrative becomes extremely confused. A base liar, Zifa, passes by the tower, sees the open door, and rushes at once to the king to declare that he has succeeded in discovering the hidden entrance. In this way Zifa becomes Shelomit's bridegroom. It soon happens that Shalom meets Shelomit, and they fall in love. Barring the road to their happiness, however, are Zifa and the scheming woman Ada. The pair of lovers have to endure much, but all ends well. It is finally revealed that it was not Zifa but Shalom who discovered the entrance to the tower. The virtuous are rewarded and the sinners punished.

Migdal Oz, however, is not really a dramatic work but a paean to love. Since the saucy and life-loving Muse of Immanuel of Rome had been silenced and the poems of Saadiah Danan had ceased to resound, songs of earthly love had no longer been heard in Hebrew literature. It is, indeed, indicated (*Metek Sefatayim*, 86) that Immanuel Frances in his youth wrote erotic

---

16. This work was also designated by the poet as a wedding poem. It was first published in 1837.

poems, but shortly thereafter became a penitent, publicly confessed his "youthful sin" (see his tercet poems in *Metek Sefatayim*, 81–85), and with no less forcefulness than the creators of the *Shulḥan Aruch* attacked Immanuel of Rome for the fact that the latter "had corrupted his way on earth with profligate songs to which it is forbidden to listen." Now, after a hiatus of generations, the free, joyous chords of love were heard once more on the Hebrew Parnassus. Poems that breathe the stormy passion of the southern sun and earth sounded again. In his work Luzzatto portrays love in the most varied nuances and degrees. The modest, bashful love between the noble Shalom and the enchanting Shelomit is interwoven with the frivolous romance of the maidservant Ayah and the boastful Zifa and with the avid desire of the magician Eri and the criminal Ada. For each kind of love the youthful poet finds appropriate images and suitable colors. With great skill he renders in vivid verses the finest nuances of the intimate feelings that tremble in young, loving hearts.

This work of the twenty-year-old poet clearly bears the imprint of an extremely significant, even if not fully mature, talent. But this talent was not destined to spread its eagle's pinions to their full span and power. The melancholy twilight era, with its leaden shadows, ruthlessly bore down on the young, tender, poetic Muse, and its wings could not endure the pressure.

In *Migdal Oz* a very characteristic passage calls attention to itself. At the end of the preface the poet notes that the story of the tower with the concealed entrance is not simply a story.[17] It is an allusion to the well-known parable of the *Zohar*[18] in which the Torah is likened to a dazzling beauty, a lovely princess who sits in a hidden tower and reveals herself in her enchanting form only to her beloved and friend; other persons, however, see before them merely a locked-up tower. In the earthly love of Shalom and Shelomit the poet perceives only a garment of mystical love. In Shalom Luzzatto portrays himself, the man who wishes to penetrate the mysterious tower where the mystical princess is concealed.

After the tempestuous movement which the messiah of Smyrna called forth, the Jewish community became frozen, as it were, in its icy despair. But messianic hopes did not die out in grieved hearts. It was hard to surrender the only available

17. It is characteristic that the tower in *Migdal Oz* bears the mystical name *Ayin*.
18. *Zohar* (Sulzbach edition), II, pp. 162–163.

consolation, and dreaming mystics and fervent ascetics who proclaimed the approaching redemption came forward one after another. After Mordecai Eisenstadt came Abraham Cardozo, Jehudah Ḥasid, Ḥayyim Malach, and many others. But the despairing people no longer followed them. Its powers were broken; it lacked the drive, the ardent feeling, to incorporate its hope, its consolation, in active deeds. Now it could only dream of messianic-mystical redemption, dream with pathological stubbornness. It was a dream while waking, a dream of despair, an opium dream, indulged in order to forget oneself, to become intoxicated and not sense the black terror lurking on all sides. We have already noted the tortuous, labyrinthine byways in which frightened Jewish thought became lost. The orthodox rabbinic world which in that era was entirely frozen within the four cubits of petrified formalism could not, given its intellectual decline, struggle successfully against messianic mysticism.

In just this orphaned generation saturated with mystical dreams appeared a young poet with a highly impressionable soul which, like King David's harp, echoed with the most marvelous tones at every touch of the external world. The magic of the mystical world locked up in the *ḥochmat ha-nistar* (esoteric wisdom) attracted Luzzatto when he was still quite young. According to the report of one of his most devoted disciples, at the age of fourteen the poet was already diligently studying the writings of Rabbi Isaac Luria.[19] The Kabbalist doctrine about the universal, cosmic role of man and his will enchanted him. He greeted with great enthusiasm the idea expressed in the *Zohar* that without man's act of will, without his deed, the divine influence cannot prevail, and that toward the streams of divine radiance which flow from above over all the breadth of the world rays of light rising from below ascend. A tremendous impression was made on him by the poetic simile in the *Zohar* which declares that the earthly world is connected with the upper worlds like the keys of a musical instrument with the strings: if the hand touches the keys, the whole instrument responds with brightly sounding chords. Luzzatto's entire poetic nature was permeated with the mystical consciousness that every step in life, every act of will disclosed in man's deeds, is strongly associated with the celestial powers and hallowed

---

19. See Yekutiel Gordon's letter in Jacob Emden's *Torat Ha-Kenaot*, 91: "When he was fourteen years old, he knew all the writings of Rabbi Isaac Luria by heart."

through their approval. He was convinced that no one had ever penetrated so deeply into the profound mystery of the divine, living spirit that is revealed in all the entities of the world as the men of the "esoteric wisdom," the sages of the Kabbalah.

An exalted poet who conceived everything in vivid images, Luzzatto soon lost the boundary between what is imagined and what really exists. On the contrary, the mystical and the hidden became in his dreaming eyes the truly real and firmly assured. The twenty-year-old Luzzatto felt in himself immense powers but did not grasp their significance. He did not understand that he was indebted for these to his great poetic talent and, instead, sought their origin in the mysterious magic of the "esoteric wisdom." He was visited by the Muses and believed that those who came to him were exalted saints, the prophet Elijah and Rabbi Simeon ben Yoḥai, who wished to reveal to him the mysteries of the "work of creation" and announce the "end," the day of redemption, for the cup of suffering was already filled to overflowing. The darling of the Muses, Luzzatto was persuaded that he was constantly accompanied by a heavenly messenger, that he heard the voice of a *maggid* (proclaimer). A man of poetic revelation and with the penetrating vision of the genuine artist, he believed that he had attained the level of *gilui einayim* (uncovering of the eyes) as a result of his ascetic life and his fathoming of the mysteries of the Kabbalah. He sensed that he was blessed with the great gift of ruling the spirits and hearts of men, but he believed that this power drew sustenance not from the spring of poetry but from Rabbi Isaac Luria's incantations and combinations of letters. A poet by the grace of God, he thought he was a heavenly messenger who had come down to the sinful world to purify and exalt it and to save the exiled people from homelessness and enslavement. In his tender, noble soul arose a dramatic struggle, filled with tragic, mystical beauty.

With remarkable impetuosity Luzzatto wrote one Kabbalist work after another, now in the mysterious and obscure style of the *Zohar*,[20] now in the beautiful image-language of the Bible. In the course of four years he composed forty works[21] and was firmly persuaded that all were written through the holy spirit; the celestial messenger, the *malach maggid* (mentor

---

20. Luzzatto wrote a *Zohar Tinyana*. He also wrote a large commentary to the Book of Ecclesiastes in the language of the *Zohar*.
21. See the letter of the rabbis of Venice to Moses Hagiz (*Torat Ha-Kenaot*, 109).

angel) dictated them to him, and he wrote them down word for word.[22] "Elijah the prophet," Luzzatto relates in his *Zohar Tinyana*, "appeared to me, opened his lips, and said: 'My teacher, my master! Blessed is your fate, for all the heavenly secrets are disclosed to you, nothing is hidden, and all the mysterious gates stand open before you.' "[23] For the time being Luzzatto kept his great mission secret, speaking of it only in the restricted circle of his comrades and familiarizing them with his mystical works. But the secret was soon disclosed. In the small circle of Luzzatto's ardent followers was Yekutiel ben Leib Gordon of Vilna,[24] who had come to Padua to study medicine. The young Luzzatto made an enormous impression on Gordon, who promptly wrote (1729) to two rabbis whom he knew—the Kabbalist Mordecai Jaffe of Vienna and Joshua Höschel of Vilna—and announced to them in emotional, exalted fashion the joyous tidings of the glorious new star who had appeared over the tents of Jacob.[25] Mordecai Jaffe deemed it necessary immediately to send copies of Gordon's letters to the rabbis with whom he was acquainted in Germany.[26] They, on their part, also endeavored to spread as widely as possible the happy news of the "glorious new star."

One of these copies was received by the rabbi of Altona, Moses Hagiz, who was renowned as a bitter opponent of the Shabbetai Tzevi movement and in 1714 had taken a very active part in the controversy over the Sabbatian propagandist Nehemiah Ḥayon.[27] The fanatical battler against sectarian "heresy" at once suspected a new messianic pretender in the young mystic of whom Gordon wrote so emotively. He therefore decided to take the harshest measures and, to this end, addressed a summons to the rabbis of Venice, who occupied the foremost place in Italy, that they see to it as quickly as possible "to tear out by the roots the noxious plague [Luzzatto and his

---

22. Luzzatto himself declared to the rabbis: "The compositions . . . that I wrote in the language of the holy *Zohar* . . . I wrote them, in my view, through a *maggid* and holy souls." His ardent disciple Yekutiel Gordon writes: "And it is now two and a half years since a holy and fearful mentor-angel *(malach maggid)* revealed himself to him and disclosed mysteries to him. And he commanded him, with the approval of the Holy One Blessed Be He and His *Schechinah*, to compose the book of the *Zohar* that was called by heaven *Zohar Tinyana.*"

23. *Torat Ha-Kenaot*, 92–93.

24. For a discussion of him, see D. Kaufmann, in *REJ*, XXIII, 256.

25. Both letters are published in *Torat Ha-Kenaot*, 91–92.

26. See *Luḥot Edut*, 15a.

27. Moses Hagiz' father Jacob was one of the rabbis who excommunicated Shabbetai Tzevi.

followers] before it spread over the whole body of the people."

The Venetian rabbis, however, were in no haste to adopt strong measures against Moses Ḥayyim Luzzatto, not only because the young mystic was already at that time famous throughout Italy but mainly because they did not wish to quarrel with the wealthy Luzzatto family which occupied the most honored of places in the community of Padua. But the fanatical Hagiz refused to rest. He was not even satisfied by the heartfelt letter Luzzatto sent him, in which the young mystic attempted to persuade him that he was free of all Sabbatian "heresy."[28] After Hagiz became convinced that the rabbis of Venice were unresponsive to his summons, he turned to the rabbis of Germany with the proposal that they place Luzzatto under the ban unless he at once promised that he would no longer devote himself to the Kabbalah, either alone or in company with others. Here Luzzatto's old teacher Isaiah Bassani intervened, and with his aid they managed to prevail on the quiet, submissive poet to issue (in 1730) a written undertaking in which he vowed with the strongest oath that as long as he lived outside Palestine he would not occupy himself with the practical Kabbalah or transmit to others any mysteries whatever in the name of a *maggid* or other "holy souls."[29] However, he explicitly stipulated that he might write compositions in Hebrew (but not in the language of the *Zohar*) under his *own* name.

For a time the controversy was stilled. It appears that a profound crisis occurred in Luzzatto's life. From dreams and fantastic visions he turned again to real, everyday life. In 1732 he married and even began to devote himself to business. The daily prose of life, however, could not long attract the poet's restless soul. Poets in general are rarely successful in business, and Moses Ḥayyim Luzzatto was no exception. His business affairs went badly, and in a short time he lost his entire fortune. At that time success also abandoned his father, and from being extremely wealthy he became a poor man. The poet, who had grown up in affluence and comfort, now found himself and his family in material distress and suffered greatly from worry about the wherewithal to live. Then the dreamer again awakened in him. From the pretty concerns of every day he sought

28. Luzzatto's letter is published in *Torat Ha-Kenaot*, 93–94.
29. The text of this document is falsified in several places in Jacob Emden's *Torat Ha-Kenaot*. The correct text, according to Luzzatto's own handwritten manuscript, which is located in the library of Jerusalem, is published in *Kiryat Sefer*, VIII, 199.

refuge in the imaginative world of hopes and dreams. He again felt himself surrounded by holy spirits, and the heavenly *maggid* disclosed to him the most marvelous secrets in the obscure language of the *Zohar*. But Luzzatto remembered his written undertaking not to put such secrets down on paper nor relate them to his disciples. Hence, he wrote only apologetic works in which he very enthusiastically defended the "esoteric wisdom." In Venice he had the opportunity to become acquainted with the manuscript of Leo de Modena's *Ari Nohem*. The bitter attacks on the *Zohar* of the extreme rationalist enraged Luzzatto, and he issued forth against de Modena's critique with a polemical work, *Maamar Ha-Vikkuaḥ*. Immediately after this work, he wrote his *Ḥoker U-Mekubbal* which follows the pattern of Joseph Ergas' *Shomer Emunim*,[30] written in the form of a dialogue between a freethinking "seeker" and a Kabbalist. The Kabbalist (it is the author himself who speaks in his name) endeavors to show that not rationalist philosophy but the Kabbalah alone can provide a definitive solution to the most important problems. Only the "true wisdom," Luzzatto asserts, can resolve the great enigma of the world: the fact that the will of the First Cause, which is incomprehensible to man's understanding, is potentially infinite and unbounded but in actuality, in the process of creation, manifests itself in the limited forms of *sefirot* and attributes accessible to man's perception.[31]

In this work, as well as in a whole series of shorter works written immediately after it,[32] Luzzatto appears in a new role —as a master of expository style who understands the secret of rendering the most complicated theosophical-philosophical issues in clear and sharp fashion. The enthusiastic mystic who dreamed and saw visions while waking was endowed with the talent of an outstanding systematizer and popularizer. This is only one of the many and, at first glance, inexplicable contradictions in the inner, spiritual life of this remarkable man. With exemplary clarity appears in these works of Luzzatto's the basic idea of the *Zohar* about the cosmic, universal role of man, the idea that only through man's active deeds is the divine nature disclosed in its fullness. The poet with his mystical

---

30. *Shomer Emunim* was first published in 1736, after the author's death. Apparently, however, Luzzatto became familiar with this work while it was still in manuscript.
31. *Ḥoker U-Mekubbal*, 8–12, 44–55 (according to the Leipzig edition, 1840).
32. *Derech Hochmah, Ma'amar Ha-Ikkarim, Kinat Adonai Tzevaot* (against the Shabbetai Tzevi movement) printed in 1863.

world outlook feels intensely that the fate of the universe, the key to the entire cosmos, is located in the depths of man's soul, for the absolute, harmonious integrity of the world consists in the fact that the general, regulative law of the world is simultaneously the *human* law, the revelation of man's spirit, of his moral consciousness. The conduct of man, his fulfillment of the commandments of the divine Torah—this, in Luzzatto's view, is a moral act of cosmic significance. The supreme pattern of life, the prototype of the whole universe, is the image of man and his striving toward God. The world can be illuminated with the divine light only in the merit of the enlightened man who bears in his heart the universal, divine righteousness.

During these years Luzzatto lived in Mantua with his father-in-law and from there carried on a very intensive correspondence with his friends in Ferrara, always admonishing them to devote themselves as much as possible to the "esoteric wisdom." But the author was under the secret surveillance of the local rabbis who followed his every step with suspicion. The rabbis of Venice, who regarded the mystically-minded poet favorably as long as he and his family were rich and prominent in the community, all at once changed their tactics now that he lived in poverty. They surrounded him with spies of the lowest kind. These followed his every step, rummaged through his effects, and searched his writings. On the basis of the material which the spies collected for them, the rabbis of Venice dispatched emissaries to Luzzatto with the strict demand that he show all his writings and again promise that he would not publish anything without the permission of the Venetian rabbinate. In this connection the following is interesting: the rabbis accuse Luzzatto not only of occupying himself with "sorcery and incantations"; he is also reproached for the sin of being overly familiar with Latin and classical literature.[33] The sensitive poet was deeply grieved by the whole network of petty intrigue and ugly espionage with which the rabbis of Venice surrounded him and therefore indignantly rejected their demands. In response, the rabbis decided (December 3, 1734) to place the stubborn Luzzatto under the ban of excommunication and burn all his writings. The verdict of excommunication was read aloud the same day with great ceremony

33. The rabbis note in their summons. "How shall one who has already wedded himself to Latin be wedded with the holy tongue and with the language of the sacred *Zohar?*"

in all the synagogues of Venice, and the text was circulated to all the prominent rabbis in Germany, Holland, and Poland. The persecuted poet had no alternative but to take the wanderer's staff in hand and leave his home. But even in his roaming through foreign countries Luzzatto had no rest from the Venetian rabbis. As soon as he arrived in Frankfurt-am-Main the local rabbis received the news that Moses Ḥayyim Luzzatto of the city of Padua, "who desires to destroy and tear down all the boundaries and fences of our Torah,"[34] was coming there. The rabbis of Frankfurt received Luzzatto with great anger. They took away from him the manuscript of his *Ḥoker U-Mekubbal* and extracted from him a written promise that from now on, under fear of the great ban and excommunication, he undertakes that he will no longer study the Kabbalah with anyone in the world either orally or from any book whatsoever —not even from the writings of Rabbi Isaac Luria and the *Zohar.* Luzzatto obtained only one concession, namely, that if he would be privileged to attain the age of forty, he would then have permission to study Isaac Luria's Kabbalah with persons of the same age.[35]

The sore trials which the persecuted, homeless poet had to endure came to an end only when he left Germany and arrived in Amsterdam, where the Sephardic community welcomed him with great honor. In order not to have to receive aid from anyone he, like Spinoza in his day, supported himself by polishing optical lenses.[36] Because of his thorough knowledge of physics and mathematics, Luzzatto obtained a high degree of perfection in the technique of his work and derived an ample living from it. According to some sources,[37] he also gave lectures for intellectually curious young people on rhetoric and natural sciences. After the stormy years of struggle and exile, the poet now enjoyed days of rest and contentment. He kept in epistolary contact with his Italian friends and disciples, and in the letters he wrote the childlike purity and tender modesty of his poetic soul is reflected in remarkable fashion.

In 1740 Luzzatto published his *Mesillat Yesharim,* one of the finest books of moral instruction in Hebrew literature. To be sure, the mystic and poet summons men to repentance, soli-

34. *Torat Ha-Kenaot,* 109–111, 114.
35. *Ibid.,* 115–116.
36. According to other sources (e.g., *Torat Ha-Kenaot,* 116) Luzzatto engaged in polishing precious stones.
37. See *Kerem Ḥemed,* VI, 1, 4.

tude, and a rigorously ascetic life, but the wrathful tone of the authors of *Reshit Ḥochmah, Kav Ha-Yashar* and *Shevet Musar*, who sought to cast fear on the reader, to drive him with the lash of terror and punishment on the way of piety and fear of God, is alien to Luzzatto. An intimate, tender, loving beauty permeates the pages of this work written in Luzzatto's masterfully polished style. "We are orphans of an orphaned generation," he laments,[38] and not with fear and indignation but with quiet, musically tender words does he teach the "orphans of orphans" and show them the way leading to true, self-sacrificial love for the Creator of the universe. Hence, it is quite understandable that *Mesillat Yesharim* was so beloved among the people. It is related that Elijah, the Gaon of Vilna, when he read this book, exclaimed: "If Moses Ḥayyim Luzzatto were alive today, I would go to him on foot to learn morality and true piety from him."[39]

In this solitary ascetic, who preached that the terrestrial world is merely a preliminary to "the world of truth" (the next world), the inspired poet who avidly perceives the marvelous wealth of colors of the world about him with his keen eye and forges what he has observed into clear, plastic images did not die. Three years after the appearance of *Mesillat Yesharim* Luzzatto published his allegorical drama *La-Yesharim Tehillah,* which is quite justly considered the cornerstone of neo-Hebrew poetry. Only when one compares this work with Luzzatto's earlier drama *Migdal Oz,* does it become apparent how much Luzzatto lived through in the intervening years. We see before us no longer the romantic poet who celebrates love in fervent songs, but the greatly tried and experienced man who has carefully reflected on the life about him and closely observed its pettiness and baseness. Luzzatto makes use of the old-fashioned form so popular in medieval drama in which, instead of living people, personified human qualities appear. But the magic of the true poet is great; even common abstractions are transformed by him into colorful symbols and obtain flesh and blood. The poet declares immediately at the outset that he has didactic purposes in mind. The personified *Mashal* (Parable or Allegory) appears in the prologue and announces that he, wisdom's constant and most faithful servant, will speak to the people and sow in human hearts the seeds of morality and knowledge. On the stage appear the son of *Emet*

38. *Mesillat Yesharim*, 46 (first edition, 1740).
39. *Nezir Elohim*, 34.

(Truth), who is named *Yosher* (Righteousness) and his friend *Sechel* (Reason), *Hamon* (Populace), Hamon's daughter *Tehillah* (Fame or Glory) and his servant *Sichlut* (Ignorance), *Rahav* (Foolish Pride) the son of *Taavah* (Lust) who was raised in the house of *Dimyon* (Imagination), *Rahav's* friend and counsellor *Tarmit* (Falsehood), *Yosher's* nurse *Savlanut* (Patience), *Mehkar* (Research or Contemplation), and King *Mishpat* (Justice or Judgment).

With an ironic smile the poet who has suffered greatly portrays the frivolousness of *Hamon* who allows himself to be led astray so easily by such trifles as *Rahav*, aided by *Sichlut and Tarmit*, and how difficult it is to persuade *Hamon* to follow the instructions of *Yosher* and his companion *Sechel*. A catastrophe must occur, marvelous signs must appear from heaven, before *Hamon* comes to his senses and realizes how grievously he has been misled. It is not surprising, given the lack of understanding of *Hamon*, that *Tehillah* is not obtained by him who has rightfully deserved her and that much injustice and barbaric cruelty take place before *Yosher* and *Sechel* finally becomes the guides of *Hamon* and succeed in overcoming *Tarmit* and the puffed-up vanity of *Rahav*.

With tender sorrow the persecuted poet portrays the contempt with which *Hamon's* servant, *Sichlut*, mocks the bearers of knowledge and culture, and in the name of *Yosher* he pours out, in splendid lyrical verses, his ardent desire to remove himself from the petty tumult of the marketplace and to find rest in the bosom of kingly beautiful and exaltedly powerful nature. But Luzzatto is very far from pessimism; despite his sad experiences, he firmly believes in the ultimate victory of *Sechel* and *Yosher*. "If we could at least once consider the world in its true form," *Yosher* exclaims (Act II, Scene I), "we would realize that our criminal opponents are so miserable and cast down that it is difficult to think of any greater revenge. Only to the superficial glance does it seem that they are 'filled with good and sated with pleasure;' in reality they are caught in a close net from which they cannot liberate themselves."

The language of *La-Yesharim Tehillah* attains genuinely classic perfection. One has the impression that here the masterful style of Proverbs and the Songs of Songs has been blended with the rhythm and symmetrical beauty of the Latin sentence in one harmonious mold. Even the present-day reader is transported by *Mehkar's* polished verses in which are portrayed in such lovely poetic imagery the life of plants, their blooming and growth, and, along with this, the feeling of supreme enchantment that *Meḥkar* experiences when he considers and determines the laws governing nature.

We completely forget that we have before us an ascetic mystic, not a thinker of ancient Greece who strolls with philosophical generosity over the blooming fields of the royally sedate Epicurus. Immediately after *Meḥkar*'s monologue young *Tehillah* appears with her prayer which, in its lyrical pathos and tenderness, attains the classic beauty of the best of the Biblical psalms.

But the fervent mystic did not die in the calm, quiet, philosophically reflective poet. *Meḥkar*'s wise words could not drive away the magic with which the "true wisdom" dominated the author of *La-Yesharim Tehillah*. As in his youth, so now the poet remained its faithful servant and admirer. Now, too, his faith was strong that in the Kabbalah is hidden the marvelous power with whose aid he, the chosen messenger of God, is destined to redeem the world and put an end to the endless sufferings of the homeless, exiled people. All the Kabbalists were convinced that only on the holy soil of Palestine can one penetrate into all the mysteries of Kabbalah; only there can the holy spirit disclose itself and the miraculous signs of the advent of the Messiah appear. For Moses Ḥayyim Luzzatto also this was an assured truth. His loveliest hope, the guiding star of his life, was the thought of reaching the land of the Patriarchs, the marvelous land of the holy spirit and the prophets. There, as soon as he reached the age or forty, he would devote himself freely, without further fear of the rabbis and their excommunications, to the wisdom of the Kabbalah and fullfill his mission. He did not have long to wait; soon he would be forty. Shortly after publishing his *La-Yesharim Tehillah*, Luzzatto left Amsterdam with his family and, like Jehudah Halevi, the poet of Zion, in his day, set out on the difficult journey. After many trials he finally arrived in Safed, the capital of Rabbi Isaac Luria's Kabbalah. At last Luzzatto had attained his goal; he had trodden the holy land of the Patriarchs. Soon now the day would come when he could openly preach the "true wisdom" and reveal to the whole world the marvelous secrets whose key only the Kabbalah holds.

But the long-awaited day did not come. The lovely hopes and grandiose plans of the ardent mystic were ruthlessly stifled by the cold hand of death. In the spring of 1747 the plague broke out in Palestine and among its first victims were Luzzatto and his entire household. He died in Acco on May 6 in the fortieth year of his life and was brought to burial with great honor in Tiberias near the grave of the famed Tanna Rabbi Akiba.

In this tragic way the life-path of the great dreamer, the unfortunate genius with broken wings, ended. So perished one of the loveliest and noblest of Jewish personalities, broken and crippled under the heavy burden of the melancholy twilight era. A pure white, solitary sea-gull appeared over the darkened ghetto. The solitary one who had not come at the right time had to perish, but his cry of anguish was not suffocated and the echo of it resounded sharply and clearly. Luzzatto was not destined to reveal the full power of his great talent, but even what he accomplished under such disadvantageous circumstances created a new era in the history of Hebrew poetry.

CHAPTER FOUR

The Controversy Between Jacob Emden and Jonathan Eybeschutz

Shulḥan Aruch rabbinism and its period of decline—The powerlessness of the contemporary leaders—Rabbi Jonathan Eybeschütz and his significance—Eybeschütz as a "seeker"; his inclination to the Kabbalah—Eybeschütz's Kabbalist work *Shem Olam*—Reconciling the God of Aristotle and the God of Abraham—Resolving the problem of predestination and free choice—Eybeschütz's world-outlook —The First Cause and the God of Israel—Eybeschütz's belief in combinations of letters—Rabbi Jacob Emden Ashkenazi as a man and writer—His autobiography *Megillat Sefer*—His battle against Eybeschütz—The significance of this battle.

E NOTED that the weapons with which the rabbis fought against the Sabbatian "heresy" were excommunication and persecution. In reality no others were available to them. The leaders of the generations well understood that "it was not quiet or peaceful in the tents of Jacob." They saw the perilous and slippery paths into which the messianic-mystical tendencies were leading, but they were powerless to struggle against the imminent danger with the weapons of persuasion, with the fervent sentiment of the inspired word. It is clear that among the disciples and followers of Jehudah Ḥasid, Ḥayyim Malach, and the like there were not only adventurers of quite low moral character, such as Nehemiah Ḥayon, but also profoundly ethical "seekers" whose tender, sensitive consciences could give them no rest. In the confused, mystical-theosophical ways, veiled in secrets, their longing souls sought an answer to the grievous enigma of life and hoped to find a definitive solution to the painful problem of the rule of evil in the world and the unredressed suffering of the chosen people, the bearer of the "holy covenant."

What could be given these restless, searching spirits by the congealed supervisors of *Shulḥan Aruch* rabbinism who squandered all their spiritual and intellectual powers on fruitless and arid *pilpul* and whose entire creativity was exhausted in gathering mountains of ever new subtleties and notes to the religious codifiers and codices of earlier generations? The greatest praise spoken of one of the most prominent rabbis at the end of the seventeenth century was the fact that he knew by heart the *Arbaah Turim* and *Bet Yosef*.[1] To guide those who roamed lost over the confused paths of mysticism, to assuage the yearning of souls seeking a solution to the painful riddle of life—this was beyond the power of the leaders of the generation who themselves believed in magic, demons, and destroying spirits, in all kinds of incantations, and in the miraculous power of amulets and combinations of letters. Thus they had nothing with which to issue forth other than the ancient weapons of excommunication and persecution. It soon became apparent, however, that these weapons could not bring victory but, on the contrary, might prove extremely dangerous for the very persons who utilized them. The leaders of the generation soon had occasion to become persuaded that they had not slain the serpent of "heresy" with their weapons but had rather greatly weakened their own authority and shaken the entire rabbinic structure.

In their battle against Moses Ḥayyim Luzzatto the rabbis triumphed. But shortly after the poet's tragic death a new struggle which agitated the entire rabbinic world and even found a certain echo in the Christian environment erupted. This time suspicion of infection with Sabbatian heresy fell on the foremost rabbinic scholar of that period, whose like was not seen in the rabbinic realm from Shabbetai Ha-Kohen to Elijah the Gaon of Vilna. This was Rabbi Jonathan Eybeschütz.

---

1. Jacob Emden, *Megillat Sefer*, 5.

Eybeschütz was born in Cracow in 1690 into a respected rabbinic family which traced its descent from Nathan Spira, the author of *Megalleh Amukot*. When he was still a child he was already renowned as an *ilui* or prodigy. As a small boy he studied in his father's *yeshivah* with grown-up men and astonished them with his learning and brilliance. When Jonathan was eleven years old his family went to Eibenschitz, where the community had elected his father rabbi. About a year later, however, the father died and the Eibenschitz community sent the twelve-year old orphan to Prossnitz in Moravia to study at the *yeshivah* of the author of *Panim Meirot*, Meir Eisenstadt. Apparently, however, he did not remain there long and later studied at the Talmudic academies of Holleschau and Vienna.

As a result of his marvelous capacities, Eybeschütz, while still quite young, acquired renown for his remarkably keen mind and enormous scholarship in the Talmud and Kabbalah. At the age of eighteen he was already president of the rabbinic court at Jungbunzlau and at the age of twenty-four principal of the famous *yeshivah* of Prague.[2] Hundreds of pupils were attracted to the young *rosh yeshivah* from the farthest countries.[3] Every Talmudic student dreamed of having the privilege of studying Torah with the brilliant Jonathan Eybeschütz who so effortlessly and with such marvelous acuteness resolved the most difficult problems of the Talmud. In addition, Eybeschütz was a "mouth bringing forth pearls" and renowned as a splendid orator.[4] With every year his fame grew and he was regarded as the great scholar of the generation, the foremost genius of his time.

His vast fame, however, did not bring contentment to the head of the Prague *yeshivah*. Nor did the wisdom of the Talmud satisfy him, despite the fact that he was its peerless master. His keen mind yearned from youth on for comprehensive knowledge. The medieval wall of isolation which then surrounded the rabbinic world was so solid and strong that even so richly endowed a person as Eybeschütz did not have the courage to break through it. The *Shulḥan Aruch* was regarded by him as the highest and limitless authority. He was firmly convinced that the men of the *Shulḥan Aruch* had produced this collective work

---

2. Graetz indicates that Eybeschütz was principal of the *yeshivah* at the age of twenty-one. Eybeschütz himself, however, relates that he became *rosh yeshivah* only in 1714. See *Luḥot Edut* (1755), 45b.

3. At the beginning of the 1750's the number of Eybeschütz's disciples had attained twenty thousand (see the proclamation of the *Vaad Arba Aratzot* in *Luḥot Edut*, 50b).

4. From 1728 on Eybeschütz was also a preacher.

through the holy spirit and everyone is therefore obliged to fulfill everything "written there."[5] "We must not even think," Eybeschütz teaches, "of abrogating any firmly established custom." Every new phenomenon is for him suspect merely by virtue of the fact that it is new, and it must be fought against. Hence he speaks with great indignation of those who visit "the so-called *Schauspiel, Komödie* and *Oper.*"[6] Eybeschütz proudly insists the he is quite familiar with the wisdom of philosophy and the natural sciences as well, but this knowledge he drew exclusively from medieval Hebrew sources. A younger contemporary of the famous Isaac Newton, he nevertheless considers it possible to speak contemptuously of the "foolish theory of Copernicus which contradicts our tradition." To be sure, Eybeschütz mentions "the Cartesian philosophical school,"[7] but there is no doubt that he had heard of the great French thinker Descartes only accidentally from the conversations he frequently carried on with prominent secular and spiritual officials.[8] Eybeschütz had thoroughly and fully studied only the medieval Jewish religious philosophers and their commentators, but he did not discover in them a satisfying solution to the basic problems which were at the center of his concern. This he found only among the mystics and Kabbalists.

When he was still quite young, his father, who was himself an ardent Kabbalist, familiarized him with the "true wisdom," and legend relates that his great-grandfather, the author of *Megalleh Amukot*, revealed to him the profoundest mysteries of the Kabbalah. Eybeschütz studied with special interest the writings of Nehemiah Hayon and Abraham Miguel Cardozo[9] and, to clarify certain points, carried on a correspondence with the Sabbatians Prosnitz, Hasid and Kamenker. This correspondence cast a certain suspicion on him, and when the rabbis who

5. In his *Urim Ve-Tummim* Eybeschütz writes: "While we are orphans of orphans, we are not empowered to argue against the *Shulḥan Aruch* and the notes of Rabbi Moses Isserles, may his memory be for a blessing, since the spirit of the Lord shone upon them and the sages of the generation established and agreed to teach and keep everything that is written in the *Shulḥan Aruch.*"

6. *Ya'arot Devash*, II, 308 (Lublin edition, 1888).

7. *Shem Olam*, 89, 257.

8. For evidence that the prominent officials of Prague would gladly converse with the keen and eloquent rabbi, see *Shem Olam*, 175.

9. In one of his works that he wrote in 1728 Eybeschütz relates: "It is more than twenty years since I became acquainted with the writings of Hayon and Cardozo" (*Shem Olam*, 31).

were battling against the Sabbatian heresy in 1725 excommunicated the three just mentioned "Shabsay-Tzeviniks," several of the fanatical fighters conceived the idea of excommunicating the rabbi of Prague along with the three. But Eybeschütz's authority at that time was already too great, and the fanatics did not dare carry through this perilous step. Nevertheless, Eybeschütz found it necessary, in order to purge himself of all suspicion, himself to pronounce on Kol Nidrei night, at the head of several other rabbis and leaders of the Prague community, the great excommunication against all adhering to the Sabbatian sect.

Heinrich Graetz, who is so unfair to all whom he suspects of having any inclination toward mysticism, declares that Eybeschütz did this out of hypocrisy and duplicity, since he himself accepted the blasphemous Sabbatian teaching that the First Cause is beyond all connection with "the work of creation" and only the first emanation of the First Cause, i.e., the God of Israel, the prototype of the ten *sefirot*, is the Creator of the world, the Lawgiver, the One who entered into covenant with the people of Israel. It is clear, Graetz adds, that Eybeschütz also accepted all the further corollaries of this heretical doctrine—that Shabbetai Tzevi is the true Messiah, the embodiment of the "Holy King," and that from the time he appeared in the world the laws of the Torah of Moses are abrogated. In all this Graetz does not take into consideration, however, that the "heretical" basic idea about the First Cause and the God of Israel was borrowed by Eybeschütz from the pious Menaḥem da Fano, who died before Shabbetai Tzevi was even born, and also that such a convinced opponent of the Sabbatian teaching as Joseph Ergas whom Graetz himself attests as "a clear mind" points out in his *Shomer Emunim* (38a) that "he who believes in the eternity of the [divine] will does not believe in dualism—God forbid."

When Graetz expresses his firm conviction that Jonathan Eybeschütz was a follower of the Sabbatian teaching, he relies on the manuscript *Shem Olam*, which was found thanks to Y. Mizes and which Eybeschütz's pupil, Simeon Buchhalter, completed in 1748. In this work, on which Graetz bases himself, Buchhalter presents, on the basis of written documents and oral conversations, his teacher's philosophical-mystical world outlook. Buchhalter's manuscript has now become available to all, since A. Weissmann published *Shem Olam* in 1891. Now everyone can easily convince himself how unjustified Graetz and, after him, the fanatical *maskil* David Kahana,[10] were with their assertion that the great Talmudic dialectician Jonathan Eybeschütz was a secret "Shabsay-Tzevinik."

Eybeschütz's pupil, Simeon Buchhalter, in his old age collected all the letters[11] and notes received from his teacher which deal with philosophical and religious-mystical problems, copied them, as he asserts, "word for word and letter for letter," and made out of them an entire composition entitled *Shem Olam*. All the epistolary material, which is written in the form of a dialogue between a rabbi and his pupil, actually revolves around two ancient and fundamental problems: how did the absolute and infinite create the material and limited, and how is the concept of *ha-kol tzafui* (everything is forseen), or God's omniscience, to be reconciled with the doctrine of free will and reward and punishment? Eybeschütz's keen mind pondered long and hard over these two questions. We have noted the reverence he had for accepted authorities. When, for instance, he mentions Moses Cordovero, he at once adds: "Would that our soul were the footstool of Rabbi Moses Cordovero."[12] He also cannot imagine that anyone should undertake "to differ with the *Sefer Yetzirah*."[13] Yet he manifests, for the retarded rabbinic world of that time, the very remarkable courage to draw from foreign sources and also to accept, as aids in his arduous search for the truth, scholars of the gentile peoples, non-Jewish philosophers and thinkers. "Everything in the philosophers that is true and right, I take from them," Eybeschütz several times repeats.[14] He has the highest respect for the authority of Maimonides not only as the great codifier, the incomparable author of the *Mishneh Torah*, but also as the indefatigable seeker after truth, the brilliant creator of *A Guide for the Perplexed*. "How profound are the ideas of this man," he exclaims feelingly, "how exalted his thoughts!"[15]

In full agreement with Maimonides, Eybeschütz constantly stresses that the divine principle, the First Cause, cannot be vested with any positive qualities or attributes whatever.[16] The

---

10. See his *Even Ofel*.
11. The letters were written in the years 1728–1730.
12. *Shem Olam*, 103.
13. *Ibid.*, 130.
14. *Ibid.*, 88, 122, etc. Of course, one must bear in mind in this connection that Eybeschütz drew all of his philosophical knowledge exclusively from Jewish sources.
15. *Ibid.*, 156.
16. Like Cardozo, Ebyeschütz constantly uses the term *Sibbah Rishonah* (First Cause) in the masculine gender.

First Cause does not even have a name, for *ha-shem hu atzmuto mamash*,[17] the name of a thing is the expression of its nature and being,[18] and the nature of the First Cause is hidden and veiled. This idea that a name is not something accidental and adventitious but expresses the nature of the thing itself is considered extremely important by Eybeschütz, who returns to it several times. "In just this," he says, "one perceives the great wisdom of Adam, who gave names to all creatures; hence, he understood the nature and essence of each living being."[19] The First Cause can also not be described by the word "one,"[20] for the concept of oneness is also an attribute; it expresses a quality. Even the Ineffable Name (the Tetragrammaton, YHWH) is not the name of the First Cause, for it signifies existence or being, and "being, too, is an attribute, a quality which characterizes the thing."[21] The title *Ein Sof* (Infinite) may also not be applied to the First Cause, for, Eybeschütz points out, in the *Zohar* and other Kabbalist works one frequently encounters the expression, "the *Ein Sof*, blessed be He." Now, in relation to the First Cause such an expression would be literally absurd, for the First Cause is absolutely veiled and hidden; He cannot be blessed, for He is beyond all changes and modification and is higher than any prayers and blessings whatever.[22] The First Cause is unchangeable, and it is ridiculous to think of any external influences on Him.

Eybeschütz, indeed, sharply and clearly poses the question: To whom actually are the prayers of men addressed? What sense does it make to cry to the First Cause, "Forgive now, pardon now?" He is, after all, beyond any change whatever; He is one and the same through all eternity. How, then, can one think of any alteration through external effect?[23] It is not the First Cause, hidden and unknown, without form or name, that radiates light and comfort to religiously longing souls; it is not to Him that ardent prayers are addressed, that eyes filled with

---

17. *Shem Olam*, 157.
18. For a discussion of this idea among the earlier Jewish mystics, see our *History*, Volume III, pp. 30ff.
19. *Shem Olam*, 165.
20. *Ibid.*, 51, 64.
21. *Ibid.*, 7–8.
22. *Ibid.*, 135, 145, 240: "Of the First Cause it may not be said, Blessed is He . . . He may not be spoken of as blessed because He is above all praise and blessing." On the same idea, see also Menahem da Fano's *Me'ah Keshitah*, No. 22, and Basilea's *Emunat Hachamim*, 31b.
23. *Shem Olam*, 23, 30, 193ff.

hope and faith are turned. How, then, can we unite, as Jehudah Halevi puts it, the God of Aristotle with the God of Abraham? How can we bridge two such basically different concepts—on the one side, the First Cause, the abstract and infinite, the profoundly hidden with the unknown name that is beyond all contact with time or space and, on the other side, the God of Israel, the Creator of heaven and earth, the God of justice and righteousness, the protector of orphans and widows, who accepts the prayers and tears of the suffering and grievously oppressed? Eybeschütz was firmly convinced that to this painful question speculative philosophy gives no answer whatever. But the question *must* be answered; in it is the key, the true essence of man's existence and life. Only in the Kabbalah, in the doctrine of the emanated ten *sefirot,* Eybeschütz affirms, can one find a final and valid solution to this life-question.[24] But it is characteristic of the great thinker and dialectician who spent all his days in Talmudic *pilpul* that he takes pains to emphasize that the *Torah she-ba-lev* (Torah in the heart) is not at all inconsistent with reason. In this, he points out, consists our greatness as Jews. We are distinguished from all other nations by the fact that in our Torah there is nothing that *contradicts* common sense. We insist only that we have, through tradition, truths that transcend man's intellect.[25]

With all the brilliance of his keen dialectic, Eybeschütz endeavors to prove logically that, both in Holy Scripture and in the Talmud, whenever the Creator, the God of Israel, and the revelation of Sinai are mentioned, it is not the First Cause Himself who is spoken of, but only His will. In this connection, however, Eybeschütz is particularly insistent that the term "will" is simply intended to indicate that the creation of the world was a *conscious* act, not a necessity or an unconscious activity, such as that of the sun in radiating its light.[26] In general, Eybeschütz concludes, the word "will" signifies consciousness, the thinking principle in creation. *Willing* means *thinking;* to will and to think are identical. "He (the First Cause), His wisdom, His wish, and His will are all one."[27]

It is not a matter of accident that Eybeschütz mentions, even

24. *Ibid.,* 89, 91, 101, 150, 174, etc.
25. *Ibid.,* 118, "God forbid to say of our perfect Torah that reason is opposed to it. It is our doctrine that our Torah is above reason, and no argument of reason is necessary to establish it, but that reason should oppose it will certainly never happen." See also p. 42 and especially p. 231.
26. *Ibid.,* 46–47. See also *ibid.,* 57–59.
27. *Ibid.,* 84, 85.

though only incidentally, Ḥasdai Crescas, the author of *Or Adonai*. He points out very definitely, though in somewhat more disguised fashion than Crescas, that the creation of the world was a matter of necessity.[28] But he also insists, as did Crescas in his day, that the notion of necessity does not at all imply that the necessary act takes place without conscious will. The divine, thinking will, or—more correctly—God's will-thought is as eternal as the First Cause Himself, for, Eybeschütz explains, "the thinking First Cause can not, after all, be separated from the thought itself." And this thinking principle, the divine consciousness and the eternal divine thought, is "creative" thought. It is the form or figure, i.e., the proto-type, of the ten *sefirot* from and through which all the worlds were created.[29]

This prototype of all existence is inseparable from the First Cause. They are united, yet not identical. And it is this proto-type, in which all the ten *sefirot* are included *in potentia*, that is the bearer of the Ineffable Name, for, as divine, creative thought, it is the source of all existences.[30] To this prototype of the ten *sefirot*, the designation "one," to indicate its unity with the First Cause, also pertains. It is this that is meant by the name "the Lord, the God of Israel." In this, too, is hidden the profound idea in the words "Hear, O Israel, the Lord our God, the Lord is One;" the meaning of this statement is that He is inseparable from and merged in a unity with the First Cause, for the thought is inseparable from the thinker.[31] And, indeed, it is only the prototype of the ten *sefirot*, not the First Cause itself, Eybeschütz several times repeats, that bears the name *Ein Sof*. "The *Ein Sof* is the thought and the name," he declares,[32] "and the reason it is called *Ein Sof* is that it has no end but does have a beginning—in the thinking First Cause."[33] In this, he adds,[34] lies the profound import of the statement of Rabbi Eliezer Ha-Gadol, "Before the world was created He

---

28. *Ibid.*, 183, 188, 208, 209.
29. *Ibid.*, 105. See also *ibid.*, p. 46, the paragraph beginning with the words, "And the ten *sefirot* were in a thin form."
30. *Ibid.*, 49.
31. *Ibid.*
32. *Ibid.*, 117. This idea, as well as the pairing of the eternal will and the master of the will, were taken by Eybeschütz—and he himself notes this—from the Italian Kabbalist Menaḥem Azariah da Fano (see the latter's *Yonat Elem*, chapters 1–2; *Pelaḥ Ha-Rimmon*, Gate Four, chapters 1–2, 4). Graetz and his fellow-battlers against the "Shabsay-Tzevinik" Eybeschütz overlooked this.
33. *Shem Olam*, 51, 53, 108, 109, 133, 152.
34. *Ibid.*, 51.

and His name alone existed": this means, He, the First Cause, and the bearer of His name, the prototype of the ten *sefirot*, who is also called the God of Israel. Not without reason, Eybeschütz notes, does the word *shemo* (His name) correspond in *gematria* to the numerical value of the word *ratzon* (will).[35] In this connection Eybeschütz makes a very characteristic observation: What I call the form of the ten *sefirot* carries among the old Kabbalists the name *Keter* (crown), and Plato, who was the pupil of the prophet Jeremiah and, as a result, had certain mysteries revealed to him, even though in a distorted form, speaks of *ḥomer ḥiyuli*, hylic matter *(materia prima)*.[36] But Eybeschütz deemed it necessary to stress most sharply that in this idea, which he took over from Menaḥem da Fano, there is no hint of dual or multiple divinity, and that it is in complete opposition to the Christian dogma of the Trinity, in which each divinity actually has its own form. "Everything is united in a complete unity," he several times reiterates. There can be no talk whatever of duality or multiplicity, for the First Cause is joined in perfect unity with its will, the God of Israel, who is the prototype of the ten *sefirot*. Just as it is impossible to separate the thought from the thinker, so is it impossible to separate from the First Cause the *shem ha-yiḥud* (divine name), which is the expression of its creative power.[37].

It is to the Ineffable Name, to the God of Israel, Eybeschütz explains, that we offer our prayers, our petitions and our tears. For with regard to the absolute First Cause, which cannot be designated by any name because in its utter simplicity it is incomprehensible, one cannot conceive that it should come into any contact whatever with particularities and individualities, or react to any influence from individual and ephemeral or accidental phenomena.[38] In regard to the First Cause it is not appropriate to say that "it is changed from justice to mercy,"[39] for no transformation whatever can occur in it. To its kind of knowledge no particularities or individualities are applicable; it embraces only the universal and the general.[40] The First Cause is the sole source from which the absolute grace of life and being flows over the entire cosmos, but it is not this absolute, unattainable, and incomprehensible source

---

35. The numerical value of both words is 346.
36. *Shem Olam* 51, 53, 108, 109, 133, 145, 152, 204.
37. *Ibid.*, 55. Cf. *ibid.*, 7, 94–95, 145.
38. *Ibid.*, 63–64, 215.
39. *Ibid.*, 207.
40. *Ibid.*, 207. Cf. *ibid.*, 63–64, 215, etc.

that concerns itself with distributing the abundance of life and happiness.[41] And it is illogical, Eybeschütz insists, to perceive in this a diminution of the power and might of the First Cause. On the contrary, this is the consequence of its incomprehensible greatness and supreme degree of simplicity.[42] It is literally ridiculous to see a limitation in the power of the First Cause on the ground that it, the absolute and infinite, which has no image or form, is by its very nature incapable of disclosing itself in the limited form of a mortal man. It cannot do this because in it, the universal source of harmonious lawfulness and regularity, the will to alter its nature and be transformed into its complete antithesis, to be changed from the universal and unlimited into the limited and accidental, cannot even be born. Eybeschütz several times touches on this point that is so important to him, and it is typical that in this connection he never passes up the opportunity to note how grievously mistaken in this respect the "heretics" and the "majority and class of mistaken ones," i.e., the Christians, are.[43]

Thus the First Cause has nothing to do with particularities, nor does it directly affect the fate of the individual. It only thinks and grasps its own universal thought and will; and this universal will-thought is the Ineffable Name, the God of Israel, the prototype and form of the ten *sefirot*. The active, creative will emanates or radiates and produces, as a result, the ten *sefirot*, through which all the worlds are created and through which is spread the bliss the First Cause bestows according to the laws of the divine wisdom and grace, which are incorporated in the divine garment of the Ineffable Name—in the laws of the Torah.[44]

It is characteristic of the great dialectician and brilliant master of Talmudic scholarship that, in this connection, he takes pains to emphasize that the Oral Torah is not less important than the Written Torah, for they are one complete and indivisible entity. It suffices to read through pages 194–195 of *Shem Olam* to be astonished once more at how Heinrich Graetz could come to the conclusion that Eybeschütz was convinced that the

---

41. *Ibid.*, 63, 67, 78–79, 215, etc.

42. *Ibid.*, 234, etc.

43. *Ibid.*, 63, 74, 90. It is thus incomprehensible how Graetz could come to the conclusion that Eybeschütz saw in Shabbetai Tzevi the true Messiah, the *Malka Kaddisha* incarnate in human form. Eybeschütz also considers it necessary to separate himself from the followers of Shabbetai Tzevi, Cardozo and Ḥayon, and advises his pupil "to remove himself from their opinions" (*Shem Olam*, 245, 253–54).

44. *Ibid.*, 192. Cf. *ibid.*, 102.

Torah was abrogated with the appearance of Shabbetai Tzevi.

Eybeschütz proceeds to the contradiction-filled problem: on the one side, the rule of providence and divine omniscience, and, on the other, man's free will and free choice. With all his brilliant dialectic he attempts to elucidate and explain this complex of extremely serious inconsistencies. In Eybeschütz's view, the knowledge of the First Cause is not at all absolute, in the form of a final decree. It merely embraces the general and universal.[45] The knowledge of the God of Israel, the proto-type of the ten *sefirot*, who does influence particularities and individuals, is also not absolute, for it, too, embraces merely the basic norms of the phenomena as they flow from the First Cause according to definite laws.[46] The God of Israel—i.e., the will-thought, the divine thought formed in will—has no need of the good deeds or the blessings and prayers of men in order to be in constant union with its source—the thinking First Cause. Man's deeds, however, have an immense significance as a conscious confirmation of the supreme laws flowing from the divine wisdom. Indeed, according to these deeds the God of Israel bestows the divine abundance of grace, for through them the divine knowledge, the divine laws of wisdom and mercy, are incorporated in life and disclosed through conscious activity.[47] Hence, we see that, in full agreement with the earlier Kabbalists, Eybeschütz expresses the idea that not only is man dependent upon divinity, but he also, with his free will, influences the upper worlds. Indeed, Eybeschütz adds that it is in regard to this recognition of the universal role of man's deeds that the Kabbalists and philosophers go in diametrically opposed directions.[48]

When Eybeschütz reiterates that the God of Israel, the divine will, is the ruler of the world[49] and that, indeed, only He can be designated by the word *Elohah* (God),[50] he deems it necessary to admonish that one must not thereby come to the false conclusion that the First Cause has no relationship whatever to the governance of the universe. The First Cause is, after all, he insists, the source of everything outside itself. Without its influence neither the prototype of the ten *sefirot* nor each individual *sefirah* would be able to disclose its creative power,

45. *Ibid.*, 217, 491.
46. *Ibid.*, 102, 174.
47. *Ibid.*, 205–206.
48. *Ibid.*, 119–20.
49. *Ibid.*, 121.
50. *Ibid.*, 102.

for the First Cause is the primordial source of all creative powers, like the heart in a living organism.[51] In this connection, Eybeschütz attempts to reconcile still another contradiction in an extremely ingenious fashion. He distinguishes in the clearest way the form of the ten *sefirot*, which, in his view, is identical with the Ineffable Name and as eternal as the First Cause,[52] from the *atzilot* of which the Kabbalists speak, i.e., the emanated ten *sefirot* which reveal themselves in their active creation.[53] But if the form of the ten *sefirot*, i.e., of the divine thinking will, is eternal along with the First Cause, how is one to explain the fact that the creation of the world took place at a definite time—not earlier and not later? Eybeschütz neatly disposes of the contradiction. This question, he points out, has in reality no ground, simply because time itself begins only *after* the creation of the world. "Before the world was created," when "only He and His Name existed," i.e., when only the First Cause and its thought-will were in being, no movement or chain of phenomena was possible; consequently it makes no sense to speak of "earlier" and "later." It is not at all accurate to say that the world was created in time. Time itself first came into being with the creation of the world.[54]

Still another interesting point is worth noting here. Eybeschütz considers it necessary to indicate several times that the views he expresses about the connection between the First Cause and the God of Israel and about the significance of the Ineffable Name and the form of the ten *sefirot* are not at all new in Jewish religious literature, that they are clearly not his own achievement. "Do not suppose," he declares, "that I here say anything novel that was unknown in previous times; I merely repeat the words of my predecessors."[55] And he endeavors to show with his customary keenness that the views he presents here are found not only among the majority of the Kabbalists since the times of Isaac the Blind and Naḥmanides to those of Rabbi Isaac Luria and Israel Saruk,[56] but also among the Geonim and sages of the Talmud. It is only that among the latter

51. *Ibid.*, 101–02.
52. *Ibid.*, 92. Cf. *ibid.*, 76, 94.
53. *Ibid.*, 201. Cf. *ibid.*, 95.
54. *Ibid.*, 198. It is interesting to note that the same idea was also expressed by Eybeschütz's contemporary, Joseph Ergas, in his *Shomer Emunim*, which was published only after the author's death in 1736 (see *Shomer Emunim*, 36a).
55. *Shem Olam*, 110.
56. Only Cardozo and Ḥayon, Eybeschütz emphasizes, actually expressed ideas which our fathers never conceived and which have no basis among the earlier Kabbalists.

they are expressed merely by way of allusion and mystery, while he renders the same ideas in a clearer form and more systematic order.[57] And indeed, in regard to this task—presenting in a systematic, clearly comprehensible fashion the obscure mystical-theosophical ideas of the Kabbalists—Eybeschütz's *Shem Olam* is an interesting literary phenomenon. This great scholar was, indeed, not well versed in the principles of grammar, but he had his own unique style and, thanks to his brilliant analytical mind, managed to set forth in clear, concrete forms the labyrinthine theosophical problems and concepts that are so extraordinarily complex and veiled in a mystical haze. Many ideas scattered about in the Kabbalist books of earlier generations only in the form of allusions and veiled parables are developed by Eybeschütz with rigorous logical consistency in clearly grounded theories and carried to their inevitable logical conclusions. In this respect *Shem Olam* is of the greatest importance for anyone interested in the history of the development of Jewish mystical thought.

In discussing Eybeschütz as a Kabbalist one other characteristic point must be noted, namely, his firm belief in the vast miraculous power hidden in the structure of the word, in combinations of letters. We have observed[58] how in one of the fathers of the Kabbalah, Eleazar of Worms, the profoundest philosophical-theological ideas co-existed very amicably with all kinds of magical formulas, incantations, combinations of letters and amulets. In Rabbi Isaac Luria and his disciples the practical Kabbalah was completely dominant. Hence, it should occasion no surprise that such an ardent devotee of the Lurianic Kabbalah as Eybeschütz was firmly persuaded that the light of the upper world discloses itself in the form of letters, that a man's soul is also "a light composed of letters,"[59] and that from these letters the man's name is put together. Like many other rabbis of that age, Eybeschütz also believed in the magical power of amulets,[60] and in Prague and later in Metz he very frequently distributed his own handwritten amulets as healing formulas and remedies to sick and suffering members of the community. In those times this was a very common phenomenon, but in his youth Eybeschütz had aroused the suspicion

---

57. *Shem Olam*, 74–75, 76, 77, 126, 127, 106, 151.
58. See our *History*, Vol. II, pp. 70–74.
59. *Shem Olam*, 10.
60. He further believed that, through magical acts, with the aid of special markings, whisperings, and incantations, one can obtain the influence of certain planets (see Eybeschütz's *Ya'arot Devash*, 1789 edition, 32).

that he was a covert Sabbatian. In addition, fate brought it about that later in life, in 1750, when he was appointed chief rabbi of the three communities of Hamburg, Altona and Wandsbeck, he encountered the bitter fanatic Jacob Emden, who detected Sabbatian "heresy" everywhere. It did not take long until the formulas and amulets which the sick received as remedies from Eybeschütz became the "rock of conflict," the shibboleth in the obdurate struggle that agitated the entire rabbinic world of that era.

The chief figure in this controversy was Jacob Emden, better known under the acronym Yavetz. Emden himself relates that at the time he was born,[61] his father, Hacham Tzevi,[62] was ill with melancholia.[63] This certainly had an unfavorable effect on the psychic character of the son.[64] Weak and neurasthenic from childhood on, he was always an angry, bitter man and pathologically irascible. The older he grew, the more frequently he would fall into profound melancholia, and in his autobiography he constantly laments his sickly condition, saying that he becomes ever more "weak from melancholy" or that "sadness prevailed over me" or that "the black sickness" fell upon him.[65] In addition, he was a man with a pathologically vast ambition, an extremely dogmatic person who reacted to every strange and independently expressed idea as if it were a personal insult. This made him "a man of strife and contention." He was undoubtedly a decent, honorable human being, but his pathological irascibility and rapid alterations of mood brought it about that his views changed very frequently and that he was so inconsistent in his actions that many accused him of hypocrisy.

Jacob Emden had a significant literary talent, and his autobiography *Megillat Sefer*[66] occupies a very honored place in the not especially rich Jewish literature of memoirs. Many pages of his work are extremely interesting from the point of view of their style and unique structure, but the frequent repetition of the same things, even in the same words, and the unneces-

61. In Altona in 1697; he died in 1776.
62. Tzevi ben Jacob Ashkenazi was rabbi in Hamburg and Amsterdam. He was one of the most prominent rabbis of his time.
63. Jacob Emden himself tells of this in the preface to his *She'elot Yavetz*; see also his *Megillat Sefer*, 18, 56.
64. Emden himself points this out, when telling of his father's illness (see preface to *She'elot Yavetz*).
65. *Megillat Sefer*, 42, 60, 98, etc.
66. First published by David Kahana in 1896.

sary interruptions for the sake of secondary issues that have no relationship to the subject at hand diminish the literary value of this best of his works, which no scholar interested in the cultural life of Germany-Polish Jewry in the first half of the eighteenth century can ignore.[67] A man with a colossal memory and a definite literary gift but with a very average mind, Emden wrote scores of works in which he showed immense learning but very little original thought. Throughout his life he had the greatest reverence for the memory of his father, Ḥacham Tzevi, whom he lost at the age of twenty-one, and with literally pathological obduracy endeavored to follow his father's ways and to emulate him in all issues of life. Since Ḥacham Tzevi had persecuted the followers of Shabbetai Tzevi intensely, was the leader in the struggle against Nehemiah Ḥayon, and, in consequence, had to flee from Amsterdam in 1714, Jacob Emden also deemed it essential to "stand on the watch" and, like his father in his day, to be a battler in the "holy war." He was always prepared to issue forth with sound and fury whenever he detected any suspicion of heresy, to fall with great force on the "enemy" with his resounding weapons: screaming tracts full of bitter attacks and wrathful accusations.

Because the Sabbatians of all shades, together with the Frankists, considered the *Zohar* the chief authority and based their entire doctrine on it, Jacob Emden, himself an adherent of the Kabbalah, went so far in the heat of battle that he had the temerity to express the, for his time, heretical idea that it was not the great Tanna Rabbi Simeon ben Yoḥai who wrote the *Zohar* and that, in general, the *Zohar* is not the unitary work of one author, since numerous additions from later times are contained in it.[68] It was this that brought it about that the later *maskilim* and Meassefim were prepared to see in the deeply pious Emden a battler for free, critical thought. The extent to which this is ungrounded is attested by the following facts. When the grammarian Solomon Hanau[69] allowed himself to note in the introduction to his *Shaarei Tefillah* that one need not rely blindly on ancient authorities, since the great scholars of a generation may also sometimes be mistaken, it was precisely Jacob Emden who was the first strongly to attack the young author for his "impudence." Also it was none other then Emden who issued the verdict that a convert who had come from

67. Emden carries his memoirs through to the year 1766.
68. See his *Mitpaḥat Soferim*, 2–3.
69. See above, pp. 149–150.

Italy could not marry a Jewish girl on the basis that "it is known to all" that the "sons of Edom" who are descended from Esau dwell in the region of Rome.[70] Along with many other Kabbalists, Jacob Emden also believed that man's soul is transmigrated into all kinds of animals, that miracles may be performed with amulets and mystical incantations. To confirm this, he relates an event that "I saw with my own eyes," showing the marvelous power manifested by a ring with "names" inscribed on it as soon as it was put on by a virgin in whom there was a *dybbuk*.[71] The story of the demons of the goldsmith's house in Posen, related in *Kav Ha-Yashar*,[72] is also cited by Emden as a sad event "known and familiar to everyone."[73]

With great anger and indignation, as is his manner, Emden attacks Azariah dei Rossi because this scholar, whom he calls "that Edomite," allowed himself to be led astray by foreigners and had the presumption to adopt a critical attitude toward certain legends quoted by the sages of the Talmud.[74] To provide some notion of Emden's polemical style, it suffices to quote the following pearls from Emden's critique of the author of *Meor Einayim*: "a spirit of perversity enticed him"; "an act of foolishness such as this"; "all his words there are altogether vain"; "he does not know what he is saying"; "a speaker of falsehoods"; "as a drunkard reels in his vomit"; "unsearchable foolishness"; "vanity opens its mouth, piling up words without sense"; "poor in understanding"; "like a simpleton, he believes everything"; "he has dug a pit and sunk in his folly"; "good for fools like himself."[75] Emden angrily cries, "This Edomite's work should not be called *Meor Einayim* (Enlightenment of the Eyes) but *Meavver Einayim* (Blinding of the Eyes).[76]

Philosophy Emden despised utterly, and he speaks with the greatest contempt of the "crazy philosophers." The hatred of this fanatic for philosophy went so far that in the catastrophe that befell the Jews of the Ukraine in the years 1648–1649 he was prepared to see a punishment for the fact that they devoted themselves excessively to Aristotle's philosophy.[77] Given such

70. *She'elot Yavetz*, 1, no. 6, 76b.
71. *Migdal Oz*, "Aliyyat Ha-Teva," 3b.
72. See above, pp. 161–63.
73. *Ibid*.
74. *Migdal Oz*, 29a.
75. *Ibid.*, 28–29.
76. *Ibid*.
77. In this Emden bases himself on the well known letter that Rabbi Solomon Luria sent to Rabbi Moses Isserles (see above, p. 57).

a view, it should occasion no surprise that Jacob Emden could not conceive how it was possible that so great a scholar as Maimonides should have written so heretical a book as *A Guide for the Perplexed*. He therefore hit upon the brilliant theory that it was undoubtedly composed by some anonymous heretic who "hanged himself from a large tree." The heretic wrote this work himself and, to lead men astray, referred to the famous author of the *Mishneh Torah*.[78] Hence, Emden strongly admonishes his readers that one must not waste time on *A Guide for the Perplexed* and that it is not at all worthwhile to reply to its falsehoods and fabricated dreams.[79]

It was this man who was the initiator and ringleader in the stubborn controversy which created such a furor in the rabbinic world. It is clear that Emden attacked Eybeschütz not because the latter had distributed amulets as protections and remedies. Emden himself also firmly believed in the immense power inherent in amulets. He raised a clamor only because he believed the content, the "names" in Eybeschütz's amulets, to be suspect. He, the spiritual heir of Ḥacham Tzevi who all his life fought against heretical sects, considered himself the faithful guardian standing watch over God's vineyard, and he had long looked with suspicion on Eybeschütz as a covert follower of the Shabbetai Tzevi heresy.[80] In addition, there was a purely personal motive. After the death of the rabbi of Altona, Yeḥezkel Katzenellenbogen, the author of *Kenesset Yeḥezkel*, the community elected as his successor not Jacob Emden but brought in Jonathan Eybeschütz and appointed him chief rabbi of the cities of Altona, Hamburg, and Wandsbeck and of the Jewish community of all of Mecklenburg. Emden saw in this a personal offense; Eybeschütz became for him not only the "heretic" and "Sabbatian" but also the intruder who unjustly occupied the rabbinic chair.

"To go forth to battle against this spiritual Goliath of the contemporary rabbinic world, who was surrounded by thousands of devoted disciples and ardent admirers," remarks N. Golubov,[81] one of the historians of this controversy, "was for

---

78. *Leḥem Shamayim*, "Avot," Chapter Two.
79. *Mitpaḥat Sefarim*, 80.
80. *Megillat Sefer*, 81–8.
81. *Voskhod*, 1900, X, 83. For discussions of this controversy, see Eybeschütz's *Luḥot Edut*, 1755 (a collection of letters and summonses); Emden's *Torat Ha-Kena'ot* (1752), *Edut Be-Yaakov* (1756), and *Shevirat Luḥot Ha-Even* (1759); Graetz (Rabinowitch's Hebrew translation), Vol. VIII, Chapter XIII, *Beilage* 7; D. Kahana, *Even Ofel* (1913)

a fanatic such as Emden so attractive that he could not resist the temptation. He entered the fight armed with all his virtues and defects—with immense learning in Talmudic and Kabbalist literature, with inexhaustible energy, with a burning desire for martyrdom, with a pathological, overly strained imagination which suspected everything because it saw everything in terribly aggravated form."

The war began over an amulet Eybeschütz gave a woman in childbirth. Eybeschütz's opponents opened the amulet and promptly brought it to Emden to explain the text written in it. Through combining the letters of the amulet according to the order of *at-bash*[82] and other ways, Emden found that Shabbetai Tzevi's name was twice repeated in it. Eybeschütz himself, as well as many rabbis,[83] correctly pointed out that, with the system Emden employed, one could very easily obtain Shabbetai Tzevi's name from any other amulet and, in general, from any text one wished. But it is beyond doubt that Emden himself was firmly persuaded that his amulet had unmasked Eybeschütz and demonstrated to the whole world that he was a hidden "Shabsay-Tzevinik." It is no wonder that the fanatic at once girded up his loins and entered into combat. He announced from the pulpit to the entire community that "he who wrote this amulet denies God."[84] This act created a tremendous sensation, and Eybeschütz found it necessary to purge himself of suspicion. On the Sabbath he delivered a sermon declaring with oaths and bans that he was innocent before God and had no contact whatever with the "false sect." "If I swear falsely," Eybeschütz exclaimed emotively, "may God send all His punishments on me."[85] And once again, as twenty-five years earlier, he issued forth with the ban of excommunication against the followers of Shabbetai Tzevi. As the rabbi and recognized spiritual leader of the community, he also placed under the ban all who devise slander against him, stir up strife, and create controversy among Jews. The leaders of the Jewish

---

and "Edut Be-Yaakov" (*Ha-Shiloah*, V); B. Katz, "Rabbi Yaakov Emden" (*Ha-Shiloah*, IV); M. Grunwald, "Der Hamburger Amulettenstreit," (*Mitteilungen der Gesellschaft für jüdische Volkskunde*, 1903); Jacob Cohen, *Ehrenrettung des Rabbi Jonathan Eybeschütz* (1870).

82. Whereby the letters of the alphabet are exchanged for each other in reverse order, i.e., the first for the last, the second for the next to the last, etc.

83. *See Luḥot Edut*, 8, 41.

84. *Edut Be-Yaakov*, 41.

85. *Luḥot Edut*, 76b.

community of Mecklenburg then ordered Jacob Emden to leave Altona within six months, and the members of the community were forbidden to visit his house.

All this, however, did not intimidate Emden. On the contrary, with the ardor of the fanatic he longed to go the martyr's way, to sacrifice himself. With still greater force and obstinacy he endeavored to expose to the whole world the dangerous "heretic" and blasphemer, and the flame of battle grew constantly stronger and embraced new communities. Eybeschütz circulated his "Iggeret Kinah"[86] to his numerous disciples scattered all over Moravia, Bavaria, and Poland and requested them to take up his cause and his offended honor. Emden, on his part, requested support from the rabbis of Amsterdam, Metz, and Frankfurt who were hostile to Eybeschütz for personal reasons. He also turned to the Council of the Four Lands, and soon the "amulet controversy" divided all of Polish-German Jewry into two hostile camps. Virtually all the communities from Lotharingia and Venice to Podolia participated in the struggle that had broken out. A whole literature of summonses, lampoons, tracts and proclamations was produced. Jacob Emden himself wrote more than ten tracts filled with insults, excommunications, and wrathful attacks. The aged Eybeschütz could not be silent. To this great scholar and outstanding Talmudist, the "writer's weakness," the desire to see his work published as soon as possible and to acquire fame as an author, was altogether foreign. His brilliant rabbinic works were published posthumously, and it was only a year before his death (1763) that, in order to pay off debts incurred by his sons, he published the first part of *Kereti U-Feleti*, a commentary to the *Shulḥan Aruch, Yoreh Deah*. In the heat of the battle with Emden, Eybeschütz, however, had no alternative; in order to influence public opinion and purge himself of the changes lodged against him, he published (in 1755) his *Luḥot Edut*, in which much interesting material for the history of this battle of rabbis is collected. The work is written in a calm, respectful tone, and the favorable impression is significantly strengthened when one compares it with Emden's virulent tracts. Emden mentions his opponents in no other way than as "wicked one," "evil dog," etc., but Eybeschütz always speaks in a calm tone: "My opponent, who is called Rabbi Jacob, the rabbi of Emden."

The opposing sides, however, were not satisfied merely with

86. Published in *Luḥot Edut*, 43–44.

tracts, lampoons, and proclamations; they also adopted the old rabbinic weapon of excommunication—exclusion from the community, declaring the person charged to be a living corpse with whom no member of the community may have any intercourse. Eybeschütz's former pupil, the rabbi of Lublin, Hayyim Katz, excommunicated all his teacher's opponents,[87] circulated the text throughout Poland, and proposed to all the rabbis that they approve the excommunication by subscribing to it. Many of the rabbis did, in fact, give their approval and proclaimed before the entire community that they confirmed the excommunication and decreed that every book in which the honor of the "great eagle," the defender and protector of the "entire exile," Rabbi Jonathan Eybeschütz, is impugned should be condemned to burning. The proprietors of presses were also warned not to dare publish such books. But the other side was not silent, either. Eybeschütz's opponents, the rabbis of Metz, Amsterdam and Frankfurt, reached a decision in 1753 that the person who had written the text of the suspect amulets is "banned and excommunicated." To this verdict several rabbis of Germany also gave their assent. As might be expected, the controversy did not proceed without denunciations and slanders. Neither side was chary of suspicion and generally considered whatever weapon came to hand fit and proper. They even sought aid and support from the secular power. Petitions were presented to the king of Denmark,[88] and several of Eybeschütz's followers used their influence with the Danish queen.[89]

Even the non-Jewish press became interested in the controversy raging in the Jewish communities, and it was reported in it that the battle had called forth a new Jewish Messiah who had just appeared. Eybeschütz himself, at a critical juncture when his opponents obtained the upper hand,[90] applied for help to his former pupil who later converted to Christianity, Carl Anton, and the latter in 1752 published a work entitled *Kurze Nachricht von dem falschen Messias Sabbathai Zevi*, which he

87. The text of the ban is published in *Luḥot Edut*, 20.
88. The city of Altona was at that time in the domain of the king of Denmark.
89. See M. Grunwald, *op. cit.*, 91.
90. On June 30, 1752, the king of Denmark issued a decree according to which Jacob Emden obtained permission to return to Altona, the leaders of the community had to pay a fine of one hundred thalers, and Eybeschütz was allowed to remain rabbi only in the community of Hamburg, as well as obliged to give a definitive response to fifteen questions put to him and to explain in a European language the text of the amulets on account of which the controversy had broken out.

dedicated to the king of Denmark. There was even a professor, Pastor David Friedrich Meherlein, so naive that he endeavored to show in a special work that from the text of the amulet in question one could clearly see that Rabbi Eybeschütz is a secret Christian; Jacob Emden and his followers are mistaken in the meaning, for in the letters it is not the name of Shabbetai Tzevi but the name of Jesus Christ himself that is hidden.

For six consecutive years this rabbinic controversy went on, ending with Eybeschütz's victory. He was again confirmed as chief rabbi of the Jewish community of Mecklenburg, and as a sign of joy and triumph his followers arranged a festival and on the days of Ḥannukah organized, with great pomp, a colorful masquerade; at the head of the procession one of Eybeschütz's tall pupils, dressed like a hussar, rode on a horse.[91]

This, however, was a very sad victory, a Pyrrhic victory that carried in itself an inevitable defeat. Eybeschütz himself notes a number of times in his *Luḥot Edut* that this controversy over amulets makes the Jewish people and its leaders a mockery and laughing stock among the peoples of the world.[92] The prestige of the Jewish spiritual leaders, the rabbis, thereby declined not only in the outside world but within the Jewish community as well. Sharply and clearly, throughout all of Jewry, the institution of the rabbinate disclosed all its corruption and rigidity. The stubborn battle which agitated the whole of German-Polish Jewry and was so filled with petty motives, with slanders and suspicions, and even with fist-fights in the synogogues and houses of study, lacked all ideological content whatever. The "stirrer of conflict," the initiator of the whole controversy, Jacob Emden, actually fought against windmills, made a great clamor about a danger which never was and existed only in his own diseased imagination. The other two great scholars of the generation, Ezekiel Landau and Joshua Falk, who were inclined toward Emden's side, played a very ambiguous role in the controversy—and this out of petty motives, out of the fact that they were envious of Eybeschütz and begrudged him his brilliant capacities and great genius.[93]

91. See *Megillat Sefer*, 84; M. Grunwald, *op. cit.*, 124.
92. *Luḥot Edut*, 40a–b, 72b, etc.
93. When Eybeschütz, in his old age, wished to settle in Prague, Ezekiel Landau, who was the official rabbi of the city, sent a petition to the empress Maria Theresa requesting that she forbid Eybeschütz to do so, because he was a vile man and a dangerous plotter. Two years later, when the aged Eybeschütz died, Landau gave a long eulogy in the synagogue of Prague, mourning the great loss and lamenting

The Results of the Controversy

The battle of the amulets undermined the authority of the spiritual leaders precisely at the time when the first rays of the Enlightenment Era appeared over German Jewry and the ideas of the French rationalists and materialists shook the solid wall separating the Jewish ghetto from the outside world. The withered world of the rabbis, which was even more weakened and discredited after the amulet controversy, lost the power to overcome the "breakers down of the fence" who suddenly appeared in the Jewish quarter. Stormily and courageously, like a foaming mountain stream on a laughing spring day, new ideas and currents irrupted into the obsolete, old-fashioned world of the ghetto. On its triumphant way the rushing stream hurled away everything—the old and congealed and rotten and, along with it, the valuable and viable. Of this in later chapters of our work.

---

that the Jewish people had lost such a great scholar who was endowed with the loveliest and noblest human qualities.

CHAPTER FIVE

The Era of the Gaon of Vilna

The decline of the Polish-Lithuanian rabbinic world—The author of *Sha'agat Aryeh* and his controversy with the community—The protest of Jehudah Margolioth and the struggle of the community council of Vilna with the *rav ha-aharon*—At the crossroads—The Gaon of Vilna, his role and significance—The new *du partzofin*.

E HAVE noted that the six-year-long Eybeschütz-Emden controversy weakened rabbinic authority in Germany and exposed the corruption of Jewish communal life, with its slanders, denunciations, and petty intrigues. The major role in this controversy was played by the rabbis of Germany and Moravia. No better, if not worse, was the situation in Poland and Lithuania. We have indicated the lifeless, congealed forms that *Shulhan Aruch* rabbinism assumed there in the second half of the seventeenth century. The spirit of original creativity died out even among the great men of the generation, the chief representatives of Talmudic knowledge. Under this reign of corruption and petrification, in which everything alive and aspiring for fresh air had to succumb, no fruitful, life-awakening ideas could flourish. The most brilliant capacities, the sharpest minds, had to become distorted and go to waste on useless trifles.

Very instructive in this respect is the career of the famed Talmudic dialectician, Aryeh Loeb ben Asher,[1] better known by the title of his collection of responsa, *Sha'agat Aryeh*. Endowed with a remarkably analytic mind, Aryeh Loeb was extremely opinionated and manifested the, for that time, extraordinary courage of not being carried away before acknowledged authorities. In his responsa he permits himself extremely sharp expressions even in regard to such recognized codifiers as Moses Isserles, Joel Sirkes, Shabbetai Ha-Kohen, and the like. One very frequently encounters in him statements such as the following: "There is no sense in his words," "He has erred greatly in this," "He does not know what he is saying," "His words are confused and incomprehensible." Aryeh Loeb recognized quite well the weak aspects of the method of *pilpul* and would often point out that, no matter how careful one might be to employ *pilpul* only to fathom the correct meaning of the Torah, it is impossible not to mingle in it sophistry leading away from the true path.[2] But his own works are also filled with pilpulistic cobwebs. Aryeh Loeb in fact manifests the most ingenious subtleties of a sharply honed, analytic mind, but he discovers nothing new; he does not express a single thought that bears the impress of creative power, of orginal thought. His refusal to abdicate before authorities did not lead him to free, critical thought or to independent ways of investigation, but to petty pride, to an insolent contempt for other Talmudic scholars of his generation. This brought him, especially in his youth, into sharp conflicts and extremely unpleasant experiences. When he was rector of the *yeshivah* in Minsk he allowed himself to mock the well-known scholar, Yeḥiel Heilprin, the author of *Seder Ha-Dorot*, with such extreme disrespect that he greatly enraged everyone and had to leave Minsk at once in great shame. Legend relates that the community of Minsk placed the arrogant *rosh yeshivah* on a filthy wagon on the eve of the Sabbath and, with cries of mockery and hooting, conducted him out of the city.[3] This controversy

---

1. Born in the region of Minsk around 1695. In his old age he was rabbi in Metz, where he died in 1785. For biographical details, see David Maggid, *Toledot Mishpeḥot Guenzburg*, pp. 35–50, and the Russian-Jewish Encyclopedia, III, 244–249.
2. For an even sharper estimate of *pilpul*, see *Sha'agat Aryeh He-Hadash*, 26b.
3. See D. Maggid, *op. cit.*, p. 36; Jehudah Leib Gordon, *Iggerot*, II, 274.

between the community and the *rosh yeshivah* can only be designated as a typical detail which did not evoke any important consequences. Of totally different significance was another controversy which erupted in regard to the rabbi in the principal city of Lithuania, a controversy which disclosed in the clearest fashion the utter corruption and demoralization of the autonomous Jewish government in Lithuania and Poland in the middle of the eighteenth century.

The persecutions of 1648 and the terrible confusions and bloody wars which subsequently took place in the Polish lands during the next decade, we have observed, brought economic and moral ruin to the Jewish community for generations. In order to buy off the wild bands and troops which then scourged the land without hindrance, the communities had to incur debts, mainly with the Catholic cloisters and religious foundations. This period of confusion weakened still farther the power of the central government of Poland which had already for many years been completely dependent on the nobility, on the views and interests of the Polish lords and the *szlachta*. After the ten-year wars the power of the *szlachta* became even greater. Every landowner or local lord was all-powerful in his area, doing whatever he wished with none to gainsay him. The dissolution and decline of the country as a whole affected Jewish social and communal life most adversely. To repay the huge debts and to ransom themselves from the local secular and religious officials so that they would not persecute them and not exercise their power against the Jewish populace, the *parnassim* and chief men, i.e., the leaders of the Jewish community, had to levy a large poll tax and other imposts on every Jew. Leading the community were the wealthy and prominent men who had influence with the landowners and in the courts of the local officials. These communal leaders, having obtained power, used to imitate the nobles and oppress the poor people. In apportioning the taxes they would engage in all kinds of duplicity, freeing themselves and their relatives from payments and laying everything on the masses, the broad strata of the population. The poor had no one to whom to complain, for the community leaders were respected by the officials and their people and could therefore do whatever they wished.

We observed in one of our previous chapters[4] that in this stubborn battle which the poor elements of the population carried on against the "notables of the city," who were the

4. See above, p. 136.

leaders in the Kahal, or community council, and also carried influence with the officials, the rabbis played an extremely ambiguous role. Some of them were courageous enough openly to attack the unjust deeds committed against the poor masses, and these protesting rabbis consequently had to suffer intense persecution from the powerful men in the community leadership. Other rabbis, however, were in league with the leaders and thereby greatly weakened the authority of the rabbinate among the masses.

We have noted the somber colors in which the author of *Kav-Ha-Yashar* portrayed the demoralization of the "powerful men" who led the community council. In even blacker colors does one of the few cultured rabbis of the second half of the eighteenth century, Jehudah Margolioth,[5] portray the wretched and servile role that the rabbis play at the banner of the corrupt Jewish self-government.

"Some of the leaders of Israel," Margolioth laments.

do not think of the glory of their Creator but only of their own. They employ all their power merely to terrorize the community . . . With their sharp teeth they consume the poor. They throw the burden of the taxes off themselves and cast it on others. As soon as one of them obtains power, he becomes proficient in all kinds of duplicities and enters into conspiracy with the vilest men. They have no mercy on anyone; they impose heavy taxation on all the beggars and poor people. And what can these unfortunate, miserable ones do? When they are told to give, they give, even when it happens—as it does quite frequently—that the payments laid upon them surpass manyfold what the rich man contributes. And so these people fall to their feet under the grievous burden. And if the sobbing and oppressed poor try to protest against these shameful deeds, it goes hard with them, for the powerful men stop at nothing to ruin their opponents. They run at once with their slanders and denunciations to the princes and officials known to them and exploit their influence in the courts. Like wolves they commit their dark deeds in the depths of night. With their base and treacherous assistants they fabricate all kinds of libels in order to obtain mastery over the community. They trample the poor with their feet and oppress the poverty-stricken masses with their heavy hand.

"Do not think," Margolioth further complains,

that one can turn for help to the great figures of the generation, to our rabbis, whose duty it is to be the protectors and defenders of the

5. On his literary activity, see below, Chapter VII.

people. For they are in league with the oppressors, walk together with the powerful men and rulers of the city, become collaborators of every mischief-maker, give protection to every swindler. They exploit the rabbi's title and authority for all kinds of evil deeds. Everything obtains the approval of the community rabbi. He who ought to be the guardian of righteousness and justice becomes the protector of robbers and bandits. The righteous judge joins the league of the swindlers . . . And these are our judges and lawgivers! Calmly they look on at the robberies and injustices that take place in the community and flatter the rich and powerful from whom every quarrel and plague come.

"The major blame for all this," Jehudah Margolioth further complains,

lies on the leaders of the community. They deliberately refuse to select proper judges and choose unqualified men, those, "who have no covenant and no Torah." All this they do out of the vice of arrogance and their thirst for power and glory. These chiefs and rulers of the community will not allow honorable and decent men to occupy rabbinic posts, so that they will not have to take account of their authority and be subject to them. They rather choose as rabbi or preacher utterly petty men who are ready to do everything which they, the powerful, wish.[6]

At the time Margolioth wrote his wrathful reproof, there occurred in the major center of Lithuania, in the "city and mother in Israel," Vilna, an obdurate struggle between the community leaders and the chief rabbi of the city, Samuel ben Avigdor, a struggle which finally undermined the power of both sides, both the rabbinic chair and the "communal chamber"—the autonomous government in Lithuania. This controversy, which lasted for all of twenty-five years, undoubtedly has a considerable cultural-historical interest, for it provides a clear picture of the moral decline which the autonomous government had attained in the second half of the eighteenth century.[7]

Thus we see in both the major Jewish communities, that of

6. See *Bet Middot*, 40–42 (we quote according to the Lyck edition of 1862); *Tal Orot*, 38 (quoted according to the Pressburg edition of 1813).
7. We have described this struggle at length in our article "Milḥemet Ha-Kahal Beha-Rav Ha-Aharon (*He-Avar*, 1918, II). In this connection we employed a handwritten register in which are gathered "documents and proclamations relative to the controversies and quarrels on the matter of the last president of the rabbinic court in Vilna." Since the journal did not survive, the second half of our article remained unpublished.

Germany and that of Poland, the same melancholy picture. Controversies and quarrels in community life reveal, on the one side, the total corruption of the Jewish government and, on the other, the moral bankruptcy of the spiritual leaders, the rabbis and guides of the generation. On the surface of communal existence we see in both communities complete spiritual and intellectual decline; however, in the depths of the people's life, complicated processes imperceptible to the superficial eye, the consequences of various social and spiritual forces, occurred. And soon the hidden was disclosed; the monochromatic gave birth to the multicolored, and the uniform obtained complicated structures and forms. The twin brothers, the Polish and German communities, which till then were seamless, separated; each attained its own unique style. Awakened from their congealment and petrification, they began independently to seek their own ways. In places these ways diverged, intersected, came together for a while, and soon unraveled again toward various sides and in different directions.

In the very city where the quarrel of the community council with the *rav ha-aḥaron* (last rabbi), Samuel ben Avigdor—a quarrel which, as we have noted, unmasked the moral bankruptcy of the rabbinic world—occurred, there lived and worked a remarkable man, one of the most extraordinary and gifted personalities of the Jewish people in the eighteenth century. He was a rigorous ascetic and solitary, completely isolated from the present world. And it was just this man who managed to restore to the congealed and dried-up rabbinic scholarship its erstwhile glory and authority. He was interested only in what had already been; his entire being, all his activity and thought, were directed to the past, the tradition of by-gone generations. Nevertheless, with his work he led, even if contrary to his own will, to new ways. He was the connecting link between the old world and the newly awakened tendencies. This man was named Rabbi Elijah bar Solomon Zalman. Among the people, however, he has been known for generations simply as "the Gaon of Vilna," the unique and chosen one.[8]

One characteristic point about the Gaon's years of study must be stressed: he was never a student in a *yeshivah*, or Talmudic academy. When still quite young he was already re-

8. Born in 1720, he died in Vilna in 1797.

nowned as a prodigy and so, from boyhood on, studied independently, following his own way. This was undoubtedly of great significance for his subsequent intellectual development. He was not under the influence of *pilpul*, the old-fashioned method of study in the contemporary *yeshivot*. Directed to his own powers, he learned while he was still very young to stand on his own views, to seek his own way freely and without hindrance in the realm of Talmudic scholarship and Torah study.

At the age of twenty Elijah left his household and home and set out into the world "to suffer exile." In the course of five years he wandered over Poland and all of Germany. There are numerous legends about this period—how gentile scholars, great professors and learned men in Berlin, were enchanted by his vast scholarship in all "seven sciences."[9] These legends contain a kernel of truth. In the rabbinic world the brilliant young ascetic of Vilna created a sensation. Rabbi Jonathan Eybeschütz testifies that "he is highly renowned in Poland, Berlin, Lissa, and all other places where he has sojourned."[10] In 1745 the Gaon returned to Vilna, where he spent his entire life. This life was devoted to a single occupation and directed toward one definite goal: study of Torah. Divested of all worldly interests and without any concern about earning a livelihood,[11] he would sit day and night in his prayer shawl and phylacteries, locked in his room with drawn shutters so that the light of the sun might not disturb him, and study constantly. He rarely spoke a word even to his own children, unwilling to interrupt his studies. Numerous legends about the Gaon's asceticism and solitude circulated in old Vilna. He, the greatest scholar in the sea of the Talmud, the savant whose like had probably not been seen in the last few centuries, refused to hold rabbinic office. A rabbi, he said,[12] must, after all, have to do with people, with wordly matters; only a private person can be completely isolated from the world, removed from corporeality and secular affairs. Only he can be involved in pure spirituality and not depart from the "tent of Torah" for a moment. In his own generation Elijah was called not only

9. See J. Lewin, *Aliyyat Eliahu*, Fourth Edition, p. 16.
10. *Luḥot Edut*, 1.
11. All the requirements of the Gaon's household were provided by the community of Vilna, which assigned to these purposes annually fourteen hundred zlotys. It also provided him with free housing and exempted him from all taxes.
12. See *Tanna Dvei Eliahu* (a commentary to the Book of Proverbs), 19.

the Gaon but also the *Ḥasid* or pious one, the man of God.[13]

Elijah bar Solomon Zalman composed more than sixty works, but not a single one of these was published in his lifetime, and many were not even written by his own hand. Yet in his lifetime, even in his middle years, he was regarded as the supreme authority in the realm of Talmudic knowledge. Both in the rabbinic world and among the common people the Gaon of Vilna became the symbol of brilliant scholarship and holy piety. Every word of his aroused wonderment, was disseminated through his disciples from mouth to mouth, was reverently written down and interpreted with numerous commentaries.

The Gaon was a first-rate scholar and investigator. Sitting locked in his room with drawn shutters, he perceived with his keen eye how abnormal and distorted the spiritual and intellectual life of his generation was. With all his authority he issued forth against the way of *pilpul* and publicly declared that this method of study "drives the truth away."[14] In that generation minds were so perverted through the overly subtle *pilpul* that a Gaon of Vilna had to come and "reveal" so elementary an idea as that, in the education of the young, one must first teach children the Bible and grammar, then the Mishnah, and only then the Gemara with Rashi and the subsequent commentaries.[15] It was for that time literally a revelation when the Gaon expressed the simple idea that the Talmud is, after all, a result of Holy Scripture, organically connected with it, and that it is therefore quite impossible to understand the Talmud

---

13. On the other hand, when the great controversy between the heads of the community and Rabbi Samuel ben Avigdor broke out, Avigdor, in his complaint lodged with the government, charged the heads of the community, among other accusations, with the sin that they would pay annually from communal funds fourteen hundred zlotys "to one Elijah ben Zalman who is called by the surname Hasid," and that, in addition, he was given free lodging and released from all taxes. See the *Acts* of the Vilna Commission, Vol. 29, pp. 468, 470:

    Eliaszowi Zelmanowiczowi, tytuiacemu sie patriarsze, czyli po hebraysku chossidowi . . . nic nie czynemu, zadnego szelaga do kahalu nieplacacemu, ani tez do zadney krobki nie importujacemu, stancya onemu arenduje, y co tydzien z kahalnych pieniendzy tym sposobem zebranych dwadziescia osm zlotych oplaca, co na rok wyniesie wydatku daremnego tysiac czterysta zlotych, y rozne onemu akkomodacye, jako to rube y daisze rzeczy kupuja.

14. *Aliyyat Eliahu*, 72.

15. His program on the education of children is given by the Gaon of Vilna in the introduction to his commentary on the *Shulḥan Aruch: Tur Oraḥ Ḥayyim* and is enthusiastically repeated in many works of his disciples. See, for example, the work of the *maggid* of Vilna, Ezekiel Feivel ben Ze'ev Wolf of Deretschin, *Toledot Adam*, Part One, Chapter 3.

thoroughly and scientifically if one is not completely familiar with the Bible, which is the foundation on which all of it is constructed. But to understand the Bible, one must first study the language in which it is written;[16] one must first of all know the ordinary sense, the meaning of the words, and only then seek in these words the secrets of the Torah concealed in them.[17] Girls also, the Gaon of Vilna stressed, should read Scripture in Yiddish translation, and in the well-known letter that he wrote home on his way to Palestine[18] he declares that his daughters should "every day read Proverbs in Yiddish translation for the sake of God, for this book is more important than all other books of moral instruction."

But the Gaon of Vilna went even further in his proposals for the reform of education and permitted himself to express ideas that literally smacked of heresy. This God-fearing man who was prepared to sacrifice himself for the least commandment declares quite definitely that to be in a position thoroughly to explore the Talmud one must possess not only Judaic knowledge but also be competent in the "external wisdoms." Astronomy, geography, mathematics, medicine and the like, the Gaon indicates, have a strong relationship to the Gemara, for without these important sciences it is impossible to understand many laws of the Torah and rules in the Talmud.

"All the sciences," declares the Gaon, "are essential for our Torah."[19] "Every defect of knowledge in the external wisdoms brings about a hundredfold defect in studying the Torah, for the Torah and science are linked."[20] Only philosophy was regarded with hostility by the Gaon. He strongly deplored the fact that such a great scholar as Maimonides allowed himself to be led astray through "accursed philosophy."[21] As we shall see further on, Elijah pointed out to his pupils how essential it is to translate scientific works and textbooks from European

16. On the Gaon's great knowledge of grammar and Hebrew philology, see M. Plungian, *Ben Porat,* 67.

17. *Adderet Eliahu,* 1.

18. For some unknown reason, nothing came of the journey, and the Gaon turned back in the middle of the way.

19. "All the sciences are necessary for our holy Torah and included in it" (see J. H. Lewin, *op. cit.,* 23; Israel Shklover in his preface to *Pe'at Ha-Shulḥan*).

20. See Baruch Schick in the introduction to his translation of Euclid.

21. Hirsch Katzenellenbogen asserts (*Kiryah Ne'emanah,* 152) that this expression "is not that of the Gaon Rabbi Elijah," but that another person "inserted these words at the time of printing." That this assertion has no foundation was long ago shown by Samuel Luria who himself saw the handwritten manuscript of the Gaon (see *Aliyyat Eliahu,* 25).

languages into Hebrew. He was a man who practiced what he preached. He himself composed works on grammar, mathematics, and geography. He wrote a textbook, *Ayil Meshullash*,[22] in which special mathematical problems connected with certain laws discussed in various tractates of the Talmud are explained. On the basis of information given in the Bible, he composed a geography of Palestine, *Tzurat Ha-Aretz*, and also drew a schematic map of Palestine so that the Jewish reader might have a clear notion of how the land of Canaan was divided among the twelve tribes of Israel (The map is published in the second collection *Perezhytoye*). He also wrote works on astronomy, grammar, etc.

The Gaon of Vilna did not have command of a single European language. He derived his scientific knowledge entirely from ancient Hebrew sources; as a result, these works of his could not have any significant scientific value. His investigations in the field of Talmudic scholarship, however, have an incomparably greater importance. Here he was undoubtedly an innovator, and the significance of his work becomes even greater when one takes into consideration that, at that time, the critical investigation of historical documents was still in its infancy, even in the scholarly world of Europe. With all his brilliant keenness and enormous scholarship, Elijah undertook to study critically and emend the texts of the ancient Talmudic literature. To be sure, every word in the Talmud was for him supremely holy, but he also knew quite well that before the Talmud came to be printed the text was copied by hand. The scribes and copyists were, after all, common mortals and, moreover, at times without essential knowledge; hence, they often unwittingly committed errors and distorted lines and even whole pages. Here Elijah demonstrated all his genius.

We observed earlier[23] that Rabbi Solomon Luria with his keenness accomplished a great deal in his critical investigation of the text of the Babylonian Talmud. Elijah therefore devoted his attention mainly to the Jerusalem Talmud, which had been very little studied. Critical investigation and emendation of the erroneous text was especially difficult by reason of the fact that the Gaon did not have at hand a sufficient number of old manuscripts; hence, he made use of the method of comparison and collation. Any text which aroused any suspicion whatever he compared with the text of the same subject in all the other

22. Printed in 1833.
23. See above, pp. 40ff.

ancient Hebrew sources. In this connection he manifested acute critical sense when he expressed his deep regret that there is no Hebrew translation of the works of Flavius Josephus which would doubtless be able to throw light on numerous obscure passages in the Talmud. With incomparable acumen and with great effort and diligence he explored critically and scientifically the text of the entire Jerusalem Talmud, numerous Midrashim, and many other important works. Having great reverence for the text of the ancients, the Gaon carried through his critical labor with extreme caution. Every emendation cost him a vast amount of time and effort; and his pupils relate that he would spend entire months of toilsome work over a correction to an erroneous text.[24] On the other hand, however, once he became convinced of the correctness of his conjecture, he fearlessly altered the text and eliminated or carried over from one chapter into another entire lines and sentences. Very frequently Elijah managed with one brief note or a word to destroy whole mountains of idle theories and ingenious subtleties elaborated by his predecessors, and what had earlier appeared to be so difficult, confused, and incomprehensible became all at once simple and clear. He would make most of his profound and valuable explanations in the form of notes on the margins of the book in question. In the Asiatic Museum of Leningrad there is a copy of the *Mechilta* on the margins of whose pages the Gaon wrote his notes and corrections, and in fact it was from this copy that they were reprinted in all later editions of the *Mechilta* under the title *Eifat Tzedek.*[25]

There is no doubt that, from the present-day scholarly point of view, the method of comparison which the Gaon of Vilna employed is not an altogether reliable one. The dissimilar texts of one and the same law or decision in different sources are not always a result of a plain scribal mistake, i.e., the fact that the

24. See Rabbi Ḥayyim Volozhiner's introduction to *Sifra De-Tzeniuta.*
25. We noted earlier that the Gaon of Vilna in his own lifetime did not publish a single one of his numerous works. Many of these were written not with his own hand. In order not to permit any undesired falsifications, the rabbis of Vilna, immediately after the Gaon's death, issued a proclamation to the effect that no one should undertake to publish any work whatsoever under the Gaon's name before a competent court determined, after a thorough investigation, that the composition in question was in fact composed by the Gaon. The most important part of the Gaon's literary legacy was published by his sons and disciples. Not all of these, however, possessed the requisite knowledge, and for this reason some of the Gaon's works appeared with numerous errors. For a full roster of the Gaon's compositions, see our article in the Russian-Jewish Encyclopedia, Vol. VIII.

copyists erred and corrupted the text. Either according to the world outlook or according to the time and environment in which the persons who edited them lived, the sources in question obtained a very different tendency and style. But this, Elijah, who lived on the boundary of two eras, could not recognize, despite all his brilliance. With his acute scholarly sense it was, indeed, clear to him that the tradition and customs of various periods are definitely associated with the Biblical legacy, with the laws and rules of the Torah. But it could not occur to him that the Oral Torah is a product of later generations, that it is the continuation, the necessary further development and supplement, of the Written Torah—a supplement which protects the written law so that it should not become rigid and petrified. The written law is only the guideline, the fundamental principle, which, whenever it is carried through in life, must assume forms that are organically linked with the time, place, and environment in question. If the forms do not change, then the law loses its ground in reality; it becomes an anachronism, a withered thing. This truth in general, however, was still foreign to that age, which had little proper feeling for historical development. Even less could it be apprehended by the Gaon of Vilna, who grew up in the narrow world view of *Shulḥan Aruch* rabbinism. The living tradition, a result of the historical process, is transformed by him into principles firmly established for all generations with a definitive vesture and form, over which life may not and must not have any dominion. In the view of the Gaon, the Oral Torah in relation to the Torah of Moses makes no innovations and introduces no new elements from the outside world and later generations into itself. Both Torot together are *Halachah Le-Mosheh Mi-Sinai* (the law of Moses from Sinai), a divine revelation on Mount Sinai in the sight of all Israel. The task of the Talmud and all its commentators is merely to interpret the laws and rules that were given for eternity, for all future ages. To be sure, the Gaon of Vilna with his sharp and critical scholarly insight realized what no other Talmudic scholar of that time perceived, namely, that the sages of the Talmud with their interpretations and explanations at times contradict the real meaning of the Torah. He notes openly and fearlessly that the Oral Torah, i.e., the Talmud, *okeret et ha-mikra*, "undermines the Torah of Moses." As a child of his time, however, he could not recognize in this a consequence of the altered conditions of life which require that a new meaning, better suited to the demands of the age, be placed in the word of the written laws. He sees in this only "the greatness of the Oral Torah," a strong proof that both together, the Written Torah and the Torah of Moses, are "the words of the living God" and *Halachah Le-Mosheh Mi-Sinai.*

Hence, it is quite logical, from the Gaon's standpoint, that he complains strongly of the later codifiers and commentators whenever he perceives in them any tendency to adjust the written law to the demands of life. This is manifested with special clarity in his commentary to the *Shulḥan Aruch,* in which he endeavors to disclose the sources and essence of each individual law. He is an extremely strict constructionist and stands firm in insisting on every iota of the law, on all the rigors and fine points associated with any commandment. He finds that one must not in this respect take account of the authority of the men of the *Shulḥan Aruch,* and he attacks in rather sharp terms his own grandfather, Moses Rivkes, the author of *Be'er Ha-Golah,* because the latter was at times inclined to be lenient in interpreting certain commandments and laws. The Gaon issues forth in the most determined fashion against all the ordinances which eminent rabbinic authorities introduced in order to make certain Sabbath rules more lenient. For instance, he concludes that outside Palestine one may not carry any object on the Sabbath even when there is an *eruv.* He also finds that the customs of the days of the Talmudic sages which had become obsolete in the course of time ought to be reintroduced.[26]

It is not the law that must be adapted to life, but life to the law—this was the Gaon's fundamental principle. Every rule, every custom, must abide for all generations; not a single letter, not the least jot, may be altered. "The commandments are fixed, and no innovations may be introduced into them," he declares.[27] And in the observance of the *mitzvot* lies the goal and purpose of human life. In the world view of the Gaon, the religious cult holds the highest of places. "The commandments are the will of God;"[28] they are the "garments of the *Shechinah,*"[29] and the whole Torah, all the acts commanded in it, are associated with this divine vesture. The commandments are the cornerstone of morality. The righteous, declares the Gaon,

26. All the biographers emphasize what a strict constructionist the Gaon was in regard to every custom or law. See for example *Aliyyat Eliahu,* 33–34, 70.
27. *Tanna Dvei Eliahu,* 21.
28. *Ibid.,* 40.
29. *Sifra De-Tzeniuta,* 47.

do not long "either for the pleasant or the useful but for the good in itself," the essence of the good—and "this is the commandments."[30] "What can be higher, what better," he demands, "than fulfilling the commandments?" For him, the great ascetic, his departure from the world was a matter of regret only because after death he would no longer be able to observe any commandments and thereby serve God. When, on the festival of Sukkot, the Gaon lay on his deathbed, he refused to let out of his rigid hand the citron and palm-branch and, in fact, expired holding on to them.

So, in this remarkable man, who stood on the boundary of two eras, the brilliant scholar lived peaceably with the pious servant who was a "Canaanite slave" of congealed dogma. As a scholar and indefatigable investigator, he considered man's highest task to be striving and searching for scientific truth. Knowledge attained all at once, without painful and laborious effort, has no value whatever for him. "For the precepts and concepts which the proclaiming angels and the princes of the Torah may have brought me but for which I myself did not labor and over which I did not sharpen my own mind," declares the Gaon, "I have no desire."[31] "The Torah is given only through toil and suffering."[32] Man must spend his entire life in the study of Torah. He must dwell on it day and night, every hour, every minute.[33] The astute scholar and investigator, however, is subordinate to the pious servant who stands watch and is prepared to sacrifice himself for the least custom, for every jot and tittle of a withered law. Blindly to observe all the customs and laws without any speculation or investigation, the Gaon insists, is the principal thing in human life, the highest level of "serving God"; and the "service of God" is, in his view, the supreme goal that requires no recompense. "Elijah," he used to say of himself, "can serve God without any world-to-come."

The Gaon of Vilna is undoubtedly one of the most tragic figures in the history of Jewish culture in the eighteenth century. His fate forcibly reminds one of Gulliver, the hero of the famous English satirist Jonathan Swift, who was cast away in a land of dwarfs, the Liliputians. Gulliver was a colossal giant

30. *Tanna Dvei Eliahu*, 39.
31. See the preface to *Sifra De-Tzeniuta*.
32. *Tanna Dvei Eliahu*, 40.
33. "For a man ought to study the Torah day and night . . . at all times and every hour" (See *Tanna Dvei Eliahu*, 7, 21).

among these little people, but the latter tied him up with a thousand slender threads while he was asleep. The giant could not rend these threads, so numerous were they; and he lay among the dwarfs bound, incapable of moving a limb. Just such a tragic figure was Rabbi Elijah of Vilna. He was a brilliant figure, a giant, but hemmed in by thousands of threads of dried-up laws and rigidified customs. A great scholar with a sharp, critical eye, he was, nevertheless, also a blind man who groped in darkness and could not distinguish the withered husk from the kernel, the dead from the living substance. The cobwebs of his darkened, isolated age obscured the light of the sun from his eagle's gaze.

As a scholar, the Gaon of Vilna undoubtedly created the most significant and valuable things which it was at all possible to create within the limits of the contemporary rabbinic world. But, with all his extraordinary gifts, he could not tear himself out of these narrow boundaries. A profound investigator with a keen, analytic mind, he was at the same time a fanatical zealot who bowed down before every dead letter of the written law. Unusually strict with himself in regard to the "service of the Creator," i.e., the observance of the commandments, he was no less strict with others in this respect. In ritual questions he was truly "a man of war," capable of persecuting anyone to utter destruction for the least trifle. Every law or custom must be fulfilled in the most rigorous fashion, and every inclination to be lenient, even if derived from reliance on respected rabbinic authorities, must be punished. When he writes to his son, admonishing the latter to take heed that his daughters conduct themselves piously and with due reverence, he notes that for disobedience, for telling a lie and the like, "you should beat them mercilessly."[34]

This intensely fanatical element in the character of the Gaon, particularly when "the service of the Creator" as he understands it is in question, makes his role in the struggle against the Hasidic movement understandable. The religious controversy which broke out at that time between the Hasidim and Mitnagdim had, as we shall see later, socio-economic causes also, as was the case in the controversy between the community leaders of Vilna and the followers of the *rav ha-aharon*, Samuel ben Avigdor. The Gaon of Vilna who played such a prominent role in the former struggle acted, however, out of purely ideological motives. Isolated from the world, he

34. *Alim Li-Terufah*, 15, 22 (we quote according to the Vilna edition of 1865).

had at first no comprehension whatever of the new movement that had appeared in the Jewish sector. But for the Mitnagdim it was extremely important to make use of the immense authority of the Gaon in this battle; hence, they endeavored to familiarize him as quickly as possible with the "heresy" and "harmfulness" of the new movement which might—God forbid—bring about "destruction of the faith."

The Gaon was necessarily hostile toward the Hasidic teaching with its slogans proclaiming that, without the living spirit of enthusiasm, the written letter of the law is dead and withered, and that in religious practice the chief thing is not the mechanical, formal observance of the law but permeating it with warm and living content, for in the religious realm morality is above cult and the conscious sentiment of conviction is more important than the mechanically performed commandment. Being the solitary ascetic he was, firmly persuaded that "the evil inclination comes only from eating and rejoicing," the Gaon had to be extremely suspicious of the statement of the Baal Shem Tov that "man must always rejoice, for God can be served not with sorrow but only through joy." The contempt with which the Hasidim regarded the arid "scholars," and the fact that they established their own Hasidic conventicles and places of worship with their own ritual, enraged the Gaon even more against the new sect. He perceived in it the direct continuation of the Sabbatian sect and a serious threat to the survival of Judaism. Hence he decided that "it is time to act for the sake of the Lord; they have nullified Thy Torah." To defend the faith one must not recoil before the harshest measures. At his direction the Hasidim were excommunicated in all the synagogues and houses of study of Vilna with black candles and loud blasts of the *shofar*.

When the community preacher, Rabbi Ḥayyim, who sympathized with the Hasidim and insulted the Gaon of Vilna behind his back, came to him at the insistence of the community to beg forgiveness, the Gaon replied with great indignation that he could forgive him for the insult to himself but for the offense "to God and His Torah" he could never forgive him or his colleagues. "Rabbi," the preacher begged, "set us a penance!" "No," was the Gaon's answer; " 'All who come to her will not return'; for the wicked there is no salvation." "Had I the power," he declared, "I would condemn them [the Hasidim] as Elijah the prophet condemned the prophets of Baal."[35]

35. D. Kahana, in *Ha-Shiloaḥ*, XX, 364.

When the leader of the White Russian Hasidim, Shneur Zalman of Lyady, undertook a special journey to Vilna to see the Gaon in person and to persuade him that the Hasidim are not at all "breakers of the fence" and do not undermine the foundations of the faith, the Gaon refused to see him on the ground that "with a *Min Yisrael* (Israelite heretic) it is forbidden to hold converse."

The Gaon's hostility to the Hasidim grew even greater after the rabbi of Polonnoye, Jacob Joseph, a disciple of the Baal Shem Tov, published his *Toledot Yaakov Yosef*, in which the foundations of Hasidism were first presented in systematic form. In his work the contempt with which the Hasidim regarded the "scholars" appears with special clarity. Furthermore, in it the pantheistic view that all things that exist are the Creator's vestments, as well as the fundamental teaching of the Baal Shem Tov that there is no clear-cut distinction not only between matter and spirit but even between good and evil, since evil is the foundation of good, are also carried through in an extremely dangerous way. At the command of the Gaon, the Hasidic writings were publicly burned in numerous places, and on a Sabbath in all the houses of study of Vilna a proclamation was issued in which the excommunication of the Hasidism was re-confirmed. In mixed language, half Yiddish and half Hebrew, all "the holy community" are enjoined to gird up their loins

to strengthen the faith of our holy Torah and to remove the thorns from the vineyard of the congregation of Israel ... And upon those who strengthen their hands and give counsel and protect them, all the excommunications fall ... Every man should remove them with both hands. Go forth and tell them that they are excommunicated and banned, separated from the entire congregation of Israel. Of course, one may not associate with them or speak with them. Also the people who belong to this sect within our community are banned under the great ban, so that they must remove their residence from our community with their wives and children ... And whoever shall violate this is excommunicated and banned, and all the curses will fall upon his head.[36]

There is no doubt that the persecuted Hasidim were involved in the accusation mentioned above[37] in which, among other sins that the leaders of the Vilna community are alleged

36. *Ibid.*, 528.
37. See above, p. 222, note 13.

to have committed, is also mentioned the fact that "one Elias Zalmanov," who is called by the surname Ḥasid, does no work and yet is supported at the community's expense with great generosity and is, in addition, exempted from all taxes. In consonance with this, the tradition that at the beginning of 1788 the Gaon was imprisoned for several weeks in the fortress of Vilna obtains a certain real foundation. To the end of his life the fanatical Rabbi Elijah carried on a bitter struggle against "the breakers of the fence," the Hasidim. A year before his death (1796) he addressed an open letter to those "who tremble at the word of the Lord and His Torah, the children of Abraham, Isaac and Jacob," declaring that everyone who bears a Jewish name and "has the fear of God in his heart" is obliged to persecute the Hasidim ruthlessly, "to drive and pursue them with all kinds of oppressions and to humble them as far as the hand of Israel reaches," for their sin is great and "they are as troublesome to Israel as leprosy." A few days before his death he once again addressed an open letter to the leaders of the community, admonishing them not to forget the controversy for the sake of heaven and to see to it that the Hasidim are rooted out. "Let no man have mercy on them or be gracious to them; let this sinful congregation be pushed away and isolated; whoever listens to them or associates with them is to be punished."

CHAPTER SIX

The Maggid of Dubno;
THE PIONEERS OF ENLIGHTENMENT

The disciples of the Gaon of Vilna—the Maggid of Dubno—New tendencies—Back to Maimonides—The truthseekers—Rabbi Solomon ben Moses Chelm, Raphael Levi the "mathematician," and Israel of Zamosc—Abba Glusk and Solomon Maimon.

E HAVE observed that the Gaon of Vilna lived at the boundary of two worlds, that he was a man of two "forms" at a crossroads. He stood with both feet in the past, and yet in certain areas he was an innovator, one of the first in the Jewish environment who pointed to new ways leading to a freer, broader world. An obdurate battler for the old *Shulḥan Aruch* rabbinism with all its rules, severities, and subtleties, the Gaon was also in a certain sense a harbinger of a new era, an era of enlightenment and secular knowledge for the Jews of Lithuania who at that time, with the collapse of the Polish kingdom, fell under the dominion of the Russian empire. With his vast authority, he became the chief pillar of all who strove for secular knowledge and whose thirsting, seeking spirits could be satisfied neither by the mysteries of the practical Kabbalah nor by arid *pilpul.* For these the Gaon was the central figure to whom all who were eager for knowledge were attracted. Even men who lived far away from Vilna turned their eyes to him. From distant places men would pilgrimage to Vilna, and anyone who had the privilege of being admitted to Rabbi Elijah's private room and speaking person to person with the great solitary and ascetic or hearing Torah from his mouth considered himself fortunate. The above-mentioned preacher, Ezekiel Feivel, relates proudly in the introduction to his *Toledot Adam* that he had the privilege of speaking personally with the Gaon all of five times.

A very unique place among the Gaon's associates was occupied by an unusual and original personality. This man was named Jacob ben Wolf Kranz, but it is the rare person who knows and remembers this name, for he became famous and beloved in the memory of the people not under his private name but simply as the Maggid (preacher) of Dubno. He was not a battler for knowledge or culture and did not seek any new ways; he was a simple preacher. Nevertheless, he was one of the new, one of the liberators, one of those who endeavored to bring into the stifling atmosphere of the house of study fresh air, the sap of life, and the odor of the green fields.

Born in 1740 into a prominent rabbinic family in the little town of Zietil in the government of Vilna, Jacob Kranz at the age of eighteen became a preacher in Mezeritz, thereafter spent a brief period as preacher in Zolkiev, all of eighteen years in Dubno, and then lived in Wlodawa, Chelm, and finally Zamosc, where he died in 1804. But this preacher was quite unlike the preachers of his era, both those who would cast fear on the people with accounts of the terrible afflictions awaiting them in hell for the least transgression and the others whose sole intent was to demonstrate to their auditors their great keenness and brilliance in *pilpul*, to overwhelm them with ingenious subtleties. Of an altogether different type was the Maggid of Dubno. In the construction of his sermons he did, indeed, maintain the old, firmly established way. Each sermon begins with a verse of the *sidra* (pericope assigned for reading on a particular week), with one of the verses that is not altogether smooth and simple and begs, as Rashi puts it, "Explain me." In the exegesis of the verse, in the unique way of interpreting it, lie all the charm and attractive power of the sermons of the Maggid.

Jacob Kranz does not build his explanations on keen subtleties; he does not abound with quotations and verses from the sacred books. He turns, rather, to common life, to the living source of popular creativity, and from there draws whole treasures, marvelous pearls and precious stones. The Jewish community was astonished not so much by his extraordinary oratorical gift but mainly by his great astuteness and profound knowledge of life. A man of insight was the Maggid, but his insight was of a very unique kind—not a pedantic but a popular one, derived not from books but from the depths of the people's life. He was one of those popular sages who absorb the wisdom of the community, of practical life itself, which is the consequence, the end-product, of entire generations. Jacob Kranz was blessed with a rare talent, of which he himself was perhaps unaware. In him was hidden a spark of the poet—the poet who thinks not in abstract concepts but in living images and similes. He had the eye of the artist which observes what is hidden to the ordinary mortal. And it is precisely the hidden that is the most important, the essence of life. The Maggid understood how to clothe abstract and complex problems in a simple and genuinely popular garment. Arid intellectual principles were transformed by him into lovely allegories and parables that bubble with knowledge of life and popular insight. Profound ideas and difficult problems obtained in this preacher a remarkably beautiful vestment, were transformed into simple anecdotes and proverbs filled with a special charm.

The stories and tales woven into the sermons of the Maggid are extremely diverse. Some of them are reminiscent of the allegories employed by the thinkers of the ancient world. Others, again, bear the impress of native popular creativity. To familiarize the reader with his unique homiletic art, we quote here a few fragments of his sermons.

It is written in the Torah, "Honor thy father and thy mother." Everything that one's father and mother request, one is obliged to fulfill. But the question arises: Whose commandment is to be fulfilled first—the commandment of father and mother or the commandment of God? Jacob Kranz answers this question in a lovely popular tale whose motif is also widespread among other Eastern peoples:[1]

Once upon a time there were three friends who decided to set out over the world to learn all kinds of wisdoms and sciences. All three agreed that they would go to different lands and at a pre-arranged time meet again at a certain place. And so it was. At the appointed

1. For a very unique Yiddish variant of this story, see the collection *Bay Undz Yidn*, 68–69.

time the three friends assembled at the specified place and each began to relate the new things he had learned in the world. One told that he had devised an amazing little mirror in which one can immediately see everything that takes place in the whole world. The second boasted that he had fabricated a chariot with which one can effect the most miraculous 'foreshortening of the way' and which can bring one to the most distant places in a moment.[2] The third related that he possessed a remarkable apple of paradise which at once cures all kinds of diseases; as soon as a sick person smells the apple he becomes well. Fatigued from the difficult journey, the three friends lay down to rest. Then the first began to look at his miraculous mirror. He saw that in the capital city there was a great tumult; everyone was running to the palace, where the king's only daughter lay grievously ill and all the doctors had already despaired of her. The three friends thereupon ascended the marvelous chariot and in a moment were in the capital city. They were at once admitted to the palace, and as soon as the sick princess had a whiff of the apple of paradise she rose fresh and well. Joy was boundless. All marvelled at the wisdom of the three friends, thanks to whom the emperor's only daughter was saved. The overjoyed emperor declared that all his treasures were too small to repay the great favor they had done his daughter; hence, he was prepared to marry her to that one of the three whom they themselves would determine. The three friends could not reach agreement, for each of them argued that he was the most deserving. The first pointed out that, had it not been for his little mirror, they would never have known of the princess's danger. The second argued that if it were not for his chariot they would not have been able to arrive with their aid in time. And the third noted that the sick princess was cured only by his miraculous apple. When it became apparent that the friends could not agree, it was decided to ask the princess herself. She replied: It is certain that for my recovery I am indebted in equal measure to all three friends; all this, however, is in regard to what is already past; as far as the future is concerned, for my coming lifepath I shall no longer require either the mirror or the chariot; only of the apple of paradise will I be in constant need, for it is the source of health and life.

After the tale comes Jacob Kranz's explanation: "Our sages say that there are three partners in a man. Three participate in his birth—the Holy One, blessed be He, his father, and his mother. Certainly a man is indebted to his father and mother for the fact that he was born, but this is something that happened long ago. Of God's grace and providence, however,

2. In the Arabic version of this story a magic flying carpet takes the place of the chariot.

he has need all his days—every minute and every second."[3]

Constructed in the spirit of the sages of the ancient world is another parable of the Maggid. He introduces the statement of an old Midrash to the effect that one of the most precious things in the world is the limitation of man's understanding (literally, a little foolishness). The Maggid asks: Is this so? How is it possible that folly is "one of the most precious things created in the world"? He then proceeds to explain the Midrash with the following story:

Once upon a time there lived a very wealthy man who was a terrible miser. He lived in constant fear that someone might discover where he was hiding his gold and silver; hence, he concealed his wealth in the most unlikely places, so that no one would know. It happened, however, that the miser suddenly died; the secret of his treasures was buried with him, and no one knew where his wealth was. The miser's house passed through inheritance to one of his relatives, who had no notion that great treasures were hidden in it. It then happened that a gold coin once slipped out of the new owner's hand and rolled somewhere, so that he could not find it. The owner searched in all corners until he decided to remove a board in the floor, thinking it possible that the coin had fallen through a crack. But how great was his excitement when he found in place of his lost coin a whole kettle of golden ducats. He continued to search for his lost coin and thereby discovered ever new treasures. When he finally found the lost coin, it was extremely precious to him and he refused to part with it, for he owed all his wealth to it.

After the parable comes the lesson. "God blessed be He," declares Jacob Kranz, "created man with a weak, limited mind. Only because man understands so little does he long all his days for what he does not grasp and what is hidden from his short-sighted eyes. The more limited a man's knowledge, the more he seeks, and ever greater become the treasures he obtains."

It is written in the Bible (Psalm 113), "From the rising of the sun to the going down thereof the name of the Lord is to be praised." But there are in the world so many idolators who do not praise the Creator but worship idols of wood and stone. In this connection, the Maggid relates the following tale: "There was once a great sage whose name resounded over all lands. An impostor came who travelled about from city to city and everywhere gave himself out as the sage. The impostor was received in every city with great honor. The sage's relatives and friends

3. *Mishlei Yaakov*, No. 81.

learned of this and became extremely indignant, but the wise man only smiled. 'Let him be,' he said to his friends; 'this impostor is spreading my fame, and the honor that is done him is, after all, intended for me!' " "The idolators," Jacob Kranz explains, "do indeed kneel before pieces of wood, but they themselves believe they bow before the true God, the Lord of life and creation. And if this be so, is not God's name praised and revered?"[4]

When the Maggid of Dubno attempts to offer consolation and hope to the exiled people,[5] he marvels at the greatness and glory of man, before whom the angels bow with reverence.[6] Always we see before us the man of insight who knows the spirit of the people so well and understands in masterly fashion how to awaken the innermost strings of its soul. Genuine spiritual nobility resounds in Jacob Kranz' little tale about the prince who found himself in disfavor with his father.[7] According to the story, a prince offended his father by some act, and the king drove him out of the palace. The prince thereupon roamed among strangers until he hired himself out as a servant to a peasant in a village. The peasant was a crude and extremely hard-hearted man who begrudged his servant the morsel of bread he gave him and burdened him with heavy labor. Many years later the king began to long for the son whom he had driven away and decided to seek him out. How shattered the father was when he saw that his son who, after all, was destined to rule over whole lands and countries, was so degraded and fallen that he was concerned with obtaining favor from the gross, ignorant peasant, so that the latter would give him enough bread and not mercilessly wear him out with burdensome work beyond his powers.

The Maggid of Dubno was admired and revered by all; he was loved not only by the common people but also by the great scholars of the time. Moses Mendelssohn, with whom Jacob Kranz became acquainted when he visited Berlin, was enchanted by the Maggid's ingenious parables and called him "the Jewish Aesop," and the rigorously ascetic Rabbi Elijah, the Gaon of Vilna, would frequently write to him to invite him to visit, and always said that the Maggid's parables and ideas cured him of every sickness.[8]

---

4. *Ibid.*, 49.
5. *Ibid.*, 16th parable.
6. *Ibid.*, 110th parable.
7. *Ibid.*, 209th parable.
8. See *Aliyyat Eliahu*, Fourth Edition, 72–73; *Mishlei Yaakov*, 5. Like the Gaon of Vilna,

Into the dry, ascetic, melancholy environment Jacob Kranz carried the cheerful, life-loving humor of the people. With his fresh and clear spirit he could be satisfied neither with the artificial cobwebs of keen *pilpul* nor with the mystical rites of the practical Kabbalah. Thus he followed where his natural endowment instinctively led him, to the living source of popular creativity. But Jacob Kranz was not the only one who at that time endeavored to seek new ways. He was merely one of the first swallows who proclaimed the coming of an intellectual ferment and the new tendencies that appeared in Polish-Lithuanian Jewry in the second half of the eighteenth century.

The *Jewish* Middle Ages, the period of cultural barbarization and regress for Jewry, we have observed, began only in the second half of the seventeenth century. The rabbinic world was rigid and congealed. Messianic-mystical tendencies became lost in a labyrinth of pathological, fantastic dreams, and crippled thought struggled helplessly in a thick forest of vast contradictions, thereby losing the boundary between good and evil, between the morally clean and the filthy and corrupted. Yet, despite the intellectual distortion and the severe economic decline, the organism of the people still possessed a sufficiency of healthy spiritual powers, and these promptly rose to the surface of communal life on the emergence of the first favorable conditions. At the very time that mystical-messianic currents gave birth to Frankism, which declared bitter war against Judaism and the followers of which issued forth with extreme hostility against their own brethren, there appeared out of the depths of the people's life a new tendency that grew on the very soil of the mystical world of ideas into the powerful Hasidic movement, a movement that had an enormous influence on the further cultural development of all of east European Jewry. New tendencies also became noticeable in the upper, learned circles. Certain elements came into existence which could no longer be content with arid *pilpul* or with mystical-messianic dreams. A select few appeared who had an inkling, even though quite obscurely and unclearly, of the great new powers with which the civilized world of western Europe was

---

the Maggid of Dubno did not publish a single one of his works in his own lifetime. Only after his death were his manuscripts published by his son Isaac and his pupil A. B. Plahm. His most important works are *Ohel Yaakov* (first printed in 1830) and *Sefer Ha-Middot* which first appeared in 1862 with a long introduction in which biographical details about the author are given. In 1886 M. Nussbaum of Przemysl took out from *Ohel Yaakov* all the parables and stories and published them in a separate work entitled *Mishlei Yaakov*.

then pregnant. Hence they sought and searched, desiring to learn the nature of the newly born.

Certain very important factors helped this along powerfully. *Shulḥan Aruch* rabbinism, on the one side, and the virulent hatred and arrogant contempt of the outside world, on the other, did indeed endeavor to raise the wall separating the Jewish ghetto from that world as high as possible. But economic interests are an extremely powerful factor in social life, and these managed in places—and as time went on, increasingly so—to break through the wall. Strong as the isolation of spiritual and intellectual life in the Jewish sector was, economically the Jews of eastern Europe were not "a people dwelling alone." Many Lithuanian cities, such as Vilna, Shklov, and the like, carried on trade with Königsberg, Danzig, and Frankfurt-am-Oder. At the fairs in Leipzig Jewish merchants from Lithuania played a prominent role, and such Galician cities as Brody traded not only with Germany but even with England. It was not merchants alone who had the opportunity to become familiar with the European world, but Jewish teachers and scholars as well. To be sure, at that time Talmudic knowledge was so widespread in Lithuania that the scholar and the merchant were very frequently combined in one person. For generations Poland had provided the German communities with preachers, teachers, and scholars. The Polish scholars would frequently come to wealthy Jewish homes which, simply out of economic considerations, could not lead a completely isolated life or remain entirely alien to the external cultural environment. We have already seen that the ultra-pious Jacob Emden complained of wealthy Jews in Germany who imitated the nobility and permitted their children to study French and play music. It was precisely in Germany that great transformations in cultural life took place at that time. In the upper intellectual strata the influence of the British philosophers and the French rationalists and enlighteners became increasingly marked. Drawing nourishment from neighboring France, Germany's spirit began to revive, and the first rays of the classical period in German national literature began to appear.

These important cultural events initially found a very weak and barely perceptible resonance in the old-fashioned ghetto. The European world was too foreign and incomprehensible to the Lithuanian-Polish travelers. Nevertheless they felt that there, in the alien world, immense spiritual treasures were hidden. They could not properly appreciate these treasures, but they nevertheless awoke from their spiritual and intellectual slumber; they began to lose their undisturbed rest. They still belonged entirely to the old world; the traditional way of life had not lost its charm for them, but they could no longer be content with the ingenious subtleties of arid *pilpul* or with the fantastic web of Kabbalist mysticism. Half awakened, they still groped in darkness, and with longing souls sought a guide who might lead them to the right path, so that they would not have to wander in the night.

At first they sought not in the external world—so far they still did not go—but among themselves, in the Jewish sector. Rabbinic literature could not assuage the thirst for knowledge that had been aroused, and precisely for this reason an interesting phenomenon appears at the beginning of the second half of the eighteenth century, namely, a powerfully renewed interest in the medieval Arabic-Jewish philosophers, especially Maimonides.[9] Again, as in former generations, Maimonides became the teacher of life, the Urim and Tummim of all who longed for knowledge, and his *Guide for the Perplexed* once more became the pointer of the way for searching young minds. It was not by accident that publishers at that time again remembered Maimonides' masterpiece. *A Guide for the Perplexed* was among the first Jewish books to come off the printing press. It was then several times reprinted, the last time in 1553. In the middle of the sixteenth century, however, Kabbalist works attracted increasing interest. The *Zohar* and the *Shulḥan Aruch* occupied the dominant places, and Maimonides' philosophical treatise no longer found a publisher for a period of almost two centuries. *A Guide for the Perplexed* became suspect; it was overly infected with the *ḥochmot ḥitzoniyyot* (secular sciences) which might bring one to heresy, lead him away from the right path, and alienate him from commandments and good deeds. Only when the renewed interest in medieval works of philosophical speculation became marked was it also found necessary to reprint the *Guide* in Jessnitz in 1742.

One of the first prominent scholars and Talmudists who showed a strong interest in medieval philosophy was the enlightened Rabbi Solomon ben Moses Chelm. We have very few biographical details about him; even the year of his birth has not been definitely ascertained. It is known that he was born in Zamosc and that in his youth he served as rabbi in Chelm and later occupied the rabbinic office in his native city. After

9. Unfortunately, the Jewish historians of culture have given very little attention to this phenomenon.

Rabbi Ḥayyim Rapoport died in Lemberg, the Polish Wojewoda Chartoriski appointed Solomon Chelm to the vacant post in December, 1771. Six years later Chelm resigned from the rabbinate and set out for Palestine. En route he stopped in Salonika, where he arranged the second edition of his major work, *Mirkevet Ha-Mishneh* (a commentary to Maimonides' *Yad Ha-Ḥazakah*). While he was engaged in this work death unexpectedly overtook him in 1778.[10]

In the interesting introduction to his *Mirkevet Ha-Mishneh* (which first appeared in 1751) Chelm relates how even in his youth he regarded the method of *pilpul* with disfavor because he had become convinced that *pilpul* only confuses young minds and is an obstacle to knowledge. Of all the medieval scholars and codifiers, the greatest authority for him is Maimonides. The author of the *Mishneh Torah* and *A Guide for the Perplexed* is, in his view, the single and incomparable one, "the great eagle with the mighty wings," the foremost Jewish scholar, a man of God of whom it may be said that "from Moses to Moses there arose none like Moses,"[11] and whose works are therefore for him "sweeter than everything in the world." Solomon Chelm was no longer content merely with the Talmud and rabbinic codes. He relates how in his youth *A Guide for the Perplexed* became for him the pointer of the way and how, thanks to it, he began to study logic, astronomy, and other sciences, especially mathematics, which became his favorite discipline.

We observed above that at the end of the seventeenth century one of the greatest rabbinic authorities of that age, Yair Ḥayyim Bacharach, the author of *Ḥavvot Yair*, deemed it necessary to stress that "contemporary generations act properly" in removing themselves from such studies as Albo's *Ikkarim*, Jehudah Halevi's *Kuzari*, and the like, "because it is good for us and for our children to believe in everything that is laid upon us without any speculation or investigation."[12] But

10. For further details about Solomon Chelm's life, see Solomon Buber, *Anshei Shem*, 207–209.
11. In his introduction to *Mirkevet Ha-Mishneh* Chelm writes feelingly of Maimonides: "The great eagle with mighty wings, father of all the sons of Eber and father of a multitude, our master Moses ben Maimon of whom it was said: From Moses until Moses . . . If all reeds were pens and men copyists, they could not write the tiniest part [of his greatness] . . . For this is Moses, the man who went free, beyond human intellect; he rose from height to height, and for him silence is praise."
12. Above, p. 140.

fifty years later the rabbi of the little town of Zamosc, Solomon Chelm, already considers it possible to battle against "the fools and obscurantists" who think there is heresy in education and in the secular sciences. Without such sciences as mathematics, astronomy, zoology, and the like, Chelm declares, one is quite unable to understand numerous laws in the Torah. Precisely for this reason, he adds, our great scholars and sages in former generations were proficient in all the sciences, in every branch of knowledge. Like the Gaon of Vilna, Chelm underscored the importance of competence in Hebrew grammar. He also practiced what he preached and himself composed a work on grammar entitled *Shaarei Ne'imah.*

Rabbi Solomon Chelm was not singular in his generation. Another ardent admirer of Maimonides was Raphael Levi Hanover, born in the little town of Weickersheim in 1685.[13] For him, too, *A Guide for the Perplexed* was the awakener and pointer of the way. With great diligence he studied natural sciences and philosophy, carried on a correspondence with Moses Mendelssohn on philosophical issues,[14] and was on friendly terms with the famous Leibniz whom he served for a time as personal secretary.[15] As was the case with Solomon Chelm, so also for Raphael Hanover mathematics was his most congenial study, and in the Jewish world he therefore became known as "Rabbi Raphael the mathematician." In 1756 he submitted to the Academy of Leyden his *Luḥot Ha-Ibbur*, and in the same year published his *Techunat Ha-Shamayim* (on calender science) which he composed, as he explains in the introduction, to make available and easily comprehensible Maimonides' masterly

---

13. He died in great old age on May 17, 1779. For biographical details, see *Literaturblatt des Orients*, 1849, 140–143.

14. A letter of Mendelssohn to Hanover is published in Mendelssohn's *Gesammelte Schriften*, (1845), V, 446–449. See also *Historishe Shriftn*, Vol. 1, 304, 340.

15. When the renowned thinker died solitary and forsaken in Hannover, the city magistracy and the clergy concluded that it was inappropriate to accompany the "rationalistically" minded scholar to the grave, and following his casket was a single admirer, his faithful disciple Raphael Levi. It is he who is meant by G. Fost in the poem dedicated to Leibniz's memory in which he writes:

> Zuletzt erscheint der Mann.
> der seines Lehrers Sarg
> Einsam um Mitternacht begleitet,
> Ein alter (?) Jude war's—und leitet
> Ihn zu der oden Grüft,
> Die dich, o Leibniz, barg.

(See *Zeitschrift für die Geschichte der Juden*, 1, 7).

Hilchot Kiddush Ha-Ḥodesh, which is like a "closed book" for the present-day Jewish scholars who have so little familiarity with mathematics and other sciences.[16]

A contemporary of Solomon Chelm and Raphael Hanover was the Galician, Israel ben Moses Zamosc.[17] In his case, also, *A Guide for the Perplexed* opened his eyes and aroused in him a thirst for education and knowledge. He immersed himself in the Jewish books of speculation, and his favorite studies were philosophy and mathematics. This, however, greatly displeased the pious inhabitants of the little town and they began to persecute the young "heretic" to the point that he had to leave his birthplace. To show how essential and important scientific knowledge is, Zamosc in 1741 printed his book, *Netzaḥ Yisrael,* in which he clarifies and elucidates many difficult and little understood passages in the Gemara with the aid of mathematics and astronomy. "There is no doubt," Solomon Maimon writes of Zamosc's work, "that Rabbi Israel was here more concerned with disseminating knowledge of mathematics among Jews than with explaining the law in the Gemara."

But this making of the sacred Gemara a secondary thing, this explaining of a topic without subtleties and *pilpul* but through algebra and geometry, was extremely repugnant to the pietistic public. It smacked of heresy. And so they began to persecute the *Netzaḥ* (as the common people called Zamosc because of his "heretical" work). He again took up the wanderer's staff and once more became an itinerant. A year later we find him in Berlin, where he obtained a position as tutor in the home of the wealthy banker Daniel Itzig. In his campaign for enlightenment Zamosc used to give lectures to intellectually curious young people and arouse in them the desire for education and knowledge. He was particularly interested in a sickly fifteen-year-old boy who had just come to Berlin from Dessau. Zamosc studied *A Guide for the Perplexed* with him and taught him mathematics and other sciences. This pupil in time became the pride and glory of German Jewry, the renowned Moses Mendelssohn.[18] Later Mendelssohn introduced his former teacher to

16. In the Berlin state library there is an unpublished manuscript by Hanover entitled *Ḥeshbon Ha-Ketz Veha-Teḥiyyah.*

17. Born in 1700. For details of his life, see I.B. Levinsohn in his *Zerubabbel,* I, 68; S.J. Fuenn in *Safah Le-Ne'emanim,* 149; S. Stanislavsky in *Voskhod,* 1886, VI, 131–137.

18. Solomon Maimon, when speaking in his *Autobiography* of Mendelssohn, gives the following description of the author of *Netzaḥ Yisrael:* "Mendelssohn was . . . a disciple of the then renowned Polish rabbi Israel of Nevish, or *Netzaḥ Yisrael,* as he was called after the title of his book. Besides his great Talmudic knowledge,

the great German figures of that era—Lessing, Nicolai and others—and these were fascinated by the original Jewish sage. Lessing praises him as a "profound and excellent mathematician." Friedrich Nicolai points out in his *Anmerkungen* to Mendelssohn's and Lessing's exchange of correspondence that Zamosc was "one of the first who aroused among the Jews of Berlin taste for the sciences," and that, as "a very excellent mind and great mathematician," he managed, despite the fact that he lived in great poverty, to attain such a high degree of learning that he was able to make important discoveries. Of Zamosc's last years Nicolai writes: "The Jews hated him as a freethinker . . . He was severely persecuted, and took this so much to heart that he fell into melancholia in his old age."[19]

Even more tragic was the fate of another battler for enlightenment who lived at the same time as Zamosc. Not even the name of this man is definitely known. There is some doubt as to whether he was called Abba or possibly Abraham. His own generation wished to erase his name from the memory of future generations, and, indeed, he would have been completely forgotten if the creator of "Peter Schlemihl," the well-known poet Adelbert von Chamisso, had not taken pity on him and described his tragic fate in his poem, "Abba Glusk Leczeka." This poem is virtually the only source we have for Glusk's sad life-story, but the source is not an altogether reliable one, since Chamisso came to Berlin as a ten-year-old child at the beginning of the 1790's, when Glusk was already long dead. Chamisso wrote his poem many years later; hence, it is extremely difficult to determine what in it is *Wahrheit* and what *Dichtung*.

---

this rabbi also had extensive and profound knowledge in other sciences, especially mathematics, which he studied thoroughly while still in Poland following certain Hebrew books, as may be seen from the work mentioned. Hence he was regarded in his region as a heretic. In this book one encounters solutions of very complex and important mathematical problems which are necessary to clarify certain obscure passages in the Talmud or to determine a law. To be sure, Rabbi Israel was here more concerned to disseminate useful knowledge among his people than to explain or determine a law, and for this purpose he took as a pretext the explanation of Talmudic laws" (*Lebensgeschichte*, Yiddish translation, 375–376.).

19. *Op. cit.*, 204–205. Israel Zomosc died in Brody in 1772. Of his manuscripts, several were later published (his commentaries to Jehudah Halevi's *Kuzari* and Baḥya Ibn Pakuda's *Ḥovot Ha-Levavot*). The rest, however, were lost, among them a large work *Aruvot Ha-Shamayim* on astronomy, with many drawings. Isaac Baer Levinsohn relates that he saw the manuscript at the home of Naḥman Krochmal, who intended to publish this work.

It has been conjectured that Abba was born near Lublin in the little town of Glusk.[20] In his case also his teachers and guides were the medieval Jewish thinkers of Arabic Spain; it was these who opened his eyes. Thanks to them, he learned that beyond the *Shulḥan Aruch* there is a wide world of ideas, and besides *pilpul* and legal responsa there are profound scientific questions and difficult philosophic problems. He became a preacher[21] and in his sermons disclosed his thoughts and doubts to the people. But his pious listeners detected heresy in his sermons and commenced to persecute him. Apparently he was forbidden to give sermons. But Abba Glusk had a fighter's nature and refused to surrender. He took up the pen and wrote numerous books.[22] These works, however, were never published; all his manuscripts were burned in the courtyard of the synagogue in Vilna.[23] He himself is reported to have been flogged and driven out of the city.[24] Abba Glusk wandered for a long time until he came to Berlin. There also he began to give addresses and to propagandize his liberal ideas among the young. This again was offensive to the orthodox, and they began to look with suspicion on the troublesome guest. The calm and sedate Mendelssohn advised him that it would be better not to be overly visible and insistent and not to disclose his free thoughts to the public. "If you wish to dwell here," Mendelssohn warned him, "better be silent and not reveal what is not suitable; better let your thought search in quietness and hiddenness."[25] "But," the *maggid* of Glusk asked him with astonishment, "if both of us keep silent about the truth, who will disclose it to

---

20. See *Ha-Karmel*, 1871, 462.
21. Some scholars conjecture that Abba Glusk and the well known *Maggid* of Glusk are one and the same person.
22. In Chamisso's poem Glusk declares: "Und dreizehn Bücher hatte Ich verfasst mit allen Fleiss."
23. See *Ha-Maggid*, 1871, 234.
24. Chamisso tells of this in his poem:
    > Ich selbst ich solte sterben, kaum heimlich war der Rath;
    > Doch fand sich ein Rabbiner, der um mein Leben bat,
    > Ich wurde bloss gegeisselt, und als man frei mich gab,
    > Da griff ich heitern Sinnes zu meinem Wanderstab.
    The author of *Aliyyat Eliahu* also tells (*ibid.*, Fourth Edition, 24) how in the courtyard of the synagogue in Vilna they flogged someone who was suspected of heresy, and he expresses the conjecture that this was Abba Glusk.
25. In Chamisso:
    > Bleib hier und lerne schweigen, wo sprechen nicht am Ort,
    > Du magst im stillen forschen, erwagen Geist und Wort.

the world, who will enlighten the people?"[26]

Once again Abba Glusk took up the wanderer's staff, roamed over Germany, Holland, France, and England, and nowhere found rest, until he finally returned to Poland. What later happened to him no one knows.

Abba Glusk was not alone in his bitter fate. In his time arose another, much more significant thinker who also had the courage openly to set himself against his environment. The name of this man could not be erased for future generations. He himself, after a long, painful road of grievous suffering and inhuman degradation, inscribed it with a firm hand in the history of European philosophical thought. This remarkable man was called Solomon ben Joshua. He was born in 1754 in a remote little town in Lithuania to a poor villager, and after his marriage earned a livelihood as a village *melamed* or teacher. For the fact that this poor *melamed* was transformed into an eminent German philosopher, one of the finest and profoundest commentators on the philosophy of Immanuel Kant, he was indebted to, besides his own brilliant capacities, Maimonides' *Guide for the Perplexed*. He himself tells in his autobiography of the tremendous impression made on him by Maimonides, who was in his view "the great, perhaps the greatest man of our people."

My reverence for this great teacher was so vast that I considered him the highest ideal of man, a supremely perfect individual; and his thoughts were as sacred to me as if they had been dictated by the supreme wisdom, by God Himself. My respect for Maimonides went so far that when my desires and passions began to develop and I was afraid that the evil inclination might overcome me and entice me to do something against his teaching, I used to recite this oath as a proven remedy: 'I swear by my reverence for my great teacher, Rabbi Moses ben Maimon, not to commit this or that.' And this oath, as far as I can remember, always actually prevented me from committing unlovely deeds.[27]

Out of gratitude to his great teacher, Solomon ben Joshua took the name Maimon as his surname, and the only Hebrew work which he published, *Givat Ha-Moreh*, is a commentary to *A Guide for the Perplexed*. In this work he attempts critically to

---

26. *Ibid.*
> Du schweigst, du Kluger, schweigen soll mein Mund!
> So sprich, wer soll dann reden und thun die Warheit kund?

27. *Lebensgeschichte*, Yiddish translation, 1928, pp. 240–241.

explore Maimonides' world of ideas with the aid of Kantian philosophy.

For this keen thinker the Jewish environment in the small old-fashioned towns of Lithuania was too narrow. With immense effort he tore himself out of it and entered the broader European world of ideas. On Jewish thought and culture Solomon Maimon had a very slight influence. All the Hebrew scholarly works that he wrote, aside from his commentary to the *Guide*, remained in manuscript;[28] he became a German philosophic writer. But this status was extremely difficult to attain. He describes his life-drama in his masterly autobiography,[29] which also has considerable cultural-historical interest, since the historian discovers in it a wealth of important information about the inner life of the Jewish community in Lithuania and Prussia in the second half of the eighteenth century.

Forthrightly and with great simplicity this splendidly endowed man relates how the terrible distress and poverty in which he lived his wandering life stained his soul with sin, corrupted his character, and broke his health and physical powers. Maimon spent his last years on the estate of a Silesian count who took pity on the homeless Jewish philosopher, and when Maimon died of malnutrition in 1800 at the age of forty-six and his corpse was taken to Glogau to be buried in the Jewish cemetery there, the leaders of the community avenged themselves on the "heretic" and "denier." The body of one of the most brilliant thinkers which the Jewish people ever produced was buried with mockery and shame, with *kevurat ḥamor* (the burial of an ass), behind the fence of the cemetery.

28. For a list of Maimon's Hebrew manuscripts, see the preface to the Yiddish translation of his *Lebensgeschichte*.
29. Translated into Yiddish by A. J. Goldschmidt.

CHAPTER SEVEN

The Harbingers of the New Era;
PHINEḤAS HURWITZ

Harbingers of the new era—Jehudah Hurwitz as stylist and enlightener—His *Ammudei Bet Yehudah*—Hurwitz's views on "the advent of the Messiah"—His *Megillat Sedarim*—Rabbi Jehudah Loeb Margolioth as enlightener—His ethical work *Bet Middot* and his *Or Olam* on the natural sciences—Phineḥas Hurwitz and his *Sefer Ha-Berit*—His attitude towards mysticism and the natural sciences; his battle against rationalism—Hurwitz's program for rebuilding the social foundations of Jewish life—On the basic principle "Thou shalt love thy neighbor as thyself"—"Love for man as the greatest joy of the soul."

O ATTAIN the truth," Solomon Maimon relates in his *Lebensgeschichte*, "I forsook my people, my family, my home." That Maimon removed himself from his people was brought about, to a certain degree, by the extremely unfavorable circumstances in which he was destined to live. But it cannot be denied that another important factor also contributed thereto. The contemporary orthodox, rabbinic world was too narrow for such a free thinker as Maimon, "the noble audacity of whose thought refused to recognize any boundaries beyond the boundaries of the mind itself." But, at the same time as Solomon Maimon, other truth-seekers of a very unique kind appeared in Lithuania. These also looked for the truth, but the roots binding them to their environment, to the ancient culture of their people, to the heritage of their fathers, remained firm and strong. To be sure, none of them was blessed with such a brilliant, analytical mind as Solomon Maimon. On the other hand, they knew nothing of a "rent in the heart," as did this profound critic of Kant's philosophical system. It could never even occur to them "to forsake their people" in order "to attain the truth." They were certain that the truth, the real truth, can be in no way inconsistent with the cultural legacy of their people, the Torah of their fathers. They merely sought new methods of discovering the truth that is implicit in the sacred Jewish books, of explicating it, and making it comprehensible to the entire people. They were sure that to attain this—and herein consisted their enlightening role— one must employ science and education. Their desire was not to tear themselves out of the familiar environment that belonged to them but to broaden and ventilate it, to open the closed shutters so that more light might enter and the dark shadows be driven away.

One of the first among them was the physician, Jehudah ben Mordecai Halevi Hurwitz. Born in Vilna,[1] Hurwitz studied medicine at Padua and afterwards, like most of the enlighteners of that generation, led an itinerant life. He travelled a great deal over Europe, spent some time in Berlin where he became acquainted with Mendelssohn, later practiced medicine in his native city of Vilna, then in Zhagory, and for a time in Mitau. In the library of the gymnasium at Mitau Hurwitz's Hebrew manuscripts, among them some poems translated from the German, have been preserved.[2] He spent his last years in Grodno, where he died in 1797.

When he was still quite young, Jehudah Hurwitz devoted himself to the study of the Jewish poets and philosophers of the Spanish-Arabic Middle Ages, and he very frequently calls them "my teachers and my masters." The influence of the Spanish-Arabic poets is strongly discernible in his manner of writing. He makes frequent use of the *makama*-style, the dialogue-form in rhymed prose. His playful *musiv*-style is at times reminiscent of Alḥarizi, the author of *Taḥkhemoni*, and of Immanuel of Rome. Hurwitz also composed liturgical poems in

---

1. The year of his birth has not been determined.
2. See R. J. Wunderbar, *Geschichte der Juden in den Provinzen Liv- und Kurland*, 1853, pp. 71–73.

the style of the medieval Hebrew poets; here the influence of Solomon Ibn Gabirol is especially felt.[3] But modern influences are also noticeable in him. These may be observed even in his first work, *Tzel Ha-Maalot*, published in 1764. *Tzel Ha-Maalot* is a collection of 365 ethical maxims written in rhymed prose. One detects the enlightening spirit of the eighteenth century when Hurwitz speaks in his proverbs of the brotherhood of man. "Know, O man, that the whole world with all its inhabitants is interconnected, like the limbs of one body."[4] The chief factor dividing the human family into hostile camps is found by this typical son of the Enlightenment era in religious hostility, which leads foolish and ignorant men astray. "But the understanding and cultured people of all nations," Hurwitz asserts, "feel themselves truly brethren, and their love for one another is great." In other maxims the author sharply assails the rich and the communal leaders, whom he calls "men of the fist" and points out that demoralization has proceeded to such an extent that one must tremble before every slanderer because he carries influence with the lord or prince.

A year later (1765) Hurwitz's major work, *Ammudei Bet Yehudah*, appeared.[5] Virtually the entire work is written in rhymed prose in the form of a discussion among three symbolic figures. These represent the three levels of human development: animal instinct, feeling and perception, and critical reason. Very interesting details characterizing the contemporary way of life are found in Hurwitz's work. These are especially valuable, for we have to do here not with a pietistic moralist but with a cultured and widely traveled physician. The author complains, for example, of the widespread plague that the wealthier classes follow the Parisian fashions and spend fortunes on luxuries which are today fashionable and tomorrow suddenly out of favor, "following the consensus of the inhabitants of the great city of Paris."[6] He complains of the Jewish men of wealth who desire to imitate the princes and higher nobility. They build splendid residences and thereby only arouse jealousy, for the others say, "See how our servants have robbed us, and with

3. Hurwitz's collection of poems *Kol Yehudah*, has remained in manuscript (on the manuscript the date 1790 is noted). The manuscript is in the private possession of Professor D. Maggid who was kind enough to give us the opportunity to examine this collection.

4. We quote according to the Baghdad edition of 1892.

5. In the introduction the author includes the letter of approbation which he obtained from Mendelssohn, who read his work in manuscript.

6. *Ammudei Bet Yehudah*, 9–10.

our money construct beautiful homes for themselves."[7] Typical also are his emotive lines about the great suffering which the Jewish people have to endure. "When I recall all the afflictions and misfortunes," Hurwitz concludes, "I believe that it would be far better for us to live among wild beasts of prey than among these people with their false civilization."[8]

The major value of Hurwitz's work, however, lies not in this but in his moral-religious outlook. In religious-philosophical questions his highest authority and guide is Maimonides. He devotes a special chapter in his work to the medieval philosopher, and speaks quite in the spirit of *A Guide for the Perplexed* about the divine nature and its attributes. Nevertheless, when it comes to ethical matters, Hurwitz refuses to follow the path of his great guide. He declines to agree with Maimonides that God can be served only with the intellect, and that the supreme level of human perfection lies not in the realm of morality but of speculative thought. Hurwitz does, indeed, acknowledge the great value of philosophy, but he insists that it is, after all, only for the few. When discussing the great role that the sciences play in man's cultural life, he considers it necessary immediately to mention the "ancient principle" that "the sciences without morality are like trees without roots."[9]

In Hurwitz's work the old historical debate that dominated medieval Jewish civilization flares up again in all its ardor—the debate between "the sovereignty of the intellect" and "the Torah of the heart," the difficult question of which has the birthright, the all-ruling intellect or the variegated world of feelings with its profound faith in divine revelation and the holy spirit. Hurwitz in fact denies the fundamental credo of the rationalists. He does not believe that man can fathom the nature of "all existences" with the aid of speculative philosophical thought and thereby create a bond between himself and the divine wisdom. For him it is beyond question that one cannot plumb the infinite depths of cosmic life with the limited human mind, and that only revelation, the Torah from heaven, is the sure source from which we can draw our knowledge of the Creator of the world. In philosophy, he asserts, we cannot find a single firmly established principle that is universally recognized; only divine revelation, which is also the cornerstone of morality and ethics, is absolute and beyond all doubt.

7. *Ibid.*, 13, 18.
8. *Ibid.*, 45–46.
9. *Ibid.*, 32.

In his view, the way to God lies not through the dizzy heights of philosophical thought but through the fertile garden of religious ethics. For Hurwitz, who remained firmly on the soil of traditional Judaism, religion and morality were still identical; in any case, morality was the end-point to which religion led. The major task and ultimate goal of man in the world is to bring the ethical to final victory, to draw near to the source of morality and justice, to divinity. In this, the author asserts, consists the supreme bliss, the greatest joy and most ardent desire of man's soul.

Here Jehudah Hurwitz touches upon the central point of his world-outlook—his view of the "days of the Messiah and the resurrection," the interpretation he gives to the national hope for the "times of the Messiah" and final redemption. As a contemporary of the humanists and enlighteners of the eighteenth century, Hurwitz in fact removes the mystical garment of the national hope concerning the coming of the Messiah and attempts to give it a more realistic substance and foundation. A child of the eighteenth century, he believes firmly in the immense power of man's inventive spirit, and he is certain that man will finally manage, with the aid of knowledge and through intensive effort, "to transform the wilderness into God's paradise." In time the world will become broad and fruitful for all mankind, thanks to man's brilliant discoveries, and "man will no longer have to complain that his life is too limited, that he cannot satisfy his needs."[10] But all this will be attained, Hurwitz is deeply persuaded, only when the moral principle will rule the world and "the light that is hidden in righteous hearts" will be revealed before all.

Quite in the spirit of Maimonides, Jehudah Hurwitz interprets the details concerning reward and punishment and the resurrection of the dead in a purely spiritual and ethical way, without any semblance of corporeality. "There is no banquet except for the soul," he points out; "the promises are entirely spiritual."[11] All the statements of the Talmudic sages referring to Leviathan and choice wine are explained by Hurwitz as merely parables and symbols. The "advent of the Messiah" is, for him, the final triumph of the moral principle over the entire world. The "days of the Messiah and the resurrection" are, in his view, the symbol or incarnation of moral triumph in all mankind. The redeemer will come not for the sake of one

10. *Ibid.*, 72–73.
11. *Ibid.*, 73.

people only but for the whole world, for all living creatures. His task is a universal one; he will bring peace and unity to all mankind, raise all men to the supreme level of righteousness and justice, and bring the glorious day that will be completely a "holy Sabbath," the day that will be "entirely good."

The Messiah, Jehudah Hurwitz insists, can therefore arrive only when the material and economic conditions of human society will be improved to the extent that they also bring about a significant raising of the cultural level. Hurwitz, the contemporary of the humanists and enlighteners, therefore deems it necessary to remove the mystical veil from Messiah the son of David. The redeemer will not appear riding on a white ass; he will be a mortal, born in the natural way of a father and mother, but "perfect both in body and in spirit." The Messiah is the supreme degree to which the human spirit can rise. He will be the shining star illuminating the way of revival and highest culture for all mankind. He will raise the downcast and wearied generations of men from the depths of shame and suffering to the heavens suffused with light and beauty. The Messiah is the chief goal, the supreme limit, toward which the children of men created by God strive and for which they hope. He is the loveliest and the highest to which mankind can and will give birth in the world.[12]

At the time Hurwitz was dreaming of universal love, brotherhood, and unity, and saw in religious hatred the major cause of contentions and persecutions, a religious struggle erupted in his home, in Lithuania and several other Polish lands—a struggle which divided the entire Jewish community into two hostile camps, Hasidim and Mitnagdim. The arid observance of the mountains of laws and commandments according to the *Shulḥan Aruch* and its commentaries could satisfy the rabbis and scholars whose minds were so deeply immersed in sharp *pilpul* and clever novellae, but for the common multitude—the artisan, the villager, the simple peasant—*pilpul* was overly difficult and incomprehensible. The daily fulfilling of commandments according to the decree of the *Shulḥan Aruch* and other codes was too cold, too common and tedious. This could not warm broken and grieved hearts, could not bring salve and consolation to darkened and wearied souls. But what glacial and scholarly rabbinism could not provide, the common people found in the Hasidic movement with its fervor and mystical feeling. Hasidism suffused the ordinary and everyday with vivid col-

12. *Ibid.*, 74–75, 88–90.

ors, warmed them with inner fire. Every word of a common prayer became a treasure of burning enthusiasm and spirituality, every commandment a garment of fearful secrets and divine intentions that raise the downcast individual to the celestial heights. Rabbinism saw in Hasidism its chief enemy. This was not merely a struggle of ideas but a struggle for power, for social existence.[13] Hence, a bitter war, with excommunications, persecutions, and terrible denunciations and libels, broke out.

Hurwitz could not look upon this calmly and issued a brochure entitled *Megillat Sedarim*[14] in which he attempted to make peace between the opponents. The work is written in rhymed prose and in the form of a dialogue. The author several times indicates the purpose of his tract. "Our brethren," he laments, "have completely forgotten the chief principle of the Torah: 'Thou shalt love thy neighbor as thyself.' They have forgotten that love is the foundation-stone of the world. They disrupt the unity of the holy people. They sow warfare and hatred, and thereby gladden our enemies who persecute us like savage beasts . . . Thus our people has remained like a ship in a windstorm without mast and sails."[15] "To you, my brethren, I turn with this scroll written in blood and tears. I plead for peace and tranquillity!"[16]

In the first part of *Megillat Sedarim* the brothers Obadiah and Ḥeshbiah carry on a discussion. The first is an ardent Kabbalist and lives in the "esoteric world," while Ḥeshbiah is a well-known scholar, one of the cleverest of swimmers over the sea of the Talmud. His realm is the *halachah*, brilliant scholarship in the law, and he has little use for the "secret wisdom." These brothers would constantly carry on intense debates between themselves, until a great hostility developed between them and they began strongly to persecute each other. Their aged father thereupon convened a rabbinic court, and the judges finally managed to make peace between the brothers. "Let the Kabbalist," the court declared in its verdict, "no longer say to the rabbinist: 'I am rich in religion, and you are poor in religion and knowledge.' And let the rabbinist no longer say to the Kabbalist: 'You are confused and base, like the builders of the tower of Babel.' "[17]

13. A full discussion of this struggle will be found in the later parts of our work.
14. Published in 1793. We have employed the Warsaw edition of 1884.
15. *Megillat Sedarim*, Introduction, p. 42ff.
16. *Ibid.*, 43, 44ff.
17. *Ibid.*, 37.

Highly characteristic in *Megillat Sedarim* is the following point. In the introduction Hurwitz remarks that besides the two battling camps, the "sages of the Kabbalah" and the "brilliant scholars of what is revealed," i.e., the Hasidim and the Mitnagdim, a third group has appeared in the Jewish quarter —the "masters of research and enlightenment." The representative of this group is the third brother, Hodaiah, who studied "Greek wisdom" and the natural sciences. At the beginning the aged father, Yedidiah, was very fearful that secular education might lead his third son to heresy and therefore waited with great apprehensiveness for Hodaiah when the latter was expected to return from distant places where he had studied all the sciences. As soon as he arrived, the father entered into a long discussion with him and, with intense joy, became convinced that his son had remained faithful to the tradition of the fathers and that the secular sciences do not in any way lead one off the right path.[18].

In close ideological affinity with Jehudah Hurwitz is his younger contemporary, Rabbi Jehudah Loeb Margolioth,[19] whom we have discussed previously. Like most of the pioneers of *Aufklärung* in that generation, this enlightened rabbi led a wanderer's life. He lived in Chotin, spent some time in Berlin where he became acquainted with Moses Mendelssohn, served as a rabbi in Busnov, Sczebrszyn, Polotsk, Lesla, and Frankfurt-am-Oder. In his work as a preacher he would also travel to many other cities where he gave sermons.[20] As a rabbi, Margolioth had occasion to become quite familiar with the behavior of the community leaders and the melancholy decline of the autonomous Jewish government. He also had the courage openly to issue forth in protest both in his sermons and his published works. Margolioth is the author of the previously quoted[21] lines in which the leaders of the community are indignantly portrayed in such dark colors. He inveighs with similar acerbity against the current system of child education which ought, in his view, to be completely reformed. With great anger he speaks of the method of *pilpul* and the men of the *ḥillukim* with their "wild dreams and foolish theories" who confuse their pupils and distort the correct meaning of the

18. *Ibid.*, 57.
19. Born in 1747; died in Frankfurt-am-Oder in 1811.
20. See *Aliyyat Eliahu*, 61.
21. Above, pp. 218–19.

text.[22] He also complains of the rabbis of his time who occupy themselves exclusively with Talmudic studies and refuse to know of any other sciences. Margolioth incidentally relates of himself that in his youth he devoted a great deal of attention to languages and philosophy.[23]

Like Jehudah Hurwitz, Jehudah Margolioth also was devoted to medieval Jewish philosophy, and it was from it apparently that he derived his knowledge of the ancient Greco-Roman philosophical literature. He frequently quotes Plato, Seneca, and many other writers,[24] but superior to all others, for him, is Aristotle. In his view, Aristotle was the one, peerless thinker, and he always mentions him in his works simply by the title *ha-ḥoker* (the seeker). Aristotle's *Ethics*, which Meir Alguadez, the court-physician of the king of Castile, had translated into Hebrew in 1405,[25] was so admired by Margolioth that he decided to compose an independent ethical work, following Aristotle's model. In the introduction to his *Bet Middot* he declares that he set himself the task of familiarizing the public with the views which the Jewish scholars—Saadiah Gaon, Jehudah Halevi, Maimonides, Joseph Albo, etc.—expressed in the realm of ethics. He wishes to present these ideas in clear, popular language, so that they may be easily understood even by those not well-versed in books of speculation.

Following the pattern of Aristotle's *Ethics*, Jehudah Margolioth divides his work into ten gates or chapters,[26] but even in the introduction he considers it necessary to emphasize the basic thesis of Aristotle's *Ethics* with which he can in no way agree. "For 'the seeker,'" Margolioth notes, "the chief thing is perfection of knowledge, immersing oneself in philosophical ideas about the divine nature. I, however, place as the cornerstone of my work perfection of the moral virtues, for with this perfection the perfection of knowledge is associated."[27] Like Jehudah Hurwitz, Jehudah Margolioth takes the view that

22. See *Bet Middot*, 31 (we quote according to the Lyck edition of 1862); *Tal Orot*, 38 (quoted according to the Pressburg edition of 1843).
23. See *Atzei Eden*, 16: "In my youth I read much in the books of the nations." In his *Bet Middot*, p. 20, Margolioth declares: "And I passed from chapter to chapter in the books of philosophy."
24. See *Tal Orot*, 61, 62, 30–31, 32, 41, 69.
25. See our *History*, Vol. III, p. 188.
26. His ethical work, which first appeared in 1777, was later considerably enlarged by Margolioth and published under the title *Tal Orot*.
27. *Tal Orot*, 1.

philosophy cannot provide definitive and absolute principles that are beyond all doubt; only the religion of revelation, the Torah given from heaven, is absolute and final. The Torah and the intellect are compared to two luminaries, but between them, Margolioth insists, is a distinction like that between the sun and the moon. Man's mind is only a pale reflection of the great light—divine revelation. On the other hand, Margolioth issues forth in the most decisive fashion against hypocritical "pietists" who refuse to know anything of speculation and secular sciences. He declares the contention that philosophy and scientific inquiry lead man away from the right path and bring him to heresy a loathsome falsehood. Thereby, says Margolioth, they merely provide an excuse for real heretics who do, indeed, desire to show that the secular sciences are incompatible with faith and therefore only ignoramuses and fools can be true believers, and that the more understanding a man is the farther he removes himself from faith.[28]

In Margolioth's view, only fools or hypocrites, who are jealous of "those renowned for their wisdom" and envy the honor given them, can attack the study of the sciences and those engaged in them. But he frequently underscores the great distinction between speculative or purely philosophical knowledge and practical knowledge. We shall see later why Margolioth admonished that philosophy should be studied from Jewish sources alone.[29] On the other hand, he strongly propagandizes for practical knowledge, chiefly the natural sciences. Just at that time these sciences were making gigantic progress. Among the contemporary intelligentsia they held pride of place; the investigation of nature and its laws was considered the most important and essential occupation. The enlightened Rabbi Margolioth appears as a faithful son of the eighteenth century. He also manifests a vast interest in these sciences and greatly deplores the fact that the Jews who, in earlier generations, were extremely active in the most varied branches of knowledge have, in recent generations, become so ignorant that "we have become a mockery and laughter among the nations of the world, and they look upon us as common animals."[30] Margolioth endeavors to show the Jewish reader how necessary the natural sciences are, both for practical life and for the study of Torah. Not content with employing every

28. *Ibid.*, 60.
29. *Ibid.*, 59–61.
30. *Ibid.*, 60.

opportunity to give his reader essential scientific information and pointing out how important the various sciences are for every man,[31] he also wrote a special work *Or Olam*, which has the subtitle *Al Ḥochmat Ha-Teva* (On Natural Science).[32]

The preface to this work is typical. In purely Oriental style the author relates how "the science of nature" appeared before him in the form of a woman veiled in black and lamented that she has become among the chosen people "like a vessel that is lost and a fence that has been pushed down," that she is "forsaken and forgotten" by all. All other peoples have the profoundest reverence for her and strive to become as intimately familiar with her as possible, but the Jewish people which, after all, was once regarded as a "wise and understanding nation" refuses to know anything of her, and there is not in Hebrew a single work which can quench the thirst of those desiring to learn about nature and its laws. Hence, she begs the author to be her savior, to gird up his loins and compose a work which will tell the Jewish reader who she is and what her significance is. The author happily declares that he is prepared to fulfill her request, to familiarize the Jewish public with the fundamental laws of nature.

One other characteristic detail in this introduction is interesting. The author can in no way understand how such a first-rate scholar as Maimonides devoted all his attention to speculative philosophy and neglected such an important science as the science of nature.

In the introductory chapter the author, following the pattern of medieval Jewish writers such as Shemtov Falaquera and others, provides a general overview in which he lists the various scientific disciplines, divided into separate categories: (1) theoretical sciences, among which he includes not only mathematics but astronomy; (2) experimental sciences, e.g., chemistry, physics, etc. (in this group the author also includes surgery); (3) metaphysics and religious philosophy; (4) ancillary sciences, such as logic, rhetoric, and the like; and finally (5) sciences dealing with the conduct of man, the social sciences, which are again sub-divided into three headings: (a) statecraft or political science, (b) economics, and (c) ethics. In the work itself, however, Margolioth deals exclusively with the natural

31. It is interesting that among the necessary sciences that a man ought to study, Margolioth includes also philology, for language, he explains, is the highest degree of human culture. See *Tal Orot*, 60; *Atzei Eden*, 13.
32. Published in 1777.

sciences, mainly chemistry. To be sure, the rabbi of Busnov still operated in his work with the old doctrine of the "four basic elements"—fire, water, air and earth—and had no notion that at the very time he was writing his little book the great Lavoisier, with his brilliant works on the oxygen in the atmosphere and the nature of the oxidization process, shattered the old views which had dominated the field of chemistry and laid the cornerstones for the structure of the modern science of chemistry. But this was not Margolioth's fault. Being the dilettante he was, he could naturally utilize in his work only the material contained in the handbooks of his time. It suffices to note that even in such a respected scientific work as Baume's *Chymie expérimentale et raisonée*, which appeared four years before Margolioth's *Or Olam* (in 1773), fire, air, water, and earth are also considered the four basic elements out of which all known bodies are constructed.

Written in a clear, popular style, Margolioth's work was remarkably successful and in a period of six years, 1777–1783, went through three editions. This indicates the extent to which interest in this kind of book had developed at that time. Hence, it is no surprise that men soon appeared who emulated Margolioth and also wrote popular books on the natural and other sciences. Among these writers, the greatest success was achieved by Phinehas Elijah ben Meir Hurwitz of Vilna with his thick volume, *Sefer Ha-Berit*, which was published in numerous editions and had, even until modern times, a large circle of readers.

The author of *Sefer Ha-Berit* is one of the most original thinkers of Polish-Lithuanian Jewry of that era. Unfortunately, we have very few biographical details about him. Even the year of his birth is unknown.[33] Concerning his appearance, the following details are reported by one of his contemporaries who knew him personally: "He was a handsome man with fine eyes, spoke calmly and sedately, and his visage testified to his wisdom."[34] Like most of the "enlighteners" of his generation, Phinehas Hurwitz led a wanderer's life and travelled through Galicia, Germany, and Holland and also spent some time in London.[35] His was a profoundly believing, mystically-minded nature. The Kabbalah with its deep mysteries was considered by him the most precious treasure of wisdom

33. He died in 1821.
34. See *Ha-Meassef*, 1809, 73.
35. See *Sefer Ha-Berit* (1797), 78.

and knowledge. The supreme authority for him was the "holy Ari," Rabbi Isaac Luria, and his beloved disciple, Ḥayyim Vital. Faithful to the tradition of the fathers, Hurwitz refused to acknowledge the truth of Copernicus' system which regards the sun as the center around which the planets, among them our earth, revolve. This, after all, is inconsistent with Sacred Scripture which teaches that "the earth standeth fast forever." Hence, the author of *Sefer Ha-Berit* firmly espouses the theory of Tycho Brahe that all the other planets do, indeed, revolve around the sun but the sun itself revolves around the earth.[36]

This convinced mystic was a loyal son of his generation and experienced with palpitations of the heart the new phenomena which at that time appeared before the world with great labor pains. He manifests considerable interest not only in the natural sciences but also in the new tendencies which then dominated the intellectual circles of western Europe. Hurwitz did not have full command of a single European language; he only understood German to some extent. Nevertheless, this gifted and intellectually curious man acquired a relatively significant sum of knowledge in various fields of science. He himself reports in this connection a very characteristic point: in gathering the necessary material, he would have an acquaintance of his who knew European languages read the passages in question in the original and he, Hurwitz, would then note down the content in plain Yiddish and later rework it in Hebrew.

Hurwitz was powerfully impressed by the humanitarian and enlightening ideas which the progressive strata of European society fervently preached at that time. On the other hand, the clearly materialist views of the contemporary rationalists were utterly repugnant to this ardent mystic. Speculative philosophy, which so arrogantly presumes to penetrate with the keenness of the mind into the "the innermost secrets" that can really be attained—according to Hurwitz's conviction—only with the aid of revelation and divine intuition, was also not to his liking. But it was beyond doubt for him that, to fathom the mysterious depths of the Lurianic Kabbalah, one must be proficient in the natural sciences. Hence, he undertook to compose in Hebrew a work which might be a genuine compendium of the various branches of science. He labored with great diligence on this work for many years. In the 1780's when

36. *Ibid.*, Part One, pp. 48–49. Hurwitz undoubtedly became familiar with Tycho Brahe's conjecture from *Maaseh Tuviyyah.*

he was living in Buchach, he finished the first part.[37] In 1790 he was gathering endorsements for his work, but he completed some chapters only in 1794.[38] Because of his great assiduity in working through the nights, he ruined his vision and for a time was blind. He then took a vow that, if he recovered and were able to complete his work, he would publish it anonymously. With the aid of the doctors of Lemberg, Hurwitz recovered and, after spending some time with the philanthropist of that city, Naḥman Reiss, went to Pressburg. There, with the help of the cultured linguist Baer Oppenheimer, he completed his book and published it in 1797, without his name appearing on it.[39]

In the introduction the author indicates that he wrote his work not for "great and wise men," nor "for all who know religion and law and with whom are wisdom and knowledge in *halachah* and teaching, nor for the enlightened who know every book and science, philosophy and nature," but for the masses, for men of little knowledge. *Sefer Ha-Berit* is, indeed, written in a clear, popular style. Despite the fact that the author frequently had to struggle against great difficulties because Hebrew lacked the necessary terminology, his style is light and fluent and testifies that we have before us a talented popularizer with a genuine literary gift. Very interesting in this connection is the following explanation which the author deems it necessary to provide in the introduction:

If there appears in places an unsuccessful expression, an awkward sentence, let this not be offensive to the reader; for you must know that the entire work is, after all, only a *translation*, because everything that is written in it I first considered and noted down in my mother tongue, i.e., in the vernacular which Jews speak in Poland, and yet my work is written in Hebrew. Hence, this is a rendering from one language which I considered in my heart to the language in which I wrote the book. Would that my work were written in the language of my people [i.e., Yiddish], as I considered it in my heart; then the style would surely be everywhere smooth and lovely."

It is doubtless a great loss for the literary development of the Yiddish language that this gifted author did not publish his

37. See *Sefer Ha-Berit*, I, 124.
38. *Ibid.*, II, 66.
39. However, Hurwitz noted his name (Phineḥas Eliahu ben Meir Vilna) indirectly through an acronym consisting of the initial letters of the words in a sentence of the book.

encyclopedic work in the "language of his people" as he "considered it in his heart," i.e., in plain Yiddish, but issued only the Hebrew translation.

The author further asserts that, despite the fact that he deals in *Sefer Ha-Berit* with very different kinds of subjects, his work is an integral one, each chapter is harmoniously connected with the next, and the varied material is organized in the best order. From a modern point of view it is quite difficult to assent to this statement and to recognize in the mixture of different themes and all kinds of scientific problems a rigorously carried-through order. But if one takes into consideration the author's world outlook and the tasks he set himself, one must, indeed, acknowledge that this large work is permeated with a definite, unitary idea which gives the diverse material a certain harmonious integrity.

In the first chapter Phineḥas Hurwitz deals with astronomical problems and familiarizes the reader with the course of the stars and planets. Then he proceeds to the four "basic elements," and this gives him the opportunity to set forth, in their general features, various scientific and technical matters. In the essay on water the author presents the causes of tides on the seashore, describes various sources of minerals, and gives certain geographical information about seas, straits, and gulfs. In the essay on earth he describes various lands, discusses the gravitational force of the earth, etc. In the next (tenth) chapter the author tells about earthquakes, ice and steam, fog and rain, hail and rainbow, thunder and lightning. In the next four chapters he deals with the fields of mineralogy, botany and zoology, and then proceeds to the crown of all creatures, man. In the sixteenth chapter the physiology and anatomy of the human body are described. In the next three is a discussion of man's psychology and forms of thinking. Especially characteristic is the twentieth chapter, in which the author speaks at length of the sources of man's concept of God and of the role of speculative philosophy.

We have observed that Jehudah Hurwitz, the author of *Ammudei Bet Yehudah*, as well as Jehudah Margolioth, with all their respect for Aristotle and his Jewish disciple Maimonides, nevertheless rejected the fundamental thesis of the Stagirite to the effect that the supreme level of man's perfection lies not in the realm of ethics but in the heights of speculative thought. The mystically-minded author of *Sefer Ha-Berit* poses this issue even more sharply. He does, indeed, speak with greatest reverence of Maimonides, and when he mentions his name exclaims enthusiastically, "There is none like him in Torah; who is similar to him as a guide in the laws and pure reverence of God?" Nevertheless, he sharply assails Maimonides' fundamental thesis that through logical argument one can establish the existence of God the Creator, in whom man must believe and whom he must love and revere. For Phineḥas Hurwitz it is clear that logical proofs are not infrequently based on false foundations and lead one to quite groundless conclusions. He ironically introduces in the tenth chapter Solomon Maimon's statement, made in his *Givat Ha-Moreh*, that in our time speculative philosophy has attained the summit of perfection. In every generation, even in ancient times, especially in the generation of Aristotle, Hurwitz notes, the philosophers asserted the same thing, but the philosophers of subsequent generations nullified their words and views. For him, the persuaded mystic, it is clear that the "mystery of the Lord is not to be explained by logic." "The mystery of the Lord is explicable only according to the Kabbalah," in "faith and not in speculation," not through *muskalot* or abstract ideas but through divine commandments, not through speculative philosophy but through revelation, prophecy, and tradition.

Most interesting in this connection is the fact that when Phineḥas Hurwitz endeavors to show how uncertain the foundations of speculative philosophy are and how limited its arguments and theories, he introduces as evidence the great revolutionary in the realm of philosophical inquiry, Immanuel Kant, and his recently published work, *Kritik der reinen Vernunft*, which created such a tremendous sensation in the learned world. With great delight Hurwitz adduces Kant's arguments that man cannot, with the aid of mere reason, recognize the true nature of what is outside himself, for all notions that man obtains from the external world are first fashioned through his perceptive apparatus and are a definite consequence of the specific forms of understanding which the human mind possesses by its very nature.[40]

Even more characteristic of *Sefer Ha-Berit* is its battle against the rationalists and materialists of that generation. Just when Phineḥas Hurwitz was writing the last chapters of his work, the historic session (November 7, 1793) at which the decision was reached that religious worship is permissible only in regard to Reason, the ruler of the world, took place in a French

40. *Sefer Ha-Berit,* I, 117–118.

convent. "This Supreme Being," declared the chairman of the session, "desires no other worship; all are to bow down before Reason which governs the world. So the Supreme Being ordains, and henceforth the cult of Reason will be recognized as the national religion." As we shall see later, the rationalist ideas of the French enlighteners obtained a powerful resonance in certain segments of the Jewish intelligentsia with whom Hurwitz came into contact. He, the mystic and fervent admirer of the "holy Ari," relates with palpable dread how the materialists of his generation insisted that the world was formed without a definite, creative will but through the accidental collocation of atoms that are eternal and in constant motion. These ideas, Hurwitz laments, have also penetrated the Jewish camp. "There are many now who break forth among the people of the Lord with heresies through philosophic speculation." With burning wrath he tells of the Jewish rationalists who assert that "Moses never went up on high and God never came down on Mount Sinai" and deny the Torah given from heaven.

The details presented by Hurwitz on how these heretical men who "break forth among the people" attempt to explain the giving of the Torah in a purely "rationalist" way are interesting. Moses was, indeed, a "great sage in natural science" and, in addition, a skillful politician and "well-versed in statecraft." To make an overwhelming impression on ignorant and crude people, he staged the great miracle on Mount Sinai. In point of fact, everything occurred in a completely natural way. Moses, the skillful natural scientist, devised all "the thunders and lightenings" with various instruments. And so that the understanding among the people might not detect this hocus-pocus, he strictly forbade anyone to come near the mountain: "Beware lest you ascend the mountain, for all who touch the mountain will surely die." And the whole Torah, will all its commandments, statutes and laws, was composed by Moses himself.[41]

For the mystical Hurwitz these rationalists who declare that "Moses defrauded the whole generation of the wilderness" are "living corpses." He does not even wish to carry on converse

41. *Ibid.*, I, 103–104. Hurwitz's contemporary Gumpel Schnaber (about him, see the eighth volume of our work) reports that some of the Jewish rationalists went even further and declared that the Torah was composed not by Moses but by Ezra the Scribe.

with them. "To dead men," he declares, "I have no desire to preach, for they cannot understand the ways of life. I address only those who do not follow the ways of the wicked; these I warn that they should not allow themselves to be led astray by these seducers and enticers."[42]

In the closing chapter of the first part Phineḥas Hurwitz notes that this is only an introduction to the second part, dealing with man's goal and purpose. And in this second section, which is strongly colored with mysticism and bears the title *Divrei Emet* (Words of Truth), there is a mixture of "all kinds of things." Naive fantasy and homiletic material is mingled with mystical sentiment and modern Enlightenment humanism. In a tender, exalted tone the author speaks to his orphaned generation: "Prophecy has long disappeared, the holy spirit has been extinguished . . ." He endeavors to console his generation, urging them not to be downcast:

Listen, my friends and my brethren! I bring you consolation. Do not despair of God's help. Surely he is the God of compassion. Know of a surety that even if prophecy has departed from us, the holy spirit still hovers over us and its gates are not closed even in our generation . . . Over every man at every hour and every place the holy spirit rests according to his deeds.[43]

The most interesting thing in this connection is the fact that this persuaded mystic who dreams of the holy spirit appears an an energetic battler for productive labor, exposes in the clearest way the abnormal economic situation of the Jewish populace, and points out that the social life of the Jews must be rebuilt on new foundations, because the sources of livelihood from which the majority of the Jewish people draw sustenance are already long dried up and mouldering. One may assert without exaggeration that all the complaints which the *maskilim* of later generations set forth against the Jewish sources of livelihood "hanging in air" and the arguments with which they attempted to demonstrate how essential it is for Jews to devote themselves to useful artisanry and agricultural labor can already be found in the *Sefer Ha-Berit* of the mystic Phineḥas Hurwitz.

42. *Sefer Ha-Berit*, 117.
43. *Ibid.*, *II, 32.*

Phinehas Hurwitz's Sefer Ha-Berit

"I arrived at the conviction," writes Hurwitz,

that every pious man who desires to follow the path of righteousness and fulfill God's ordinances must have command of a trade, so that he may support himself from the labor of his own hands and not have to depend on another's help. Hence, every father is obliged to teach his children some trade that may support them. As our sages said, "Just as a father is obliged to teach his son Torah, so he is also obliged to teach him a trade." Thus it is greatly to be deplored that in our generation the majority of our people are so haughty that they consider artisanry a disgrace and regard every kind of physical work with contempt. Men consider it shameful to earn a living through their own labor and believe it much more honorable to live from swindlery and usury. And it is this neglect of useful trades, this contemptuous attitude towards physical labor, that brings about the terrible moral decline of the whole community. For necessity and want lead men to many ugly deeds. What can persons do who have no luck in business and also have no trade? Indeed, we see among us how men steal and rob both from Jews and Christians and commit the greatest vileness and the most shameful deeds. Thus God's name is desecrated among the nations of the world, for these say: "Consider the chosen people which stems from the holy land! There is no base thing that they do not do, no swindle in which they are not expert, no fraud in the whole world of which they are not masters." The gentiles think that for this the Talmud, which Jews study day and night, is to blame; this work is what teaches them to be such clever swindlers. But if Jews learned trades from which to earn a livelihood, they would not commit such false deeds.

Hurwitz especially assails the *talmidei ḥachamim,* i.e., the rabbis and scholars, because they do not even think of teaching their children a trade. They desire to make of all their children only rabbis and rabbinic judges. But not everyone, Hurwitz maintains, is suited to become a rabbi or scholar. And it is just for this reason that there are among us Jews so many good-for-nothings and *shlimmazelniks* who are not fit for anything and incapable of undertaking anything. All these good-for-nothings become school teachers; hence, it is not surprising that among us there are more teachers than pupils. The teaching profession does not yield a livelihood, and all these teachers are extremely poor, leave their wives and children, and roam around various cities, seeking a morsel of bread. For all this their parents, who did not teach them a trade when they were children, are responsible.

"When, then, my brethren," Hurwitz exclaims,

will you come to your senses and understand that a child must be taught a trade, and that our sages were quite right when they said that he who does not teach his son a trade will be required to give account for it? Especially here in exile, where Jews may not own fields or vineyards and where we are also forbidden to practice many other professions and occupations. It is precisely artisans whom the states in which most of the Jews live gladly support. They grant them numerous concessions, give them rights of residence, and exempt them from part of the taxes. Why should we provide a pretext to other peoples to say of us: "Here is a people which lives among strangers and consists entirely of idlers and loafers. They do not wish to work and live from the labor of their hands, but occupy themselves only with deception and fraud, support themselves through usury, and suck the blood of the surrounding population."[44]

And the "surrounding population," the "strangers," the "peoples of the world," Phineḥas Hurwitz endeavors to show, are, after all, our own brethren. He, too, like Jehudah Hurwitz, the author of *Ammudei Bet Yehudah*, had become familiar with the new world of ideas in western Europe which dreamed of equality and brotherhood among all "who bear a human form." With all the ardor of his mystical-poetic soul the author of *Sefer Ha-Berit* attempts to break through the isolation of his brethren. He wishes to proclaim to them the tidings that the golden dream of the prophets is about to be realized. He desires to arouse in them the belief that the dark night of hatred and barbaric cruelty is already over and the glorious sun of love for man and justice will soon illuminate the world. *Ahavat Re'im* (Love of Neighbors) is the title of the thirteenth chapter, which is really the heart of the entire work. "The essence of love of neighbor," Phineḥas Hurwitz proclaims at the beginning of the chapter,

is love for the whole human kind, no matter of what nation a man may be and what tongue he may speak; for every man bears the same form and is involved equally with us in the habitation of the world. Man is not created for himself alone but for all mankind, with which he is firmly grown together and without which he can have no existence, for, lacking the aid of the community, the individual

44. *Ibid.*, II, 40–42.

perishes.[45] The entire human species is like one complex organism, and every individual is like a small segment of a whole body.[46]

"Every Jew," Hurwitz teaches, "must know and remember that what is written in the Torah, 'Thou shalt love thy neighbor as thyself' does not mean that one should treat with love only a fellow-Jew, but rather every man of whatever people he may be, for every man who bears the image of God is your brother. To love one's neighbor means to love all mankind, for all mankind is like one body."

"Hear now, O sons of Jacob," the author of *Sefer Ha-Berit* exclaims, "let love and brotherhood be inscribed on your banner! Extend the hand of peace to all peoples of the world!" Love for neighbor, Phinehas Hurwitz insists in this connection, is not at all a matter of utilitarian value; we have here no question of usefulness and convenience. This is a moral obligation inscribed in man's soul and conscience, an obligation stronger and higher than love for wisdom and knowledge, higher than love for truth, higher even than love for the Torah. And this sacred obligation applies to every man without distinction, whether he be servant or master, king or laborer, neighbor or stranger. The supreme commandment, "Love your neighbor," applies to all men in the world equally.[47]

The chapter *Ha-Ahavah Veha-Simhah* (Love and Joy) concludes Hurwitz's work like a harmonious closing chord. Fervently the author declares that "love is the greatest joy of the soul," that without love there can be no joy, and that love for man is merged at its highest level with the infinite joy of love for God. "O mortal man," Hurwitz exclaims feelingly, "remember how your heart and thought ought to be filled day and night with the consciousness that God's holy name rests on your head!"

Sefer Ha-Berit, which appeared anonymously, enjoyed enormous success. Everyone wanted to know who its author was. Some asserted that this work was written by none other than the Gaon of Vilna; others, again, insisted that Moses Mendelssohn had written it. The book was distributed not only throughout all of Europe but also in Egypt, Algeria, and Morocco, and in a short time two thousand copies were sold.[48] A Christian printer quickly (in Prague in 1799) published the

45. *Ibid.*, II, 48.
46. *Ibid.*, II, 46.
47. *Ibid.*, II, 4.
48. See the second introduction to the Vilna edition of 1818.

first part of *Sefer Ha-Berit* without the author's knowledge. This edition, however, was so distorted and erroneous that Hurwitz considered it necessary soon to reprint the work, now under his full name, with numerous alterations and addenda.[49]

49. Especially enlarged in the second edition is the thirteenth chapter entitled "Ahavat Re'im."

CHAPTER EIGHT

The Maskilim of Shklov;
MENDEL LEVIN

[Baruch of Shklov as enlightener—Mendel Levin (Lefin) as stylist—His activity as an enlightener—His *Hochmat Ha-Nefesh*—Shklov as center of enlightenment—Joshua Zeitlin as philanthropist and patron—The free academy in Ustye—Naftali Shulman—The enlighteners at the crossroads.]

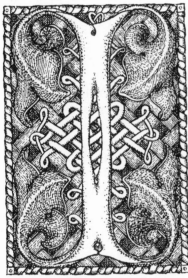

N THE introduction to the second edition of *Sefer Ha-Berit* Phineḥas Hurwitz declared that he was renouncing his author's rights and, in order to disseminate knowledge among Jews, granting permission to anyone who wished to do so to reprint his work, provided only that he publish both parts together—not the first alone, for he, Hurwitz, considers this part, dealing with the natural sciences, merely a preliminary to the second, which is the most important because it treats moral and religious questions. Of a completely different type was Hurwitz's contemporary, Baruch Schick, better known as Baruch of Shklov, also a popularizer of the natural sciences. Purely philosophic and ethical questions did not interest him at all, and his entire literary activity had only one definite purpose: to spread knowledge of mathematics and the natural sciences in Jewish circles.

Baruch ben Jacob was born around 1740 in Shklov into a rabbinic family. In 1764 he had already received ordination as a rabbi. Talmudic-rabbinic literature, however, did not fully satisfy him. He tells of the great thirst he had in his youth for the secular sciences; even at that time he was dreaming of enlightening activity and of spreading knowledge among the Jews with the aid of Hebrew translations. Schick was already a rabbinic judge in Minsk when he decided to leave his home and set out to study abroad. After long wanderings he arrived in London, where he studied medicine and also became a member of a Masonic lodge.[1] He left England a trained physician, and then his years of wandering over various European cities began. He spent some time in Prague where he gave lectures on mathematics,[2] and also visited Berlin where he made the acquaintance of the poet Naftali Herz Wessely and other *maskilim*, or enlighteners.

His European education and scientific knowledge did not shake Baruch Schick's strictly orthodox outlook. In religious questions, in the matter of preserving the tradition of the fathers, this cultured physician and natural scientist was hardly distinguished from any other Torah scholar of Vilna or Minsk. An ardent battler for secular knowledge, he never even imagined that this might bring one into conflict with the religious outlook. Schick's first appearance in literature was associated with *Yesod Olam*, the major work of Asher ben Yeḥiel's disciple Isaac ben Joseph Israeli.[3] At the home of the rabbi of Berlin, Hirsch Levin, Schick read an incomplete manuscript of this important mathematical study which had never been published. He immediately decided to make it available to a large circle of readers and published it in 1777 in Berlin.[4] In the same year Schick also published in Berlin his *Ammudei Shamayim*, a scientific commentary to Maimonides' work on the calendar, and a brief textbook on anatomy entitled *Tiferet Adam*. Shortly thereafter he left Berlin and, passing through Vilna, visited the Gaon of Vilna. The Gaon congratulated him on his enlightening work and, in connection with this, noted that one who lacks knowledge in other sciences also remains extremely backward in the wisdom of the Torah, for the Torah and science are intimately associated.[5] "The Gaon of Vilna," Baruch Schick relates, "advised me to translate as many scientific

1. See the *Russian-Jewish Encyclopedia*, X, 680.
2. In the introduction to *Keneh Ha-Middah* Schick relates: "And I taught my pupils in the holy community of Prague, all of them wise men, perfect in Torah and fear of heaven."
3. See our work, Vol. III, p. 151.
4. Because the manuscript was defective, *Yesod Olam* was printed incompletely in this first edition. A complete edition of Israeli's work was published in 1846–1848 by B. Goldberg, who employed another manuscript.
5. Schick tells of this in the introduction to his translation of Euclid.

works as possible into our holy language, in order to spread knowledge among our people, so that the nations of the world might no longer have a pretext for reproaching us for our ignorance and no longer arrogantly ask, 'Where is your wisdom?' "[6]

To disseminate secular knowledge among Jews and to "stop the mouths" of the nations of the world, so that they would no longer mock the "chosen people" for its backwardness in the "external wisdoms"—these two motifs resound not only in the just quoted words of the Gaon of Vilna; they are also heard in many other scholars of that era. The rabbi of Slonim, Rabbi Samson,[7] who in his youth spent some time in Germany and later assiduously studied German scientific books *sub rosa*, praises Baruch Schick's enlightening work greatly in his endorsement of the translation of Euclid. The enlightened rabbi is certain that, as a result of Schick's scientific editions, there will be a gradual "cessation of our sin" in having removed ourselves so far from all secular sciences. He hopes that Jews will quickly become "no worse than anyone among non-Jews" and that wisdom will increase among them "as the waters cover the sea." He considers it necessary to add in this connection that, thanks to Schick's activity, "the enemy's impudent mouth will be silenced"; he will no longer have occasion to mock the chosen people, of whom it was said, "Surely a wise and understanding people is this great nation," or ask of it contemptuously, "Where is your wisdom, where your understanding?"

At the same time the endorsements of the rabbis of Shklov, Tzevi Hirsch and Ḥanoch Henach, to Schick's *Keneh Ha-Middah* (on trigonometry) were also written. "One must welcome such books, thanks to which knowledge increases among us and we will not have to draw from foreign sources." The rabbi of Minsk, Rabbi Israel, also points out that, as a result of Schick's work, wisdom will rise among Jews like a bubbling spring and the peoples will be persuaded that all scientific matters can easily be treated in the chosen language.

Firmly convinced of the great importance and utility of his enlightening work, Schick, in his above-mentioned introduc-

6. *Ibid.*
7. Solomon Maimon went to this enlightened rabbi as a young man thirsting for knowledge in the middle of the winter from Nesvish to Slonim, in order to obtain from him a couple of scientific books in German (see Solomon Maimon, *Lebensgeschichte*, I, 105–106).

tion to Euclid, strongly assails the opponents of secular knowledge. "In the bitter exile," he complains,

as strangers and forsaken aliens, we have remained backward in all realms of knowledge. The wisdom of our wise men and the understanding of our understanding men have been lost. Science has been forgotten and mutilated among Jews. And if anyone has the courage to take upon himself the double yoke of Torah and science, he is attacked from all sides. The great host of opponents consists of two classes. To the first belong people for whom all the ways of wisdom are hidden, and they therefore revile every science; openly and shamelessly they mock knowledge and education, declare wise men fools and simpletons and, in order to make them hateful in the eyes of the common people, also brand them as heretics and deniers. But far worse than they are those who belong to the second class. These are the hypocrites who wrap themselves in the mantle of piety and humility but are immensely arrogant and grudging and cannot forgive anyone of whom it is said that he has more wisdom than they. They consider that the whole world was created to bow before them and to grovel in the dust at their feet, and the more wise a man is the more they despise him. Stealthily they undermine him, multiply controversies, and persecute all men of knowledge in order to aggrandize themselves and to gain the upper hand. The desecration of God's name which they thereby perpetrate does not trouble them at all. These hypocrites and frauds have brought it about that the people of Israel hate all sciences and are smitten with "the plague of blindness." They have brought it about that we are a mockery and a shame in the eyes of all nations, because we have removed ourselves from all the sciences which, in former times, were the pride and crown of our fathers but are now in the possession only of the gentile nations.

Schick, who was quite active as a practicing physician and was therefore known in the entire region as "Rabbi Baruch the doctor,"[8] also intended to compose a popular handbook, *Sefer Refuot* (Book of Remedies). In his short textbook of hygiene and medicine *Derech Yesharah* (published at the Hague in 1779), he even indicates that his *Sefer Refuot* is ready for printing, but he did not publish this work. What Schick did not fulfill, two other enlighteners of that era, Dr. Moses Marcuse, "the doctor of Königsberg," of whom we shall speak at length in the later parts of our work, and Mendel Levin (Lefin) successfully accomplished.

8.   Several sources even report that Baruch Schick, while living in Slutzk and holding the position of rabbinic judge there, was also at the same time body physician to Prince Radziwill.

Mendel ben Jehudah Loeb Levin was born in 1749 in the little Podolian town of Satanov and therefore was also called Satanover. Because he later lived for a rather long time in the town of Mikolayev, he is also known by the name Mikolayever.[9] Educated in the old, strictly pious way, Levin spent his youth entirely on the Talmud and rabbinic codes. By accident Joseph Solomon Delmedigo's *Elim* came into his hands, and this work of Galileo's talented pupil aroused in the young Satanover interest in mathematics and other sciences. He studied the works of the medieval Jewish religious philsosphers with great industry. The profoundest impression was made on him by Maimonides' *Guide for the Perplexed*, and in later years, in order to render Maimonides' work accessible also to those who could not bite into the difficult, cumbersome style of Ibn Tibbon's translation, he translated the *Guide* into clear and comprehensible Mishnaic Hebrew.[10] To make Maimonides' philosophical work even more understandable, Levin wrote a work entitled *Elon Moreh*, a kind of introduction to the *Guide*. This work, however, remained in manuscript, as did also the last two parts of his paraphrase of the *Guide*. Like Phinehas Hurwitz, so Levin, as a result of his great assiduity, overstrained his vision and contracted an eye disease. To treat his disease, he went in 1780 to Berlin, which had long attracted the small-town enlightener as a major center of culture. There he frequented Mendelssohn's home, where he became acquainted with Solomon Maimon, Lessing, Reimarus, Teller, and many other German writers. Levin spent all of four extremely fruitful years of study in Berlin. He learned German and French[11] thoroughly; these languages gave him the opportunity of familiarizing himself with modern literature and science. The rationalist ideas of the contemporary *Aufklärer* found in him an ardent disciple. In 1784 Levin left Berlin and for many years led a wandering life. He spent a rather long time in the little town of Mikolayev which belonged to Prince Adam Chartoriski. In the name of Mordecai Suchostaver, Levin's pupil, Gottlober

9. For bibliographical information on Mendel Levin, see Gottlober, in *Ha-Maggid*, 1873, Nos. 28–40 and in *Ha-Asif*, I, 6–7; M. Letteris, in *Zikkaron Ba-Sefer*, 38–40, and in *Ha-Meassef*, I, 1862 edition, 96–97, 182–186; Israel Weinles (*Ha-Olam*, XIII, Nos. 39–42), who employed Levin's still unpublished archives; N. M. Gelber, *Aus Zwei Jahrhunderten*, 39–57; J. Weissberg, *MGWJ*, 1927, 54–62.

10. The first part of this paraphrase was published after Levin's death by his pupil Suchostaver in 1829.

11. Levin's knowledge of French is underscored by Mendelssohn in his *haskamah* to *Sefer Refuot*.

reports the following incident from Levin's life in Mikolayev. Prince Chartoriski once happened to visit the crockery ship in Mikolayev belonging to Levin's wife, the good woman who provided a livelihood for the family. On the table he noticed a thick German book, a mathematical work by the famous scholar Wolf. Learning that this book was studied by the shopkeeper's husband, he became eager to make his acquaintance. The prince was thrilled to recognize in the small-town shopkeeper a man of European education, a friend of Mendelssohn's, and a thorough scholar of Kant's philosophy. Levin became a frequent visitor in Chartoriski's home. The latter often aided him materially and provided him with the possibility of publishing his works.[12] Levin, for his part, would familiarize his patron and protector with the rich knowledge that he had gathered in Berlin and in later years. The poet M. Letteris relates[13] that he himself saw at the home of Naḥman Krochmal a manuscript of Levin's dealing with Kant's philosophy, written in French especially for Prince Chartoriski. Very likely it was also at Chartoriski's suggestion, when the "Four-Year Sejm" (1789–1792), which concerned itself with the question of reforming the condition of the Jews, opened, that Mendel Levin composed his French brochure in which he addresses the Polish government with his project on improving the situation of the Jews.[14]

While the mystic Phineḥas Hurwitz stresses the abnormal economic condition of the Jewish community and insists that the social foundations of Jewish existence must first be reconstructed, the rationalist Levin is interested above all in the cultural aspects of reforming Jewish life. He emphasizes in his brochure that Maimonides was one of the great teachers and leaders of the Jewish people, but mysticism unfortunately bar-

12. In the introduction to his *Refuot Ha-Am*, Levin notes that Chartoriski contributed a considerable sum toward the publication of the book "for the benefit of our brethren, the children of Israel." In his letter to Simon Veit, Levin notes: "I am always supported by my good prince" (*Historishe Shriftn*, I, 813).

13. *Zikkaron Ba-Sefer*, 40.

14. The brochure, which is now extremely rare, is called *Essai d'un plan de réforme, ayant pour object d'eclairer la nation juive en Pologne et la redresser para ses moeurs*. It is beyond doubt that Levin wrote his brochure in French, for he was not very familiar with Polish. The first person who noted that Levin was the author of this very rare brochure and also provided information about its content was N. Gelber, *Mitteilungen zur jüdischen Volkskunde*, 1914, 46–48. In the fragment of Levin's letter published by Israel Weinles (*Historishe Shriftn*, I, 814) he notes: "So I issued 91 of my French brochures for the purpose of the Constitution of May 3 in Warsaw." See Max Erik, *Etiudn Tsu Der Geshikhte Fun Haskole*.

barized the people and led them away from the straight path.
And now in the era of Enlightenment, when Moses Mendelssohn and his disciples summoned the Jewish people back to
Maimonides' rationalist ways, a new mystical movement filled
with barbaric superstition and inimical to education and enlightenment has become greatly strengthened in the Polish-
German settlement. The most radical remedy, therefore, is to
reform Jewish education. The matter of education is regarded
by Levin as the cornerstone of Jewish reform. A new network
of normal schools must be established, and a great deal of
attention given to enlightening work, to opening the eyes of
the people, to fighting with the lash of satire against superstition, against all the miracle-workers and *baalei shem* (masters of
"names") with their incantations and amulets.

Levin himself was temperamentally little suited to the role
of the fighter utilizing the whip of satire; he therefore set
himself purely enlightening tasks—to disseminate and popu-
larize knowledge among his brethren.[15] He was persuaded that
honor and gratitude are deserved only by the scholar who is
not content with accumulating much information for himself
but also exerts all his powers to disseminate his knowledge
among the broad strata of the people.

In this connection the following detail is interesting. In 1819,
when the aged Levin was living in Brody, the local *maskilim*
celebrated his seventieth birthday in a small group. The profound philosopher Naḥman Krochmal, who was one of Levin's
disciples and devotees, was present at the celebration. At that
time Krochmal was already renowned for his comprehensive
knowledge, but he was a retiring soul and had never published
anything. For this Levin could not pardon him, and on the
evening of the banquet that had been arranged in his honor he
addressed Krochmal with a rather sharp speech of reproof. "Of
what use," he said to him,

would the sun with all its splendor be, if it did not spread its rays over
us? Of what avail for us would be the fact that God's spirit rested
upon the prophets, if these men had not taken pains to disseminate
their holy spirit among the common people and not deemed it necessary, despite all persecutions and sufferings, to go through the streets
and market-places and proclaim, "Come hither, O sons, return! Hear
the word of the Lord and see!" But you who are in a position to bring

15. Levin himself makes this point in an uncompleted Hebrew work in which he
discusses the question of reforms and of introducing home industries among Jews.
(See Israel Weinles' work in *YIVO-Bleter*, 1931, II, 350).

light to the people, you whom God has appointed to open the eyes
of those groping in darkness, to free souls languishing in captivity—
you sit locked up in your room, content with having gathered much
knowledge for yourself, and your hand refuses to wield the pen!

Levin, indeed, was one who practiced what he preached.
When he was still living in Berlin he conceived a whole series
of popular scientific editions for the masses. In 1789 his *Iggerot
Hochmah*, popular essays on the natural sciences, appeared.[16] In
this work all the virtues of Levin's unique style already appear.
The "enlighteners" of Berlin, the Meassefim, endeavored to
imitate the Biblical style and utterly refused to take account of
the great changes that had occurred in the development of
Hebrew through the course of the post-Biblical period. But
Levin very successfully employed the rich treasures of the
clear, pithy Mishnaic Hebrew, and thereby his writing became
fresh and vivid. He appears as a genuine master of style in his
later handbook on hygiene and medicine, in which he stresses
in the introduction that he took special pains to write in a
lucid, popular fashion, so that his work "would be easily and
quickly comprehensible."[17] At Mendelssohn's suggestion,[18]
Levin reworked into Hebrew the medical work of the physician Tissot, which was extremely popular at that time. This
work *Refuot Ha-Am* was so well done that it was at once distributed throughout the diaspora, and Jewish communities
would purchase several copies of the work to present to rabbis
and supervisors of hospitals, so that these might know how to
behave with an ill person and fulfill the commandment of
attending the sick in the proper way.[19]

16. Fragments of this work were published in *Ha-Meassef*, 1789, 81–92, 136–144.
17. Levin's works in Yiddish will be discussed at length in later parts of our *History*.
18. Mendelssohn himself notes in his *haskamah* to *Refuot Ha-Am:* "And after he trans-
    lated [Tissot's work] for the inhabitants of Europe, for each people according to
    its language, I encouraged and strengthened the heart of my friend the sage to
    translate it into Hebrew for the benefit of our brethren, the children of Israel, who
    cannot read the books of the nations or understand their tongue." This *haskamah*,
    which is dated the 12th of Adar 5545 (1785), was first published by Levin in his *Moda
    Le-Vinah*. There the first chapters of *Refuot Ha-Am* were published, together with
    the previously mentioned *Iggerot Hochmah*, and later in the complete edition of
    Refuot Ha-Am (Zolkiev, 1794), together with the *haskamot* of the rabbis of Lemberg,
    Brody, Zolkiev, and Frankfurt-am-Oder.
19. The author himself notes in the introduction to *Refuot Ha-Am:* "Whoever desires
    to fulfill the precept of visiting the dangerously sick should finish this composition
    and afterwards frequent hospitals and attend to them as is explained here, until
    his eyes are enlightened to order things clearly according to the demonstration,

After Levin had completed his handbook on curing physical diseases he decided to write another "book of remedies," a book of remedies for the soul, a work that might be a guide in the realm of ethics and aid in the development of man's moral consciousness. This work is entitled *Ḥeshbon Ha-Nefesh*. Levin wrote it in the last years of the eighteenth century but published it only ten years later, in 1808, in Lemberg. In ordering the moral rules and ethical principles which are here considered a sure aid to "an inventory of the soul" and "the work of education in virtue," Levin sets for himself as a pattern the popular works on "the art of improving morals" of the renowned Benjamin Franklin. But Levin did not intend merely to present the principles of self-education in his work. Much more important is the manner in which he explains the basic principles of Jewish religious ethics. The traditional concepts of Judaism are interwoven with the spirit and world-view of the close of the eighteenth century. The foundation of Jewish ethics appear here not in a mystical or pilpulistic-rabbinic garment but in more modern forms. In explaining the principles he set forth, Levin not infrequently introduces arguments from the natural sciences and bases himself on psychology and the physiology of the senses.[20] In full consonance with the views of the medieval Jewish moralists and religious thinkers, Levin also insists that man is morally superior to the angel, for the angel has no free choice or will; he is merely a passive reflection of the divine "attribute of mercy." But man, who does have free will, strives on his own account and, through obdurate struggle and intense moral suffering and agony, attains the "quality of lovingkindness." "Man's soul," Levin concludes, "deserves recompense for its great sufferings."[21] And when he speaks of the supreme level of bliss which man can attain, he appears before us as a true son of the "enlightened" eighteenth century. Along with the pleasure man enjoys when he performs righteous deeds and does good "to every creature," Levin also enthusiastically mentions the supreme feeling of bliss which permeates man when he delves into the mysteries of nature and explores the laws governing everything that exists.[22] Also interesting is his remark that the peo-

---

and then he will be able to begin one by one to keep and to act in matters of healing, easy things at first; and God will prosper his hand."

20. See, e.g., *Ḥeshbon Ha-Nefesh*, 106, 115, 117ff. (we quote according to the first edition).
21. *Ibid.*, 5.
22. *Ibid.*, 5 and 29.

ples of antiquity perceived in the Creator above all the God of tremendous power, the God of vengeance and righteous judgment, but the Jews perceived God's true greatness in His compassion, in His grace and holiness. The children of Israel were the first to realize that true knowledge of the Creator is based not on fear but on love and devotion.[23]

Heshbon Ha-Nefesh enjoyed enormous success. In many communities of Galicia and Podolia special fellowships whose ordinances were set up according to the moral principles of Mendel Levin's work were formed at that time. Some decades later, in 1844, when Levin had long been in his grave,[24] the well-known founder of the *Musar* movement, Rabbi Israel Salanter, reprinted *Heshbon Ha-Nefesh* as an excellent handbook for moral self-development.

A convinced rationalist and great friend of the Berlin Haskalah, Mendel Levin nevertheless stood closer to the authors of *Ammudei Bet Yehudah* and *Tal Orot* than to Mendelssohn's disciples. In his French essay written for the outside world, for the representatives of the government, he does indeed propose normal schools with Polish as the language of instruction, but he himself set as his task—as we shall see later—to familiarize the people with its finest cultural treasure, the Bible, in the vernacular of the masses, the Yiddish "jargon" which was so despised by the "enlighteners" of Berlin. And rationally-minded as Levin was, he nevertheless deemed it necessary especially to insist on the great role of the religious cult in self-education.[25]

In evaluating Levin's enlightening activity, one must take into consideration his importance as the link between the first Galician and Lithuanian harbingers of the Haskalah movement. Levin spent his old age in Brody, and there soon became the focus around which all who labored for knowledge and culture gathered.[26] But he was also closely associated with the progressive leaders of another important commercial center, Shklov. At the close of the eighteenth century Shklov played no lesser role as a center of commerce in White Russia than did

23. *Ibid.*, 94.
24. Levin died in July, 1826 in Tarnopol where, not long before his death, he completed his autobiography written in German and still unpublished: *Nachlass eines Sonderlings zu Abdera*, "which is concerned with philosophical speculations on Kant's system."
25. See Levin's interesting letter of 1817, published in *Bikkurei Ha-Ittim*, 1827, 5–8.
26. Among Levin's associates and disciples was the young Naḥman Krochmal, the subsequent author of the classical *Moreh Nevuchei Ha-Zeman*.

Brody in Galicia. Large mercantile fairs were held there, and the Jewish merchants of Shklov carried on extensive, multi-branched trade. The academician Vasily Severin, who visited Shklov at that time, relates in his memoirs: "The populace of Shklov consists chiefly of Jews, and their number has attained a total of twelve hundred souls. Their occupation consists mainly in commerce; they trade in silks, lace, linen, and all kinds of haberdashery."[27] When the Jews of Bokhara in 1802 applied to the community of Shklov for some information they required in connection with the trade they then carried on with certain Russian centers, the Jews of Shklov in their long reply[28] regarded it as necessary to stress that Shklov is a "city and mother in Israel," a city "filled with sages and scribes." The inhabitants of the city are wealthy merchants; the majority of the merchants are Jews, who travel to distant lands and thence bring all kinds of merchandise and distribute these throughout the entire region.

It was just this important mercantile role of Shklov, its close connection with centers elsewhere in Europe, that brought it about that Shklov became a city "filled with sages and scribes." The role of Shklov as a cultural center became even greater when a Hebrew press was established there in the 1780's. Leading the cultural center of Shklov at that time was the wealthy merchant and astute Talmudist, Joshua Zeitlin.[29] Highly respected by Prince Potemkin, Zeitlin obtained the commission to provide the Russian army during the Turkish war with forage and supplies. As a wholesale contractor who carried on extensive business affairs, Zeitlin accumulated an extremely large fortune and became one of the wealthiest Jews in Russia. He settled on his own estate, Ustye, in the region of Shklov, and eventually a kind of "free academy" was formed there. At his court Zeitlin built a spearate house of study with the most precious sacred vessels and Torah scrolls that he had brought back with him from Turkey. He provided numerous students and scholars with all their material requirements so that they might spend their time in quiet study. For their scholarly work a very rich library was available.[30]

At this extraordinary "free academy" men of the most varied

---

27. We quote according to Korobkov's work in *Yevreyskaya Starina*, 1910, 362.
28. In 1928 a photographic reproduction of this printed answer was published in the second volume of *Perezhytoye*, 276–277.
29. Born in Shklov in 1742, died in 1822.
30. See S. J. Fuenn, *Kiryah Ne'emanah*, 477.

intellectual interests gathered. There Rabbi Menaḥem Naḥum wrote his commentary to the *Tosefta*, entitled *Tosafot Bikkurim*, while at the same time Mendel Levin wrote his *Ḥeshbon Ha-Nefesh* and Baruch Schick organized a special laboratory to carry on chemical experiments. Among these a very unique figure, Benjamin Zalman Riveles, a disciple of the Gaon of Vilna, moved about softly. He led the life of an ascetic, ate no meat, and touched no liquor. A man of means, he abandoned all his business interests and settled on Zeitlin's estate so that he might devote himself without hindrance to scientific matters. Riveles was not content with Talmudic-rabbinic literature alone.[31] His familiarity with European language gave him the opportunity to study natural sciences diligently. He was especially interested in medicine and botany and established at Ustye an arboretum in which he collected the most varied plants, from which he would prepare all kinds of remedies and treat his acquaintances. "With his virtues and manner of life," Joshua Zeitlin's son-in-law, Mordecai Nathanson, writes of him, "Riveles reminds one of the ancient pious men and ascetics known as the Essenes."[32]

The fact that the Jewish merchants of Shklov not only carried on business with foreign firms but were also suppliers and associates of the Russian nobility and officials makes it quite understandable that as early as the last two decades of the eighteenth century there were in this major White Russian center a number of persons versed not only in European languages but in Russian as well. One of the first in this field was Naftali Herz Shulman. The historian S.J. Fuenn asserts that Shulman was so thoroughly competent in Russian that he even composed a work in the language.[33] But we have very little information about this interesting person. We know only that Shulman spent his youth in Vilna, where he was renowned as a grammarian, and that in one of its schools he studied Maimonides' *Guide for the Perplexed* with a small circle of intellectually curious young people.[34] Shulman was also reputed to be quite proficient in Latin. At the end of the eighteenth century he was in Shklov where, in 1803, he reprinted with various supplements Benjamin Mussafia's well known lexicographical work, *Zecher Rav*. Shulman's introduction to this work is interesting.

31. Riveles in 1804 published a Talmudic work entitled *Geviei Gevia Kesef*.
32. *Kiryah Ne'emanah*, 279.
33. *Safah Le-Ne'emanim*, 147.
34. On Shulman's visit to the Gaon of Vilna, see M. Plungian, *Ben Porat*, 58.

First of all, we learn from it that he also wrote but did not publish several other works, including a dictionary in which all the words that occur in the Targumim, the Babylonian and Jerusalem Talmud, the *Zohar*, Midrashim, Kabbalist books, and books of speculation are explained. He also composed a work specifically devoted to *darchei ha-limmud* (ways of learning). Shulman also speaks of reforming elementary education in the introduction to *Zecher Rav*. Like the Gaon of Vilna, he notes the abnormal manner of educating children among Jews. But in him new motifs are heard in which the influence of the Berlin Haskalah is felt—above all, hostility to the Yiddish "jargon." He emphasizes that he translates Biblical words into Latin,[35] Russian and "the pure German language, not the jargon we speak." In this connection, he also admonishes that one should accustom children to explaining the words of the Bible only in pure German and not fabricate other words, for Jews speak a mixed, corrupted dialect.

Even more interesting is the announcement printed at the end of *Zecher Rav*. Apparently the "enlighteners" of Shklov at that time were thinking of establishing a weekly journal in Hebrew; hence, Shulman utilized *Zecher Rav* to publish on the last page an announcement about the projected journal. This announcement undoubtedly has a cultural-historical significance; we therefore quote it here verbatim:

My brethren, there are now in every city and even in the small towns not a few persons who thirst for knowledge. But the great impediment lies in the fact that suitable books are lacking and there is no one from whom to obtain the knowledge necessary to learn how to perfect oneself in the realm of science. I have therefore decided to publish each week news and information about all the events occurring throughout the world. These announcements will be taken from the newspapers and magazines appearing in Hamburg, Petersburg, and Berlin, and also from newly published scientific books. In this way each will find in the weekly journal what interests him most. The merchant will read about commerce and political events, and the lover of science about scientific discoveries. Whoever has anything new to report in the field of science, let him notify me and I will inform all our readers about it through the paper. In this way much knowledge in the realm of various languages, mathematics, geography, the natural sciences, etc. will be disseminated among our people. Whoever wishes to subscribe to this paper, let him apply to Shklov

---

35. To reduce the cost of printing, Shulman printed *Zecher Rav* only with the German translation, without the Latin and Russian.

at the address of my pupil, Ḥayyim Bomharz, and when a certain number of subscriptions will have been gathered I will transmit all the further details to you.

But Shulman did not convey the promised "further details" and nothing came of the projected newspaper. It is not difficult to imagine the reasons that caused the failure of this literary undertaking. Just at the time that Shulman's announcement appeared it became clear that an end was coming to the peaceful coexistence of Torah and *Ḥochmah* (traditional Judaism and science), of ancestral piety and the orthodox outlook, on the one hand, and the "external wisdoms" and new enlightening ideas, on the other. We shall see in the later parts of our work that it was precisely the *maskilim* of Shklov who played a definite role in this.[36] This conflict developed slowly, but it became inevitable as soon as the fundamental tendencies of the Berlin Haskalah, whose influence was felt ever more intensely among the "sages and scribes" of the White Russian "city and mother in Israel," manifested themselves sharply and clearly.

We have observed that the first harbingers of Haskalah who appeared in the compact Polish-Lithuanian Jewish community still remained firmly on the soil of the traditional world outlook. Secular knowledge among them was subordinate to religion and the tradition of the fathers. They still lived the old, isolated cultural life. The new tendencies of that era influenced them only to the extent that they attempted to adapt certain elements of secular knowledge to their old world-view. We have seen how intensely interested they were in the natural sciences with their great discoveries, how eagerly they adopted the humanitarian ideas of the *Aufklärer* of that era. But they decisively rejected the rationalist doctrine, and to the materialist-utilitarian world-view they opposed a romantic-mystical one, based on emotion and intuition.

The intellectual awakening in the last quarter of the eighteenth century among the Jews of Prussia, with their major cultural center in Berlin, however, assumed completely different forms. A whole series of cultural and social factors which we shall discuss at length in one of the later parts of our work greatly strengthened in the Jewish populace in Germany at that time the drive to rush as quickly as possible out of the narrow "four cubits" of the isolated ghetto and to link itself

36. On this, see our article in *Yevreyskaya Starina*, Vol. XII.

with European culture and civilization. Only in the time of Frederick II did the financial and industrial bourgeoisie begin to play a prominent role in the capital city of economically backward Prussia. And the position of dominance in this young and quickly growing community was taken by—apart from some Frenchmen—Jewish bankers, manufacturers, and wholesale merchants. The Jewish colony became the majority within the intelligentsia and financial aristocracy of Berlin. Frederick II, who significantly increased the civic disabilities of the Jewish populace at large with his severe laws and burdened them with extremely oppressive taxes, at the same time vested in the wealthy Jewish entrepreneurs and large-scale merchants "general privileges." In consequence of this, the number of "privileged" Jews, men possessing great fortunes, in the Prussian capital grew ever larger. Frederick II was, indeed, a bitter enemy of the Jews, but his ardent desire to enrich the land as quickly as possible, to transform Prussia into an industrial state, contributed greatly to the fact that the Jews, especially those of Berlin, obtained the opportunity to accumulate great wealth. The Seven Years' War, as a result of which many Jews became rich through military contracts and other enterprises, strengthened the social position of the Berlin Jews even more.

Despite the fact that in the economic realm they attained great power, the Jews of Berlin remained under the heavy yoke of medieval disabilities and the restrictions of their *Kammerknecht* status. These men, even the wealthiest among them, had "privileges" granted to them, but no human rights. The younger generation, the children of the Jewish bankers and merchants, however, already possessed, in addition to wealth, education—modern European education. Raised in the narrow, old-fashioned ghetto, they were literally dazzled by the Christian European world with its external splendor. The contrast between the happy and life-loving Berlin of Frederick II and the ascetic, medieval Jewish quarter was too great. Mendelssohn, as we shall see later, facilitated this process of Europeanization, the association of the Jewish youth with the Christian world and German culture. The rationalist ideas of the French "enlighteners" that were so strongly favored in the salons of Berlin became extremely popular in Jewish progressive circles as well. In these Voltaire became especially loved and honored. His clever sallies, his sarcastic mockery and smile of contempt, were highly *sympathique* to the Jewish youth educated on *pilpul* with its keen subtleties.[37] In the traditional, in what had been inherited from the fathers, Jews began to see only mildew, something completely reactionary and withered that must be set aside as quickly as possible. When everything is assessed from the one-sided rationalist standpoint, which rejects all that cannot justify its existence by utilitarian or logical arguments, it is quite understandable that the legacy of the fathers, the traditional, must be denied. After all, it cannot demonstrate its rational character, its logical necessity.

At the end of the 1770's this process was still in its infancy, and for the time being it was still difficult to foresee what forms it would later assume. Nevertheless, even at that time the more keen-sighted realized that the paths of the Berlin "enlighten-ers" and of their Polish-Lithuanian comrades were diverging. This became quite clear in the first important cultural-literary undertaking in which these two groups were to participate jointly, namely, the edition of Mendelssohn's Torah transla-tion with the new *Biur* or commentary which the grammarian, Solomon Dubno, was to provide. This, however, belongs to a later era, the era of the Berlin *Aufklärer* which we shall discuss in subsequent parts of our work.

37. "Voltaire," Heinrich Graetz rightly points out, "had far more followers and ad-mirers in Jewish houses than in German."

Bibliographical Notes

The German-Polish
Cultural Center
Book One

CHAPTER ONE

THE CENTER OF CULTURE IN ANCIENT KIEV; ABRAHAM KIRIMI AND MOSES OF KIEV

There is an extensive literature on the history of the Jews of eastern Europe. Among the most valuable works are the following: J. Aronius, *Regesten zur Geschichte der Juden im fränkischen und deutschen Reich bis zum Jahre 1273* (1887–1902); M. Balaban, *Yidn In Poiln* (1930); S. W. Baron, *A Social and Religious History of the Jews*, Vols. 2, 3, and 8 (1957 et seq.); P. Bloch, *Die general Privilegien der polnischen Judenschaft* (1892); M. Brann, *Die Geschichte der Juden in Schlesien*, 5 vols. (1896–1910); I. N. Darevsky, *Le-Korot Ha-Yehudim Be-Kiev* (1902); S. M. Dubnow, *A History of the Jews in Russia and Poland*, 3 vols. (1916 et seq.); D. M. Dunlop, *The History of the Jewish Khazars* (1954); A. Eisenstein, *Die Stellung der Juden in Polen im XIII und XIV Jahrhundert* (1934); I. Halpern, *Yehudim Ve-Yahadut Be-Mizraḥ Europa* (1969); idem, editor, *Bet Yisrael Be-Polin*, 2 vols. (1948–54); idem, "The Jews in Eastern Europe from Ancient Times to the Partitions of Poland, 1772–1795," in L. Finkelstein, ed., *The Jews: Their History, Culture, and Religion*, 3rd edition, Vol. 1 (1966), 287–320; A. Harkavy, *Altjüdische Denkmäler aus der Krim* (1876); G. Kisch, *The Jews in Medieval Germany* (1949); M. S. Lew, *The Jews of Poland: Their Political, Economic, Social and Communal Life in the Sixteenth Century as Reflected in the Works of Moses Isserles* (1943); M. Lowenthal, *The Jews of Germany* (1936); J. R. Marcus, *The Rise and Destiny of the German Jew* (1934); B. Mark, *Di Geshikhte Fun Yidn In Poiln* (1957); R. Mahler, *Toledot Ha-Yehudim Be-Polin* (1946); I. Schipper, *Kultur-Geshikhte Fun Di Yidn In Poiln Be-eysn Miltalter* (1926); idem, *Di Wirtshaftgeshikhte Fun Di Yidn in Poiln Be-eysn Mitlalter* (1926);

D. B. Teimanas, *L'Autonomie des communautes juives en Pologne aux XVIe et XVIIe siecles* (1933); I. Trunk, *Shtudies In Yidisher Geshikhte in Poiln* (1963); F. H. Wettstein, *Le-Korot Ha-Yehudim Be-Polin Uve-Yihud Be-Cracow* (1918); B. D. Weinryb, *The Jews of Poland: A Social and Economic History of the Jewish Community in Poland from 1100 to 1800* (1973); and idem, *Texts and Studies in the Communal History of Polish Jewry* (1950).

On Abraham Kirimi, see E. Deinard, *Massa Krim* (1878), 178–180; A. Firkovich, in *Ha-Karmel*, 3, (1863), 53f; S. J. Fuenn, *Kenesset Yisrael*, Vol. 1 (1887), 62f; and M. Steinschneider, in *Hebräische Bibliographie*, 11 (1871), 38f.

On Moses of Kiev, see *Kitvei Rabbi Avraham Epstein*, Vol. 1 (1950), 301–07.

CHAPTER TWO

JACOB POLLAK, MOSES ISSERLES, AND SOLOMON LURIA

On Jewish education and scholarship in eastern Europe, see S. Assaf, *Mekorot Le-Toledot Ha-Hinukh Be-Yisrael*, 4 vols. (1925–43); H. H. Ben-Sasson, *Hagut Ve-Hanhagah* (1959); and A. Menes, "Patterns of Jewish Scholarship in Eastern Europe," in L. Finkelstein, editor, *The Jews: Their History, Culture, and Religion*, 3rd edition, Vol. 1 (1966), 376–426.

On Jacob Pollak, see M. Balaban, "Jakob Polak, der Baal Chillukim in Krakau, und seine zeit," *MGWJ*, 57 (1913), 59–73, 196–210; F. H. Wettstein, in *Ha-Maggid* 5 (1896), nos. 17, 20–21; and idem, in *Ha-Eshkol*, 6 (1909), 218–22.

On the use of *pilpul* in the study of the Talmud, see N. S. Grinspan, *Pilpula Shel Torah* (1935); idem, *Melechet Mahashevet* (1955); L. Jacobs, *Studies in Talmudic Logic and Methodology* (1961); and E. E. Urbach, *Baalei Ha-Tosafot*, 2nd edition (1957).

One of the few items of Shalom Shachna's work that has been published is his "Teshuvah Be-Din Sivlonot," published by J. L. Fishman (Maimon) in *Sinai*, 4 (1939), 218–20. On Shachna and his work, see S. A. Horodetzky, *Shelosh Me'ot Shanah Shel Yahadut Polin* (1945), 15ff; and Ch. Tchernowitz, *Toledot Ha-Posekim*, Vol. 3 (1947), 38ff.

A new edition of Moses Isserles' *She'elot U-Teshuvot (Responsa)* was published, with introduction and notes, by A. Siev (1970). On Isserles and his work, see O. Feuchtwanger, *Righteous Lives* (1965), 79–81; S. A. Horodetzky, *Le-Korot Ha-Rabbanut* (1911), 81–

121; M. S. Lew, *The Jews of Poland: Their Political, Economic, Social and Communal Life in the Sixteenth Century as Reflected in the Works of Moses Isserles* (1943); A. Siev. *Ha-Rema* (1957); idem, *Rabbenu Mosheh Iserlesh* (1972); and Ch. Tchernowitz, *Toledot Ha-Posekim*, Vol. 3 (1947).

The 1582 edition of Solomon Luria's *Hochmat Shelomoh* was recently reprinted in four volumes (1972). Luria's *Hanhagat Maharshal* was published from a manuscript, with introduction and notes, by Y. Raphael (1961). On Luria and his work see, S. Assaf, *"Mashehu Le-Toledot Maharshal,"* in *Louis Ginzberg Jubilee Volume* (1946), 45–63; S. A. Horodetzky, *Kerem Shelomoh* (1897); idem, *Le-Korot Ha-Rabbanut* (1911), 123–44; S. Hurwitz, *The Responsa of Solomon Luria* (1938); A. Siev, *Ha-Rema* (1957), 49–59; and Ch. Tchernowitz, *Toledot Ha-Posekim*, Vol. 3 (1947), 74–91.

CHAPTER THREE

DISCIPLES OF ISSERLES AND COMMENTATORS ON THE SHULHAN ARUCH

A new edition of David Gans' *Tzemah David*, with introductions in Hebrew and English and an index, was published in 1966. A German translation of parts of *Tzemah David* by G. Klemperer (edited by M. Gruenwald) was published in 1890. On Gans and his work, see Gruenwald's introduction in Klemperer's translation of *Tzemah David*; G. Alter, *Two Renaissance Astronomers* (1958); M. Steinschneider, *Copernikus nach dem Urteil des David Gans* (1871); idem, *Geschichtsliteratur der Juden* (1905); and S. Steinherz in *Jahrbuch der Gesellschaft für Geschichte der Juden in der Čechoslavakischen Republik*, 9 (1938), 171–97.

On Abraham ben Shabbetai Sheftel Horowitz, see H. H. Ben-Sasson, *Hagut Ve-Hanhagah* (1959); Ph. Bloch, "Der Streit um den Moreh des Maimonides in der Gemeinde Posen um die Mitte des 16. Jahrhundert," *MGWJ*, 47 (1903), 153–69; and S. A. Horodetzky, "Me'ah Shanim Shel Perishut Musarit," *Ha-Tekufah*, 22 (1924), 290–302.

On Mordecai ben Abraham Jaffe, see M. Amsel, "Mi-Toledotav Shel Rabbenu Ha-Levush," in: Mordecai Jaffe, *Levush Malchut*, 2 (*Levush Ha-Hur:* 1964); S. M. Chones, *Toledot Ha-Posekim* (1910), 314–18; S. A. Horodetzky, *Le-Korot Ha-Rabbanut* (1911), 145–74; and S. B. Nissenbaum, *Le-Korot Ha-Yehudim Be-Lublin* (1900), 25–27.

On Samuel Edels, see H. H. Ben-Sasson, *Hagut Ve-Hanhagah*

(1959), index; S. M. Dubnow, *A History of the Jews in Russia and Poland*, Vol. 1 (1916), 129–30; S. A. Horodetzky, *Le-Korot Ha-Rabbanut* 2nd edition, (1914), 183–90; R. Margulies, *Toledot Adam* (1912); and J. M. Toledano, *Sarid U-Falit* (1945), 74f.

On Meir Lublin and his work, see S. Buber, *Anshei Shem* (1895), 132f; S. A. Horodetzky, "Ha-Maharam Ve-Halach Nafesho," *Ha-Goren*, 1 (1898); idem, *Le-Korot Ha-Rabbanut* (1911), 175–82; idem, *Shelosh Me'ot Shanah Shel Yahadut Polin* (1945), 68–72; B. Katz, *Rabbanut, Hasidut, Haskalah*, Vol. 1 (1956), 65–69; J. Loewenstein, "Toledot Maharam Me-Lublin," *Ha-Goren*, 1 (1898), 39–54; J. Meisl, *Die Geschichte der Juden in Polen und Russland*, Vol. 1 (1921), 312f.; S. B. Nissenbaum, *Le-Korot Ha-Yahudim Be-Lublin* (1900), 31f.; I. Rivkind, "Dikdukei Soferim," in *Alexander Marx Jubilee Volume: Helek Ivri* (1950), 427f.; J. Rosenthal, "Le-Korot Ha-Yehudim Be-Polin Le-Or She'elot U-Teshuvot Ha-Maharam Me-Lublin," *Sinai*, 31 (1952), 311–38; and Ch. Tchernowitz, *Toledot Ha-Posekim*, Vol. 3 (1947), 120f.

On Joel Sirkes, see M. Kossover, "R. Yoel Sirkish," *Bitzaron*, 14 (1946), 23–31, and S. K. Mirsky, "R. Yoel Sirkish: Baal Ha-Bah," *Horeb*, 6 (1942), 41–75.

On Joshua Falk, see H. H. Ben-Sasson, *Hagut Ve-Hanhagah* (1959), index; Ch. Tchernowitz, in *Ha-Shiloah*, 6 (1899), 233–40; and idem, *Toledot Ha-Posekim*, Vol. 2 (1947), 213ff., and Vol. 3 (1947), 112–20.

On Shabbetai ben Meir Ha-Kohen, see S. M. Chones, *Toledot Ha-Posekim* (1910), 586–90; C. B. Friedberg, *Keter Kehunnah* (1898); B. Katz, *Rabbanut, Hasidut, Haskalah* (1956), 108–11; idem, in *Sefer Ha-Yovel Le-Yitzhak Baer* (1960), 335f.; S. Knoebil, *Toledot Gedolei Hora'ah* (1927), 87–95; and Ch. Tchernowitz, *Toledot Ha-Posekim*, Vol. 3 (1947), 138–58.

CHAPTER FOUR

THE MAHARAL OF PRAGUE, EPHRAIM OF LUNTSHITS, AND YOM TOV HELLER

An edition of *Yosif Ometz* by Joseph Juspa Hahn (Nördlingen) was published with corrections, addenda, notes, and a biography of the author at Frankfurt-am-Main in 1928. The biography is signed with the letters *Shin Tzadi*, but the writer is unknown.

On Hahn and his *Yosif Ometz*, see S. Esh, "Shinuyyim Be-

Sefer Yosif Ometz Veha-Reka Ha-Histori," in *Kovetz Le-Zichro Shel Eliezer Shamir* (1957), 155–162; M. Horovitz, *Frankfurter Rabbiner*, Vol. 2 (1883), 6–18; J. Horovitz, in *Festschrift . . . A. Freimann* (1935), 35–50; and idem, in *Festschrift . . . J. Freimann* (1937), 78–93.

On the work of Jephta Joseph Yozpa, the sexton of Worms, see A. M. Habermann, *"Minhagei Hodesh Adar Mi-Toch Sefer Minhagei Virmaiza Le-Rabbi Yosef Yozpa Shammash,"* in *Sinai: Sefer Yovel* (1958), 482–90.

A selection from the writings of Jehudah Loew ben Bezalel, the Maharal of Prague, is to be found in A. Kariv, ed., *Kitvei Maharal Mi-Prag: Mivhar* (1960). M. Z. Kasher and J. J. Blacherowitz edited and published for the first time from manuscript, with an introduction and notes, *Perushei Maharal Mi-Prag . . . Le-Aggadot Ha-Shas . . .* (1958). For a bibliography of the Maharal's works, see Y. Kohen-Yashar, *Bibliografyah Shimmushit Shel Kitvei Ha-Maharal Mi-Prag* (1967).

On Jehudah Loew ben Bezalel and his work, see C. Bloch, *The Golem: Legends of the Ghetto of Prague* (1925); B. Z. Bokser, *From the World of the Cabbalah: the Philosophy of Rabbi Judah Loew of Prague* (1954); M. Buber, *Bein Am Le-Artzo* (1945), 78–91; T. Dreyfus, *Dieu parle aux hommes; la révelation selon le Maharal de Prague* (1969); A. Gottesdiener, "Ha-Ari Shebe-Hachmei Prag," in *Azkarah Le-Nishmat Ha-Tzaddik Ha-Rav Rabbi Avraham Yitzhak Ha-Kohen Kook*, Part Three, (1937), 253–443; B. Gross, *Le eternité d'Israel*, 2 vols. (1968); idem, *Le messianisme juif* (1969); A. Kariv, ed., *Kitvei Maharal Mi-Prag: Mivhar* (1960), introduction; A. F. Kleinberger, *Ha-Mahashavah Ha-Pedagogit Shel Ha-Maharal Mi-Prag* (1962); the review of Kleinberger's work by G. Vajda in *REJ*, 123 (1964), 225–33; A. Mauskopf, *The Religious Philosophy of the Maharal of Prague* (1949); O. Muneles, ed., *The Prague Ghetto in the Renaissance Period* (1965), 75–84; idem., in *Judaica Bohemiae*, 5 (1969), 103–7 and 117–22; A. Neher, in M. Zahari and A. Tartakover, eds., *Hagut Ivrit Be-Europah* (1969), 107–17; idem, *Le Puits de l'Exil; la théologie dialectique du Maharal de Prague* (1966); G. Scholem, *Zur Kabbala und ihrer Symbolik* (1960), 209–59; and F. Thieberger, *The Great Rabbi Loew of Prague* (1954).

On Ephraim of Luntshits, see H. H. Ben-Sasson, "Osher Ve-Oni Be-Mishnato Shel Ha-Mochiah Rabbi Efrayim Ish Lantzitz," *Zion*, 19 (1954), 142–66; I. Bettan, "The Sermons of Ephraim Luntshitz," *Hebrew Union College Annual*, 8–9 (1931–32), 443–80; idem, *Studies in Jewish Preaching*, (1939), 273–316; M. Gruenwald, *Rabbi Salomo Efraim Luntschitz* (German, 1892); G.

Klemperer, "The Rabbis of Prague," *Historia Judaica*, 12 (1950), 33–66; and H. R. Rabinowitz, *Deyokena'ot Shel Darshanim* (1967), 137–49.

A bibliographical listing of Yom Tov Lippmann Heller's works is to be found in I. Halpern, "Ḥibburei Rabbi Yom Tov Lippmann Heller U-Ketavav," *Kiryat Sefer*, 7 (1930–31), 140–8, 482. Heller's *Megillat Eivah* was edited by M. Koerner and translated into German by H. Miro (1837).

On Heller and his work, see I. D. Beth-Halevy, *Rabbi Yom Tov Lippmann Heller* (Hebrew, 1954); S. M. Chones, *Toledot Ha-Posekim* (1910), 167–72; B. Katz, *Rabbanut, Ḥasidut, Haskalah*, Vol. 1 (1956), 91–97; G. Klemperer, "The Rabbis of Prague," *Historia Judaica*, 12 (1950), 33–66; J. L. Maimon, ed., *Le-Chevod Yom Tov: Ma'amarim U-Meḥkarim;* (1956); and Ch. Tchernowitz, *Toledot Ha-Posekim*, Vol. 3 (1947), 127–37.

CHAPTER FIVE

LURIANIC MYSTICISM IN POLAND; ISAIAH HORO-WITZ

An English translation of Isaac Troki's *Ḥizzuk Emunah* was issued by Moses Mocatta in 1851; the work was recently reprinted with an introduction by Trude Weiss-Rosmarin (1970). The second edition of a German translation, along with the Hebrew text, was published by David Deutsch in 1873. On Isaac Troki, see J. Mann, *Texts and Studies*, Vol. 2 (1935), passim.

Letters of autobiographical significance written by Isaiah Horowitz from Palestine are to be found in A. Yaari, *Iggerot Eretz Yisrael* (1943), 210–21. On Horowitz's life and work, see S. M. Chones, *Toledot Ha-Posekim* (1910), 580–83; H. G. Enelow, "Isaiah Horowitz: His Life and Times," in *Selected Works*, Vol. 4 (1935), 1–40; A. L. Frumkin and E. Rivlin, *Toledot Ḥachmei Yerushalayim*, Vol. 1 (1928), 146–158; S. A. Horodetzky, *Ha-Mistorim Be-Yisrael*, Part Four (1961), 54–113; idem, "Meah Shanim Shel Perishut Musarit," *Ha-Tekufah*, 22 (1924), 305–323, and 24 (1928), 389–415; idem, *Olei Tziyyon* (1947); G. Klemperer, "The Rabbis of Prague," in *Historia Judaica*, 12 (1950), 33–66; P. Pesis, *Ateret Ha-Leviyyim* (1902); H. R. Rabinowitz, *Deyokena'ot Shel Darshanim* (1967), 243f.; and A. Shochat, "Al Ha-Simḥah Be-Ḥasidut," *Zion*, 16 (1951), 30–43.

On Nathan Spira, see J. Ginzburg, "Neshamot To'ot," *Ha-Tekufah*, 25 (1929), 488–97; S. A. Horodetzky, in *Iyyim*, 1, Section

Four (1928), 54–61; idem, *Shelosh Me'ot Shanah Shel Yahadut Polin* (1946), 127–32; and G. Scholem, in *Revue d'histoire des religions*, 143 (1953), 34–36.

CHAPTER SIX

THE MASSACRES OF 1648 AND THEIR ECHO IN LITERATURE

On Bogdan Chmielnitzki, Jewish life in the Ukraine at the time of his rise, and the Jewish massacres of 1648, see S. Ettinger, "Maamadam Ha-Mishpati Veha-Hevrati Shel Yehudei Ukrainah Be-Meot 15–17," *Zion*, 20 (1955), 128–52; idem, "Helkom Shel Ha-Yehudim Be-Kolonizatzyah Shel Ukrainah," *Zion*, 21 (1956), 107–42; I. Halpern, *Yehudim Ve-Yahadut Be-Mizrah Europah* (1968); M. Hendel, *Gezerot 1648–1649* (1950); J. S. Hertz, *Di Yidn in Ukraine* (1949); J. Israelsohn, in: *YIVO-Historishe Shriftn*, 1 (1929), 1–26; J. Katz, in *Sefer Yovel Le-Yitzhak Baer* (1960), 318–37; J. Shatzky, *Gezerot Tah* (Yiddish, 1938); F. Vernadsky, *Bohdan, Hetman of Ukraine* (1941); and N. Wahrman, *Mekorot le-Toledot Gezerot 1648 ve-1649* (1949).

A new edition of Nathan Nata Hannover's *Yeven Metzulah* by J. Fichman, with notes and comments by I. Halpern, was published in 1946. Hannover's chronicle was translated into English by A. J. Mesch under the title *Abyss of Despair* (1950).

On Hannover and his work, see J. Israelsohn in *YIVO-Historishe Shriftn*, 1 (1929), 1–26; I. Nacht, in *Reshumot*, 1 (1946), 164–67; M. Weinreich, in *Tsaytshrift far Yidishe Geshikhte, Demografye* . . ., 2–3 (1928), 706–16; N. Prylucki, "Bibliologishe Notitzn," *YIVO-Bleter*, 1 (1931), 414ff.; and J. Shatzky, *Gezerot Tah* (1938), 9–159.

For the work of the other major chronicles of the Chmielnitzki massacres, see J. H. Gurland, *Le-Korot Ha-Gezerot Al Yisrael*, Vol. 4 (1890). See also I. Halpern, "Sheviah U-Fedut Be-Gezerot Ukrainah Ve-Lita 1648–1660," *Zion*, 25 (1960), 17–56. On a previously unknown manuscript of *Tzok Ha-Ittim* by Meir ben Samuel of Sczebrszyn, see A. Yaari, in *Kiryat Sefer*, 16 (1940), 375–379.

Book Two

CHAPTER ONE

THE PERIOD OF INTELLECTUAL DECLINE

On Yair Ḥayyim Bacharach and his work, see S. Freehof, *Responsa Literature* (1955), 84–87; idem, *A Treasury of Responsa* (1963), 171–75; D. Kaufman, "Jair Chayim Bacharach: A Biographical Sketch," *JQR*, 3 (1891), 292–313, 485–536; idem, *R. Jair Chajjim Bacharach* (German, 1894); and A. Marx, in *Essays in Honor of J. H. Hertz* (1942), 307–11.

On Tobias Cohn, see E. Carmoly, *Histoire des médecins juifs* (1844), 248ff.; D. A. Friedman, *Tuviyyah Ha-Rofe* (1940); and A. Levinson, *Tuviyyah Ha-Rofe Ve-Sifro Ma'aseh Tuviyyah* (1924).

A new edition of David Nieto's *Ha-Kuzari Ha-Sheni* was published in 1958, with an introduction by J. L. Maimon (pp. 5–20) and a biography by C. Roth (pp. 261–75). On Nieto and his work, see J. J. Petuchowski, *The Theology of Ḥaham David Nieto: An Eighteenth Century Defense of the Jewish Tradition*, 2nd ed., (1970); and I. Solomons, *David Nieto and Some of His Contemporaries* (1931).

On Jehudah Briel, see M. S. Ghirondi and G. H. Neppi, *Toledot Gedolei Yisrael U-Geonei Italyah* (1853), 127–29; J. Rosenthal, "Sifrut Ha-Vikkuaḥ Ha-Anti-Notzerit: Bibliografiyah," *Aresheth*, 2 (1960), 158, 166; S. Simonsohn, *Toledot Ha-Yehudim Be-Dukkasut Mantovah*, Vol. 1 (1963), 332, n. 427; and M. Steinschneider, "Die italenische Literatur der Juden," *MGWJ*, 44 (1900), 88–89.

On Solomon Aviad Sar-Shalom Basilea, see Ghirondi-Neppi, 36–39; M. Mortara, *Catalogo dei manoscritti ebraici . . . di Mantova* (1878), 45–47; S. Simonsohn, *Toledot Ha-Yehudim Be-Dukkasut Mantovah* (1964), index; and S. Wiener, *Mazkeret Rabbanei Italyah* (1898), 37–40 (third pagination).

On Shabbetai Bass, see J. Bloch, *Studies in Jewish Bibliography and Related Subjects* (1929), and A. M. Habermann, "R. Shabbetai

Meshorer Bass: Ha-Bibliograf Ha-Ivri Ha-Rishon," in *Yad Le-Kore*, 3 (1953), 157–63.

An edition of Yeḥiel Heilprin's *Seder Ha-Dorot* was published, with a preface, by N. Maskileison (1878); this work was reprinted in 1956. On Heilprin, see B. Z. Eisenstadt, *Rabbanei Minsk Ve-Ḥachmehah* (1898), 14–16; and B. Katz, *Rabbanut, Ḥasidut, Haskalah* (1957), 141.

On Isaac Lampronti, see M. Benayahu, "Yitzḥak Lampronti Ve-R. Shabbetai Elḥanan Min Ha-Zekenim," *Sinai: Sefer Ha-Yovel* (1958), 491–503; B. Cohen, in *Sefer Ha-Yovel Le-Chevod Alexander Marx* (1943), 41–57; J. A. Klausner, "Ktav Yad Lo Noda Shel 'Musarim' Le-Rabbi Yitzḥak Lampronti," in *Kiryat Sefer*, 36 (1960–61), 123–36; B. Levi, *Della Vita e dell' Opera di Isacco Lampronti* (1869); idem, *Sefer Toledot Ha-Rav Ha-Gadol Yitzḥak Lampronti* (1871); and I. Sonne, in *Horeb*, 6 (1941), 76–114.

CHAPTER TWO

ETHICAL LITERATURE

On Jehudah Ḥasid (Segal) Ha-Levi and his followers, see M. Benayahu, "Ha-Ḥevrah Kedoshah Shel R. Yehudah Ḥasid Ve-Aliyyatah Le-Eretz Yisrael," *Sefunot*, 3–4 (1960), 133–82; I. Halpern, "Ha-Aliyyot Ha-Rishonot Shel Ha-Ḥasidim Le-Eretz Yisrael (1946); and S. Krauss, in *Abhandlungen zur Erinnerung an Hirsch Perez Chajes* (1933), 51–94.

On Tzevi Hirsch Koidonover, see E. Tcherikover, "Di Geshikhte Fun A Literarishen Plagiat: Ver is Geven Der Emeser Mekhaber Fun Kav Ha-Yashar?," *YIVO-Bleter*, 4 (1932), 159–167.

On Elijah ben Solomon Ha-Kohen of Smyrna, see H. H. Michael, *Or Ha-Ḥayyim: Ḥachmei Yisrael Ve-Sifreihem*, 2nd ed. (1965), 188–90; S. A. Rosanes, *Divrei Yemei Yisrael Be-Togarmah*, Vol. 6 (1945), 291; G. Scholem in *Sefer Ha-Yovel Le-Chevod Alexander Marx* (1950), 451–70; and S. Werses, in *Yavneh*, 2 (1940), 156–73.

CHAPTER THREE

MOSES ḤAYYIM LUZZATTO

A considerable number of the works of Moses Ḥayyim Luzzatto have been published in new editions in recent years. A. M. Habermann published a vocalized edition of *Sefer Ha-Melit-*

zah in 1949 and of *Leshon Limmudim* in 1951. Yonah David published a similar edition of *Maaseh Shimshon* in 1967 and of *Migdal Oz* in 1972. A collection of Luzzatto's plays, *Sefer Ḥa-Maḥazot*, was edited and published by S. Ginsburg (1927). Ginsburg also edited a collection of Luzzatto's poems, *Mosheh Ḥayyim Luzzatto: Sefer Ha-Shirim* (1945). The Hebrew text of *Mesillat Yesharim* with an English translation by Mordecai M. Kaplan appeared in 1966. Luzzatto's *Kelalei Ḥochmat Ha-Emet* was translated into English under the title *General Principles of the Kabbalah* (1970).

A full biography of Luzzatto's printed works and manuscripts is to be found in N. Ben-Menaḥem, *Kitvei Ramḥal* (1951).

On Luzzatto and his work, see M. Benayahu, "Ha-Maggid Shel Ramḥal," *Sefunot*, 3 (1961), 299–336; S. Bernfeld, *Kämpfende Geister im Judentum* (1907); Y. David, *Ha-Maḥazot Shel Mosheh Ḥayyim Luzzatto* (1972); S. Ginsburg, *The Life and Works of Moses Ḥayyim Luzzatto* (1931); idem, *R. Mosheh Ḥayyim Luzzatto U-Venei Doro*, 2 vols., (1937); A. Kahana, *Toledot Rabbi Mosheh Ḥayyim Luzzatto* (1911); F. Lachover, *Al Gevul Ha-Yashan Ve-Ḥadash* (1951), 29–96; I. Tishby, "Darchei Ḥafatzatam Shel Kitvei Kabbalah Le-Ramḥal Be-Polin Uve-Lita," *Kiryat Sefer*, 45 (1970), 127–154, 300, 628; idem, "Yaḥaso Shel R. Mosheh Ḥayyim Luzzatto El Ha-Shabbeta'ut," *Tarbitz*, 27 (1958), 334–57; idem, *Netivei Emunah U-Minut* (1964), 169–203; and I. Sonne, "Avnei Vinyan Le-Korot Ha-Yehudim Be-Italyah," *Horeb*, 6 (1942), 76–114.

On Abraham ben Shabbetai of Zante see M.S. Ghirondi and G.H. Neppi, *Toledot Gedolei Yisrael U-Geonei Italyah* (1853), 32, No. 76; and A. Rubens, *Jewish Iconography* (1954), No. 2006.

CHAPTER FOUR

THE CONTROVERSY BETWEEN JACOB EMDEN AND JONATHAN EYBESCHÜTZ

On Jacob Emden and Jonathan Eybeschütz and the long controversy that raged between these two scholars of the eighteenth century, see B. Brilling, "Eibenschutziana," in *Hebrew Union College Annual*, 34 (1963), 217–28, and 35 (1964), 255–73; M. J. Cohen, *Jacob Emden: a Man of Controversy* (1937); G. Scholem's review of Cohen's book in *Kiryat Sefer* 16 (1940), 320–38; J. J. Greenwald, *Ha-Rav Rabbi Yehonatan Eybeschuetz* (1954); M. Grunwald, *Hamburgs deutsche Juden* (1904), 89–124; Y. Raphael, in *Aresheth*, 3 (1961), 231–76; B. Katz, *Rabbanut, Ḥasidut, Haskalah,*

Vol. 1 (1957); J. Katz, *Exclusiveness and Tolerance* (1961), index; R. Margulies, *Sibbat Hitnagduto Shel Rabbenu Yaakov Me-Emden Le-Rabbenu Yehonatan Eybeschuetz* (1941); M. A. Perlmutter, *Rabbi Yehonatan Eybeschuetz Ve-Yahaso El Ha-Shabbeta'ut* (1947); G. Scholem, *Leket Margaliyyot Le-Ha'arachat Ha-Sanegoryah Ha-Hadashah Al R. Yehonatan Eybeschuetz* (1941); idem, "Le-She'elat Yahaso Shel Rabbi Yehonatan Eybeschuetz Le-Shabbeta'ut," *Zion*, 6 (1940–41), 96–100; and D. L. Zinz, *Gedulat Yehonatan* (1930).

CHAPTER FIVE

THE ERA OF THE GAON OF VILNA

On Aryeh Loeb ben Asher and his work, see H. D. Y. Azulai, *Shem Ha-Gedolim* (1852); A. Kahn, "Les Rabbins de Metz," *REJ*, 12, 295ff.; and H. H. Michael, *Or Ha-Hayyim: Hachmei Yisrael Ve-Sifreihem*, 2nd ed. (1955).

On Jehudah Margolioth see B. Dinur, *Be-Mifneh Ha-Dorot* (1955), 264–65; J. Klausner, *Historyah Shel Ha-Sifrut Ha-Ivrit Ha-Hadashah*, 2nd ed., Vol. 1 (1952), 85–86; and R. Mahler, *Divrei Yemei Yisrael: Dorot Aharonim*, Part One, Vol. 4 (1956), 40–44.

Sefer Ha-Gra, edited by J. L. Maimon (1954), contains a biography of Elijah, Gaon of Vilna, and essays on his thought, as well as selections from his writings. In *Talpiot*, Vol. 4 (1949), 155–356, 409–13, are a number of essays on the Gaon by various authors and a bibliography of his works by J. Dienstag.

On the Gaon, see also M. G. Barg, *Ha-Gra Me-Vilna* (1948); H. H. Ben-Sasson, in *Zion*, 31 (1966), 39–86, 197–216; I. Cohen, *History of the Jews of Vilna* (1943); S. J. Fuenn, *Kiryah Ne'emanah*, 2nd ed. (1915), 144–70; L. Ginzberg, "The Gaon, Rabbi Elijah Wilna," in *Students, Scholars and Saints* (1928), 115–24; S. J. Jazkan, *Rabbenu Eliyahu Me-Vilna* (1900); B. Katz, *Rabbanut, Hasidut, Haskalah*, 2 vols. (1956–58); I. Klausner, *Ha-Gaon Rabbi Eliyahu Me-Vilna* (1969); idem, *Vilna Be-Tekufat Ha-Gaon* (1942); B. Landau, *Ha-Gaon He-Hasid Me-Vilna* (1965); M. S. Samet, in: *Mehkarim Le-Zekher Tzevi Avneri* (1970), 233–57; S. Schechter, "Rabbi Elijah, Wilna Gaon," in *Studies in Judaism*, First Series (1896), 73–98; M. Silber, *The Gaon of Wilna* (1905); I. Unna, *Rabbenu Eliyahu Me-Vilna U-Tekufato* (1946); and M. Wilensky, *Hasidim U-Mitnaggedim*, 2 vols. (1970).

CHAPTER SIX

THE MAGGID OF DUBNO; THE PIONEERS OF EN-
LIGHTENMENT

A new edition of the parables of the Maggid of Dubno, *Emshol Lecha Mashal: Mishlei Ha-Maggid Me-Dubno*, was published by M. Lifson in 1956.

On the Maggid see I. Avigur, in: *Yahadut Lita* (1960), 346–52; I. Bettan, "The Dubno Maggid," *Hebrew Union College Annual*, 23 (1950–51), Part 2, 267–93; H. A. Glatt, *He Spoke in Parables* (1957); J. L. Maimon, *Sefer Ha-Gra* (1954), 160–75; and A. B. Plahm, introduction to J. Kranz, *Sefer Ha-Middot* (1860).

On Solomon ben Moses Chelm, see Berik in *Sinai*, 61 (1967), 168–84; S. Buber, *Anshei Shem* (1895), 207–9, No. 525; H. N. Dembitzer, *Kelilat Yofi*, 1 (1888), 140a–144b; and G. Scholem, "Shetei Ha-Eduyyot Ha-Rishonot Al Havurot Ha-Hasidim Veha-Besht," in *Tarbitz*, 20 (1948–49), 228–40.

On Israel ben Moses Ha-Levi Zamosc and his work, see S. J. Fuenn, *Keneset Yisrael* (1877–90), 690–92; G. Kressel, *Leksikon Ha-Sifrut Ha-Ivrit Ba-Dorot Ha-Aharonim*, 1 (1965), 755–56; H. Lieberman, "Ketzad Hokerim Hasidut Be-Yisrael," *Bitzaron*, 32 (1955), 113–120; R. Mahler, *Divrei Yemei Yisrael Be-Dorot Aha-ronim*, Part One, Vol. 4 (1956), 26–30, 260–63; and G. Scholem, "Ha-Polemos Al Ha-Hasidut U-Manhigehah Be-Sefer Nezed Ha-Dema," *Zion*, 20 (1955), 73–81.

On Abba Glusk, see A. Kohut, *Mendelssohn und seine Familie* (1886), 51–53, and Stanislavsky, in *Voskhod*, 12 (1887), 122–28.

Solomon Maimon's *Gesammelte Werke*, edited by Valeris Verra, have recently been published in six volumes (1965–71). A new edition of his Hebrew work *Givat Ha-Moreh*, edited by S. H. Bergmann and N. Rotenstreich, was published in 1966.

Maimon's *Autobiography (Lebensgeschichte)* was translated from the German by J. C. Murray and published in 1888; the work was reprinted in 1954 with an essay on Maimon's philosophy by S. H. Bergmann. Another translation into English of the *Autobiography* was published by Moses Hadas in 1947. N. J. Jacobs provided a valuable bibliography of writings on Solomon Maimon in *Kiryat Sefer*, 41 (1965–66), 245–62.

An extensive literature has been produced on Maimon's writings. Among the most important works are: S. Atlas, *From Criticial to Speculative Idealism* (1964); idem, "Solomon Maimon's Treatment of the Problem of Antinomies and Its Relation to Maimonides," *Hebrew Union College Annual*, 21 (1948), 105–53;

idem, "Maimon and Maimonides," in *Hebrew Union College Annual*, 23, Part One (1950–51), 517–47; idem, "Solomon Maimon's Conception of the Copernican Revolution in Philosophy," in *Harry A. Wolfson Jubilee Volume* (1965); idem., in: *Journal of the History of Ideas*, 13 (1952), 168–87; S. H. Bergman, *The Philosophy of Solomon Maimon* (1967); I. Boeck, *Die ethischen Anschauungen von S. Maimon in ihrem Verhältniss zu Kants Morallehre* (1897); S. Daiches, "Solomon Maimon and His Relation to Judaism," in *Aspects of Judaism* (1928); L. Gottselig, *Die Logik Salomon Maimons* (1908); M. Gueroult, *La philosophie transcendentale de Salomon Maimon* (1929); F. Kuntze, *Die Philosophie Salomon Maimons* (1912); F. Lachower, *Al Gevul Ha-Yashan Veha-Ḥadash* (1951); C. Rosenbaum, *Die Philosophie Salomon Maimons in seinem hebräischen Kommentar gibath-hammoreh zum moreh-nebuchim des Maimonides* (1928); N. Rotenstreich, *Sugyot Be-Filosofyah* (1962); and A. Zubersky, *Salomon Maimon und der kritische Idealismus* (1925).

CHAPTER SEVEN

THE HARBINGERS OF THE NEW ERA; PHINEḤAS HURWITZ

On Jehudah Hurwitz, see S. J. Fuenn, *Kiryah Ne'emanah*, 2nd ed. (1915), 178f.; B. Katz, *Rabbanut, Ḥasidut, Haskalah*, Vol. 2 (1958), 122–28; and J. Shatzky, *Kultur-Geshikhte Fun Der Haskole In Lite* (1950), 21–23.

On Jehudah Loeb Margolioth and his work, see B. Dinur, *Be-Mifneh Ha-Dorot* (1955), 264–65; J. Klausner, *Historyah Shel Ha-Sifrut Ha-Ivrit Ha-Ḥadashah*, 2nd. ed., Vol. 1 (1952), 85–86; and R. Mahler, *Divrei Yemei Yisrael: Dorot Aḥaronim*, Vol. 4, Part One (1956), 40–44.

On Phineḥas Hurwitz, see S. A. Horodetzky, *Yahadut Ha-Sechel Ve-Yahadut Ha-Regesh*, Vol. 2 (1947), 387–405; and R. Mahler, *Divrei Yemei Yisrael: Dorot Aḥaronim*, Vol. 4 (1956), 45–52.

CHAPTER EIGHT

THE MASKILIM OF SHKLOV; MENDEL LEVIN

On Baruch Schick of Skhlov, see B. Katz, *Rabbanut, Ḥasidut, Haskalah*, Vol. 2 (1958), 134–39; J. Katz, *Jews and Freemasons* (1970); R. Mahler, *Divrei Yemei Yisrael*, Vol. 4 (1956), 53–56; and N. Schapira, in *Ha-Rofe Ha-Ivri*, 34 (1961), 230–35.

On Menaḥem Mendel Levin (Lefin), see M. Erik (Merkin), *Etiudn Tsu Der Geshikhte Fun Der Haskole* (1934), 135–51; N. M. Gelber in: *Aus Zwei Jahruhunderten* (1924), 39–57; idem, in: *Abraham Weiss Jubilee Volume* (1964), 271–305 (Hebrew part); S. Katz, "Targumei Tanach Me-Et Menaḥem Mendel Lefin Mi-Satanov," *Kiryat Sefer*, 16 (1939–40), 114–33; J. L. Landau, *Short Lectures on Modern Hebrew Literature*, 2nd. ed. (1938), 187–92; J. S. Raisin, *The Haskalah Movement in Russia* (1913), 99–101; Ch. Shmeruk, in *Yidishe Shprakh*, 24 (1964), 33–52; J. Weinles, in *Ha-Olam*, 13 (1925) Nos. 39–42; idem, "Mendel Lefin-Satanover," in *YIVO-Bleter*, 3 (1931), 334–57; and M. Wiener, *Tsu Der Geshikhte Fun Der Yidisher Literatur In 19ten Yorhundert* (1945), 38–44.

On Joshua Zeitlin, see S. J. Fuenn, *Kiryah Ne'emanah* (1915), 271–73, and S. J. Horowitz, in *Ha-Shiloaḥ*, 40 (1923), 3–6.

Glossary of Hebrew and Other Terms

Glossary of Hebrew and Other Terms

Active Intellect: Among the Jewish and Arabic Aristotelians, the universal "Intelligence" which serves to control the motions of the sub-lunar world and especially to develop the human faculty of reason, which, in the infant, is merely a capacity or potentiality—a "material" intellect.

Ashkenazim: Since the ninth century, a term applied to the German Jews and their descendants, in contrast to the Sephardim (see below). After the Crusades, many Ashkenazic Jews settled in eastern Europe and from there migrated to western Europe and America. In recent centuries they have constituted the overwhelming majority of the world Jewish population.

Combinations of Letters: A method of exegesis of Biblical and other texts through combinations and permutation of the constituent letters of their words, practiced by many Kabbalists. It was also believed by some Kabbalists that supernatural and miraculous results could be obtained in practical life by the application of this method.

Ein Sof: (literally, "without end" or "infinite"): In Kabbalist thought, the undifferentiated unity of the unknown God, the *deus absconditus* as He is in His own being before His self-revelation through the *sefirot* (see below).

Gaon (plural, Geonim): The spiritual and intellectual leaders of Babylonian Jewry in the post-Talmudic period, from the sixth through the eleventh centuries C.E. The head of each of the two major academies of Babylonia, at Sura and Pumbeditha, held the title Gaon. The Geonim had considerable secular power as well as religious authority, and their influence extended over virtually all of the world Jewry during the larger part of the Geonic age. The title Gaon is occasionally applied in a general honorific sense to a very eminent Judaic scholar.

Gemara: The second basic strand of the Talmud (see below), consisting of a commentary on, and supplement to, the Mishnah (see below).

Gematria: A system of exegesis based on the interpretation of a word or words according to the numerical value of the constituent letters in the Hebrew alphabet.

Golem (Hebrew, "shapeless mass"): An automaton, particularly one in human form, supposedly created supernaturally through magic, especially through the invocation of mysterious divine names.

Ḥacham: (Hebrew, "wise man"): Originally, an officer of the rabbinic courts in Palestine and Babylonia. Later the term was applied to an officiating rabbi in Sephardic communities.

Halachah: (in Hebrew, "law"; derived from the verb *halach*, "to go" or "to follow"): The legal part of Talmudic and later Jewish literature, in contrast to Aggadah or Haggadah, the non-legal elements. In the singular, *halachah* means "law" in an abstract sense or, alternatively, a specific rule or regulation; in the plural, *halachot* refers to collections of laws.

Ḥalitzah (Hebrew, "taking off"): The ceremony of "removing the shoe" prescribed by the Bible (Deuteronomy 25: 9–10) in the case of a man who refuses to marry the childless widow of his brother.

Ḥannukah: (In Hebrew, "dedication"): An eight-day festival commemorating the victory of the Maccabees over Antiochus Epiphanes in 165 B.C. and the subsequent rededication of the Temple in Jerusalem.

Haskalah: The movement for disseminating modern European culture among Jews from about 1750 to 1880. It advocated the modernization of Judaism, the westernization of traditional Jewish education, and the revival of the Hebrew language.

Haskamah: (pl. Haskamot): Approbations or authorizations by respected rabbinic authorities, sometimes inserted in Hebrew books. The practice of inserting *haskamot* became particularly widespread after the synod of rabbis in Ferrara in 1554 decided that Hebrew books should obtain prior approval by Jewish authorities in order to prevent suppression or censorship by the officials of the Church. Later a *haskamah* was frequently solicited by the author of a book as testimony of his work's scholarly value and its orthodoxy.

Ḥiddushim (Hebrew, "novellae" or "new things"): Commentaries on the Talmud and subsequent works of Rabbinic literature that seek to deduce new facts, principles, or interpretations from the implications of the text.

Ḥilluk (plural, ḥillukim): Subtle distinctions or refined analyses in interpretation of the Talmud or other rabbinic texts.

Hoshannah Rabbah: The popular name for the seventh day of the Sukkot or Tabernacles festival.

Ineffable Name: (YHWH, the Tetragrammaton or *Shem Ha-Meforash*): The particular name of the God of Israel in the Bible. Its original pronounciation is no longer known, though it is generally conjectured to have been Yahweh. By the second century B.C.E. it was no longer pronounced, except by the High Priest on the Day of Atonement, but read as *Adonai*.

Kabbalah: The mystical religious movement in Judaism and/or its literature. The term Kabbalah, which means "tradition," came to be used by the mystics beginning in the twelfth century to signify the alleged continuity of their doctrine from ancient times.

Kapparot-Shlogn: The custom, practiced on the eve of Yom Kippur or the Day of Atonement, of swinging a fowl over one's head while praying that the fowl, when slaughtered, will expiate the sins of the individual as his substitute. The practice was sanctioned by some rabbinic authorities and ridiculed or banned by others.

Karaites: A Jewish sect, originating in the eighth century C.E. in and around Persia, which rejected the Oral Torah or Oral Law and wished to interpret the Bible literally and to deduce from it a code of law without reliance on Talmudic tradition. Major factors in the evolution of the Karaites were their ardent messianic hopes and their ascetic tendencies.

Kelipah(plural, kelipot): Literally, "husk" or "shell." A mystical term in Kabbalah, denoting the forces of evil.

Maskil (plural, maskilim): An adherent of Haskalah (see above).

Meassefim: Contributors to the Hebrew *Ha-Meassef,* which, in the late eighteenth century, served as the major organ of the Haskalah (see above) movement in Germany.

Messiah, Pangs of the (in Hebrew, *Ḥevlei Ha-Mashiaḥ*): The woes and troubles, especially those inflicted on the Jewish people, that were expected to precede the advent of the Messiah.

Midrash (pl. Midrashim): The discovery of new meanings besides literal ones in the Bible. The term is also used to designate collections of such Scriptural exposition. The best-known of the Midrashim are the *Midrash Rabbah, Tanḥuma, Pesikta De-Rav Kahana, Pesikta Rabbati,* and *Yalkut Shimeoni.* In a singular and restricted sense, *midrash* refers to an item of rabbinic exegesis.

Mishnah: The legal codification containing the core of the post-Biblical Oral Torah, compiled and edited by Rabbi Judah Ha-Nasi at the beginning of the third century C.E.

Notrikon: A method of abbreviating Hebrew words and phrases by writing only single letters, usually the initials.

Parashah (plural, parashot): The Hebrew word meaning section, and signifying, in the synagogal reading of the Pentateuch, either the weekly portion (sidrah; see below) or, more particularly, the smaller passages read to or by each person who is called to the reading of the Torah.

Parnass (from the Hebrew term *parnes,* meaning "to foster" or "to support"): A term used to designate the chief synagogue functionary. The *parnass* at first exercised both religious and administrative authority, but since the sixteenth century religious leadership has been the province of the rabbis. The office of *parnass* has generally been an elective one.

Pesaḥ: The festival, commonly referred to as Passover, which commemorates the exodus of the Israelites from Egypt.

Pilpul: In Talmudic and rabbinic literature, a clarification of a difficult point. Later the term came to denote a sharp dialectical distinction or, more generally, a certain type of Talmudic study emphasizing dialectical distinctions and introduced into the Talmudic academies of Poland by Jacob Pollak in the sixteenth century. Pejoratively, the term means hairsplitting.

Rosh Yeshivah: The principal or rector of a Talmudic academy, or *yeshivah* (see below).

Sanhedrin: A Hebrew word of Greek origin designating, in rabbinic literature, the assembly of seventy-one ordained scholars which served both as the supreme court and the legislature of Judaism in the Talmudic age. The Sanhedrin disappeared before the end of the fourth century C.E.

Seder (in Hebrew, "order"): The ritual dinner conducted in the Jewish home on the first night (and outside Israel, the first two nights) of Pesah. The story of the exodus from Egypt is recounted and a number of symbols related to it are included in the ritual.

Sefirah (plural, Sefirot): A technical term in Kabbalah, employed from the twelfth century on, to denote the ten potencies or emanations through which the Divine manifests itself.

Semichah (in Hebrew literally, "placing" [of the hands]): The practice of ordination whereby Jewish teachers, beginning in the Talmudic age, conferred on their best pupils the title "rabbi" and authorized them to act as judges and render authoritative decisions in matters of Jewish law and ritual practice.

Sephardim: The term applied to the Jews of Spain (in Hebrew, Sepharad) and afterwards to their descendants, no matter where they lived. The term Sephardim is applied particularly to the Jews exiled from Spain in 1492 who settled all along the North African coast and throughout the Ottoman empire.

Shechinah: A term used to imply the presence of God in the world, in the midst of Israel, or with individuals. In contrast to the principle of divine transcendence, Shechinah represents the principle of divine immanence.

Shofar: The horn of a ram sounded on Rosh Ha-Shanah, or the New Year, as well as on other solemn occasions, e.g., the ceremony of excommunication or at a time of epidemic or famine.

Shtadlan (a Hebrew term from the Aramaic, meaning "persuader"): The name given to a Jewish representative or lobbyist, skilled in diplomatic negotiations and having access to high officials. The shtadlan carried on his activities to promote the welfare and interests of the Jewish community.

Shulḥan Aruch: The abbreviated code of rabbinic jurisprudence, written by Joseph Karo in the sixteenth century, which became the authoritative code of Jewish law and is still recognized as such by Orthodox Judaism.

Sidra[h] (plural, sidrot): A Hebrew word meaning "order" or "arrangement," and signifying a section of the Pentateuch prescribed for reading in the synagogue on the Sabbath. There are fifty-four *sidrot*, permitting the reading of the entire Pentateuch in the course of one year.

Simḥat Torah: A holiday on the last day of Sukkot, or the Festival of Tabernacles, celebrating the annual completion of the synagogal reading of the Pentateuch and the commencement of a new cycle of reading.

Talmud: The title applied to the two great compilations, distinguished as the Babylonian Talmud and the Palestinian Talmud, in which the records of academic discussion and of judicial administration of post-Biblical Jewish law are assembled. Both Talmuds also contain Aggadah or non-legal material.

Tashlich: A Hebrew term meaning "thou wilt cast," and referring to the custom, observed on Rosh Ha-Shanah or the New Year, of praying near a stream or body of water and (at one time) throwing bread crumbs to the fish.

Tosafists: The French and German scholars of the twelfth to the fourteenth centuries who produced critical and explanatory notes on the Talmud.

Vaad, or Vaad Arba Aratzot: The autonomous national organization of Polish-Lithuanian Jewry, originating in the sixteenth century and taking its name from the four "provinces:" Major Poland, Minor Poland, Red Russia, and Lithuania.

Yeshivah (plural, yeshivot): A traditional Jewish school devoted primarily to the study of the Talmud (see above), and rabbinic literature.

Zohar: The chief work of the Spanish Kabbalah (see above) traditionally ascribed to the Tanna Simeon ben Yoḥai (second century) but probably written by the Spanish Kabbalist Moses de Leon at the end of the thirteenth century.

Index

Index

Index